LOVE'S FIRE WORKS

... the Rule-Breaker

Andrew Carey

authorHOUSE®

AuthorHouse™
1663 Liberty Drive
Bloomington, IN 47403
www.authorhouse.com
Phone: 1 (800) 839-8640

Published by AuthorHouse 12/14/2015

ISBN: 978-1-5049-6164-6 (sc)
ISBN: 978-1-5049-6365-7 (hc)
ISBN: 978-1-5049-6165-3 (e)

Library of Congress Control Number: 2015919433

Print information available on the last page.

*Scripture quotations marked NIV are taken from the Holy Bible, New
International Version*®*. NIV*®*. Copyright © 1973, 1978, 1984 by International
Bible Society. Used by permission of Zondervan. All rights reserved. [Biblica]*

*Scripture quotations marked NASB are taken from the New American
Standard Bible*®*, Copyright © 1960, 1962, 1963, 1968, 1971, 1972, 1973,
1975, 1977, 1995 by The Lockman Foundation. Used by permission.*

*Note: The New International Version and The New American Standard from
the Biblesoft PC Study Bible are the biblical translations used throughout,
unless otherwise noted (in which the New King James Version was occasionally
used). Also, certain scriptures are italicized at times for added emphasis.*

*The book can be purchased through the Authorhouse bookstore
or at Andrew's website: "presenceandglory.com".*

ACKNOWLEDGMENTS

I thank Jesus Christ who walked through love's fire before me. He made a way and is my way.

I thank my wife Kathy for the crucial part she played in the birth of what is found in this book and for her willingness to allow our story to be told for advancing Christ's kingdom on this earth. Kathy's faith allowed her to hang onto hope through humanly-impossible fireworks. I love her deeply and even now am emotional as I write this. I pray that Kathy would be blessed abundantly for her faithfulness to endure through our fireworks so that Christ's testimony through us could go forth on this earth.

I thank Jason for his extensive and valuable feedback on several earlier drafts that caused a transformation in the readability and power of the book's message. I am thankful to my graduate students in the spiritual classes – Kapri, Andrew, Odette, Ethan, Tammy, Adam, Craig, Nydika, Denija, Angie, Stephanie, Megan, Nancy, and Jenelle – for their invaluable input that caused adjustments to crucial foundations (especially the yearning-turning foundation), as well as for bringing more of my practical story to the forefront. Their thirst for Christ and His ways inspired me.

I appreciate my sister Laurie for reading an earlier draft and giving feedback. And I thank her, Mike, Joel, and Michelle for all of their support especially during the worst part of my fiery journey.

Many thanks to my men's group for their wisdom and passion to follow Christ and also for their tremendous unity and support during really difficult periods as well. Thanks to World Harvest Outreach for being family and for all of the ways they were used to support and further awaken me. Thanks to Phil, FUSE, and many others who have encouraged me through regular fellowship.

I also want to thank my SU colleagues and counseling students as a whole who have encouraged and supported me in my journey.

Thanks as well to Team Pearl at Authorhouse for their work in producing a quality final product.

This book is also written in memory of Shirley, an amazing person, wonderful colleague, and close friend who made all who were with her feel like they were the most important person on earth. She lived the kinds of truths expressed in this book.

CONTENTS

INTRODUCTION

I have one request. Please consider not telling others about this book's conclusions or "answers" about certain life issues. I ask, instead, that you share what happened to you because of reading the book. Let others experience and know the fruit in your life from reading it. A tree is known by its fruit.

You may think that this is a strange request, or maybe that I'm crazy. But I do have purpose behind this request (at least most people would tell you that I'm not crazy).

The book is confidential because I share vulnerably about my life.

Just kidding. I do share vulnerably, but my reason for asking you not to tell people *about* the book is based on Jesus' example of a similar directive. So I am in good company.

Jesus healed a man from leprosy and told him to tell no one (Lk. 5:14). Have you wondered why Jesus directed him and numerous others to tell no one after He did a miracle in them? Me too. But then He healed me from my own unresolvable struggles.

My own healing may have awakened me to Jesus' purpose. I believe that Jesus wanted people to encounter His works rather than superficial words about outcomes. I believe that He also wants you to encounter *His* works in my life that are beyond my abilities, determination, or inadequacies. That's why I personally share God's works in my life rather than presenting you with some

1

neatly-wrapped package as the outcome. My life is still messy at times, but God is in it.

I don't think that you can read this book without experiencing significant awakening. *Love's Fire Works* was forged by fire. Trials expose the deep in people. My trials have exposed the deep in me and will likely touch deep areas within you whether you struggle with anxiety, depression, perfectionism, addiction, or identity and relationship issues. Sharing at a practical level about my trials, as well as God's works to bring healing through them, adds greater understanding for your journey into restoration. I share my inner world connected to the circumstances I faced so you can learn how emotions, inner experiences, and spirituality facilitate or hinder awakening.

God has used trials to lift me spiritually, and He showed me a picture of what this spiritual lifting was like. God has a way of putting things into proper perspective, and He did that for me through a brief vision in full color during the height of my trials.

I saw a woman holding a door open for me. Her hand was still on the door knob as she whispered, "Come in here, quickly." I understood that she was inviting me into a new spiritual room. I also knew that not just anyone could walk nonchalantly through that doorway as seen by the woman's whisper, as well as her intent to close the door quickly behind me.

As I walked through the doorway I knew that she was a kindergarten teacher. Then I saw a long rectangular table with highchairs around it. She motioned for me to sit in the highchair closest to the door.

That was all I saw of the vision. Its meaning became clear as I paused. The woman was the Holy Spirit who had invited me into a higher spiritual room. Her invitation was just a whisper, which required me to be alert to hear her. The highchairs indicated that this room was like kindergarten compared to the rest of the kingdom. I realized that I was just scratching the surface of God's infinite realm that was higher than mine. I saw that I was barely learning these kindergarten ways as seen by me being in the chair nearest to the door (meaning the most recently admitted child).

The vision put things into perspective. I've gone through fire to enter kindergarten and I'm fortunate to be the least in the room!

I am thankful for the fire. I believe that the vision is about all who are willing to embrace the fire in their lives. God has further delivered me through my fiery furnace that had no way out except "Christ in me," who was with me in the fire. I'm always a work in progress, but God has further delivered me from worldly systems and rules, from the fear of people, and from hiding who I truly am. He has faithfully freed me into more of my true identity that gives testimony to the value planted within all of us.

You may want to read only bits or to the extent that God stirs your heart, and then leave those places bubble a while before reading further. Then you will not race past the Spirit's works within you. This book is meant to provide you with an experience, not to be treated like another manual of standards you are required to perform. I pray that all of us would be lifted into kindergarten and beyond (to infinity and beyond, as Buzz Lightyear would say). I pray that Christ would use these fireworks to burn away more of the earthly fog in your life and to make you a living testimony of God's image on this earth.

Be blessed by *Love's Fire Works*.

CHAPTER 1

Love's Passionate Pursuit

Encounters with a Greater Love

I love to tell three stories about my experiences with an unquenchable love, and to share the song that God birthed through me during this season. These experiences are a wonderful testimony of God and His passionate, unquenchable love for people.

God met me during prayer leading into my three significant experiences. I sensed that I had received a call to be a voice about God's greater love. I initially felt resolute with a clear sense of purpose. Before long I found myself telling Him that I personally did not know His greater love (though He had been teaching me about His love for a while). He has been faithful since that time to chip away at the lesser love and to establish the greater.

I also received a vivid dream prior to my three experiences. In the dream there was a town and surrounding countryside with a great river running through it. Many people were sick and suffering throughout the town and surrounding area. Something was wrong.

Doctors ministered in futility to those who were sick. I felt compelled to go upstream to find the source of the problem.

Just upstream from the town I encountered a wall of thorns and brush; it was too thick for me to continue along the river bank. I circled out wider and went a considerable distance upstream. As I made my way back to the edge of the river and began walking downstream again, I saw a major sewage plant hidden in a wall of thorns. I saw all the sewage pouring into the river.

As I watched workers go in and out of the building I noticed that they were aware of the problem. I saw them laughing about their intentional destruction.

I made my way back to town and told some friends about the sewage plant's activities. Immediately they helped me direct a missile towards the plant, and we blew it up (with love, of course)!

Within days we saw people being healed and the town and land transforming into the beautiful place that was meant to be. Within a couple of weeks the land was lush green with flowers and blossoms blooming in all their glory. The people became fully healed, whole, and joyful.

Then I awoke, and God pressed upon me the meaning of the dream. The river is God's love. The wall of thorns and brush is our fallible human nature and the sewage is its lies about love that make people sick. God's river of love will fill and heal the land after the lies are blown up. Eternally ruined.

Our fallible human nature with its lies must be stripped away to awaken our Christ nature and its river of Love that will fill and heal the land.

Love's fireworks. That's my calling.

Story 1 – A Mountain of Love

My first encounter with God's greater love involved a flight attendant.

My wife Kathy and I were flying back from Peru where we had just visited our middle son who was living and working with natives in the Amazon Jungle region. During the flight the pilot urgently stated over the speaker, "Flight attendants, we will be encountering turbulence; take your seats!" Normally pilots try to sound calm so as not to overly excite the passengers but that was not the case this time.

After another fifteen seconds we hit the most turbulence I had ever experienced. The plane bucked like a wild bronco. "Coincidentally" the only vacant seat in the plane was beside me against the isle.

As I held onto my seat during the turbulence I looked beside me and saw only a hand on the armrest at the edge of the isle. A moment later I saw a flight attendant who had fallen to the floor peeking over the armrest at me. She asked with urgency, "Is this seat vacant; can I sit here?" I quickly stated that the seat was free.

As soon as she sat down she looked squarely into my face and asked with great curiosity, "Are you a pastor?" I said "No." About half a minute later she leaned towards me and asked a second time, "Are you *sure* you're not a pastor?"

Again I said "No." Meanwhile I was shocked that I found no words. I was convinced at this point that God wanted something more but felt completely inadequate to communicate further.

In hindsight I felt like this inability to communicate was for me to know that every bit of this experience was from God and had nothing to do with any earthly ability of mine. Normally I would talk easily with others, and in this case I would have checked further about her questions regarding whether or not I was a pastor. But I was blank for no logical reason.

Within several minutes (with me still being silent!) the flight attendant mentioned that the turbulence must be over. She left the seat and resumed her duties. I thought I missed what God wanted. But the jet's intense bucking reemerged after about three more minutes, and I looked up again only to see the same flight attendant wobbling and hanging onto the armrest.

She sat down and immediately asked with even greater insistence, now a third time, "Are you *sure* you're not a pastor?" I finally felt free and stated, "No I'm not a pastor but God is very important to me."

Several seconds later the flight attendant said, "Oh, I'm sorry; I didn't mean to make fun. I didn't realize you were reading the Bible." I had thought that maybe she asked about me being a pastor because she had seen the Bible in my hands. She, in fact, had not seen the Bible until this point and had gotten embarrassed thinking that I might believe she was making fun of me.

After I clarified that I wasn't offended she asked very specifically what I was reading. I was reading a passage about prayer, which had also been the theme of God's work on my heart during the trip. Coincidentally, the question most urgent within her heart was about prayer. She asked questions with such thirst and tenacity that it led into lengthier conversation about visiting my son in Peru, as well as into other spiritual experiences.

At a certain point during our conversation I wrongly assumed and stated that God must be important to her. I assumed this because I thought, "Who sits down beside you, a person they don't know, asks several times if you are a pastor, asks very insistently what you are reading from the Bible, and then fires off many questions about God in your life?" But she looked sheepish and guilt-ridden when I had assumed God was important to her. She stated that she wasn't a Christian, that she was doing her own thing in life, and that her grandmother kept praying for her because she saw her as having her back to God.

Instantly I became overwhelmed and shocked by the powerful wave of love that overtook me. This powerful experience was well-beyond me as an individual. Here is the essence of the words that came through me: "The Lord loves you and wants to be with you with an overwhelming love that doesn't depend on labels or actions. His love is ever-pursuing you just to be with you, and *nothing will ever, ever change that.* You could still run from Him or have your back turned to Him twenty years from now, and that will never change the fact that the Lord wants to love you powerfully and to be with you. His love is not dependent on you. He just wants you to open up to know His enormous love that is always for you and pursuing you."

More than those words I experienced an indescribable mountain of love coming through me that permanently impacted me. I still weep when I pause about that experience.

The utter reality of this love was beyond my greatest imagination. I experienced an unquenchable love coming through me towards this flight attendant that I knew absolutely nothing from her end could hinder. The security, peace, rest, profound desire, compassion, freedom, and unwavering acceptance of this love were beyond anything that words could ever express. They were beyond this world.

Following this exchange the flight attendant was so joy-filled and lifted up spiritually that she asked if she could give me a hug, as well as to do something, anything, for me and my wife. A flight attendant has never before asked to give me a hug! After giving me a big hug she asked if she could give us free wine.

After she brought us wine and went about her duties I could not yet drink. Nor could I talk. I was overwhelmed with emotion and then began experiencing something like an out-of-body experience where I watched what had just occurred through me.

I sobbed uncontrollably for about ten to fifteen minutes as I re-watched God's limitless love come through me to the flight attendant. I saw His tenacious and profound mountain of love for her, which then powerfully struck me how tenacious and profound His love was for me and for all people. I saw that His love for us had nothing to do with our actions.

God's love cannot change because it is *who He is*. He just wants us to receive and know the fullness of that overwhelming love. He wants oneness. Withness (this word says it best to me). We simply have unending lies interfering with us experiencing His supernatural love. The lies cause sickness and suffering, and they need blown up!

I hope that you have experienced to some degree the love that overwhelmed me and the flight attendant. I know that the passionate, unquenchable love I experienced is real and well beyond the kind of love that anyone I know walks in during life. You may need some space to take in this experience before reading my next encounter.

Story 2 – Love Accomplishes Justice

Three months later God continued His works to reveal new aspects of greater love to me. I was facilitating a counseling group that included a woman who had been struggling with relationship issues. The content was left vague to protect her identity but the story is true.

During a group counseling meeting this woman began revealing the pain in her life. She had experienced tremendous loss connected to both her parents. She also experienced unimaginable abuse and loss after she had married and then divorced. She never dreamed that she would find gentle care, support, and love … especially from any man.

After this woman's marriage had ended she happened to reconnect with a past male friend, and they became romantically involved. The problem was, he was married.

She expressed to the group "How can I be a Christian woman and do such a thing? I've been miserable." The group responded to her with a healthy balance of acceptance of her as a person along with honesty about their concern regarding inevitable consequences. But she left group with the situation unresolved in her mind.

Following the group time she approached me individually and squarely asked, "Do you think I should break it off with this man?" I knew that she knew the "correct" answer, so I paused.

In the meantime the Spirit rose up in fullness and I spoke with compassion that brought tears to my eyes (and believe me, I didn't know or plan what came out): "The problem isn't the sin. Sin is the outcome. The issue is that you have a hole in you that doesn't trust God and His love. You have unending reasons and pain that cause you to think you can't find any other man that will love you. No wonder you want to hold onto him. But the issue most important is for you to come to know God's greater love. He passionately loves you. I will pray that you know His love so that you would trust Him and His leading. He will be good to you but it starts with knowing His love."

I prayed with her to receive that love. As she was leaving she looked at me and said, "I didn't expect this. I know that I just experienced God's love; thank you."

I know that if I had encountered that situation several years earlier I would have followed her lead. I would have focused on the sin like she thought *should* happen. I could feel those vibes from her ("correct the mistake first and *then* God will accept and be with you"). This experience caught me off guard and showed me once again a greater love like I had experienced with the flight attendant.

You might feel like I was too easy on this woman if you haven't yet been touched by God's greater love. All I can say is that I've

11

constantly been learning and experiencing more of God's grace, love, and goodness beyond what I had experienced or been taught previously.

By the way, there is a happy ending to this story. In the next group counseling meeting the woman beamed with peace and joy. She surprised all of us by sharing that she had ended the affair.

People grow when they receive love-filled honesty and are given the freedom to be. Had I put pressure on this woman, I would have hindered her direct relationship with God. God seems to restore life and justice in situations when we support people to look to God directly by faith (as opposed to them staring at their sins or others' judgment and pressure to act in new ways). Pressure is not love, and far beyond many people's awareness, they frequently pressure others to change.

Greater love accomplishes justice. I am sure this woman encountered further challenges in her journey to know this greater love. But I know and she knew that she had been touched by a greater love that broke our rules and worked a miracle beyond what either of us had expected.

The more I grow the more I am surprised and overwhelmed by God's love that is beyond this world. Greater love truly frees and restores us from our bondages rather than placing the pressure of performance upon us.

Story 3 – The End of the Rainbow

This third story is about a rainbow. God conveyed His overwhelming love to me through an experience with a rainbow, which resulted in a song. This experience occurred three months after the previous one and was about knowing a greater love.

Have you ever been at the end of a rainbow? Better yet, in it? I know that sounds miraculous. I have been told that it is scientifically impossible, but it happened to me.

I'm not talking about a dream, vision, or spiritual realm experience, or even about being under a rainbow. I literally mean *at* as well as *in* the end of a rainbow.

I had always heard the myth about finding the gold at the end of the rainbow. I never imagined being in the end of a rainbow with the colors shining directly on me.

The experience happened after I had been visiting friends in North Carolina. Once again I had seen God furthering His love in me and my friends. I left my friends and began my trip home. I thanked God for our fellowship and felt tremendous joy about being part of His kingdom.

I knew that I was undergoing spiritual work to see God's love as utterly faithful, in spite of any unfaithfulness on my part. I was beginning to see that even judgment was part of God's love and faithfulness. I somehow knew this and yet was not at a place of being able to see it clearly enough to express it.

I paused with God while I drove and sensed that I was to open up and let Him express a song through me. The Lord had worked in me previously to create songs that expressed His present works. I sensed that He wanted a song about His faithful love that loves us as we are. Little did I know that the Lord would center this song on a rainbow.

The words and the melody flowed as I began letting God's joy about love be expressed through me. I sang endlessly during this six-hour return trip to Pennsylvania. I am sure that other drivers seeing me concluded that I had lost touch with reality.

I stopped for a bite to eat and then began driving again. The song and great joy overtook me more fully (you have to know me to picture this). I looked to my right and saw a gorgeous rainbow.

It was the most brilliant rainbow I had ever seen, with a fully visible second rainbow above it. At one point the road turned directions and I looked ahead and saw the road going straight beneath the rainbows, as if it were the entrance to the Promised Land. They were breathtaking.

Meanwhile I belted out the song as the road turned another direction where I could not see the rainbows briefly because of trees. Then it happened – the impossible.

The road again turned while I was still singing with no restraint about the Lord's love. I looked up at the height and center of the top of the now single rainbow that was angled off to my right side. I began to notice the direction that the closer end of the rainbow was coming. It was coming down from its middle towards me. My eyes kept following the rainbow from the middle downward to the closer end until the road turned slightly more. I could now see that the rainbow was angled precisely at me and the thought struck me as I saw all the colors around me, "Its end is right on top of me! I'm *in* the end of the rainbow!"

I could clearly see the brilliance of the end of the rainbow and its colors on the road in front of me, on the hood of my car, across my windshield and dash, and onto my shirt and lap. I saw the colors glowing all around me for at least five minutes as I continued driving. And, no, I hadn't had any wine or mind-altering substance (unless ice cream counts)!

In the past I have been almost underneath the center of rainbows once or twice but I have never been close to being at or in the end of a rainbow. This was unbelievable.

Then the road changed directions and I was no longer in the rainbow. I could see it as I normally saw rainbows, with the ends somewhere else. I watched that rainbow and its brilliance for a good hour and a half until darkness finally came. Even that was a new experience; it was spectacular until dark.

The whole way home I either sang or contemplated further about what had happened and *when* it had happened. I was meant to see God's rainbow at the same point that He was working a song through me about the faithfulness of His love – a love that is faithful during and through judgment. Hasn't God's rainbow always meant that?

People have often viewed God's judgment as separate and apart from love. His love is bigger than that. God's love encompasses His judgment, which is His stripping works to free us from our false self and its lifeless ways. That is what God's love did for the woman having the affair. Greater love freed her from lesser ways that had hurt herself and others.

God's rainbow has always been a promise of His faithfulness. That is His faithful love that never retreats one step from us. Not sin, not forgetting Him for a day, not running with our backs to Him for 20 years, or not even hurting others can separate us from His love that passionately desires to overtake us. Why? Love (and its judgment or stripping works) frees us from all the unloving things we do. *God knows that we will continue all our unloving ways until we come to know love.* We have no chance to stop our lesser ways without our holes being filled by love. Love is the security and way for trusting and following Christ. Greater love is the fullness that needs no lesser things to fill holes. Jesus was a picture of that for us.

God knows that we have no chance at higher life without knowing His greater love. That's why He passionately pursues us with His love. But there is another reason. God revealed to me through the rainbow experience that each of us is the gold at the end of the rainbow. He created the gold that is imprisoned within our fleshly body, and He passionately pursues what is lost until it is found.

Our souls are the treasure hidden in a field, or like sheep that are sometimes lost. Jesus expressed the widow's great joy over finding the lost coin, and the joy of the man selling all that he had upon finding the one pearl of great worth. Jesus' parables point towards God's passionate love that works towards finding what is lost, and they express the tremendous joy He experiences upon the lost being found. We are that sought and valued gold that brings Him inexpressible joy when He finds it.

Read the resulting song below as a prayer about God's faithful love.

<u>A Song – True Love is a Rainbow</u>
(Love Loves Us First)

1.

Only Love loves us first,
Even before we are able to do what's good.
Knowing Love is the place of peace
And security for the strength to do what's right.
Do we really know this kind of Love?
For we're truly nothing without Love.

Love alone heals our hearts of stone,
And it gently births a surrendered way of being.
For only Love can soften our hearts
And transform pain into a humble love for all.
So faithful is this True Love.
Like a rainbow is True Love.

Go to Chorus

2.

Showing Love comes from knowing Love
And from trusting Love and its ways that make us free.
For only Love desires what's true,
So it patiently frees all the good that's hidden within.
Do we really know this kind of Love?
For we're truly nothing without Love.

To carry Love means to die with Love
So that Love alone would be the voice crying out through us.
For Love remains as a faithful friend,
And it never gives up till it brings new life without end.
So faithful is this True Love.
Like a rainbow is True Love.

Chorus:

For this Love is the greatest gift of all,
For only Love sets us free.

Oh I will surrender to Love,
Oh I will surrender to Love. 2x

For knowing I am loved will reach those I love,
Knowing I am loved will reach those I love. 2x

Nothing without Love

My experiences are interwoven throughout this book so you can see practically what helped and didn't help during my trials. What I experienced most is this: the security of God's love allowed me to awaken through, rather than resist, my trials. I always thought I knew love, but I see now that there was a greater secure love I had not yet known. I look back and see how I had stepped in empty ways to fill holes when I didn't know love's security, as well as how securely I acted when I waited on God's peace before stepping during difficulties. I was far from perfect during this process, but I believe that God revealed many foundational truths to me for participating with Him to awaken more of heaven on this earth.

The more God has opened my eyes through trials, the more I have seen that nothing grows or awakens into His kingdom without love. Nothing. God's love makes a way for the kingdom, and not knowing His love cripples us.

Jesus' parable of the talents (money, symbolizing God's riches) demonstrates what happens when we don't know His love. The first two servants used the master's talents to gain more talents and then received greater kingdom authority as a result. But the wicked servant said (Matt. 25:25-26), "And I was afraid, and went away and hid your talent in the ground; see, you have what is yours."

"I was afraid." I relate to that. In the parable, the wicked servant was wicked *because* he didn't know love. Fear moved him. Fear caused him to hide the true "in the ground." Fear caused me to hide the true within me and, instead, to live in the performing false self. That false self is the fearful fallible human nature (what the scriptures translate as the sin or flesh nature; see Rom. 8:5-8).

Earlier in my journey I anxiously strived to live perfectly and to achieve great things only to find myself constantly empty. Then anxiousness gave way to panic attacks. That was my fallible earthly nature that did not know love. Fear, because of not knowing love apart from performance, governed me. In the end, I learned that fear increased when fear caused my decisions. Fear led me and became stronger when I participated with its urges, and its emptiness clung to me like glue during and after the striving.

The scriptures convey that I am nothing and can profit nothing for myself or others when I do not know love (1 Cor. 13:1-3). I now see the utter truth of that. Without love, I could never *be*. I could not rest. I could not express my true self, the Christ nature within, when I didn't know love or peace. I had buried the talent. I had buried Christ's riches, my true self, and lived in an empty shell that tried to perform a taskmaster's tasks. Not knowing secure love caused fear and lies to move me in false ways. I performed, hid, or reacted to life circumstances.

I *am* nothing if those false ways govern me. Those false ways are the fallible nature scrambling for survival; they are not my true self.

God's other attributes (e.g., holiness, justice, and righteousness) will profit me nothing without love as their way. I can have faith that moves mountains but without love I am still nothing. I thought I was standing in faith by trying to trust God during my panic attacks, but in actuality, not knowing love caused me to be self-absorbed. I was consumed by one quest: How do I get rid of these crippling panic attacks?

Love is fullness of security, and lack of love is emptiness and insecurity that gives way to selfishness in spite of good intentions.

Consider Peter and Jesus' other disciples and how fearless they were when love (Jesus) was securely at their side. Think about that immediate loss of courage when Jesus was taken to the cross. Think about all the lesser motives that powerfully moved the disciples when they didn't know love's security. Fear overpowered them, and their Christ-like attributes disappeared.

Fear and all kinds of death prevail when I do not know love. I cannot be a vessel of God's higher ways when I am not grounded in His secure love. Without love I would be under delusions of carrying out justice and righteousness … because underlying self-serving motives would move me to regain lesser versions of security as a substitute for that missing love.

God is love, and perhaps love is God's beginning for all of life. Love is meant to be the starting point for babies. That is all the more true for spiritual birth.

Love is the Way. It is the greatest gift of all. Love is the greatest testimony of the heart of God.

Discerning Love

I shudder at points when I again get in touch with the depth of the panic attacks I experienced. I share about how God awakened me from them later, but for now I emphasize the importance of recognizing whether you truly know love or not at any given moment. That is crucial.

Knowing love leads one way and not knowing love leads another. At each moment you face in life, you can participate with the fearful false self or with the secure true self. I didn't know this during my panic attacks and wish I had. I could have avoided endless struggles and grief! But I believe that God allowed the struggles to birth some of these lessons more deeply for me as well as for others who desire to hear them.

I was under the fallible nature's lies anytime I thought that I was unacceptable and should be further, different, or beyond who I was. I was also under deception when I believed that life or others should have been beyond where they were. My inability to rest or take a break from achieving, helping others, or contributing positively to life demonstrated that I was hooked on these lies about needing to be further than where I was.

Now I personally recognize these lies anytime I experience an uptight, anxious, restless, or insecure foundation within me. I also recognize this insecurity when I believe the world's messages that pressure me and others to get somewhere different (such as should, shouldn't, need to, have to, or must). Those words are almost always used by people to pressure the performing false self.

You might interpret my words to mean that there is something wrong with performing or achieving in life. That is not my meaning. I still achieve. The difference has to do with my foundation or motive. I used to achieve to gain love, security, or significance; that was the false self. Now I pay attention to only achieving if it comes from a place of peace, from a place that is already secure and significant. That is the true self, and rest or peace is the proof of whether or not I am secure. Succumbing to "shoulds or musts" that don't allow me to rest is the proof of the insecure false self.

Counseling is my profession. I constantly watch human nature to learn all that I can. I believe that this issue of knowing secure love or not is far deeper and elusive than people think. For years I could have said the right words about being loved, but the evidence was, "Could I rest?"

Can *you* rest from striving? Agreed, you likely have times where you can rest. But do you think you could remain aware of being loved and significant if you rested for a week or month from being productive, achieving, and helping others?

I still would have answered "yes" to those questions. Until it was tested for a month. I had never actually stopped being productive and doing good deeds, but as soon as I had, I fully believed the onslaught of lies that came against me: "What good are you? What are you contributing? You don't make any difference. If you're not doing good, you might as well be thrown away."

I only saw what was in my heart after it had been tested. I saw that I didn't really know the truth of love apart from performance. I saw that I had always been on the slippery foundation of the false self. The imposter.

I now regularly watch these areas that pertain to whether or not I know God's secure love. It is foundational to how I live life. I also learned that I will frequently *feel* like God is dissatisfied with me every time I join with the lesser nature. But as soon as I awaken from that lesser nature I regain awareness that God fully loves me just as I am.

I facilitate an exercise with counseling students to emphasize these dynamics. I ask them to pay attention to how a significant other may be frustrated with and unable to accept them regarding an aspect of their life. I ask students to become aware of their inward experience in that place.

I tell students to imagine that they told me about that "problematic area," as if I know everything about that aspect of their life. Then I tell these students to imagine that I completely accepted them whether or not that area changed and whether or not I agreed with their behavior. They become aware that my love of them does not depend upon their change or perfection.

I usually see relief on some of their faces. I then ask them to imagine that the very person who has conditionally treated them has had a miraculous change of heart. The students imagine that their significant other has finally conveyed to them that they love them as they are regardless of change (even though that person still may not agree with their present way of being).

At this point I usually see even greater relief on students' faces. I ask them about what they noticed inwardly. They describe the initial tension and anxiety connected to their significant others' conditional love. Then they describe the peace, freedom, and security that filled them inwardly when they knew they could be accepted in spite of unwanted behaviors.

That exercise gives them a glimpse of God's love that always accepts us, even during His stripping works of our lesser ways. That is His unfailing love, which is essential for our awakening and growth. This exercise enabled students to become awakened to their true self, to their Christ nature within that knows and is secure love. This true self, also described as the new self in the scriptures, is the foundation for knowing and expressing Christ's love on this earth.[1] Our part is to participate with being awakened to this rock foundation.

These students' anxiety during the conditional love they experienced actually hindered growth. Just like test anxiety chokes out student learning, conditional love causes people anxiety and it chokes out growth. That's why the scriptures say that we are nothing and can profit nothing when we don't know love. We aren't receptive and cannot embrace Christ within when our souls are afraid. I have experienced this many times in life.

Significant others hinder the very change they want in you when they can't accept you first as you are. Likewise, you will hinder the change you want in your significant others when you judge or reject them for not behaving or believing as you think they should. Harsh tones demonstrate the negative judgment that usually impacts far more than the often well-meaning good intentions during interactions. Conditional love judges and separates people from one another; it chokes out life. People's conditional ways of "love" are the thorns that choke out God's word within us. The true self then remains buried inside while the false reacts, rebels, or tries to perform regarding the outward pressures.

The shift in the students resulted when they knew they could be loved just as they were. They did not have to be different or beyond where they were to be acceptable. *Experiencing* secure love allowed their true self to come forth. To awaken.

Secure love allows people the freedom to choose. No pressure. No judgmental tones that convey the right answer that has to be chosen.

We may encounter unwanted consequences for choosing certain actions, but love always allows free will. One way or another we reap what we sow, but love allows the freedom to choose, sow, and reap accordingly.

A Passionate Lion

Jesus' love embraced and gathered people regardless of belief differences, labels, or sins. Jesus loved prostitutes, fishermen, tax-gatherers, lepers, the poor, a Roman centurion, Pharisees (Joseph of Arimathea and Nicodemus who were open to His love), and another Pharisee (Saul who became Paul) who initially oversaw the beating and killing of Jesus' followers. Greater love breaks rules.

Jesus loved everyone because He allowed tares (weeds) to remain among the wheat.[2] He allowed imperfections along with the true. Jesus said (Jn. 10:10), "The thief comes only to steal, and kill, and destroy; I came that they might have life, and might have it abundantly."

Jesus wanted us to receive abundant life and He knew that we would neither love nor receive love if we did not allow imperfections. Jesus knew that nothing would grow without love, so His primary message to all was love.

Jesus' love did not always look like love, especially when He interacted with the religious leaders. What was the difference?

Part of the difference was that Jesus defended those who were "poor" and without love. Jesus stood with those who had no one at their side and against people's messages that worked to steal, kill, and destroy love.

Jesus was a passionate Lion about one kind of weed. Jesus allowed other weeds to be left unchallenged but He regularly exposed the false fruit of one particular weed. Jesus destroyed any message that worked to steal, kill, and destroy *love*.

Why didn't Jesus stand against the Romans even though they stole, killed, and destroyed? The Romans could not steal, kill, and destroy love. The Romans were not the people's standards of love and could not take that from the Jews. But the Jews' religious leaders could.

The religious leaders were the people's standards of love, and Jesus stood like a Lion against their unloving messages and false heavy loads they placed on the people (against all the shoulds, ought to's, and musts!). Jesus stood against the destructive messages that came from those who were supposed to be God's ambassadors of love (just as God stood against Jonah's "love" of Nineveh; see the book of Jonah).

Jesus tore down all that stole, killed, and destroyed the truth of God's love for people. Jesus was grieved at the religious leaders' hardness of heart that constantly tore down love.

Jesus was the Rule-Breaking Lamb that laid down His life to destroy the earthly ways of power and force for meeting needs. But He was also the Rule-Breaking Lion that came to destroy all that would steal, kill, and destroy love.

Love's fireworks broke my rules and stirred my heart to become a releaser of people's true self that no longer demands that we be different or further to be loved. I pray that we would no longer judge and separate from one another because of belief differences, labels, or denominations. Allow the weeds in yourself and in others, and become part of God's love that burns brighter than those separating ways.

CHAPTER 2

Fire, Fire

Greater Love

Do you want greater love on this earth? I know that I do. The secret is this: allow suffering, and desire real relationship with God and one another in the midst of suffering. Do not resist love's fireworks designed to awaken you into more of your true self. *Trust that Love is fully with you and for you during whatever difficulty, sin, or darkness you encounter.* Knowing love's security and faithfulness during trials helps you to let go of all the lesser things and to enter into greater relationship with God and one another. Then you become love on this earth as you were meant to be.

I feel a call on my life to be a voice of Christ's greater love. Equally important, I am a trumpet that alerts us to embrace the necessity of Christ's stripping works that awaken us from the lesser nature to embrace our Christ nature within (Col. 1:27). Our ongoing journey is to shed the false and embrace the true. Love's fireworks help us do that.[1]

Love's fireworks were life-changing for me. I wouldn't trade them for anything, although I fiercely struggled at times during the fire. My references to "fire" and "love's fireworks" in this book are about the difficulties that come upon people in life. I see these difficulties as God's purposeful fire, not because He is angry, but because He works to help us let go of lesser ways and securities that have kept us blind and imprisoned. I look back and see many of my previous ways as futile and restrictive, and I know that I could not have been freed from those lesser ways without hitting impossible roadblocks during my journey.

My story includes struggling daily with panic attacks earlier in my journey and then enduring marital trials for over two and a half years. God purposed each fire to produce higher comfort and relationship than I had known.

The difficult people and circumstances I encountered during those two fires were counterparts to awaken higher life within me. That higher life was the higher comfort that no longer needed to come from outside of me (although God worked through various people to awaken me to His comfort that was already within). All that felt like sandpaper to me was purposely designed to awaken me to higher secure love in place of my lesser securities. Fire stripped away the lesser to awaken the greater.

Looking back, I handled life very differently during each fire. If you are stuck in trials, pay attention to the two overall ways I handled life because one was healthy and the other one wasn't. My unhealthy way during the panic attacks was to strive in the false performing self that could never rest or receive true comfort. Then my healthier way of being during the marital struggles was to let go of outcomes so that I could watch and join with what Christ seemed to be working. That way of surrender caused me to abide in my true self who knew peace, rest, and secure love.

The panic attacks demonstrated my prior ways of performing to meet the demands of "religion" and rules, believing that life and self were controllable, and striving endlessly to accomplish unending goals, which hindered my ability to accept and be present with "what is" in life. I could not even know acceptance of myself during my unending striving to get somewhere different than where I was (although I thought I accepted myself at the time).

The more recent marital struggles demonstrated how I had changed. I had awakened to a freer spirituality without rules, a greater acceptance that life and self were not controllable, and rest, peace, and the ability to be present in the midst of chaos. I had learned to accept that life and God were bigger than me and still for me, which allowed significant awakening throughout the marital struggles. I had become able to receive and give comfort even during horrendous struggles. I had come to a place of making decisions from freedom and peace rather than from shoulds or expectations.

The panic attacks initially caused me to hit an insurmountable wall. I believe that hitting an impossible wall was necessary. Foundational change came from recognizing that life and self were not always controllable. That was pivotal; it allowed me to rest from the striving. I had seen previously that stopping the panic was beyond my human nature's ability. The panic had blindsided my performing false self, which began shifting me onto the foundation of my true self. Then the marital struggles released me further into my true self that knew Christ was with me in all things. Fire had matured me to embrace Christ within when life became humanly impossible.

Have you encountered situations where you intuitively knew that change was beyond your human ability or control? If you haven't, pride in your human ability will still run your life. You will still believe that the power of change is within your human ability, which leaves you susceptible to placing that enormous load on your shoulders. Or, susceptible to having panic attacks when you can't be superhuman! Placing that load on human ability will still be religious rules to live up to, even if you don't look to any kind of formal religion. My rules, that determination and willpower would accomplish anything, were a relentless taskmaster. It was my deeper (but false) religion. That is, until "fire-fire" changed me ... the fire of panic attacks, and then the fire of marital trials.

When life is beyond my human ability now, I am completely fine with acknowledging that I am humanly unable and that I need higher power to accomplish the impossible. I now see humanly impossible situations as opportunities rather than obstacles. Every humanly impossible situation or difficulty is an opportunity to acknowledge human inability so as to further awaken into my Christ nature within. The true self. (I refer to this inner true nature either way throughout the book; please don't let labels hinder your awakening into the true!)

Paul said (Phil. 3:15), "All of us who are mature should take such a view of things." Do you want to be mature in Christ? I believe that accepting the sufferings of Christ as part of your walk is crucial. The sufferings of Christ continually awaken your soul into your true self. That is what I call the fire.

My soul awakens and matures into more of my true self when I "know Christ and the power of His resurrection and *the fellowship of sharing in His sufferings,* becoming like Him in His death, and so, somehow, to attain to the resurrection from the dead" (Phil. 3:10). That statement is not simply about being resurrected after we physically die. Paul's meaning was that the earthly life is regularly traded for the heavenly life during our sufferings. That's what Paul meant by maturity.

I awaken to more of Christ's resurrection life every time I embrace rather than resist His purpose for trials. I regularly ask during difficulties, "What are You after in me?" I have come to the place of truly trusting that God works absolutely all things together for good no matter what things look or feel like.[2] I ask for the grace to join with His will during trials, and my earthly will falls away while His higher will takes more place within my soul.

I didn't begin with this surrendered way in my journey. Originally, I neither experienced grace nor revelations during trials. Why? I was asleep. Immature. I had concluded that God wasn't in the trials, judged myself as defective when circumstances didn't change, and resisted His works. But many scriptures exhort us to stay alert or awake because Christ comes in times and ways we do not expect (Lk. 12:40). Isn't life like a wild animal at times that simply won't cooperate with what we want? Difficulties are our greatest times of awakening when we embrace what we are to gain through them.

As I awakened a little more in my journey I considered that God at least allowed the trials. I judged myself less and received occasional revelations afterwards. I had started to see a connection between me embracing trials and receiving greater revelations.

Finally I became awake. I began to trust that Christ was always and fully in the trials and that He was for me. I stopped judging myself and embraced the fire, and daily I received extensive revelations during the trials. Why did the revelations come more quickly?

Space and freedom for the Spirit's work happened most during the trials, as long as I didn't shun them. I learned that I matured most in Christ during trials. I knew that the extreme pressures were opportunities to leave more of the earthly behind and to be lifted more into His nature. So I learned to participate with Christ, to "eat of Him" rather than of the world during trials. Participating with Christ's will was my food, just as Jesus had said that doing the Father's will was His food (Jn. 4:34). I watched for and ate of His higher life constantly during trials.

I know that I made plenty of mistakes along the way, but I kept paying attention to discerning what Christ was working during the trials, and to keep surrendering to His higher will. As I did, the trials helped me to exchange lies for truth. God continually uprooted my refuge of lies, which made room for more of Christ within my soul (Isa. 28:17-18). Resurrection life increased in me as death's lies decreased.

At an experiential level, I gradually became stripped from striving to be different or more than I was during difficulties to pausing and sensing what Christ was working. I saw that He was not after me being superhuman in my lesser nature, but instead acknowledging my human nature's inability so as to become further shifted into my Christ nature. Just learning to pause more in the midst of difficulties allowed more freedom for Christ to work from within.

I have learned to be extremely patient during trials just as love is patient. I have learned to allow time for love's fire to burn away my lesser rules and ways. As I allowed Christ to strip away lesser ways, inner suffering decreased because I further awakened to the greater. I awakened more to Christ and love, within and around me. I came to recognize that love was with me and for me even during devastating circumstances. I saw that patiently allowing suffering was foundational for establishing Christ's kingdom on earth.

I will be quick to strike back in situations if I do not allow suffering. I will be quick to fight for my rights when God and life do not give me what I think I should have. That is not greater love.

I will also be quick to fight, judge, and defer to lesser ways when I do not allow suffering in the lives of my significant others. That is challenging. But with the goal of avoiding suffering I will quickly direct my significant others to get a divorce, fight against difficult situations, or escape life's trials. Or I will put more pressure on them to change something that is currently beyond them. That is not greater love. That is not how Jesus loved those closest to Him. He allowed suffering (remember His friend Lazarus, as well as John the Baptist in prison?).

I do not mean that we should seek suffering. I am also not advocating for passively remaining in situations that call for healthy boundaries with others (where continued destruction would hinder our growth if God wanted a situation to discontinue). But I am saying that life frequently brings suffering to strip us from lesser ways. Participate with those fireworks that free us into clarity beyond the earthly fog.

Embrace the sovereignly ordained suffering. Watch for the wind of the Spirit during life circumstances similarly to how trees bend with heavy winds. With patience you can sense which way the Spirit moves. Maybe you are to endure one situation and to remove yourself from another. See and join with Christ first; then your actions will be from Him. If you don't sense His peace during trials, then wait till you do. Otherwise, your actions will come from fear or emptiness, which brings further destruction.

All people suffer. The rain like the sunshine is a necessary part of life. Storms come upon all. Why?

Suffering frees us.

Beautiful People

The most beautiful people have endured suffering and gleaned its wisdom. Elisabeth Kubler-Ross in her grief and loss work regularly witnessed this powerful truth. People who have suffered are the most trustworthy to love with God's love because suffering burned away the fog.

They see clearer. They no longer think they have control over life's higher purposes.

Suffering has caused these beautiful people to lose the bondage of worldly rules and to find life's wisdom beyond those limiting ways. These awakened people won't blurt out superficial answers when you suffer. Their words are full of compassion, which means "to suffer with." Like Jesus these beautiful people will neither separate from nor judge you for what you face. Their words are full of life and the testimony of Jesus' way. They are wellsprings in the desert.

During my own suffering I encountered people who had not been stripped by love's fireworks, and they quickly applied concrete rules to how life should work in my situation. I felt judged. I felt treated as if I were dense and just not willing to carry out the simple remedy. At those times, I wanted to curl up in a corner and hide from life for a while (you will see what the word corner symbolizes later).

I knew that those people were well-intentioned but I felt the sting of the world's expectations that I could not meet. That was their lesser nature blindly "helping me" because they had not yet been stripped of it. That is why Jesus said on the cross (Lk. 23:34), "Father, forgive them; for they do not know what they are doing."

I also encountered a few people who saw my situation beyond concrete rules (where one size fits all). These individuals had suffered through their own fireworks. They were not so quick to judge and confine life experience to simple formulas. They were more discerning; they were patient. Love allows the stripping works for gaining higher, clearer wisdom beyond the earthly fog.

The power to lose hope during trials comes from concluding that trials should not exist. Much of humanity hides behind the façade that life is under control, as if personal trials don't or shouldn't exist. We act like something is wrong when we think we've been doing everything right and then encounter trials. People's everyday façades regularly scream forth the lie to us that we are alone, different, and even defective when we encounter trials that are beyond us. Divided we are conquered, and we lose hope.

Accept periodic trials as inevitable and necessary for all people to awaken into greater love. Greater love will come to pass on this earth as more people embrace suffering as good. Light is meant to shine forth from life's places of darkness. That is Christ's way. The poor of worldly circumstances become rich *in faith* (Jam. 2:5). The outcast, orphan, and widow (those who have no one earthly at their side) come to find a greater love that supports them from the inside. Christ fights to be known by those who suffer. He fights for those who are alone in this world. He wants to become their refuge. But we must let go of lesser ways to receive more of our Refuge.

In some ways I became an outcast and an orphan during my fireworks. But that fire burned away some of my lesser heavens and earth. Suffering revealed to me a higher heaven and new earth. God's fire faithfully broke through the limiting world's ways to free me. Love's fire works … the Rule-Breaker. Always and all ways.

Love's fire is *for* us, and it is inescapable. That is my testimony.

Campfire Intimacy and Wildfire

Do you want to receive heavenly riches? Christ's rest, peace, freedom, and secure love in spite of the earthly chaos around you? I do, and I now gain more of those riches regularly.

I don't mean to imply that I am not fazed by trials and human weakness during fire. As long as gaps exist between earthly and heavenly ways, God will use fire to awaken me to what is currently beyond my human ability. Every time I experience those gaps, I will initially struggle and feel weak. The difference is, now I know that I can receive greater comfort each time I encounter earthly impossibility. I intellectually agreed with those words previously, but not until the fire tested me did I learn how to truly receive support in the midst of difficulties. I now have a way of escape from the lesser things, and God regularly desires to establish higher comfort within me each time I encounter my human weakness. How can I truly comfort others if I do not first receive this higher secure comfort in the various aspects of my life? In any area of my life where I have not awakened to true security, my false performing self will interfere with me being a vessel of true comfort for others.

Continuously receiving God's higher comfort is His primary goal for us during fire. Looking back, that's what most stands out to me overall about God's purpose for fire in my life – receiving His higher comfort. But what actually happened to me during the fire? In the big picture, what did God change at a practical level within me that awakened me to His higher comfort (I progressively share the actual life dynamics and events as I continue)?

The Lord initially worked through the panic attacks for me to rest and unhook from "old moves" to be able to receive *heavenly* comfort, support, and security in place of earthly securities (whether that was from Christ in others or from Him directly). My inability to rest and receive support for a long time was a primary hindrance to uprooting the anxiety and panic attacks. The rural Pennsylvania culture included a strong work ethic, self-sufficiency, and no cracks in the armor, which meant no emotions. The culture almost seemed to ooze, "Let me alone, I can do it" and was counter to receiving (let alone asking for) support. I couldn't see that God wanted me to learn to receive support rather than to be the one always giving it! God desired balanced relationships. I saw later that I had unknowingly maintained level difference in relationships when I was always the one giving to others.

As I received higher comfort and became shifted more onto the true foundation, God then worked in me to continue His works. That built or expanded His spiritual house in me and through me. I could now give comfort to others in ways that I had gained comfort.

Both major fires in my life, the panic attacks and marital trials, also increased intimacy. How? Fire stripped away my ability to walk independently from others, caused me to be more vulnerable with people, and heightened my ability to know God as well as my true self more deeply. Impossible human circumstances had not allowed me to be a lone ranger anymore. Nor had those fiery circumstances allowed me to remain unaware of what I held to be true from deeper within me.

Early in the panic attacks I clung to an ideal image that walking in heavenly ways meant never struggling. Without knowing it I had tried to perform this heavenly feat by behaving those ways while much of my inner world had not yet been transformed. Then after the panic attacks I had actually begun to walk in considerable peace even during outward difficulties. One of the primary differences was that I had begun to be more vulnerable with others when I did struggle. The deeper connection through vulnerability regularly reestablished and maintained my overall peace.

Vulnerability with others who were safe allowed them to be with me during the struggles, which allowed me to know more fully that Christ was with me and for me during struggles. Others receiving my honesty about "what was" in my life, rather than trying to fix my situation, allowed me to be more present during difficulties. Being present continually awakened me to more of my true self and to God.

I learned to accept "what is" about myself and life, whatever the case may be. I saw acceptance as a primary pathway for my true self to emerge. That acceptance of "what is" is God's secure love of us; and friends who received me that way during my trials helped me to further awaken to His love that first loves me where I am. So I sought those few people around me that were brave enough to truly be present with me about the trials rather than those who tried to fix whatever didn't feel good. That presence and acceptance of "what was" awakened me to higher comfort while still in the fire. But I saw that my awakening and receiving higher comfort could not have happened without me first being vulnerable about my struggles and weakness with those who were safe.

My more recent marital trials, then, cemented my vulnerable way of walking that quickly awakened my true self who knew higher comfort. The more I received inner comfort during vulnerability with others, the more I awakened to the transformational path of vulnerability about "what is" in life. The ironic part is, the more I awakened to the path of vulnerability, the more I seemed able to walk in peace even in the midst of horrendous trials. The way of vulnerability had become my way for receiving higher comfort, especially during humanly impossible situations.

Vulnerability during fire increasingly caused realness. Real relationship and connection with others and my true self (Christ within) was the foundation for no-more-alone.

Fire-fire continually shifted me inwardly from a false foundation to my true foundation. From my false performing self to my true self, from earthly will to heavenly will, and from resisting higher ways during fire to honoring Christ's ways of peace and peacemaking anytime peace did not exist. Sometimes peacemaking included boundaries with others where I vulnerably expressed what I could not do in my human nature. These shifts kept replacing my inflated false self's image, guardedness, and individuality with vulnerability and intimacy. As God established these new works within me, I received His higher comfort. I could finally receive "goodness" in deeper places as I more fully acknowledged my need. Then as God established His foundation within me, He worked as a fire through me to awaken others to these ways that establish higher comfort. The scriptures refer to these two fiery works as "grace, grace" but are sometimes described in other ways.[3]

During fire I kept letting go of whatever earthly outcome looked like the right one so that I could see what Christ was working on my behalf. Often, God's fire caused me to let go of common earthly ways and beliefs that had become automatic (e.g., as long as I do such and such, then the right outcome should occur). I was amazed at how predominant common formulas are in others regardless of religious or spiritual labels, or among those who had no label at all. These dominating formulas govern our lives more than we know. They are a false foundation. Really, a false religion within us.

Humanity's lies are endless and love's fire recycles like waves during our earthly journey to uproot those lies. These waves of fire are frequently unseen by others who do not know us intimately, but everyone goes through the fire. Periodic fire awakens me, which keeps ensuring that I'm a safe vessel for awakening others into their true self. Occasionally being salted by fire prevents me from returning to the inflated false self for too long, because only my true self can further awaken others into their true self. We carry within us a resource, power, and love far beyond our imagination. My fiery experiences have awakened me to that fact, and I now burn like a fire to release others further into this true self. Trust that the fire of life does that.

The book's title, "Love's Fire Works ... The Rule-Breaker," has two meanings. God's fiery works break our earthly rules to shift us onto our true self's foundation (our Christ nature), which is our higher comfort and security. That higher nature then, becomes much like fireworks in the sky that awaken others to their true nature, security, and comfort. The fire's initial purpose is to gather us around a campfire for deeper comfort and intimacy with God and one another. Then it purposes to become a wildfire that sparks, moves, and blazes into the sky causing many other campfires.

My fiery panic attacks mostly caused me to learn how to receive higher comfort (the campfire), and then the marital fireworks furthered that foundation while causing me to be a fuller vessel of comfort to others (a wildfire). God used fire-fire to work comfort-comfort. Fire awakened the true self and comfort within me; then the fire worked through me to awaken the true self and comfort in others.

I was astounded to see, after experiencing fire-fire and comfort-comfort at a practical level, that the scriptures point this out in various ways. "Lord, Lord" is an expression of intimacy in the scriptures, and I believe that that intimacy only comes about through fire-fire (Matt. 7:21).

God sometimes said a person's name twice when they followed Him closely ("Abraham, Abraham"; "Moses, Moses"; "Simon, Simon"; see Gen. 22:11; Ex. 3:4; Lk. 22:31). If you look at those related scriptures, you will also see that the Lord used each of their names twice when He was working fire in their lives – with Abraham who was about to sacrifice Isaac, with Moses at the burning bush who was about to go through the fiery trials of Egypt, and with Simon Peter who would be sifted as wheat through the coming cross. God fervently loved each of them but also brought fire into their lives to further intimacy, as well as His kingdom works in and through them.

The double name symbolized intimacy that came through fire. I understand that now. More than I knew throughout my life, I could not become truly intimate with people until I encountered fire-fire. I still have difficulty being intimate with those who come across like they are superhuman, as if they have no weakness and that fire does not touch them in life (I used to be that way!). I have difficulty partly because those ways of living life trigger my old ways, which I now know are lies. I just occasionally fall for those lies when I am in an atmosphere that gives the strong impression that people can float through life untouched by fire. Or, as if they are untouched by human weakness. That's why I believe that God desires greater vulnerability in us, which allows greater intimacy. The realness of vulnerable and intimate relationships establishes greater insulation against the lies that we should be perfect in our human nature.

As my personal fires increased I also gained clarity in my journey with God. I began to see peacemaking and walking in peace as the center of God's two graces. I look back and see my panic attacks mostly as the gut-wrenching peacemaking work that shifted me from the performing self to the true self. From my will to Christ's will and from no peace to peace. Then God used me to touch others with peace when they saw an unexplainable peace within me during much of my marital upheaval. It made no earthly sense to others for me to trust God while total chaos existed in my personal life. That peace touched many people.

I do want to add, however, that I endured the marital trials differently than how I had during the panic attacks. Rather than performing and trying to handle the difficulties well outwardly while in total disarray inwardly, I felt more whole and honest with myself and others during the martial trials. Overall, I was in much peace during those struggles but was also very honest with key friends when my faith wavered. I had matured since the panic attacks.

God worked in other ways through Kathy's and my direct contact during the marital upheaval. He furthered my true foundation but also used me as a peacemaker with Kathy for further establishing her true foundation. Enduring and standing firm for peace when there was no peace further established Christ's foundation in both of us. Honoring heavenly will above earthly will established Christ's peace. Eventually.

If I do not experience inner peace in my life, it demonstrates that I am not fully one with the Spirit of Christ within me. At those times Christ wants to work through me to be a peacemaker. Making peace where there is no peace furthers Christ's will and kingdom on earth, whether that is within me or between me and others. This peacemaking gathers all into Christ's will. Intimate relationship begins when we further unite in Christ's will. Sometimes that means holding fast for a season.

If I am already at peace and one with the Spirit of Christ within me, He will use me to touch others with peace and intimacy. Intimate relationship spreads through touches of peace. I look back and see how my human nature could not achieve peace or truly intimate relationship. Fire-fire alone brought heaven's peace and intimacy into my life. Intimacy began and deepened with the first fire; it became contagious and spread through the second one.

When I trusted that God was with me and for me during the first fiery work, it gradually became a campfire. The first fire gradually unhooked me from the lesser nature and its reliance on the world's futile system. As I let go of those lesser ways and rules, I awakened into more of my true self. That foundation became a campfire where my whole being was focused on and knew the fire's peaceful goodness. That intimate campfire continually increased in me and through me as I cherished it.

Then that campfire threw sparks and became a wildfire that burned away the earthly in others, further awakening them

41

to Christ within (only Christ's higher nature and works cause awakening, which are evident throughout this book). That wildfire continues to unhook others from worldly striving so as to finally be still around the campfire as well. We all have unending earthly ways needing stripped so that we can experience more of the campfire's peace and intimacy. Our journey is fire-fire to go higher. We continually awaken into the true through fire.[4]

What happens at campfires? No one strives to get anywhere. No rules, structure, or expectations. The unity of campfire songs sounds forth into the atmosphere. There's peace, rest, and freedom to be.

In that atmosphere of being rather than doing, I become more relational. I am not so goal-oriented that shuts out relationship with God and others. I enjoy marshmallows and smores with friends. People become philosophical around the campfire. Deeper. Why? The Spirit in us yearns to draw deep to Deep, and we are more able to do that as we unhook from worldly striving and busyness.

God's first fire awakens us through trials to get us to be still around the campfire and become aware that God is God. He gathers us around His fire to know Him and one another more deeply, which causes us to become aware of ourselves more deeply. True identity comes forth around the campfire. We begin to trust Christ's fire that purposes to work good on behalf of us and others.

Once God's first fire awakens and gathers us to join Him and others in campfire intimacy, He begins His wildfire. Wildfires move. They spread beyond human control. After Israel saw that God was God when He delivered them from Egypt's fiery trials, He then regularly moved with them as a pillar of cloud and fire in the desert (although they were only to move as He moved).

That is us. God's wildfire is a collective fire that is easily blown by the wind of His Spirit on behalf of the desert of this earth. The wildfire collectively spreads and burns away the earthly fog to awaken people to God's greater mysteries (one of the greatest ones is the true self within us, which is the mystery of Christ). As more people become shifted over from the false foundation to the true, more of Christ's fullness within humanity will become expressed on this earth.

In my counseling program where I teach, I have a saying: "True self releases true self." It's amazing how much one person communicating from the real ignites others to do the same, even if that is the honest sharing of deep pain. Almost always, one person's risk to be in the true causes a ripple effect of others speaking from deep to Deep. That is a campfire that ignites a wildfire.

God constantly works campfire intimacy and wildfire to cause earth to become as it is in heaven. The campfire collects. The wildfire collectively moves. The campfire unhooks us from futility so as to know Christ in one another in deeper ways. Then we become part of His wildfire that spreads His comforter over others with the comfort we have received (2 Cor. 1:4).

Fire, fire. Grace, grace. Comfort, comfort.

Training

God taught me about long-term suffering during my lengthy fires. Why does suffering sometimes last so long? Why do we go through lengthy periods of trials that are centered on certain issues?

Sometimes trials continue when I resist embracing their messages. But not always. Sometimes lengthy trials are necessary to uproot longstanding patterns, ones that much of the world, religious or otherwise, embraces. The unending trials cause me to acknowledge human weakness and to cry out for Christ beyond all I've known. Sometimes these unknown ways are unseen mysteries.

We only need to observe life and we will see that cyclical trials occur. Don't you experience trials that come in waves at points? I do. These trials are training times with breaks in between. They are God's works to uproot lesser ways to free us into higher, more fulfilling ways.

We can read the scriptures with fleshly lenses or higher spiritual lenses. God's "wrath" and judgment in the Bible are always about our false performing self that is opposed to Him and to who we truly are. That lesser nature hurts and hinders us and we only let go of that nature to the extent that it no longer works for us. Life's trials are God's judgment, help, and stripping works for causing futility to the human nature in order to awaken us to our Christ nature.

That is the meaning in the scriptures (Rom. 8:18-21), "For I consider that the sufferings of this present time are not worthy to be compared with the glory that is to be revealed to us. For the anxious longing of the creation waits eagerly for the revealing of the sons of God. For the creation was *subjected to futility*, not of its own will, but because of Him who subjected it, *in hope that the creation itself also will be set free* from its slavery to corruption into the freedom of the glory of the children of God."

Don't those scriptures cause all of life to make sense? God's goal is to awaken us through periods of earthly frustration. Seasons of training.

Doesn't life teach us that we encounter futility fairly regularly with some breaks in between? The futility is not because of an angry god but because of a God who passionately wants to free us from life's doubt, anxiety, and conflict into freedom, peace, and love. I can honestly say that because of my trials I am far freer from doubt, shame, fear, rules, and other lesser ways that hide who I am (although the journey continues). His stripping works are worth it.

The Voice in the Fire

The testimony of all my fireworks speaks throughout these writings. The order of the fireworks was purposeful. I know that I could not have survived the marital fireworks without having gone through my earlier season of panic attacks.

I had walked with great anxiety for ten years. The last few of those years became full-fledged panic attacks ... until I learned to hear God's voice in the fire.

I first heard God's audible voice during a season where my panic attacks were increasing while teaching at Morehead State University in Kentucky. I had been paying attention to my thoughts at times, wondering whether some of them were God speaking to me. I sensed that some of the thoughts that popped into my head were not ones I would have been inclined to think.

Then I saw an advertisement for a teaching position at Shippensburg University (SU) in Pennsylvania. SU was where I had received my master's degree in counseling. I had always wanted to teach in that program but had never seen an opening that matched who I was. Now, ironically, after nearly ten years of teaching at four other universities in four other states, a position fit me (I always tell people that I kept changing universities because no one would keep me).

Not only did SU fit me, but I could not have written a position description more precisely to fit who I was. Ironically, Kathy and I had decided that Morehead was where we would live out our lives. We loved the rural country feel and the friendships we had made. But surprisingly, Kathy seemed to consider the possibility of moving. I had not had time to think about it after her saying that and then left for work.

Later that morning I happened to mention about this job opening with another faculty member who was spiritual. She asked if I was going to apply, to which I immediately conveyed that it was unlikely. She then asked, "Did you check that with God?" That question halted me in my tracks for a moment because I normally checked with God about everything.

So I went into my office, closed the door, and I sat down at my desk with my eyes closed and asked God, "Should I apply?" The way I handled decisions up to this point was to imagine that I made a decision one way and see what I experienced within me, and then do the same while imagining the opposite decision. I usually paid attention to which direction I experienced more peace and wholeness within me.

This time caught me completely off guard. As I paused, I experienced a pure higher presence and clarity beyond what I had known to this point in my life. I saw huge gold letters while hearing the words very loudly within my head, "You will be at Shippensburg!" As I heard and saw those words (with an exclamation point at the end), I saw many flashes of my life up until this point and I knew that all of life worked together for me to be at Shippensburg. I knew that this move would be difficult and yet completely right for what God was working spiritually in my life (as well as in Kathy's and in my three sons).

I knew that none of this was my own thinking or answer. "Yes" or "no" would have answered the question I had asked. Had the response come in that form, I still wouldn't have known whether it was truly God or not. It could easily have been what I thought I "should do," or it could have been me answering the question the way I wanted it answered.

But I knew the answer was real. I was depressed for the next month and a half (until the deadline for applications) because I desperately did not want to go back to Shippensburg where I was raised. I knew that the culture was more rigid, unemotional, and did not allow for gray areas in life. I had gradually been growing emotionally and spiritually, and I was afraid I would get shut down in these important areas of my life. I was depressed because I dreaded moving there and yet knew I would ultimately heed this spiritual directive I received. I liked the idea of not being so far from Kathy's and my families but was still greatly concerned about me disconnecting from my true self that I was just beginning to know.

I put off writing the cover letter and revising the resume until four days before the deadline. Then I quickly threw them together and put them in the mail with 3 days to spare. At the time I couldn't imagine undergoing intense interviewing with the horrendous panic attacks I was experiencing, and yet I intuitively knew I would get the job no matter what! I knew that I would have to teach a class to the panel of faculty members interviewing me. That seemed impossible to me at the earthly level, and yet my spiritual encounter had ensured me that the new job would come to pass.

Needless to say, all went miraculously well with the interviewing process. That is not to say that I did not experience panic attacks. I just experienced them in between the actual interviews and teaching demonstration! I remember having a panic attack while walking with a faculty member to her office, and I was afraid of totally losing consciousness. As I regained awareness and my footing, I thought, "If they only knew; they might not want me as a student in their counseling program, let alone teaching their students about how to facilitate mental and emotional and health!"

If I Die, I Die

My anxiety and panic attacks were like Jesus' words to the church of Smyrna being tested for ten days (Rev. 2:10-11). Ten days for me had been ten years of anxiety. The number ten in the scriptures isn't about an actual length of time but about a season of refinement.

I hope I don't scare you by my testimony. Please don't believe that going further with God means that you will suffer horribly for years! Part of my testimony is that I suffered that long because I hadn't learned to honor God's voice in the fire. The more that people awaken to honoring God's voice in the fire, the more support we embrace from Christ and one another, which greatly decreases the severity and length of our suffering. But the battle will continually resurface until the lesser nature surrenders and loses its grip over us.

God does not battle against us but against the false performing self that hinders our true self. The scriptures say (Psm. 30:5), "For His anger is but for a moment, His favor is for a lifetime; weeping may last for the night, but a shout of joy comes in the morning." Being awakened into the fullness of our Christ nature is the everlasting morning that comes after a brief night of weeping in the human nature.

Our lesser human nature screams with powerful messages that we need to be better, further, or more than we are to be acceptable. No rest. Being competent in the human nature is essentially a rite of passage for teens to become adults.

We strive and finally become "competent" in that nature. Then God begins to strip us from that nature that learned to become strong in itself. The stripping feels like torment. Hell. Why?

We strived so hard to become competent in the lesser nature that we clung with a death grip to that "success" that was so hard-earned. The scriptures portray those lesser ways as fortified cities with high walls within us (Hos. 8:14; Isa. 2:12-15). Its streets are rigid ways that we are bound to; they are humanity's rules, expectations, and pressure to be competent. Those entrenched ways become a relentless taskmaster within us that allows no freedom, life, or love. The fortified cities must come to ruin, and that lesser nature will weep and gnash its teeth in the process (that is hell!).

As stripping had increased in my life during heightened anxiety, I cried out to God "What's wrong? I'm trying as hard as I can to follow You and nothing's working anymore!" I had still been clinging to earthly ways that had worked previously, and now I was receiving tremendous pressure from God to help me let go of those ways. I just didn't know that for quite a while. The lesser ways needed humbled for the greater to be exalted.

My battle was not yet finished at the ten year point, but I had begun surrendering to the higher voice in the fire. I still remember the turning point during my first few years at Shippensburg.

God opened my eyes during prayer one day about how I had strived in futility for years to bring change through increased prayer and new actions based upon scriptural principles. As I paused and faced that reality I heard God say, "Lift no finger for thirty days." His voice had finally come with clarity from the fire.

I disbelieved what I heard. I thought I would die if I did nothing for thirty days when that anxiety and abandonment overwhelmed me. You may think I am exaggerating. I am not.

I thought I would literally die if I followed God's way of surrender during the fire. But I knew by this point that none of my efforts had worked or were going to work to bring deliverance. So I seriously considered doing nothing during the panic and abandonment. I imagined and wrestled in agony about what life would be like for my three sons and Kathy if I died. That's how serious it was for me. But God comforted me about Kathy and the boys. So I thought, "If I die, I die." [5]

I encountered terrifying ups and downs that first week. I felt like I was going before the firing squad in the minutes leading into teaching classes. At points I thought God might do a miracle and at other times I felt utterly alone. But I remember talking to Kathy by the seventh day about a subtle change I began to notice.

I told her that I didn't feel like anything outwardly had changed but that somehow my faith deeper within me felt faintly stronger. I didn't know how or why, but I felt like I was beginning to get girded up by Christ within me.

I realized later that the subtle new faith was Truth in place of a lie within my soul – I hadn't died! I could no longer be haunted by the lie that I would literally die if I did nothing about the panic and abandonment. That was my soul embracing more of the Christ nature within me rather than lies. (And, that fear of death within me was actually the false self that knew that more of it *would* die.)

By the seventh day I knew enough to know that I would continue walking this way of the cross – God's voice from the fire – not just for thirty days but for the rest of my life. I paused about how my thinking had changed. I now knew that Christ was absolutely in everything and that He was reaching and delivering me personally.

No outside help. No effort on my end. Christ was alive and real, and He was within me.

Christ would not have received the credit when change came to that lost place if I had still been striving, praying harder, reading scriptures more, or looking to some new thing that would deliver me. I would have concluded that my hard work had caused the change, and then my human strength rather than Christ would have received the testimony.

By lifting no finger to save myself for thirty days the scriptures came true (Psm. 46:10), "Be still, and know that I am God." I knew that Christ alone saved me when I exerted absolutely no energy towards change, and change happened.

God reached me when I trusted the cross' way of surrender during fire. I had previously been aware that God was real and good in many ways, but behind this one door in my heart I had no clue that He was with me and for me. That place was a deeper void where I believed nothing could reach or deliver me.

I needed to be still to know that God was God in that place where I knew nothing of Him. I was much like a researcher with all variables constant except for the one being tested. I needed to know that no other variable moved except the unseen God of the universe who met me in that lost place. True testimony!

Ten years with no change, and then through surrendered trust in Christ, finally, change came. Not all at once, but gradually through now surrendering to the voice in the fire.

Old ways and beliefs had become broken by the Rule-Breaker. I came to know experientially God's tested word within me as true.

Love's fire had burned away the old and revealed the new. One nature became humbled and the other exalted. That's what happened to me ... for me. Like Christ, I painfully endured a crown of thorns before receiving a heavenly crown of life.

No human effort or worldly help could take credit for me receiving a crown of life in place of death. God, through Christ's fiery way of the cross, received the glory.

Panic Clothed

The panic attacks leading into my early years at Shippensburg University were essentially spiritual nakedness, although I had not thought of it as that at the time. During this traumatic season I had encountered nowhere earthly to lay my head (like Jesus said about Himself; see Lk. 9:58). I believe that God wanted me to experience the inability to meet my needs through the earthly realm to awaken me to higher ways. He was available to support me and wanted to provide that support, but I had not yet known how to turn to Him as comfort in that place that seemed void of anything good.

At a practical level I was not to look outwardly at Kathy, childhood, or the world for excuses about the abandonment I experienced within me. I was no longer to strive to fill that hole in my soul. God wanted to free me by me becoming still and naked before Him with no one else to hide behind (which God also accomplished in Kathy through the marital fireworks).

I am not saying that you should not have the support of others around you. Look for Christ's support wherever that comes from. But you will not experience true support when your eyes are fixed on people's human nature to deliver you rather than on Christ within them being your help. There's a difference. The "senseless" stripping will continue till you are awakened to the two natures within people and that only Christ's higher nature delivers you.

In that place of only me and Christ I became convicted of the lesser nature's uselessness in me and in all people. My eyes opened more deeply to these two natures within. I saw that my needs were never met by anyone's lesser nature and that it was futile to expect that. I also came to see that only Christ, whether that was Him directly or His higher nature coming through me or others, truly met my needs. I saw that it was always Christ.

You are no longer blind when you see these two natures and desire to participate with the Christ nature amidst the stripping works. You may periodically encounter fogs or miss-steps but overall you have found the way.

Nakedness finally freed me from the futility of striving. I became further clothed in my true self, in Christ, and my eyes became clear from looking outwardly for peace, freedom, and love. Others' Christ nature allowed me to experience and awaken to the Christ nature within me, but my peace, freedom, and love ultimately came from within. Panic had been clothed by Christ, which prepared me for my marital fireworks. That was also the beginning of my eyes being freed from staring at outer darkness. Then my marital fireworks further freed me from that log in my eye.

CHAPTER 3

Behold, Love's Fiery Testimony

A Glimpse of My Fiery Journey

I would have published a lesser form of this book about three years earlier but I was convicted to no longer hide anything about my life. That changed my writing. It changed this book.

I received feedback that I was not to go half way in my writing – put it all out there or don't say it at all. I wrestled with that because I didn't want to share in a way that could cause people to judge anyone who was part of my trials. Also, the choice was not mine alone. Kathy and I had been experiencing marital difficulties, and sharing my story was dependent upon her being willing to share.

I'm sure this rule of protecting people's privacy was compounded by the fact that I am a counselor who must maintain confidentiality. But this rule had become an idol bigger than God in my heart, and it caused me to stay hidden more than God desired.

So I continue to share as real and practical as I can while remaining respectful of all people involved. No one deserves to be judged because we are only able to love to the degree that God has awakened us. We love to the degree of His mercy and grace.

A funny incident happened to me a few days after I received feedback from three people about fully revealing my heart in this book. Actually, the incident didn't just happen to me. I did it to myself.

I had been giving myself haircuts and grabbed the clipper for another one. I put the clipper's 3/8 inch attachment on the counter, plugged in the clipper, and blazed away. I looked into the mirror with shock and saw a bald stripe straight back the middle of my head. I had forgotten to put on the 3/8 inch attachment!

Here I was, a 55 year old grandfather with a bald stripe down the center of my head with about an inch of hair on each side (a skunk stripe, bright in the middle and dark on both sides). Thinking that this was a bit extreme for my age, I cut off the rest of my hair. I later told my youngest son who came for a visit that I had originally given myself a No-hawk (rather than a Mohawk).

A few days later I sensed that my shaved head was by God's hand. I had never forgotten previously to clip on the attachment. I saw that God sovereignly worked to have me exposed to reinforce His message to me about not hiding. And that is how I first felt upon seeing my surprise haircut. Exposed!

I was clear that God wanted me to be utterly real. He wanted me to give testimony to love's fireworks at a practical level. I was to bare everything. And the words "be real" were used several times in the preaching I heard the following day.

These coincidences pushed me over the hump. The decision to bare everything was difficult for me because I was convicted not to release the book until Kathy and I were united about sharing our story. That seemed like the equivalent of God having to move heaven and earth at the time. It potentially meant death to this book that I had suffered and died for (at least that's how I felt)!

Would God actually work the impossible? Part of me knew that I was to go for it all by letting go of it all. No timeline. No pressure or energy about making any outcome happen.

So I prayed. I wrestled with God and asked if it was His desire for me to include my personal story of Love's fireworks in this book. Then during a period of stillness, I saw a full-color glimpse of Kathy saying, "It needs to be released." The glimpse was just enough for me to commit to God to not publish the book until Kathy said those words (or at least the spirit of those words). I even wondered if my addition of "at least the spirit of those words" was me already hedging on my commitment. I asked for the grace to hold fast.

Later that day, and at various other points when that glimpse became fainter I thought, "What did I do?" But God gave grace for me to stand firm about my commitment to Him.

Kathy did end up saying those exact words over two and a quarter years later, just prior to me using the manuscript to teach a spiritual course at the university. I was planning to teach the course without our story as part of the manuscript unless Kathy said otherwise.

Kathy's words about releasing the book were emotional for both of us because they were the completion of what the Spirit initiated over two years earlier with the glimpse I had seen. God's timing of it was a miracle to me. I happened to look at the date just after Kathy said those words and didn't know why I did so. I knew that I had specifically looked, not for the time, but for the date for some reason.

The date was 6/24 of 2014. God had often used numbers to draw Kathy's and my attention to some issue addressed in the scriptures. Later when I paused about 624, Isaiah suddenly popped into my mind. I had preached on Isaiah 61 and 62 over two years earlier. Isaiah 61 in the NIV translation uses the word "bestow" several times and is about God bestowing His heavenly riches in our places that had been barren. I also knew that Isaiah 62 was about bestowing a new name.

Could it be that Isaiah 62:4 was that new name? My heart stirred, wanting to see whatever this new name was. I then went to those scriptures and saw that verses 2 and 3 described God bestowing on His followers a new name and what that experience would be like. Then verse 4 conveyed what that new name is! You will likely be astounded by that new name and how perfectly it fit Kathy's and my trials as well as the outcome God had worked for us.

Isaiah 62:4 states, "No longer will they call you Deserted, or name your land Desolate. But you will be called Hephzibah [My delight is in her], and your land Beulah [Married]; for the Lord will take delight in you, and your land will be married."

"Your land will be married." Wow! I sat in wonder as I digested the magnitude of what had just happened.

The Lord had done that actual work within and between Kathy and me. He had taken us from a long period of desolation to being truly married in His higher works and ways. All who experienced our situation knew that restoration was humanly impossible.

To me, 624 was a miracle that put God's stamp on *Love's Fire Works*. It was God's timing after His many works to bring restoration. It was a miracle after many other miracles along the way. I now knew, because my hands had completely let go of the book, that God desired its release. I also believe that Kathy and I felt emotional about releasing the book because its release seemed to be the completion of God's purpose for the trials we endured.

About two weeks later I accidentally came across another 624 verse when exploring a completely different topic than marriage. I saw in the scriptures that the angel of the Lord had shown Himself to Gideon, called him a valiant warrior, and then came to him exclaiming peace. Then Gideon built an alter to the Lord and called it "The Lord is Peace" (Jdg. 6:24).

That was also my experience on 624 (June 24th). Similar to Gideon I felt like fire had come from heaven and then brought me peace. I felt like God confirmed and released that peace to go forward on 6/24 of 2014.

Fortunately love's stripping works awaken us when we look to Christ. The hell of labor births life. The hell and death of winter bring forth spring. Our inexpressibly painful trials bring wisdom and higher life when we look to God during them.

In varying degrees, hell and death are necessary to make a way for life. That's God's word that is demonstrated through Jesus' earthly walk. That's also been my experience.

At the beginning of our upheaval, Kathy and I had a passion to go further with God, so love's fire went further. We tried to help a relative survive a life and death battle (I will call him Bob). He had made some unwise life decisions and was now struggling to regain stability. He had been hospitalized for a season without any improvement. We brought him to live with us, mainly to provide a healthy peaceful place while finding him the help he needed. That lasted four months to the day.

That was the beginning of our hell on earth for a season. Just prior to bringing Bob home to live with us the Lord clearly conveyed to me, "This is for a testimony of Me." Of course I had my versions of what that testimony would look like.

Heroic faith. Miraculous healing. Living happily ever after.

Not long into this four month battle I felt utter inadequacy rather than heroism. I saw my helplessness to make a difference. Here I was, a counselor and spiritually passionate person whose identity was healer, and I could not touch the gravity of the situation.

Communication with Bob was impossible. Nothing penetrated his distorted world. At times he remained suicidal, and whatever decisions we made connected to him were filled with life and death consequences.

Not only did I see my inadequacy but I felt people's judgment about why I was not able to bring the good outcome. People regularly questioned why Kathy and I made one decision versus another during this intense battle. I poured out my heart to follow Christ as best I could, and nothing seemed good enough to bring change or to satisfy the many armchair quarterbacks.

But God used my season of inadequacy to ignite regularly passionate prayer. Deep called to Deep. I thirsted for more than the world could give me during this wilderness. I prayed tenaciously for God to teach me His higher ways beyond what I currently knew. I especially prayed for Him to deliver me from fear of people's judgment.

God answered. Eventually. I just didn't expect Him to answer the way He did. He broke my rules and ways for a lengthy season to awaken me to higher ways.

Another extended family member wanted a shot at reaching Bob, so he took Bob from our home after exactly four months. But Bob remained unreachable. Bob was then hospitalized, and, most importantly, God began working more fully on Bob's heart. After this whole ordeal, Bob knew that God had stirred up faith in him during this period. How did God do that?

Honesty had finally occurred between Bob and his wife. Real connection rather than falseness about crucial issues finally occurred. God then used Bob's wife to cause him to know he could still be loved in spite of some serious mistakes. She had loved and forgiven him for things he had felt were unforgivable. That forgiveness caused Bob to know experientially that God could forgive him, which brought peace back to his relationship with God.

God's love coming from outside of Bob (from his wife) caused him to awaken to the love he carried within him … just like had happened to me. For me, that love had come in the form of acceptance during human inability (which allowed me to forgive myself for "weakness"). For Bob, love had come in the form of forgiveness for wrongs.

Forgiveness took the power out of the wrongs. Lack of forgiveness would have retained that power (Jn. 20:23).

Soon, Bob began spending more focused time with God. He was released from the hospital and never went back. Medication was no longer needed, his job and family were restored, and he walked faithfully with God.

Love's fireworks had caused Bob to let go of lesser ways and to be awakened to God more fully … as well as to his true identity as a child of God fervently loved by Him. God had brought Bob to the warmth, peace, and intimacy of His campfire that unhooked him from striving and isolation.

Bob had not been reached by us in some evident miraculous way like I originally pictured. But Bob changed. His lesser ways of life were replaced with a higher, freer way of walking in his true self. We were very thankful for Bob's restoration into a man with God's higher wisdom.

Suffering beautifies us. Love's fire works to bring beauty from the ashes.

Meanwhile, the trauma connected to Bob living with us exposed unseen marital gaps for Kathy and me. Kathy felt separation between us. She wanted greater unity and security and was frustrated that she could not get that with me. In an attempt to cause some kind of awakening in me, Kathy left and moved in with her parents.

I was stunned.

Life suddenly blindsided me at no choice of my own. One moment I was minding my own business trying to follow God as well as I could, and the next moment I was slapped in the face with an unreturnable-to-the-familiar season. One moment I defined myself as a caring husband and the next moment I found myself in the category "separated."

Love's Fire Alarm

Please hear my compassion for Kathy, me, and all of us connected to this story. We only grow or awaken through knowing love. But sometimes our lesser loves need broken for us to further awaken to the greater. That is true for each area of our life. Freed from our lesser securities we are able to embrace more of true Security.

Our story is one of utter brokenness and helplessness on one hand, and transformation and beauty on the other.

I want to honor Kathy for her willingness to allow me to share our story. I also want to honor her God-ordained part in this fire. She was a fire alarm. Kathy's heart expressed more than could be said and knew more than could be seen. It was a lengthy time before God's purpose that was initiated through her became visible.

Have you felt like a fire alarm who feels deep gaps where more is to be worked but you can't fully see or express what that is? Or have you been on the receiving end of a fire alarm with its sight on you and yet there is nothing understandable about the gaps or any way forward to bring restoration? Both parts are the groaning of the Spirit that is deeper than words. Both parts are necessary.

Kathy was the Spirit's fire alarm. I was the fireman who kept my sight on accessing the Living Water that would eventually put out the fire. But various people thought that I should be able to immediately put it out, as if it was under my control. At least that's how I felt viewed by Kathy and others during the intensity of the flames.

I instinctively knew that the fire was well beyond earthly control. I knew that I had no power to put out the fire. In the Spirit I knew that Christ meant for the fire to blaze for a while, and for a season I withdrew from the chaos to a "cave" so as to watch and join with what God was working.

I knew enough to know that Kathy's senses were real but I could not be what she wanted no matter what I said, did, or prayed. I believed her. But, to me, it seemed like she thought I would be transformed into what she needed if I believed her. And she was temporarily unable to stop focusing on me to obtain what was missing. That, too, was part of how God brought further awakening.

I found in the end that there was a higher role for me to play but I could not see that from the beginning. Nor could anyone around me provide input for how to become what was missing. I can now say that I see a way that neither I nor those around me knew at a practical level. I also knew that I was not to see this unknown way until God completed numerous works He desired. God was working the times and seasons and they weren't in Kathy's and my control even though we wanted them to be.

This unseen way that I was to learn was about *how* to more fully lay down my life for my friend.

Many people are aware of the importance of laying down their lives like Jesus did. But few are aware of how to lay down their lives when words or loving actions in general will not work. In other words, the often advised "Kill her with kindness" (win Kathy with good deeds) would not work.

Fierce Fireworks

I was shocked when Kathy left and moved in with her parents. I felt betrayed, hurt, and grieved. Both Kathy and I had been impacted and were afraid of people's judgment and expectations when Bob initially had not been healed. I also felt as if Kathy saw me as the reason for the upheaval. That was still by God's hand.

I felt expectations and pressure (from Kathy and from within me) to be what she needed for regaining security. Little did I know that these higher fireworks were still answers to my prayers. They just didn't feel like answers for a long season.

Prior to these fireworks Kathy and I had occasionally encountered maritally what we saw as "the spot." My history connected to the spot was to try too much in the human nature to please Kathy, which only established a temporary external security (kind of like her wanting me to be her knight in shining armor and me trying to be that knight for her).

We had made progress in me not being her perfect knight and her not desiring a perfect knight. But everything went through the roof during the last phase of Bob living with us. I felt as if God resorted to a beyond-human level to uproot those dynamics and to awaken us to more of His mysteries.

I continued to seek what God desired in me through this extreme upheaval. From the panic attacks in my life I had learned to see God in everything and to pay attention to what He was after in me. That was my main focus, along with me knowing that I was not to try to superficially be Kathy's source or rock (which had interfered with Christ being that Rock). I knew that I was to learn more about how to support her in this process, but at this point, I could do nothing except wait and pray until God revealed more.

That was difficult. It was gut-wrenching to know that Kathy suffered while I did nothing tangible about it. But I was clear within my heart that nothing I currently knew would alleviate the suffering. Chasing or outwardly appeasing that part in Kathy that did not know security (and frequently wanted it through me) was not going to work. I had previously gone that direction many times.

Some people disagreed with me and judged me as an uncaring husband. I who was known as a caring, understanding counselor was now seen as unloving to my wife. My earthly identity was shattered.

The gravity of the situation initially overwhelmed me in spite of my desire to awaken to God's purposes. I grieved sporadically for about six weeks after Kathy moved out. At times I felt despair and hopelessness. At other times God met me personally and provided spiritual sight for enduring a lengthy season of trials (although later I questioned those encounters when certain people around me challenged my walk).

Kathy and I went as a couple to several places for help. But nothing brought sense to the upheaval. People who tried to help received little direction from God and expressed being confused about our situation.

Individually I sought some spiritually grounded people for support. The input I kept getting from them was similar to what my spirit knew. Pay attention to what God was after in me day by day without having my sights on Kathy. That girded me up for walking by faith during these trials.

Inwardly Christ's leading was similar to how He had led me during the panic attacks: lay down my earthly desires so I could see and join with His work. I had learned that failing to lay down earthly desires blinded me spiritually. But laying down my desires during this season still brought no clarity about our marriage. At times it struck me that it might be an unknown way. If it was, I could not see it.

Everything I sensed personally as well as the input I received from my support people was to wait on God. Nobody seemed to receive anything further. No clear direction.

Their input confirmed the bigger picture I sensed from God – everything between Kathy and me was locked up for a season in spite of our trying to participate with Him. In fact, the week after Kathy moved out, God met me one morning in the kitchen with clarity and a higher sense of His presence. God emphasized to me that He desired this work and that it would bring us greater fullness and peace than we had known and that it would be used to awaken others. I remember feeling great relief even though God conveyed that this work would take well over a year. I initially told people that this would be a long God-work, possibly a year or more. But the work ended up being about two and a half years from the point that we had brought Bob to live with us.

I knew that working at communication was temporarily impossible, even with others' support. The evidence since things had erupted had consistently demonstrated that. Of course imperfections existed on both our parts, but scrambling to change certain imperfections was not the fire's purpose. God was not an ogre god demanding that we somehow change certain sins. He was more loving and patient than the world or religion had conveyed to me. But it didn't mean that the fire for stripping flesh nature was pain-free!

My ongoing spiritual sense was that God sovereignly worked this situation to be beyond all human control. God desired a prison where earthly answers were unavailable. The unavailability of lesser answers caused the deep within us to seek higher answers through Christ. The verse that most came to mind about our situation at various points was (Rev. 3:7), "He ... who opens and no one will shut, and who shuts and no one opens." I believe this word applies to many others during this spiritual season.

Your heart will sense this just as mine did. Let go. Allow love's fireworks. Allow the cross. Step forward only as you receive light and peace; otherwise, wait.

Hell and death in various forms were allowed for a season. It was a long season for us. Kathy's dad died a few months after she had moved into her parents' place. Later, we could see that it was God's timing for Kathy to be there to help her parents during their season of loss. But the loss of Kathy's dad was a tremendous blow to us on top of our already-intense fire. My relationship with Kathy's family had been temporarily uprooted even though her brothers still desired to have me be a pall bearer for the funeral. Some people who witnessed our struggle concluded that I should have worked harder at communication with her and that not doing so meant that I didn't really love her. That simply blew me away, after all I had consistently demonstrated for years! Kathy also believed that about me during much of our upheaval, and it devastated me (although God intended this void of certain earthly supports during this season for stripping away more of my earthly crutches).

At one point I feared that all friends and people I knew would simply judge me as a bad husband. I felt alone. I even had a glimpse of touching experientially what Jesus might have experienced when everyone around Him abandoned Him and no longer believed the truth about Him. At that very moment I remembered previously asking God to deliver me from the fear of people (when we initially tried to help Bob). I saw that people's judgment was God's fire and an answer to my prayers. Thank God for help!?!

God pressed upon me that I could not be delivered from the fear of people if I was still filled with people's approval. Ugh. Christ as my Rock in that place only became true when people's approval and provisions were temporarily burned away by fire. Only by being emptied of people's approval could Christ become my substance and truth in that place. God has surely awakened more of my soul to be on His rock versus me relying on people's approval. God was faithful to answer my prayers but it sure took fire to reach me in that deep place.

That's what seemed most unfair to me when God initially brought these fireworks. I had already grown significantly in following Christ rather than doing what I did to please Kathy or others. But apparently God knew I would stop short of that full work. He had a much freer way in mind for me.

I know that without the trials I endured I would not have had the courage to speak boldly about areas that conflict with many people's religious views. The clarity and depth of the spiritual truths conveyed in these works would not have existed. These trials have further produced in me Christ's greater love and works that do not bow to people's lesser ways (although I have considerable work still to be done!). I knew that God also initiated these trials through Kathy for me to learn more about the gaps she sensed, but awareness of this only came through further birth pangs.

Encountering True Testimony

I often wondered if Jesus' unusual directive to tell no one about His miracles was because He didn't want further earthly attention. I also thought it might be because He didn't want to go to the cross before the acceptable time.

I believe that these explanations are part of Jesus' reasoning. But I never felt resolution that these reasons were Jesus' full purpose behind His unusual statements to people He healed. Only as I began writing this book did I learn what I believe was Jesus' fuller purpose – one that brought greater focus and clarity to the overall message that burns within me.

Immediately after exhorting a leper to tell no one about the miracle Jesus told him to show himself to the priest for a testimony to them (Lk. 5:14). The underlying purpose, as is always true with the scriptures, was for then and for now. Jesus wanted the priest to *encounter* the healed leper and His works that occurred.

Showing the works is testimony of the works. Those works speak louder than telling others about some end result.

I share my own testimony in this book so that you will encounter God's works in me rather than empty words. Through sharing my journey or testimony you get to experience God's ways and works that delivered me from the impossible in my life. Telling you about how spiritual concepts and principles are supposed to work without revealing the works themselves would have left you empty.

Had the leper only stated the end point of being healed, others would have encountered no spiritual experience or testimony of God. It would have been empty words. Jesus wanted more than that.

People can see or hear about an end result and still not know God. There is no testimony. People must encounter the works and the experience of the one going through those works to learn of God. That's why Thomas, the apostle who doubted, wanted to encounter the resurrected Lord. He wanted to know for himself. Being told outcomes usually remains hearsay to us.

Telling people about the final outcome of a good novel or movie defeats the whole purpose of them having their own genuine experience that moves or changes them. They are robbed of an encounter. Simply telling others about the outcome of a book puts that book into a particular box based upon superficial words. The label attached to it might be way off base.

That can happen with this book like it can with any book. I can say up front that this book doesn't fit under any specific label. These works have not been heavily influenced by any single person, book, or theology even though I have been impacted by a wide variety of people.

There are many forerunners to various ideas found throughout this book. I thank them for their messages. But I have not read a book with the particular unified scriptural interpretations that come through these writings. The ideas behind what I've written mostly come from the scriptures as well as from the Spirit and love's fireworks in my own life. I speak what I've experienced.

So with this book I ask that you let the tree be known by its fruit. Fruit speaks louder than words. It gives testimony. True testimony brings life-filled relationship with one another – the birthing works of God.

Scattered

While Kathy and I were separated I noticed how God filled my gaps regarding knowing Him. I knew God and His goodness in many ways but I had certain gaps within me that hadn't known Him.

Christ is the gap filler, the One who completes what is incomplete or unawakened in our souls. But He completes us through first scattering us.

During my fireworks I learned that God first scattered me, and He showed me where He scattered me *to*. I was scattered to where Jesus told us that we would be scattered to during the cross. Jesus said (Jn. 16:32), "But a time is coming, and has come, when you will be scattered, each to his own home …"

I was not scattered to a physical home but to what I knew, to the familiar. I was scattered to the lesser securities found previously in my life (just like Israel wanted to go back to Egypt)! For Peter it had been love of fishing rather than love of people.

During my panic attacks I was scattered to my old "home" of striving and achieving as my security. Then during my marital fireworks I was scattered to my old home of not being a villain. Acting in a way that caused others pain in life was not to exist. This overall way was good, but to me it was a rule higher than God. Somehow God seemed unavailable to me when He initiated a "new move" that went beyond my box of "being nice," of what ideally "should be." I could not hear Him as easily at those times because my heart had not wanted any course of action that might mean me being perceived as a villain. He could not easily reach me when it meant me stepping in ways that could cause others to have to face their pain (Kathy and I remaining apart for a season allowed her to more fully face deeper areas within herself rather than focusing on me).

Jesus' actions sometimes evoked hurt in others. The Pharisees come to my mind.

Sometimes Jesus denied what people wanted. Other times His responses caused people's flesh nature to react. Jesus said to Peter, "Get behind Me Satan." Jesus delivered a man from the legion of demons and then disallowed that man to come along with Him.

Rejection. Scattered. Love has boundaries that confuses and humbles human nature at times.

But the scattering was purposeful. Just prior to Jesus' statement about being scattered to our own homes He conveyed a picture of a woman painfully giving birth and described how her sorrow would be turned to joy (Jn. 16:20-23). Jesus added that the disciples would ask no questions when their joy became complete. I relate to this.

God's sovereign goal through the cross that scatters us is to bring completion in our places that do not know Him. I did not know Christ in ways that followed the Spirit fully in spite of being misunderstood and potentially judged by others as uncaring.

Christ was shaking my fleshly tree so that false leaves fell away. That hurt. But Christ filled more gaps within my soul where I had not known true security that was not dependent on earthly affirmation. He filled more of those empty places with Himself. Higher life, like a child, must be born within the soul.

I saw that sorrow was turned to joy and that I had no questions when God planted this higher life into my soul in areas that hadn't known Him. I saw how He had worked His cross to awaken me more fully in Him, and I found that I became fully satisfied in each newly awakened area of my life. That was wholeness in those areas. Completion.

Completion requires first being scattered to your own home. You must be scattered to your worldly ways that have brought false security. How many times must you run to your false securities before letting go of them? A dog returns to its own vomit (that expression always sounded disgusting!). During the cross and times of upheaval human nature returns to what it has known – old food that was really a lot of crap! During the cross you will return to rejecting others before getting rejected if that has been your way. Or, you will return to being outward directed during conflict rather than to acknowledge your fallibility or fear if that has been your way.

During my panic attacks I had returned to handling everything with no support because that had been my home. Then during my marital cross I returned to not being the villain because that had also been my home. How did God accomplish restoration in me when He allowed and even sovereignly worked this return to my own home?

I returned to my lesser ways and *no longer experienced those ways working*. Then, from deep within, I finally let go of the lesser for Christ to complete (or awaken) me in that place of need. I let go of more false leaves to receive more eternal ones within my soul.

I needed to experience my old ways as no longer satisfying for me to surrender into Christ being the Way for me in each aspect of my life.

Ask for spiritual eyes during times of the cross. Ask to see what your home or way has been that Christ is working to uproot. Christ wants to uproot our lesser roots so that He can be our never-failing Root. Ask for the grace to surrender old ways, ways that you may have seen as truth. Let go of old ways so that the new would be planted in the good ground that bears God's fruit. That good ground is the soul opened up to and embracing the true seed in new places.

God gains testimony when He completes your soul in that place where your old home is no longer your refuge. Then Christ becomes your refuge and others encounter His finished works in place of lesser ways. More heaven on earth.

The Third Way

Early in my marital struggles I attended a spiritual retreat where God uprooted more of my old ways and ignited a passion in me to be who I truly am. He used this retreat to birth my true identity more fully.

I asked in advance where this retreat was located but no one could tell me because it was on a Pennsylvania mountain in the middle of nowhere. To my surprise I found upon arrival that this retreat occurred on the very mountain and road where I was born and raised till age ten. During free time I walked from the retreat location to my birth home.

What a coincidence! God physically took me to my own earthly home and roots. I had been scattered physically and spiritually to my old home. That very weekend God shifted me from a familiar earthly way of passivity to a higher Home of standing in whom I truly am. I saw it as a sign and wonder.

I was a follower rather than a leader much of my life. Follow the rules and authorities' leading was my overall way. Teaching and doing counseling gradually caused me to walk in more of who I was, but I still held back fuller expression of the real me. God used the marital fireworks and the retreat to further burst me forth from the outer shell that always hid me. At the least, I clearly saw God's deep desire to further release me into my identity while at the retreat. I saw that He was presently doing that work through difficulties that could not be overcome without the true coming forth. I saw that I had no way out except faith. He was not against me but was purposely stripping away the earthly nature so that I *would* stand. He was for me and desired to gird me up to stand in my true identity in the difficult places.

Seeing God's purpose while at the retreat reminded me of a friend's vision about me. He had received the vision at the beginning of my lengthy marital trials. I believe the vision also applies to people as a whole.

In my friend's vision he saw me standing in front of two houses. I faced those two houses, one to my right and one to my left. A man came from the house on my right and stood facing me, angled just off to my right. Another man came from the house on my left and also stood facing me from just off to my left. The man from my left was very angry. In his anger he scraped my scalp open with his fingernails as I stood in place, and it bled. Then he went back into his house. The man on my right stood watching the whole event and then returned to his house without saying or doing anything.

My scalp miraculously healed as I stood in place. A few moments later a raging beast came from the angry man's garage. The beast was the size of the garage. Full of rage it charged me as fast as it could. I did nothing but stand firm in faith as I faced it. As the beast neared me it saw my unwavering faith and collapsed into a heap at my feet.

As I contemplated my friend's vision I saw that the two houses are two worldly ways. One way used power; the other avoided power. Each person symbolized an aspect of human nature that comes from the void of not knowing true support and love. The void of love causes a void of security. At some level human nature recognizes its insecurity and selfish tendencies towards power to try to establish security.

Using power depicts the flesh nature's deep awareness of lack and how it uses power to try to force or take what will bring security. Then flesh becomes angry when it can't get what it lacks. That anger sometimes increases into a beast when flesh blatantly sees its selfish and destructive ways. It attempts to destroy anything that appears like power in others because of hating its own destructive power.

Avoiding power, in contrast, symbolizes flesh being deeply aware of power's destructiveness, which causes it to fear power in self and others. That avoidance of power is accompanied by passivity, lack of inner support, lack of deeper relationship, and susceptibility to being used or abused.

All people have participated with both worldly ways, although people tend to lean in one direction or the other during trials. But using or avoiding power fails to establish the security that can only be found in God's love. Using or avoiding power interferes with knowing love because lies govern those worldly ways.

I knew that I had always tended towards passivity in life, symbolized by the man on the right that silently watched the painful interaction. I knew, throughout my life, that I had tried to avoid impacting people negatively by holding back in relationships and life circumstances. I saw how that passive man in the vision stood by watching yet avoiding the painful interaction. He didn't get involved. I know that passive way in life. Yes, it avoids pain in some ways but communicates that injustices don't really matter. Keep everything conflict free as much as possible. But then the wrongs continue because of no intervening interactions.

The vision taught me that God desired to gird me up to stand in Truth rather than to walk in either of the two worldly ways. Rather than pretend (like the passive man had done) that the man who used power did not hurt anyone, I was to stand and face that man. I was not to try to change him nor to turn some other direction. Only by standing fast in faith and being upright and clear in my true self would the man of power lose power. The scriptures (Eph. 6:11-14; Heb. 10:23; Mal. 3:2) say much about standing firm and holding fast, and numerous times they ask some form of the question "Who will stand in the day of the Lord?"

The day of the Lord is supposed to come upon all for testing His word within us (and is not just some single final day or outcome). God wants the worldly forces to come against human nature within us to strip it away and cause us to stand in who we truly are. We must lose one life to gain the other. God *wants* us to gain true life. He wants to gird us up and help us stand in the Truth rather than to succumb to the lies during those worldly forces. Human nature is *not* to stand during those times but the true is. That is the inevitable narrow gate that all people must go through, although awakened individuals are more aware of participating with God when encountering that gate's stripping works.

During the testing I experienced both kinds of worldly forces that caused me to question God's love. And when the lies did not cause me to fold from the inside, the world sometimes brought an even larger beast from the outside that attempted to threaten me (the judgment, anger, or condemnation from others). But those more significant tests were to cause me to awaken into an even more secure foundation of love.

God's constant goal during my encounters with those worldly forces was to refine me like gold (Mal. 3:2). He wanted to use every single trial I faced *to help me stand* through the tests that were meant to strip away the lesser nature and its lies. That was my ongoing experience, and the vision portrayed that.

The kingdom cannot be established by the two worldly ways seen in the vision. Those ways are rooted in fear because of not knowing love. Force or passivity that comes from not knowing God's love will not stand. Fortunately God showed me a third way, the way of Christ.

The third way of standing in the Truth brought Life into my hopeless situations. It was not passivity; it was about standing and walking in my true identity. Sometimes being awakened into my true identity meant waiting during trials, which appeared passive to most people. But this third way was about participating with God's stripping works to bring forth my true identity.

I did not achieve this third Way by striving or forcing myself to be more than I presently was. This way emerged through trusting that God wanted me to be who He made me to be. If you cannot trust that God wants to comfort and gird you up during the fire, find someone to stand with you in trust.

All of life points to the Truth, but the Truth could only set me free when I came to experientially know Truth. That is what love's fire births – a personal encounter with Truth. The scriptures say (Jn. 8:32), " … and you shall *know* the truth, and the truth shall make you free." Intellectually knowing the truth was not enough to free me. I only came to know the truth as well as freedom when I experientially encountered Christ's eternal works. I encountered His inner riches of peace and love in spite of horrible circumstances. Only then did I come to know my true self more fully and that He was for me in all things.

Love is in the Tree

Love is in the Tree

Part of standing in my true self meant allowing God to strip away the false while He awakened, or filled up my soul with, the true. To do that, I needed to see with Christ's eyes about "all things working together for good" rather than with fleshly separating eyes.

Our greatest enemy of awakening to Christ's never-failing love is the fleshly mind that perceives separation from God and each other. The fleshly mind has deceived us.

Fortunately love seeks to fill gaps. That's what is meant by the scriptures (Prov. 10:12), "Hatred stirs up strife, but love covers all transgressions." Love fills up what is empty, clothes what is naked, and covers or completes places of lack.

The scriptural counterpart to the above verse adds more to the picture of love (Prov. 17:9), "He who covers a transgression seeks love …" We don't know love when we hide or cover up our transgressions. We would never hide our imperfections if we truly knew love. We would not cover ourselves with false leaves if we knew true love that fills all gaps.

All human actions can be reduced to one of two motives in life, which are often beneath our awareness: we are motivated by love to fill other's gaps when we know love, and we are motivated to fill our own gaps when we don't know love. Our flesh nature that does not know love works in false ways to fill our perceived gaps; and our Christ nature that knows love works in His higher ways to fill others' gaps (although sometimes our flesh nature outwardly tries to fill others' gaps as a false means for filling our own).

This section's picture of two trees is a great illustration of our Christ nature and flesh nature. The tree filled with leaves is our tree of life within us. That is our already-completed Christ nature. We experience no nakedness, void, or insecurity when we abide in that nature. The tree is restoration itself and is full of eternal healing leaves that seek to fill gaps within all souls, including our own.

The tree with missing leaves is our flesh nature. We experience gaps, abandonment, nakedness, and insecurity when our souls abide in the flesh nature. That is the same nakedness that Adam and Eve recognized when they participated with that lesser nature. They didn't feel clothed or complete so they hid from God. Their souls hadn't truly known love, which was evident when the serpent was able to convince them that God wasn't trustworthy. That distrust of love caused their lesser actions. Not knowing or trusting love from within was the true sin that gave way to outer sin.

Haven't you experienced thoughts that lifted you into higher loving places versus ones that pulled you in lesser ways? Doesn't that sound familiar, kind of like the angel in one ear and the devil in the other? That is the two natures within us that draw our attention.

Don't you experience insecurity, emptiness, or abandonment at times? I do. And don't you also experience total security and awareness of love at other times? That shows which nature we are in at the moment.

But what flounders back and forth from nature to nature? From kingdom to kingdom?

That is our soul with its free choice. In the picture we could have drawn the soul in between and just below the base of the two trees. Our soul looks to one of the two trees throughout life for fulfillment.

The soul is our journeyer. It is like a cup that seeks to be filled. It consists of the mind, will, and emotions, and becomes filled with what it seeks. The soul becomes built up in Christ when it seeks and joins with the Christ nature. Yet our soul's growth is simply an awakening to our Christ identity placed within that is already complete.

Unfortunately our souls have chosen the lesser nature for much of life, and we feel the void and insecurity of those choices. Our souls have been filled with created matter that seems to fill the void for a time, but God shakes those false leaves away at points to awaken us to the true (Heb. 12:26). That is why King David said (Psm. 23:3), "He restores my soul."

We journey through life encountering the periodic shaking of our individual trees. That shaking continually awakens us out of the imposter tree that has relied on created matter. That is the Rule-Breaker breaking old ways and rules because He wants to increasingly establish our souls in the true that cannot be shaken.

Christians, people from various religions, and humanity as a whole also encounter the shaking of their trees. Through a gradual shaking we collectively see a little clearer as some of the longstanding false leaves fall away to awaken us more to the true. God keeps coming as the Rule-Breaker to free us into His higher ways of unity and love rather than judgment and separation. Perfect love eventually casts out judgment and separation.

At present our judging flesh nature has drawn judgment to itself. We reap what we sow. We have judged and separated from one another. Marriage has always been broken to some extent even though we have tried our best. And God has increased the shaking in recent years. Why? He wants to break us out of the old and into His higher ways that we could not yet embrace.

Pictures can never capture the complexity of our internal world. The picture of the two trees mainly illustrates the tree with leaves that can be shaken versus the tree with unshakable leaves. But, more accurately, I see the flesh nature as a false shell (like an acorn shell) that imprisons the Christ nature within it, which to me is the foundation of who we are. God intermittently causes more cracks in our superficial flesh nature, which then further allows the Christ nature to break forth like an oak tree in those places. That freed Christ nature, in turn, continually awakens others to their Christ nature. Our journey is to stand in that Christ nature, our true self.

CHAPTER 4

Servants of Conscience

<u>Shadows</u>

Both Kathy and I tried to stand in the true self as the shadows fell away during fire. We had previously done many things to please one another rather than to let each other "feel the weight of who we were." My one son had said that phrase to me earlier in my journey and it stuck. I had been trying to let people feel the weight of who I was following the season of panic attacks, but this way of walking went to another whole level when Kathy left. She had felt compelled to leave. Kathy had tended to use me as a shield in front of her in life, which hindered her from more fully knowing her own unique identity and purpose. It seemed as if God used this time for her to pay attention to what she sensed from the inside and to be true to those nudges.

It felt devastating and messy to me, but I knew that God was working to cause her to stand more fully in her identity. Her true self. I knew that God was also furthering my identity through this fire. I saw that God birthed and released identity every time we held onto and followed how He uniquely met us individually. Our individual God-connections mostly happened when we paid attention to inner nudges and inclinations that gave us a sense of inner peace and wholeness when we followed those nudges (even if that resulted in outer upheaval).

The messiness sometimes looked and felt like God was nowhere to be found. We both appeared blind to many. But God was working from within us to further establish each of us in our true self. More than we knew, we still had tendencies to follow the crowd, the common way, as if numbers make something true. I think that many people walk this way without knowing it, at least until fire causes them to see that the common way is not necessarily true.

I regularly unhooked from other people's ways as right when fire no longer allowed those ways to work for me personally. I saw that I became established on solid ground when I let go of others' rules about how life was supposed to be, and, instead, remained true to this unseen deeper leading that made me whole. I also saw wholeness come about in Kathy the more she honored this inner leading as well, one that took us apart for a season. This process just took a while because of the pain that occurred during the upheaval.

The part that stood out most to me was how neither of us could have become more whole or complete in Christ without God meeting us personally in a way that connected with our inner being. This played out at the earthly level in two different directions for us.

For a season we had met spiritually in "home churches." But after our marital upheaval, Kathy felt led to return to the Catholic Church. I felt led to continue in the home church, but later began meeting at a local protestant church. That separated us all the more at the earthly level. Some of you who are protestant oriented could judge Kathy for being off track and might feel compelled to pray for her to "see the light." Some of you who are Catholic could judge me and conclude that I am the one needing awakened. And, possibly, some of you who are not in formal churches could judge both of us as still being blinded by religion.

Fire revealed to me that God works through many ways to reach and awaken people. Everything has its place. Honor how God *does* work in people's lives, and let Him pull out any possible weeds in His time. God regularly connected with me when I was performance-oriented earlier in my journey. I saw Him as outcome oriented and that He didn't really care about my emotions or pain as long as I "got the job done." I now look at that phase of my life and think "Yuck!" And yet, God knew that He could begin connecting with and awakening me through that avenue. It was a main way for me to initially relate to and receive Him. Now, if I happen to be performance-oriented, everything seems to fall flat, and God seems distant. That is no longer an avenue of our connection. He has graduated me to the place of surrender to His peaceful will as our connection while still honoring the emotional and inner support needed on my journey.

The scriptures provide many examples of God initially meeting His people in lesser ways (like granting Israel an earthly king instead of them walking with Him directly; see 1 Sam. 12:12). Then God "changed" in the New Testament, or at least many people who read the Bible conclude that He had changed. God had not changed. He simply met people initially in the only way that they would recognize Him as God (which in the Old Testament, people only honored power and would only acknowledge that God was God when He showed Himself in ways of power). That's why God stated repeatedly to His people in the Old Testament, "Then they shall know that I am God." That's also why the New Testament scriptures state that God had been *willing* to show His wrath (Rom. 9:22; NAS). He had been willing, but it was not who He truly was; it was not His heart.

I had previously been troubled about how God appeared one way in the Old Testament and another in the New Testament. Now I see that it pertained to people's inability to receive who God really was. This paralleled how I could only receive God initially as wanting my performance. Now I see that that was never truly His nature. He simply met me in the only ways that I would initially receive Him.

That's why I am always thankful (afterwards!) for God's fire that strips away my lesser ways of viewing Him. During this season, fire stripped away from my eyes the labels and shadows that keep people separate. They are not the real. I saw that the true is within and that all else is a shell. God meets us in a way that connects with us. He meets us to the extent that we let Him, and usually that means starting with where we are.

Some of you are powerfully moved when people share their experiences. You are designed that way and will likely be stirred by my personal stories. Others may be moved upon gaining understanding of how something works and may need to see it make sense scripturally before letting my personal stories touch you deeply. That is because you are designed that way, and you will likely pay closer attention to those sections in this book. But God knows how to reach you best, and usually you will have an inner sense of what that is. Honor God's ways that connect with you.

In the end, my testimony is that Kathy somehow began to get girded up through her return to the Catholic Church. I knew that that wouldn't have happened in the protestant church (and hadn't previously, because of what connected to her heart and what did not). During my still times, I sensed that that was completely right for her even though it took us in two different directions at the earthly level. I also sensed much peace and wholeness that I was to be where I was, and not in the Catholic Church. Christ especially met me most powerfully when I was alone with Him or with my likeminded men's group. To me, God seemed to be after a higher testimony of unity than Kathy and me being together at the same physical place. The Testimony was that unity does not require the same label or external way of connecting with God. Rather, higher unity was demonstrated through our sacrificial love that embraced one another beyond labels or differences. Our sacrificial love embraced God's ways of uniquely connecting with each of our souls.

The journey to this higher testimony of unity, though, was a long one. After the initial upheaval of Kathy leaving to move in with her parents, I gained much practice at standing in my true self while feeling totally blind about the earthly outcomes God desired. We occasionally had contact, but communication remained impossible at those times. Spiritually, those times seemed like birth pangs and labor (I am a bit outside of my expertise here since I have not given birth!).

The labor is the difficult work prior to the time to push. Pushing to give birth before its time will not work. Any good doctor or midwife knows this. In a sense, labor is the lengthy preparation where no immediate reward is received, other than knowing that each painful contraction brings you a bit closer to labor's purpose. Only after the appropriate time to push does the reward of life come forth.

That was my sense for a long season. Kathy and I were in the midst of labor and could do nothing to bypass these intense birth pangs. While this labor could not bring birth to a good earthly outcome for a season, each contact between us seemed to birth many spiritual revelations. I share some of those that came to light during this intense season. Also, because I look to the scriptures to provide wisdom and direction for participating with Christ, I share how my interpretations of key ones gradually changed through the fire.

Shadows about myself, life, and the scriptures kept falling away, and the real kept getting birthed through the earthly contractions. I began to see all earthly things as shadows of the real, and that my role was to continually participate with Christ and His unseen realm rather than to pursue earthly goals.

Inner Knowing Versus Ideas

I saw that words and labels often limit understanding. Even the name "Christ" is likely viewed differently by many people, which is why I want to describe the Unseen Christ and how to recognize Him at a practical level (doesn't that sound impossible?).

I learned that the power to know the truth beyond words and labels comes through experiential knowing. Inner knowing, as contrasted with ideas that come from others. That's why fire is necessary in our lives. Fire causes people to leave the shadows and to experientially and personally touch Reality, which, to me, is Christ. Fire caused me to further let go of my *ideas* of Christ and to personally relate to Him as a true Person within myself and others. That is the true self. Some of you may prefer to think of Christ as Reality within people and within life as a whole.

The trick for awakening beyond shadows, however, is to recognize the Spirit of Christ versus the spirit of the world. Mistakes were to be expected, but getting through my marital trials depended upon what spirit I participated with overall. Both the Spirit of Christ and the spirit of the world were (and are) in both Kathy and me. Kingdom against kingdom is in all people. That is our ongoing battle for being lifted further spiritually, because what we participate with, grows.

My earlier panic attacks awakened me to being able to distinguish between these two natures within myself and people as a whole. Then my marital upheaval caused me to watch closely for, and participate with, the Spirit of Christ rather than the spirit of the world in the midst of difficulties. Much of this chapter, as well as several others, addresses this unseen realm, which is hard to do. Emotions, thoughts, and other inner experiences are part of this unseen spiritual realm.

I recognized the Spirit of Christ when I paused and took space during difficult situations. During those times of space I regained inner peace and life that signaled what decisions made the most sense. That peaceful way was the Spirit of Christ that testified that He was still living, and that He was with me and in me regardless of chaotic circumstances.[1] This way of walking was not about ideas, but about me inwardly paying attention to knowing Christ experientially. Personally.

In contrast, the spirit of the world usually became evident within me during difficulties when I failed to pause and find space to be. Lack of inner peace and wholeness then continued, and I found no peace or higher life to participate with. I was usually fearful at those times and would become more defensive during communication with Kathy. That was the spirit of the world that treated Christ like He was neither living nor in Kathy or me.

Inwardly paying attention during the upheaval for the Spirit of Christ within me kept awakening me to see many of the scriptures in ways that went well beyond the teachings I had encountered previously. That's why I feel compelled to share these new understandings of certain scriptures. They provide fresh ways for relating to and connecting practically with Christ's unseen realm. I saw that the words on pages could not capture or contain Reality and only pointed towards Reality. They were symbols of a Living Reality that could only be known by experience. I know that the scriptures say that the Old Testament events and ways were but shadows of the true, but even the New Testament cannot give us Christ's reality. Only Christ Himself can. He is the Living Word that we carry.

Jesus said to the Jews (Jn. 5:39-40), "You search the Scriptures because you think that in them you have eternal life; it is these that testify about Me; and you are unwilling to come to Me so that you may have life."

The scriptures overall provide direction for recognizing how to participate with the Unseen Christ, but they are not Christ. Even Jesus' teachings were but parables and mysteries that pointed towards Himself as the Living Word who is meant to be our fullness within. We experience more of that wholeness anytime we participate with that Christ nature. Soul joined with the Christ nature is our true self. That is true life.

I experienced many ups and downs throughout Kathy's and my upheaval. Mountains and valleys, though most were valleys for a lengthy time. The trials caused Kathy and I to let go of our expectations regarding earthly outcomes and to keep embracing Christ within us as our peace and security. Through letting go of our perceived necessary outcomes, God tumbled fleshly mountains and completed or filled in the felt valleys with true security and peace.

King David said (Psm. 23:4), "Even though I walk through the valley of the shadow of death, I will fear no evil." That is a powerful statement. The earth is the valley of the shadow of death. This "valley" is about the gaps we feel during our earthly journey, and other scriptural passages about "mountains" being made low are about God humbling the earthly nature that raises up to try to fill those gaps. But those gaps are merely shadows; they are not real. That's why King David called his earthly journey "the shadow" of death.

Death (as well as all the suffering it causes on this earth) is only a shadow. While death and suffering feel very real and powerful to our earthly nature, we are all eternal beings that will continue journeying after this earth. Beyond death, because death is a shadow.

See the scriptures with eyes of the Spirit.[2] See what the words, physical realities, and shadows express about Unseen Reality. Christ is Spirit, not a limited physical being. Know Him by the Spirit.

Unawakened Living or Following Conscience

Much of what I experienced during my upheaval regularly stripped me from looking at life as well as the scriptures through earthly eyes. I saw that restoration of Kathy's and my marriage had no chance if I focused on the marriage as the end result. Doing so would have caused me to focus on some preconceived notion of "the right earthly outcome" rather than on what Christ was working during the difficulties. Earthly marriage was only a shadow of the real. In the end, I realized that pursuing any outcome above following my sense of Christ's leading in the moment would not work. I also saw that as I watched fervently for Christ, I began recognizing Him more frequently, whether He showed up in me, Kathy, or someone else.

I recognized Christ through a sense of peace or wholeness, stirring of the Spirit, drawing of my attention, quickening of my heart, or by a heightened keenness of senses about a matter. As I discerned those times or areas where I sensed Christ's higher presence, I paused to open up to that higher presence to see what other thoughts, words, or potential actions came to the forefront. Upon receiving new learning or direction, I already felt strengthened for any potentially new steps because that new direction came with the Spirit's strength for carrying out those steps. But I learned to pay attention to discerning and following Christ above all.

The hardest times, though, seemed to be when Christ didn't show Himself much about resolving the issue of marriage. Periods of silence about direction occurred when it seemed most critical to hear from Him. Many times, it seemed totally illogical for me to wait until I sensed what Christ might be working, especially when everything between Kathy and me appeared to be on hold. So I occasionally thought, "I might as well try what Kathy wants since I am not yet sensing any new steps to take." Several times, those new attempts were about approaching people or a counseling ministry for help, when I could tell within my heart that God was not yet moving in that way. I sensed further labor was needed and that it was not yet time to give birth. That was my sense because I had experienced no peace about those steps even when I had left go of needing any certain outcomes. But I had talked myself out of what my heart knew at points, mainly because I thought that I might not have an accurate sense of peace in the midst of the upheaval. But looking back, my heart knew. Peace was still the most effective indicator of the areas where Christ was working and regarding what He was working in those places.

My learning about following Christ above all else brought some of Jesus' difficult statements to life, such as (Lk. 14:26), "If anyone comes to Me, and does not hate his own father and mother and wife and children and brothers and sisters, yes, and even his own life, he cannot be My disciple." I began seeing many of Jesus' statements and the scriptures as a whole as symbols of unseen ways.

Did I get through my marital fireworks by hating Kathy? Of course not. The scriptures point towards a spiritual, not a natural, reality (though our natural reality is deeply affected by the spiritual).

Many people on this earth dislike the scriptures because they have not understood their deeper meaning and symbolism, and people have used them hurtfully when the literal meaning was not the intent at times. "Hate" in the Greek, for example, means hating one thing *as compared* to another; it also means loving one thing less than the other. In other words, I hated Kathy's and my false earthly nature as compared to our Christ nature. I learned to love Christ in us far more than the earthly. My love of Christ (and Christ in people) began establishing higher will that caused me to love Kathy and others far better than my earthly love was capable. I wanted to follow Christ's will that would further establish Kathy's and my true self.

I initially became sensitive to following higher will during my earlier panic attacks and then my sensitivity greatly increased during the marital trials. Greater inward heavenly riches became established through me following higher will, which meant to "hate" or love-less all things compared to following Christ. I would have said that I already followed Christ fully in my life, but those trials caused me to follow Him beyond where I had been.

I learned that following Christ is much about following conscience. During the marital trials, Kathy needed to follow her conscience and I needed to follow mine. Following our consciences demonstrated when we were being true to following Christ, which at first seemed devastating at the earthly level (although, be careful not to blindly follow wounds, emotions, or earthly wants).

If either Kathy or I had done what we did for the other at the expense of following Christ, it would have been a false foundation that would have crumbled at some point. My goal of pleasing her no longer remained above following Christ. God wanted each of our motives to be about following the True above all else. We also needed Christ's voice through others on our journey, which sometimes helped awaken us further to Christ's voice within us.

But in the end we needed to follow conscience to follow Christ. Be servants of conscience.

You can tell when you are not being true to deeper nudges from your conscience. Part of you knows that when you follow those inner nudges you become more whole and that, when you don't, you sense lack of fulfillment. Lack of inner peace.

Jesus asked (Matt. 16:15), "Who do you say I am?" That was about direct relationship with nothing in between. That is conscience. That is our Rock. Higher will. You will experience more wholeness and completion when you directly follow conscience. That is the pure in heart with no conflicting goals. That is also inner peace between you and Christ.

Following conscience is different than the scriptures' reference to each person in futility doing what is right in their own (earthly) eyes. That is earthly thinking and goals that separate people from each another.

Conscience is higher, beyond the individual. Even when Jesus' mother Mary indicated for Him to do something about the wine that had run out during the wedding feast, He initially didn't think it was His time to reveal who He was. But after consideration, Jesus recognized that the Father had worked through Mary to initiate this new season (Jn. 2:1-7). Jesus stepped only after His own conviction. That was Jesus staying true to the Spirit of the Father working within Him (which had also worked through Mary to stir the Spirit within Jesus). Jesus remained true to Conscience, to Higher will.

Like Jesus, Kathy and I received higher food and drink when we participated with Higher will. What we participated with grew. Higher life within us took a while, but peace and wholeness gradually grew as we participated with peace's nudges. We honored peace's leading over what the other person wanted, or what each of us individually wanted. That peaceful way demonstrated honoring conscience. Peace could not have grown otherwise (although it was a long process).

The more people participate with conscience, which is the works of Christ in their hearts, the more they are aware of and find value in honoring conscience. All people who honor conscience, whether they know it or not, receive a higher drink (though they may not know that it is from Christ within). Jesus said (Jn. 7:37-38), "If anyone is thirsty, let him come to Me and drink. Whoever believes in Me, as the Scripture has said, streams of living water will flow from within him."

Jesus did not mean to get a drink from some "external idea or name" of Christ. He meant for us to participate with Him who is within. That is your drink of Living Water. That's why Jesus said that streams of living water will flow from within us. He begins to flow more within us as we increasingly come to Him for drinks.

Throughout life we are faced with choices that either honor conscience or the world's louder voices around us. Honoring the louder external voices disconnects us from our Source; it hinders awakening. Regular inner growth, or soul awakening, cannot happen without the experience of free choice. Experience is the best teacher, and freedom of choice (which God always gives) allows us to have direct relationship with Him and to experience the consequences of our choices.

We do not experience for ourselves what our choices bring when we merely follow others' beliefs or ways. That is indirect. Following others disallows inner growth or awakening because we become disengaged from true life within when we simply perform what others tell us to do. We become disengaged from conscience, disengaged from Christ within. Christ said to follow Him, not others.

We are spiritually asleep when we disengage from conscience. Unawakened living is death.

Many people blindly follow the unspoken rules of "the world's system" rather than following conscience, and that system still governs all of us more than we think. The mountain of expectations from culture, family, schools, and organizations constantly pressures us to conform to that culture and to be the same as everyone else. One major ongoing unspoken rule is that we must strive to be further or different than who or where we are to be acceptable. We can be accepted or loved *if* we do all the right things. *If* we follow all the unspoken rules around us.

But God speaks to us, "Come out of her, My people" (Rev. 18:4). No longer conform to the world (Rom. 12:2). God is the Rule-Breaker who desires to free us from systems and rules so that we can walk in direct free relationship with Him. That is walking in our true self. That is walking with a clear conscience between us and Christ.

Jesus told us to be salt and to be at peace with one another. That is about allowing flavor and differences. Following Christ honors uniqueness and gathers uniqueness into loving relationship much like a symphony with all the beautiful instruments harmonizing to bring a glorious sound. Following Christ and becoming the unique salt that we are means following conscience. That is awakened living.

Conscience is the True

Do you believe that a higher will than your earthly one establishes more of heaven on earth? People's conscience gives evidence of a higher will. Conscience is from Christ planted within, even before people fully know to turn to Him.

For a while I had earnestly wanted God to teach me how to communicate more effectively with people who neither look to God nor use the same spiritual terminology as me. Out of the blue one morning during stillness the word "conscience" popped into my mind (which then caused this whole chapter). I wasn't even focused on God giving me an answer at this particular time, but I instantly realized that this was God's answer to the question I had been asking. That's why I believe that God very much wanted to highlight this area. I also believe that this revelation came through the birth pangs I was enduring with Kathy; experiential learning and higher spiritual sight kept coming to me during this season of heightened earthly pressure.

Immediately I became excited because the scriptures in Romans came to mind, and I knew that God was showing me something foundational about all people. Paul said, (Rom. 9:1), "I speak the truth in Christ — I am not lying, my conscience confirms it in the Holy Spirit." Paul's statement is also translated as "My conscience bears witness to the Holy Ghost." But I wondered if this meaning pertained to everyone or just to Paul and followers of Christ.

I then researched the meaning of conscience in Romans 2:15, which focused on the Gentiles, or those who did not look to God. I was astounded. The Greek word is *suneidesis* and means "coperception." It comes from the root word *suneido*, meaning "to be aware of, to be informed of, or to be privy of." Wow, this passage focused on people who were not awakened to God!

Conscience is the experience of a person, along with God, perceiving what He perceives. That is coperception. Not just those who have been awakened to God, but all people – together with God – become privy or aware of His perceptions when their conscience speaks to them. Unawakened individuals are simply not aware that their conscience is God speaking to them. This has profound spiritual implications about all people. In other words, this discovery makes clear that all people carry Christ within but that some are simply unaware of Him. This understanding also discredits the idea that Christ only "comes into people from some

95

outside place" upon making some simple confession. Instead, Christ is already within people, and as people turn to Him within, a veil of blindness is removed. For it states (2 Cor. 3:16), "But whenever anyone turns to the Lord, the veil is taken away."

Here is the Romans 2:15 passage: "…they show the work of the Law written in their hearts, their conscience [coperception] bearing witness and their thoughts alternately accusing or else defending them." God created all people with a conscience that defends them when they are in accordance with Him and accuses them when they are not. Conscience works to gradually awaken people into God's higher unity, ways, and love.

All children are born with conscience. They are born with this sensitivity.

At the same time, severe wounding in life can sear peoples' consciences. That's why the scriptures say that people "*suppressed* the truth, their thinking *became* futile, they did not *retain* the knowledge of God, they *separated* from God by hardening their hearts, and they *lost* all sensitivity and *became* callous" (Rom. 1:21, 22, 28; Eph. 4:18, 19). Do you hear how clearly the scriptures convey that unawakened individuals had already possessed God's truth and inner riches and then lost *sensitivity* to them? "They exchanged the glory of the immortal God" for lesser things (Rom. 1:23). Their souls carried the One but became filled with the other. Filled with the lesser.

Unawakened living blindly follows the crowd rather than conscience. That causes tragedies. Holocausts.

Awakened living means following Christ within. And following Christ means following the nudges from our conscience that are beyond following the world's rules. Conscience is the source of the still small voice within, and the more you pay attention to following conscience, the easier it is to hear that voice. It takes sensitivity and practice to be in tune with your inner experiences where that still small voice originates. The world does not walk this way.

Sacrificially follow your inner nudges from Christ.[3] Sacrificially pursue His nudges through your conscience rather than allowing the world's systems and rules to move you. Motive makes a difference. You will receive earthly or heavenly rewards depending upon your motive. When you only seek and are moved because of earthly rewards, you will be limited to earthly goodness. But when you sacrificially follow conscience, you honor Christ above all, and He will be your increase. That means more heavenly life while on this earth.

The Awakening of Christ Within

At one point, numerous people around me were trying to get me to pursue Kathy. It was difficult for me to hear and honor conscience directly when those voices around me were pressuring me to do what they thought should work. During those competing and overpowering voices, I learned to seek Christ's voice first, even if that was the least voice … a faint voice amongst the loud ones.

Hear the symbolism in Jesus' statements that pointed towards honoring Him within us (Matt. 25:35, 36, 40): "For I was hungry and you gave Me something to eat, I was thirsty and you gave Me something to drink, I was a stranger and you invited Me in, I needed clothes and you clothed Me, I was sick and you looked after Me, I was in prison and you came to visit Me … I tell you the truth, whatever you did for one of the least of these brothers of Mine, you did for Me." What "least" brothers of Christ did He mean?

Whatever I do for Christ within others and for Him within myself, I do for Christ.

I more fully learned to honor "the least of these" within others and within myself during my marital fireworks. The "least" was often the still small voice of peace amongst the loud ones. That is how I continually awakened and passed from death into more of life through that time of great adversity. I awakened further by losing one life (the loud one) and gaining the other. I lost the fleshly life and honored the least voice of Christ during those trials, whether that voice was within me or within others.

Christ in me has clear voice in certain aspects of my life. Another way of saying this is that my conscience has clear voice at certain times over other times. Those times seem to happen most when I am alone with Him, with Kathy at certain times, or with my men's group or other likeminded individuals. In other areas, Christ has a somewhat limited voice in me, like when I am with those who are only somewhat likeminded, or when Kathy can only somewhat hear my Christ voice.

In still other areas, Christ has little to no voice in me. In those areas, usually when I shrink back from others who don't accept or understand Christ's voice in me, He is small in me. When I say that Christ is small in me, I mean that He does not have much room for voice within me at those times. Christ isn't actually small in those areas. I just unknowingly restrict His strength or freedom within me at those times (because He allows my choices and inclinations).

In those restricted areas, Christ is kind of like an infant in me, and He needs me to give Him a cup of water to drink, food because He is hungry, or clothes because He is naked in those places. Christ needs me to visit Him there, because He is like a stranger to me; He is imprisoned there by my earthly nature.

Sometimes I don't recognize that Christ needs a drink within me until life isn't working well. That is when I see my need to be attuned to Him and to honor His faint voice within me. That gives Him a drink and strengthens Him in me (which also gives me a true drink). Sometimes in those difficult places, I even recognize my inability to give Christ a drink. So I ask for His grace to participate with Him where I feel afraid or unable, or I ask others for support to trust Him there.

My most difficult times were when Kathy and I had direct contact and I felt pressure to be different or more than I was. I knew in my head that I did not have to be more than I was, but the fear in my heart showed that I inwardly bought that lie in those moments. I could neither hear nor sense Christ at those pressurized times and mainly communicated that I needed some space to hear and honor Him before we talked further.

During the trials I learned that my continuous purpose was to awaken Christ within me and within others in all aspects of life. I regularly recognized more areas where Christ had been like an infant within me who needed a cup of water. When I gave Him a drink, I had done it unto Him because I had done it to the least of these.

Jesus said that if you want to be great you must become the least, the servant of all (Mk. 9:35). This statement held double meaning. Jesus meant honoring the least, the child of Christ, in all people; but doing this also required being the least in the flesh nature. This had become my goal. I wanted to be a servant to the least voice of Christ in all, which also meant regularly laying down my fleshly life and earthly desires.

Jesus' flesh nature was the least of all, the servant of all, and He fulfilled His destiny by emptying Himself and becoming the name greater than all names. He continuously "fed" or awakened His true nature by losing the earthly and honoring the heavenly. That lifted Him into His full glory as well as awakened others into their glory that is one with God. Jesus' walk as a servant revealed heaven to the earth; it revealed and fed the Greater to the lesser.

My eyes are now opened more fully to that way that serves people by awakening them to their true self. Jesus said that the kingdom is within us (Lk. 17:21). His words about us doing whatever we do to Him when we've done it to the least began with the following statement (Matt. 25:34-36), "Come, you who are blessed by My Father; take your inheritance, *the kingdom prepared for you since the creation of the world*. For I was hungry and you gave Me ..."

Why do we do what we do unto Christ when we do something to anyone? Christ was Spirit from the beginning (not a limited physical person), and we were originally designed with Him in us. Jesus' point about receiving His unseen kingdom within us is connected to attending to Him during times of need. During my intense trials, how was I supposed to inherit this kingdom within that had been prepared for me since the creation of the world? Jesus' words already told me how. I must attend to Christ within myself and others during times of need (thirst, hunger, naked, etc.). I must serve Him first, and through doing so, I continually receive more of His kingdom. My true inheritance.

Two kingdoms are within us. The earthly kingdom within us that doesn't know love screams for attention and wants us to live selfishly to meet needs. The heavenly kingdom is Christ within who desires to find room or place within our souls, even if it seems like He is only a faint child's voice. He desires to find voice and expression on this earth. Honor Him; honor conscience!

Do you honor Christ's faint voice within yourself and others over worldly voices? Doing so gives Him a drink and He is strengthened within. Even if Christ's voice is well-disguised and is only like an infant trying to come through you or others, do you long for His voice to come forth? Do you look past people's rough earthly edges and seek Christ's voice from within them ... even with unawakened individuals or those using different terminology than you? I am deeply passionate about this and believe that it is the way to Christ's unseen realm becoming visible on this earth!

Jesus said to His disciples about the rewards of serving Him especially through trials (Lk. 22:26-30), "… You are those who have stood by Me in My trials. And I confer [bestow] on you a kingdom, just as My Father conferred one on Me, so that you may eat and drink at My table in My kingdom and sit on thrones, judging the twelve tribes of Israel."

"I confer on you a kingdom?" True ruling with God's image on this earth is what we were called to do from the very beginning (Gen. 1:26, 28). Do you want to rule and make this earth as it is in heaven? That's the kind of rule God desires. Christ demonstrated this way to rule and He called us to this same walk.

Discern Christ within yourself and all people. Stand by Him through trials. Sacrificially love, long for, and serve Christ within wherever you find Him. Then He bestows more of His kingdom of peace upon you and those you serve. You give Christ food, clothe Him, and visit Him who is imprisoned when you embrace Christ within yourself and your brothers and sisters.

Care for conscience within all people in the midst of earthly voices and needs. Beyond terminology or religious labels. Hear and honor people's conscience that bears witness of Him more than getting them to hear your preferred terminology! Then you will receive and establish more of Christ's kingdom on this earth.

Who did the Apostle Paul say was the least of the saints? Himself. Paul followed Jesus' way that made his earthly nature least so that Christ would be full in him. Paul also labored to bring forth Christ in all people, which also meant helping them become least in the earthly nature at times.

The way to greater works on this earth is through greater love. Sacrificial love that serves Christ in all. That is why Jesus told us that the greatest commandment is to love God and love our neighbor (Mk. 12:30-31). Can you hear that truly loving God and neighbor as ourselves is loving Christ within all? Jesus also said that He gave us a new command, that we love one another as He loved us (Jn. 13:34). That meant sacrificially laying down our lives for one another just as He did.

During my trials, Christ awakened Kathy and me to the degree that we sacrificially cared for Him in her and in me over our earthly voices. Would I attend to Christ and His voice in me or would I attend to my lesser nature's voice that felt alone during the trials? Would I attend to Kathy's earthly voice when that nature wanted earthly security from me beyond what was possible given God's times and seasons?

The same was true for Kathy, and for me towards her. Would she attend more to Christ within her or to her earthly nature? Would I attend to Christ who was imprisoned within her in certain ways just like Christ was within me? Would I give Christ within Kathy a drink so that He could mature within her soul as well as in my own areas where we had not given Him food or drink?

For writing this book as well, Christ was like an infant or young child in me in certain areas (remember me at the kindergarten table?). Risking to write in ways that went beyond prior rules of what it meant to be a Christian was initially scary to me. But my purpose was to feed and clothe Christ within me and you rather than to please people. I was to visit Him when He was still imprisoned within us rather than to succumb to fear about what my earthly nature thought it needed. Sometimes that meant asking for grace.

Our journey consists of ongoing battles between the Christ nature and the earthly nature. Two competing kingdoms within. Jesus said (Lk. 16:10, NKJV), "He who is faithful in what is least is faithful also in much; and he who is unjust in what is least is unjust also in much." Be faithful with the Little. Seek and serve the slightest voice of Christ within yourself and others, and you will become the greatest. You will rule the way you were meant to rule on this earth.

Christ is fully within you and desires to be awakened in various aspects of your life. He wants you to listen for Him like a mother listening for her infant's voice. A mother is constantly aware of the child's voice.

Old Wine to New Wine

To be prepared is to be emptied. Jesus emptied Himself to become fullness. Christ kept emptying me to make room for the new. Many of my previous ways of viewing and handling the scriptures changed during my trials. Pressuring myself to believe, have no fear, and to carry out certain scriptures in practice, or to do the impossible gradually gave way to acknowledging human weakness and asking for Christ's grace during difficult circumstances. Overall, I was further emptied of human strength, which allowed space for more of Christ's strength to work within me.

Jesus demonstrated the importance of emptiness before doing any of His other miracles when He turned the water into wine at the Cana wedding feast (Jn. 2:1-11). The miracle doesn't start with Jesus turning water into wine. The miracle could not take place without the old wine running out. Emptied.

Only after the wine ran out did Jesus ask some servants to fill the purification jars with water. That event signifies the need for our souls, in each area of our life, to be emptied of the earthly nature. It must run dry. In each area of difficulty Kathy and I needed to reach the end of our earthly abilities for Christ's living water within to take its place. Then our souls, filled only with

Christ's living water in those places, were able to become Christ's glory (symbolized by Jesus turning the water into wine).

Wine represents glory. The glory of the grapes with protective skins must become crushed to produce the glory of the wine. Kathy's and my old wounds with their protective shells would not work anymore. They had kept the true beauty hidden, and also prevented true connection. But fortunately, ruined earthly nature produced heavenly glory. We learned to be more vulnerable and present in the moment in certain areas where we had never been able. Our vulnerability and openness about the real was the juice that came forth from the pressed grapes (Kathy and me). That was the new wine or glory that became true drink for us and for others. Until then, in those stuck areas Kathy and I were separated individual grapes with our protective shells still in place.

Jesus emphasized later that the new wine must be put in new wineskins and that, as long as the old wine remained, people would conclude that the old wine was good enough (Lk. 5:37-39). Old wineskins are unawakened souls that conclude that the old wine is good enough, so they remain filled with old wine. Old ways. Unawakened souls continue to serve the earthly nature and its own individual glory.

New wineskins are awakened souls who have recognized the need to pour out the old wine, seeing that it is no longer good. These awakened souls have seen the futility of the earthly nature. They keep allowing the old to be emptied so as to receive the new. These awakened souls recognize the need for the periodic crushing of the grapes to increase the heavenly wine and glory on this earth.

Goats and Sheep

I'm sure you have notice my increased use of scriptures in this chapter. I feel compelled to share how my awakening about life paralleled my awakening regarding the scriptures. I do so because I see how my previous scriptural interpretations hindered Christ's love through me, interpretations that many people still hold to be true. If the increased use of scriptures is difficult for you because of them being used negatively in your past, I pray that my use of them would cause you to see them with God's higher life, wisdom, and compassion in them.

I endured greater stripping works throughout this season. I began to see these God-works as purposeful for stripping the lesser nature from the Christ nature in all people *rather than as separating people from people.* The scriptures overall are about kingdom versus kingdom within humanity, and not about person versus person or people versus people who bear different labels.

I saw that God did not favor Kathy or me during the difficulties. He did not favor Catholic versus protestant. Rather, God constantly worked to further strip both of us from the earthly nature to awaken each us into more of our Christ nature. The true self. That is God's continuous work in all people. No one is exempt.

Earthly versus heavenly nature within people is also symbolized by Jesus' reference to the goats and the sheep. Remember that Jesus was addressing the unseen kingdom within? Leading into His words about doing what we do unto Him, He said (Matt. 25:32, NKJV), "All the nations will be gathered before Him, and He will separate them one from another, as a shepherd divides his sheep from the goats." Translations from one language to another are sometimes inadequate. "One from another" is one possible translation from many. This passage could have numerous meanings.

One possible meaning could be about one physical person or group of people from another, but that meaning is not consistent with Jesus' following words about building His unseen kingdom.

Jesus focused on the fact that we do unto Him when we do it to the least. How can that be? Jesus was addressing the unseen spiritual realm within us. The kingdoms are within. One way sacrificially honors Jesus as well as Him in our brothers and sisters, and the other way does not.

Christ's goal is a continual work of separating the goats from the sheep, meaning the goat nature from the Christ nature in all of us. Who is truly righteous? Only the Christ nature, the sheep nature. Who is the wicked? Only the selfish earthly nature, which is the goat nature. Separating "one from another" is the sanctifying work of the Spirit that separates one kingdom from the other within people.

The sheep know and honor Christ's voice. The goat nature does not. We only come into knowing and truly possessing our inheritance (the Christ nature) when we honor Christ's voice within us above the lesser loves of the world. The souls turned towards the Christ nature within oneself and others will receive more of the inheritance, and the false earthly nature will continue to come to eternal ruin, whether during this earthly journey or afterwards for those who have still clung to it.

Had I had the label of Muslim, Buddhist, criminal, Jew, or Atheist, I believe that God would have been for the true me. His fire would have kept stripping away my goat nature to awaken me to my sheep nature, just like He would have been doing with Kathy regardless of her label.

All of this journey is beautiful. In spite of all the pain and ugliness on this earth, God sees us as beautiful. We see this in the Song of Songs when the Bridegroom calls to His bride (Song 4:1-2), "How beautiful you are, my darling! Oh, how beautiful! Your eyes behind your veil are doves [meaning purity of the Christ nature beneath our fleshly veil]. Your hair is like a flock of *goats descending* from Mount Gilead. Your teeth are like a flock of *sheep* just shorn, *coming up from the washing*. Each has its twin; not one of them is alone."

Hair like a flock of goats?! The words in these passages always sounded crazy to me until I understood that they were symbolic and held much spiritual meaning. This passage states that "Each has its twin." Its counterpart, which always offers choice. *God keeps working His works so that the goat nature descends and the soul joined with the sheep nature becomes washed and ascends.* One nature increases as the other decreases in our souls. One continually (eternally) comes to ruin as our soul joins with the other to become lifted in eternal life. That is the washing. Also amazing to me is how God sees this whole process as beautiful even though we often condemn ourselves for mishaps along the way!

"Hairy goats" represents the earthly nature (goat nature) and parallels the Old Testament's tent curtain made of goat's hair that surrounded the Tabernacle. Christ was the Holy of Holies in the center of the Tabernacle with the tent of goat's hair surrounding it. That is Christ within us and our earthly goat nature that imprisons Him. Isn't the Old Testament tabernacle a great picture of how God created humans?

We also know that God hated Esau and loved Jacob before they were born (Rom. 9:13). Why? God didn't hate the true person. Esau and Jacob symbolized flesh and spirit, the earthly nature and the spirit nature. Esau, whose skin was like goat's hair, represented the superficial flesh nature that sells the true inheritance because of loving the earthly more than the heavenly. His brother Jacob represented the true spirit person of God who pursues the heavenly.

Can you see in the Song of Song's how much God sees our whole journey as beautiful? He seems to see our journey as a dance or love song that gradually woos us into knowing His sacrificial love that goes well beyond our superficial goat's hair.

Andrew Carey

Mustard Seeds

I regularly learned new ways when old ways no longer worked during the fire. My discernment of Christ and His faint voice had increased. I learned to hear or sense Christ and his leading in new ways. Sometimes those ways were initially garbled and undiscernible, but as I watched and paid further attention to those places, hidden treasure emerged.

We only need to observe life to see that we must start small anytime we desire to begin a new hobby, job, or relationship. That's why the scriptures say (Zech. 4:10), "For who has despised the day of small things." Isaiah also stated (11:6) "… a little child shall lead them."

In any new area of awakening, a little child has to do with the little child of Christ within us. Kindergartners! I speak to our souls, "Join with Christ within even if He seems but a child!" We must become as a child in every place Christ desires to establish Himself anew within our souls and on this earth.

Jesus told us that the kingdom was like a mustard seed that is "the least of all the seeds" within us (Matt. 13:31-32, NKJV). He also told us to become like little children to enter the kingdom, and to choose the least or lowest place of honor to become promoted (Matt. 18:3; Lk. 14:8-10). Choose the lowest place, and Christ will call you "Friend" (Lk. 14:10). Choose the still small voice rather than the loud ones in your life. That is conscience.

The above messages are similar to and parallel Jesus' overall messages to lose the earthly life to find true life, to become poor to become rich, and to become the least to become the greatest. That narrow gate is consistent. It is opposite of the world's ways and is always about humbling the earthly to exalt the heavenly.

There is no other way to ascend but to descend first through the small gate. The way up is down. This message surely ripped away any chance of Jesus being made an earthly king, which He did not want anyway.

For Kathy and me to embrace new ways, we needed to allow ourselves to be like little children who had many mishaps along the way. It would have been easier for me to brace myself and still appear strong in my earthly shell like I had always done. But God desired increased vulnerability and my acknowledgment that, at points, I had no clue of how to go forward as a couple. Only as we surrendered our "go to" ways and slowed down did Christ have room to utter almost inexpressible thoughts and feelings through us that began to give glimpses of direction.

Serve the child and even the infant Christ in others where they may not be able to express adequately what's on their heart. Jesus said that He was glad that the Father hid kingdom ways from the wise and intelligent and had revealed them to "babes" (Matt. 11:25). The humble. Jesus also said that God had ordained praise from the lips of infants, meaning babes with inexpressible words, even non-speaking (Matt. 21:16).

How often have you been unable to put words to the meaningful things of Christ? Things that others could not receive from you? How often have you encountered others who have tried to express the things of Christ, but you could not yet receive them? Inexpressible words.

Being the greatest means becoming a child as well as to welcome, accept, and embrace other children. That honors *new beginnings* of Christ (the Alpha) in certain areas within self and others, as well as in the various situations we encounter. To make any headway at points, Kathy and I needed to allow one another to be toddlers attempting wobbly new steps. That required patience and space connected to one another at times of heightened emotions.

Jesus also said that welcoming children is the same as welcoming Him, and the word He used for children in that passage meant infants or half-grown children (Mk. 9:34-37). Humble yourself as a child who continually starts anew in various aspects of your life, and also be a servant of the infants and children around you. Be a servant of all who struggle to express Christ. That might be those who have been wounded or it might be natural children. Trust that Christ is in, and desires expression through, all people.

Serve those who barely grasp new aspects of Christ, and serve those who are *half*-grown as well. In many aspects of the kingdom we are only half-grown because we must embrace counterparts to become fully grown. Kathy was my primary counterpart, and I gradually learned to identify and embrace what was Christ in the midst of what seemed different or opposite from me.

CHAPTER 5

Kingdom Counterparts and Crumbs

Unintelligible Groanings

During fire, people's pain groans with expressions deeper than words. But there's meaning behind that pain. Kathy's pain, after all that had happened during the time of Bob living with us, was beyond words. Unintelligible. I'm sure that mine was too, although I tended not to be as in touch with some of those deeper experiences and to think that I was doing fine when I really wasn't.

Looking back, I see that the whole experience could have gone a little more easily had we known that God's higher purpose was for us to not expect anything more or different from each other and, instead, to be safety for one another being exactly where we were so that we could express the unintelligible. That is where Christ could be found most easily. Expression from the deep without trying to get anywhere. That is where previously unseen mysteries awakened in us like beautiful flowers blossoming for the first time in the spring.

God definitely works through people sometimes not being safe with others, because those hurtful rough edges can shake others loose from their normal ways and into "new moves." Into higher ways. But at some point, safety for people to be where they are must exist for the unintelligible to come forth. Our unintelligible areas could not come forth until experiencing greater safety.

Kathy could not initially verbalize what her insides knew through experience. That is, she could not communicate about the gaps she felt, which essentially left me guessing about what was needed. I felt unable to fill those gaps that I somehow sensed that God wanted to use me to fill. We didn't know during much of this season that God was more fully birthing our true identities, ones that were very different from each other. The rough edges were initially shaking loose old ways but we could not yet see or embrace the new moves. I believe that is because we weren't yet to find those new moves at a tangible level so that more time and space allowed a fuller establishing of our deeper identities that had been planted within. These unique identities were birthed through groanings, which eventually caused our identities to become more fully visible and embraced by one another.

Kathy's make-up was to be sensitive to deep places of lack, which called our attention to areas where God wanted to further shift us from earthly to heavenly ways. My make-up was to wait beyond, or withhold from, lesser earthly moves so that God had the space and freedom to fill those places of lack with His higher ways. Said another way, Kathy usually exposed areas where God wanted to go further, and I usually paid attention to God's time and way for fulfilling or lifting us into those higher ways. She was more in touch with need, and I was more in touch with the necessary safety and space for needs getting met. God wanted us to rest in His safety, much like an incubator, while He brought birth to more of the unseen within us.

We could not fully see our unique identities early in our upheaval. But we were both necessary, and the fiery circumstances awakened and established our identities that needed to work together as one. The upheaval had caused groanings that were the Spirit's beginnings of yet unembraced aspects of our identities that God wanted expressed through us. It just took a while to fully understand and accept that we were supposed to be different in these respects. Different and yet working together as one. I needed to honor Kathy's expressions (sometimes big emotions or reactions) about unseen places of lack, and she needed to honor my sense of God's time and higher ways to fulfill those places (sometimes appearing to her as a bump on a log who didn't really "get it" when I didn't take visible action).

The scriptures say that the Spirit helps us with groanings deeper than our understanding (Rom. 8:26). These unintelligible groanings especially come through counterparts that are often like unspeaking babes to us. Counterparts are opposites. I'm sure you've heard the expression that men are from Mars and women are from Venus. That's what Kathy and I, and counterparts as a whole, are like. Kathy and I were designed with two very different functions. But fortunately the Spirit helped us by "taking hold of the opposite together" (which is the deeper meaning of that passage).

Just as the scriptures say that God is longsuffering, He wants us to endure, bear with, and forgive one another during perceived gaps and differences. Counterparts must work together with the Spirit who takes hold of and gathers people's differences to awaken their souls to more of the unintelligible Christ who is in and through all things.

Marriage is God's clearest symbol for a godly relationship where two who are different come together as one. Counterparts. That is about us being in union with God, but also about our unity with one another's true self on this earth. That is how earth becomes as it is in heaven.

113

This was God's foremost purpose for Kathy's and my struggles: to embrace what seemed different or even oppositional to us as God's sovereign works to birth more of Christ in each of our souls. God desired for us to embrace more of the unintelligible Christ within one another that would awaken us into higher unity and also into more of His mysteries.

I believe that our awakening through "the marriage of counterparts" was meant to be a testimony for awakening many others to this mystery of mysteries. Marriage has been translated as a profound mystery and even the mystery *of* mysteries (Eph. 5:32). That means a mystery that continually births other mysteries. I now believe that marriage symbolizes God's central path of Christ-like relationship for awakening His greater love on this earth, which is about seeking the true treasure in all people in spite of any of the earthly rough edges.

Ongoing marriage of counterparts, of that which appears different or even difficult, is the way to kingdom fullness. That unity of counterparts pertains to you with difficult people, events, or even aspects of yourself that seem not to go together. Ongoing marriage is a primary way to access God's higher power that becomes visible in gaps or conflicts. Ongoing marriage is Christ's keys of the kingdom that continually bind and loosen heavenly and earthly ways (Matt. 16:19). We must continually leave, be loosed from, and be the least regarding earthly things so that we join, become bound to, or sealed with heavenly things. That is the way of marriage – leaving our previous origins and cleaving to what we have not yet fully known.

Kathy and I gradually received more of each other's true self through paying attention to the unintelligible areas in one another. We received more of our specific spiritual identities and "names" from within one another as we learned to "hear" and embrace these unintelligible areas. I learned to recognize Kathy's initial reactions to felt gaps as areas where God desired something further or new. These were at least times for deep prayer if nothing else, and when we prayed, both Kathy and I usually felt more whole, as if a higher purpose had been fulfilled. Kathy learned to recognize that my unique part was needed in those places of felt gap as well. I usually had a sense of how Christ wanted us to participate with Him at those times.

Just as Christ left the secure home of His Parent to love and gather people, we must leave the secure home of our parents to love and gather Christ in one another. Leaving earthly father and mother to be married symbolizes leaving earthly origins and ways, which we use to define and separate ourselves from one another. It symbolizes leaving earthly identities. Only through leaving the earthly mind that sees people as separate do we recognize that we are truly one family under heaven; only then are we in the loving Christ nature enough to understand more of His sacrificial love that surpasses earthly knowledge (Eph. 3:14-19). This love gathers.

Marriage is God's continual pathway to honor Christ's name that is above all names. To me, that means honoring Christ who is bigger and embraces all true individual names ... the true self in all people. Through Kathy and I serving Christ in one another, through the "marrying" of our individual identities and names, we gradually awakened to and received more of the name above all names. More of the kingdom.

There are over 100 names in the scriptures for God and Christ. Why so many names? Names in the scriptures were descriptive of one's character, the true substance of a person. The problem is that names are not only descriptive but restrictive. That's why Christ is the name above all names. The meaning of the name of Christ goes beyond all titles and labels, beyond all cultures and peoples. And marriage symbolizes the continuous gathering of two into one. That is Christ's gathering of all names under His name and nature, which establishes heaven's unity on earth.

Ongoing marriage of counterparts awakens us to receive more of the true inheritance placed within us. The scriptures emphasize that although we are owners of all … we do not truly receive that inheritance until the time set by the father (Gal. 4:1-2). Receiving the inheritance is beyond the heir's control. There is a time and season for everything (Eccl. 3:1). Also, receiving an earthy inheritance is usually a one-time event whereas receiving our heavenly inheritance is an ongoing unfolding "day."

Kathy and I gradually received more of our inheritance planted within us according to the Father's ordained way and times, which took far longer than we would have liked. This ongoing ordained way humbled our earthly nature because the way required losing one life to gain another. When Christ within us was persecuted, imprisoned, naked, thirsty, or hungry, He wanted us to visit and feed Him who was within rather than to gratify our earthly nature.

I fully awakened to this spiritual unseen way of marriage because of the intensity of my trials. This spiritual way of marriage is far more real than earthly marriage. While God established marriage for the earthly journey, it will come to an end because it is ultimately only a symbol of a *spiritual* way. Jesus said (Lk. 20:34-36), "The people of this age marry and are given in marriage. But those who are considered worthy of taking part in that age and in the resurrection from the dead will neither marry nor be given in marriage, and they can no longer die; for they are like the angels. They are God's children, since they are children of the resurrection."

Marriage will no longer exist. Why? Because unity will already exist in heaven as well as through Christ's resurrection within people while on this earth. So marriage's way of two becoming one will no longer be necessary.

Spiritual marriage while on this earth is about sacrificially loving one another so that each other's Christ nature comes forth (resurrects) to express His higher ways. Receiving more of our inheritance happens through "marrying" more of Christ in one another. Marriage's "leaving and cleaving" means leaving the earthly nature in yourself and others so as to cleave to "new land." The Promised Land.

Go and know the land of Christ within yourself and in others. In doing so, you will continually feed the hungry, clothe the naked, and visit and strengthen the prisoners. The unintelligible that desires release.

God told Abraham that He would give him the land wherever he walked (Gen. 3:17). That is always true for all of us. Wherever we place our foot, we reap what we sow. We reap what is worldly when we walk according to the worldly, and we reap what is heavenly when we walk in the heavenly (although the reaping may not be in the immediate moment).

Counterparts

Counterparts are our greatest opportunities for awakening, and marriage of counterparts is the means for awakening.

I regularly took space to be with God during heightened times of conflict and upheaval with Kathy, which helped me to see life from God's higher perspective. The world's duality versus heaven's unity stood out to me. I saw that God had set up everything with duality on this earth. He had set up everything with counterparts: up and down, light and dark, day and night, higher and lower, and good and bad. These counterparts were necessary for recognizing differences, and for learning and choice.

Somehow God's fire had been awakening me to see that I regularly had choice when experiencing counterparts. During difficult circumstances, or times where I felt like Kathy could not receive me, or when I didn't like certain ways I was made (like not being a take-charge person), I began experiencing these "problematic" counterparts as felt gaps where God most desired to establish His higher works and ways.

I began seeing all obstacles as God's greatest opportunities for me to watch and listen for the unintelligible at those times. I always had a choice. I could maintain an earthly mindset of "this versus that," which I knew would produce more of earth's separation. More of Kathy's and my differences that could not go together. Or, I could put on the mind of Christ, whose name was higher than our individual names, which would produce more of heaven's unity on earth. I began to see that Christ (or His name) was always above and governing over the earthly, and that problematic counterparts were always His opportunities for more of Kathy's and my unintelligible true self to come forth. I saw that "this versus that" was earthly, and that "this *and* that" was Christ's higher way that gathers into His unity. Not every aspect in Kathy or me was the true, but I saw that there was always at least some aspect that *was* true and was meant to be established through the difficulties. I saw that Christ always wanted me to pay attention to what He was working difficulties for. What unintelligible aspect was the treasure that He wanted me to embrace during any of the problematic counterparts I experienced?

Occasionally during upheaval I could find no higher life from within people in the midst of interactions. Sometimes the higher life I was meant to embrace was not from within them, but simply from joining the way I sensed Christ wanted to awaken me while people or obstinate external dynamics remained unchanged. Watching for higher life this way was part of paying attention for the unintelligible. The hidden treasure.

As much as I was able, I embraced various counterparts as God's purposeful opportunities to awaken me to more of His higher life. Sometimes those counterparts were Kathy's friends or established relational connections who were not open to any reality on my part. Other times those counterparts were difficult circumstances where it seemed that no right or even good decision was possible. Still other counterparts occurred when experiencing two poles within me, where I simultaneously experienced great compassion and anger at points, or felt a clear leading to set healthy boundaries while also feeling strongly pulled towards enabling. All of these difficult experiences were counterparts and opportunities for me to awaken to higher ways.

God's primary way to increase wisdom and discernment in me during my journey was through counterparts, especially difficult ones. Life's gray areas, not the clear-cut ones, accomplished that work. And lengthier obstinate unchanging circumstances were meant to birth deeper unseen areas within me that I couldn't see until much later.

What is it that makes you anxious when you encounter situations that feel beyond you? Isn't it that you have not yet possessed the required skill or ability? That's true for me. That is when life (or God) is presenting us with situations that require new or higher developmental skills than we have used before. That is what difficult counterparts and life's gray areas are meant to call forth from within us.

The Simple or Wise Way

Discernment is required for counterparts to unite. The scriptures say (Prov. 10:13), "Wisdom is found on the lips of the discerning."

Discernment means going beyond the simple ways of "This is all good; that is all bad." Our awakening is limited when we cling to clear-cut boxes of all-or-nothing. That is the common fleshly way and perspective for maintaining false security.

We can cling to a false sense of security, to all that is familiar that we've previously experienced as right, when we conclude that anything different or difficult is bad. Protestant is good; Catholicism is bad; clear-cut religious ways are good; and the gray, sometimes less-definable spirituality is bad. Isn't this what happens at times? Historically we have seen imperfections in others (especially counterparts), and sadly that has sometimes meant receiving nothing from them. Usually because of underlying fear. Because of wanting clear-cut boxes for our earthly nature to feel secure. But that is always in place of faith that requires higher security in the midst of earthly uncertainty.

The earthly nature sees with simple eyes of either-or and black or white. "But sound wisdom has two sides" (Job 11:6). Heaven's wisdom on earth knows that two sides form a greater whole. Counterparts in unity display heaven's higher ways.

Humanity has been asleep to the two sides of wisdom. Flesh's common way has been to judge and disagreed with one another; for advantage it discounts one thing to elevate another. But Christ's body on earth is presently being raised to a greater love that lays down the fleshly eyes of either-or.

That is why wisdom calls out to the simple who lacks discernment (Prov. 9:1-6), "Leave your simple ways and you will live; walk in the way of understanding." We are called to leave the earthly and to cleave to wisdom that comes from the fullness of Christ in humanity. We are called to love God and our neighbor with *all* our heart, soul, and mind so that we don't cling only to our individual loves and perspectives. That is a sacrificial walk and is part of Jesus' meaning when He said to lose our life to find true life. We must continually lose the simple fleshly ways of this versus that and grow in God's discernment that gathers rather than separates. Jesus gathered.

Also calling out to the simple is the woman Folly. The scriptures say (Prov. 9:13-18), "The woman Folly is loud; she is undisciplined and without knowledge ... calling out to ... all who are simple." Both Folly and Wisdom call out at the city's gates, which means during life decisions or doorways that build earthly or heavenly "cities" (Prov. 8:34; 9:3, 14). Both call out from the city's highest points, which means at our most stretching points regarding what decision is the higher path. I continually came to see the deeper meaning in all of these scriptures the more that fire awakened me.

Flesh wants the security of humanity's common ways, which utilize simple rules and formulas that require no faith. That is the lower path of this versus that. But we are to seek after the *hidden* wisdom just like God wanted me to seek the unintelligible within Kathy, myself, and others (Prov. 2:2-6). We attain wisdom when we fervently seek her like hidden treasure, and we only find hidden treasure in difficult-to-find places. Gray areas. God used difficult life circumstances to increase my discernment and wisdom. That was the primary way for me to awaken from flesh's clinging to simple, unloving ways. Simple rules could not love. Remember when I mentioned earlier about beautiful people who have learned wisdom through suffering and how they do not blurt out simple formulas to fix us during our trials? Suffering stripped them so as to leave flesh's simple ways.

God granted Kathy and me higher life through counterpart circumstances or people, which required greater faith and discernment than we had yet embraced. Along the way, I found the richest delicacies through people who had been treated as outcasts. One of my friends is mildly mentally disabled. One day he explained to me how airplanes were previously made with bigger windows but are now made with smaller ones for structural stability. Now airplanes can fly higher and through more turbulence with greater stability.

As my friend shared his discovery the Spirit stirred within me and revealed how we only advance higher spiritually through narrower pathways. We are less able to see and find the way, but once we have seen the way we receive greater stability. Hidden treasure! That is part of what Jesus meant by the narrow gate that few find.

My friend shared his discovery with me at the same time I was writing about the wise way that requires greater discernment than the simple way. This experience caused me to learn again this way of using spiritual discernment with anyone I encounter. I especially pay attention to counterparts, anyone whose life style is different from mine, people who are different from me spiritually, and especially people who have suffered. These gifts are sometimes unintelligible, but they are constantly available.

Diversity is a pot of gold for increasing wisdom and expanding vision. Counterparts uniting become God's dynamite that explodes beyond the world's rigid ways. We become enlarged, and our vision becomes enlarged by embracing and seeing through the eyes of each unique member of God's body of people across this earth. But only loving discernment embraces more of Christ within one another.

We must search for wisdom and gain crumbs wherever we may find them. That was part of Jesus' meaning when He told His disciples to gather all the leftover crumbs of broken bread so that "nothing may be lost" (Jn. 6:12). We are all broken and imperfect humans, but crumbs of the Christ nature are always available in all people to enlarge our souls into Him.

King David said (Psm. 23:5), "Thou dost prepare a table before me in the presence of my enemies." God provides spiritual food for us in the presence of our "enemies," and that is especially true when encountering enemies that again turn our need to God. Our enemies are not people. Our only real enemy is the flesh nature that is the false part within all of us.

But there is always food. Crumbs can be gleaned from counterparts with rough fleshly edges, whether those edges happen to be in awakened individuals or not.

Jesus told the story of the rich man and a poor man named Lazarus who longed even for crumbs from the rich man's table (Lk. 14:21). People have often viewed that story as only about physical food, but I also see it as about spiritual food. The rich man cared neither for giving spiritual crumbs to Lazarus nor for gaining crumbs from him; and he learned later about the folly of that simple way.

Just before Jesus' story about the rich man He emphasized the importance of pursuing heavenly riches rather than earthly ones (vs. 13). Then Jesus confronted the Pharisees about how they justified themselves to one another regarding money and divorcing their wives (vs. 14-15, 18). Jesus said in the midst of these statements that they were forcing their way into the kingdom and then exhorted them with a huge "but."

Jesus emphasized that no one could advance further into His kingdom apart from His word, way, and higher nature (vs. 17). Lesser nature that maneuvered and justified itself by people's standards with one another would not work. Jesus' message about adultery was partly that we are unfaithful and betray *Him* when marital counterparts divorce. We commit adultery and betray Christ within when we "divorce" one another, whether that is in marriage or our many other relationships. That is why Jesus immediately told the next story about the rich man and Lazarus.

Jesus' story is not unrelated. He had just emphasized how marital counterparts divorce themselves from one another, and then He immediately described how the rich man did that with poor Lazarus. Jesus' point was that we cut off our love from Him when we cut off our love from one another. We betray Him. We've done it to Him when we've done it to the least.

We must walk in faith beyond the rough fleshly edges within others to receive more crumbs of Christ's nature. And seeking those crumbs beyond what initially feels like a "no" sometimes brings tremendous healing and restoration.

The story of the Canaanite woman wanting her daughter restored portrays seeking crumbs from Christ in spite of several "no's." Jesus conveyed "no" twice but she persisted in asking a third time saying (Matt. 15:27), "Yes, Lord; but even the dogs feed on the crumbs which fall from their masters' table."

Jesus exclaimed that she had great faith. Her respectful persistence illustrated how to gain Christ's crumbs amidst experiencing "no's" at the earthly level. We are to extract the precious from the profane within people. We must seek Christ's crumbs amidst earthly rejection, pain, and trials, and those crumbs may turn out to be essential to our restoration.

Elisha also received a "yes" after he persisted through three of Elijah's "no's" (2 Kng. 2:1-14). Elisha could have stayed at three different places where God had previously visited His people. Those were tests to see if Elisha would stay in old places of food or move on with Elijah to new places of food. History can teach us, but faith goes beyond history. We must continually stretch beyond the familiar to awaken further into our true self.

Fortunately Elisha went on with Elijah and received a double portion of Elijah's spirit. That is symbolic of Christ giving a double portion of His Spirit to His people after they go on with Him through three "days" of testing (through three days of "no's"). That is the cross. The word within us is tested and experienced before we become one with it.

Elisha receiving the double portion is also symbolic of followers of Christ receiving the latter day's greater works *after* they let go of old ways that are not His fullness. Elisha had to let go of the lesser to go on and receive the greater.

Kathy and I would not have received more of Christ's fullness without receiving His crumbs that came through His body (through one another as well as others). The flesh nature's rough edges were part of the testing. We were called to lay down our lives to the "no's" to receive Christ's crumbs that resulted in fuller restoration.

Paul told us to receive all the *hidden* treasures of wisdom and knowledge within the mystery of Christ by being knit together in love (Col. 2:2-3). Why did Paul emphasize receiving hidden treasures through the mystery of Christ and being *knit together*? The mystery of Christ is "Christ in us (all of us), who is the hope of glory." Also, the deeper meaning of "knit together" is to compact or drive together into unity." This sounds a lot like how dynamite is made – counterpart substances packed tightly together (which I will discuss shortly). Paul conveyed that we receive Christ's hidden treasures through sacrificially loving Him in people while on this earth, which is where we find the fullness of Him.

Christ constantly governed and established His realm through Kathy and me by opening up locked places through our sacrificial love of one another. We found hidden treasure when we pursued and sacrificially loved Christ within one another and did not hold onto our individual "loves" too tightly. That is how Christ gradually worked through us to establish His sovereign name above our individual names.

Jesus said we are to love our neighbor and told the Jew's a story to illustrate who their neighbor was (Lk. 10:29-37). The story portrayed a man being beaten on his journey from Jerusalem to Jericho. The man lay on the road half dead. A priest and then a

Levite walked past him without helping. Then a Samaritan came by, helped him, and offered him care.

Jesus chose a Samaritan to illustrate who had been a neighbor. Why? Jews had *no* dealings with Samaritans (Jn. 4:9). Cut off.

There is much meaning in that passage. Part of the meaning is that we tend to cut off relationally people who are able to contribute the most to us. They might be the very source of our restoration; they are the counterparts that complement us and awaken us from our blind areas. Christ wants us to care for our neighbors (those we've cut off). He wants us to open up beyond "simple's" separating way of labeling or confining people to one box versus another.

We are called to lay down labels. Lay down categories, groups, denominations. We must lay down our lives for those who rub us in wrong ways, live different life styles, and believe differently than us. We must lay down our lives to love counterparts. *That* is how the Spirit within the body of Christ will have the freedom to work through us to breathe new life into humanity! In that way we finally become a true house of God with angels ascending and descending upon a ladder that visibly connects heaven and earth.

Jesus' story about loving our neighbor was about a journey to Jericho. Jericho symbolized victory, as well as God's people entering the Promised Land. Jesus' story emphasized that the way to live in the victory of the Promised Land is for us to love our neighbors who we have historically cut off from ourselves. Let us lay down our lives for our neighbors; for counterparts.

The Food of Champions

You must embrace the cross, the way of laying down your life, to eat the food of champions. You know that the breakfast of champions is Wheaties, right? But what is the food of spiritual champions?

Wisdom, which is Christ, the Living Word within us. Wisdom comes in many ways, shapes, and sizes, and we must lay down our lives for her.

The difference between spiritual champions and others is that champions constantly eat God's food rather than the world's. They hunger for God's ways rather than the world's ways in every situation they encounter. They don't settle for people's teachings, knowing that all people and authorities are fallible. Instead, they watch and listen for the Living Word that can come through any person or during any situation. They long for what stirs their heart, or for what they sense they were meant to hear or learn. They are open to thoughts, words, or ways that touch their own heart a little deeper than the world's empty words and ways. As they become a student of life and practice this way of "eating," a hunger awakens within them for the Master's teaching in all things. The Master then continuously teaches because the student is always ready.

Champions can't stop eating. They find morsels of God's light during darkness. They find a meal in the presence of their enemies. They find crumbs of Christ in many places that food appears to be unavailable.

I experienced two brief visions (one immediately after the other) that highlighted messages about the food of spiritual champions. I saw many sheets hanging on a wall and that each sheet was a testimony of Jesus through people. I saw the most recent sheet hanging on the wall, and it was sagging. I instantly knew that the nail attaching its left edge to the wall needed taken out and moved further to the left to keep it from sagging. I also knew that it meant that the sheet needed stretched further before that testimony was finished for all to see. I felt that the sheet was about my current fireworks but also sensed that it was about the body of Christ on earth still needing stretched through the cross. I sensed that the stretching centered on food.

Then I saw a dishwasher and its silverware container. The container was lopsided because of too much silverware on one side; it was tipping over. The container needed silverware on the opposite side (counterparts) to cause it to stand upright. The silverware was for eating food.

I knew that the vision represented eating spiritual food through the many members in the body of Christ (whether or not people currently label themselves this way). I saw that the missing silverware on the opposite side was about presently unseen or unutilized members of God's body on this earth.

I also knew that the body of Christ currently used members whose spiritual food was more visible. I saw how people elevated others deemed as authorities and those with visible gifts.

I understood that God now wanted to bring balance and fullness to His Living Word in people through unseen instruments. I sensed that the body of Christ was to emphasize seeking food through instruments that are typically overlooked, discounted, or treated as outcasts. The world gives credibility to worldly kings, queens, and princes but Christ especially seeks those who are humble, poor, and unnoticed. The "healthy" do not need the Physician. The "unhealthy" or those who acknowledge areas of lack regularly draw more of the Physician to themselves.

God emphasizes human weakness as our pathway for increase so that no person can boast in their earthly nature (1 Cor. 1:27-29).[1] Kathy's and my marriage was certainly not worth boasting about during the fireworks. In fact, we were viewed as the foolish, shameful things that did not know up from down! But, in time, the unhealthy and the broken drew the Physician.

Christ desires to use the humble and those not deemed as authorities to bring greater light and fullness in this coming season. Christ is not against people in authority positions but He desires balance in His body to cause it to stand upright. Many current church practices have emphasized earthly authorities or those with polished gifts rather than seeking Christ more fully in the unintelligible places. Seeking Christ in people who do not fit the norm or who have rough edges has not been commonplace. But Christ desires to bring more abundant honor upon those that have been deemed weaker, unnecessary, or less honorable (1 Cor. 12:22-23). The poor, the outcast, the stranger, and the prisoner.

God desires to use His body's "weaker" parts who are different or have rough edges, but we must desire and eat God's word through them, rough edges and all. Jeremiah said (Jer. 15:15-16), "… Know that for Thy sake *I endure reproach. Thy words were found and I ate them* …" Jeremiah suffered others' reproaches towards him, but he found God's words amidst that suffering and ate them. He didn't conclude that the "bad" shouldn't exist. Jeremiah trusted God's sovereignty over the suffering, which allowed him to be fed with more of heaven in spite of people's hateful actions towards him. Jeremiah recognized what God was after within him during those trials, and he ate that word of God.

We become God's spokespersons when we learn to eat His whole word even in the trials. God said to Jeremiah when he was enduring persecution (Jer. 15:19), "… and if you extract the precious from the worthless, you will become My spokesman." Jeremiah was a spiritual champion who found God's word in many unseen places, and God used him as a mighty spokesperson.

God wants to awaken His word within us individually during trials. I constantly ask, "What are You after in me Lord?" Especially during trials I pay attention to how God might want to stretch and lift me further in faith. I watch for His word that I am to eat.

This is not passivity but active discernment about what God is after in me and then joining with that work. Christ is always after something further in me when I encounter difficulties beyond my present abilities (He does not demand anything but *wants* to give me a gift when I humbly acknowledge my human inability and agree with Him by faith about what He is working).

Many people turn away God's high-protein food in their lives. Those places of higher food require greater trust in God. I will fail to find God's food if I perceive some circumstance or person not to be as they "should be" in life. Shoulds, shouldn'ts, musts, and need to's reveal unacceptance of "what is." First accept "what is" without preconceived shoulds and then ask for what Christ is after in those places. He wants to take your fingers off of all aspects of your out-of-control situations so He can fill the gaps with more of heaven's reality. Only after fully surrendering can you see to join with what Christ is working.

Our earthly nature views difficult circumstances or people through all-or-nothing boxes and cuts off potential learning. That is the flesh's separating way, which prevents us from eating God's word that is present in the midst of those "enemies."

I will invalidate the Christ nature within others if I distrust them. Without knowing it, I previously distrusted and closed my eyes to Christ in others. I had closed my eyes (and soul) to the spiritual food to be gained through others because I had judged according to fleshly separating eyes. I used to think that I could only gain heaven through those who looked like a polished Christ. Forgive me God.

I agree that I cannot trust anyone's flesh nature, but that does not necessitate treating people like lepers, as if there is no Christ nature desiring expression from within them. I cannot distrust Christ in others and love them at the same time; and I distrust Christ when I distrust Christ in the least of us.

God desires to forgive (meaning removal of lesser ways) His people for this kind of distrust, but we must sincerely ask Christ to uproot the lies that hinder us from loving as He loves. We will only ask this of Him if we recognize that we are sometimes still blind in those ways.

Ask for trust during love's fireworks. Ask for trust during God's use of imperfect counterparts. Ask for trust to know that God will prepare a table of food for you in the presence of your enemies. You can never not find food! Ask that you would receive whatever crumbs are available, whether that is through a person or from Christ directly during obstinate difficulties.

Safety is crucial for seeing people's hearts. Without safety I will usually only see people's rough edges (which are usually their attempts to act significant or cover up the gaps they feel when fearful of judgment). Safety allows me to truly see another. Safety allows me to see myself.

I will be less honest in the moment with others when I feel unsafe with them, and without knowing it, I will be less honest with myself. I have seen that I am less vulnerable and real when I am fearful, and then I become less self-aware and less God-aware. That's why I occasionally need space to be still with Christ when I am fearful during heightened difficulties.

I saw Kathy's freedom instantly expand connected to me when she finally saw and felt my heart. Kathy had regularly said that she couldn't see me during our fireworks. I knew that that was true and wanted to be seen by her, but I felt like she could not see me no matter what I did. She also expressed that she felt like I could not see her.

We were both afraid.

Fear had regularly conveyed false pictures of ourselves to one another, and we needed to know safety for the true to show. Only through God gradually increasing inner support and safety could I reveal my heart to Kathy in a way that she could see and hear it. I expressed my heart to her previously even with emotions at times, but not as fully. Only through safety could the deep be expressed in greater purity. Then the true could be seen. My Christ nature became more visible to her through safety. Then deep called to Deep within one another. When my heart expressed the deep, it touched the Deep within her.

It was just like in the movie Avatar when the couple said to one another, "I see you." They were an example of seeing with purity into the Christ nature of one another (though it wasn't called that). The trials had removed the planks from their own eyes, and they experienced tremendous unity when they saw with pure eyes.

Lack of safety from either Kathy or me caused our hearts to hide even in the midst of "communicating." I don't think we as a people have awakened to the profound importance of safety for people's souls to be brave enough to keep embracing the Christ nature within one another.

I received a powerful vision that highlighted the importance of safety and trust. It also taught me more about the food of champions. I saw me looking straight ahead while standing very peacefully. It appeared as if I was seeing into the future. Then I saw a huge reddish-orange horse eating food from my shoulder. It stood towering over me from behind my left shoulder while it ate. That's all I saw but it was with full clarity and color. I was also keenly aware of what I experienced emotionally while the horse ate from my shoulder.

Has a horse ever eaten food from your hand? Even with gentle horses you don't want a finger sticking up while feeding them or you could lose it. In fact, I knew a woman whose horse ate a chunk from her shoulder when she wasn't looking (and her shoulder didn't even have food on it!).

That's what struck me powerfully when I saw this vision. I knew that I was fully at peace and trusted that the horse would not hurt me while it ate. I was so peaceful and trusting of the horse that I knew that it made no earthly sense. Then I was drawn to its color. I couldn't take my eyes off of the horse's color.

Several days later I researched the word "horse" in the scriptures. Again I was drawn to the horse's color in my mind. I was also drawn to the scriptures in the book of Job about the horse's majesty (39:19-25). I contemplated those scriptures as Kathy walked into the house; she asked if I wanted to watch the movie Secretariat later. I agreed that that sounded good and was struck by the coincidence.

We had never seen that movie. Right from the beginning a narrator stated the scriptures in Job about the majesty of the horse. I was astounded. The Spirit stirred within me. A little later I saw the first side view of the full grown Secretariat. I realized it was the identical color and side view of the horse I had seen in my vision. I knew that there was a connection between my vision and Secretariat.

As I continued to watch the movie I nearly fell out of my chair when the characters emphasized that Secretariat could not stop eating! A champion.

Then I remembered that a well-known prophetic man had communicated about the coming of future spiritual champions from among the followers of Christ. He compared these champions to Secretariat and had emphasized that their hearts would be enlarged through stretching God-ordained experiences. I can't recall details but I remember that he stressed that Secretariat's heart was over two times larger than other horses' hearts. A double portion?

Our hearts become spiritually enlarged through trials when we lay down our lives for one another (like Jeremiah did). Trust that the Christ nature within one another will come forth when we seek it with all our heart. Seek and you *shall* find.

I try to set my sight on and seek the Christ nature within others rather than staring outwardly at fleshly waves. That is seeking the kingdom within them and all else becomes added. Weeds fall away on their own and the wheat becomes revealed.

The vision centered on trust. Safety allows the expression of hearts. We must love others by laying down to their rough edges rather than making quick judgments that shut down life within them. Allow the weeds. God is faithful to weed out all that is not Him by the end. We don't need to do that sifting work for Him.

I eat spiritual food when I embrace the Christ part of others and desire those crumbs. More importantly, I am then able to feed and grow champions when I trust the deep within them. I feed others when I see their crumbs for me and lift those crumbs upon my shoulders. I feed and strengthen them by receiving their gift. I affirm the Christ nature in them and say, "I see you!" Their soul is built up in Christ to believe in the champion they are. That affirmation of their Christ nature continually unhooks them from their lesser nature because love fills gaps.

I am learning to trust that the Christ nature in others wants to come forth but has not been received by the world. I am not to be part of the world's persecution that frightens others' souls from joining their Christ nature. I am to be a safe ear for a faint Voice trying to be awakened within another's soul.

I will fail to see Christ's fullness within others when I am not safe. Especially in conflicts and differences of belief, I genuinely try to hear what another's heart feels compelled to believe or express even if that is mostly unintelligible. Most times that is the Christ nature desiring expression.

Not always. But I will not discover people's unexpressed Christ from within unless I first desire to hear their deep place without initial judgment or conclusions. God brings tremendous food through the rich diversity within His body of people. Those who trust will become champions and will feed champions like Secretariat.

Allow God to protect you rather than resorting to fleshly protection at others' expense … and at the kingdom's expense. Trust is the way forward. That is the connector. Trust is Christ's faith within us that becomes His joints and ligaments for connecting the body of Christ on this earth. Trust is what the vision highlighted to me more than all else.

Two other coincidences happened connected to the Secretariat vision.

I shared the vision at my weekly men's breakfast. The vision reinforced what others saw about the need for greater trust and unity. Afterwards I left in my car and pulled onto the street behind a tractor-trailer truck. The huge words on the back of the truck right in front of me were "Triple Crown." God's timing was amazing!

Then I finished writing this section on the food of champions (all but this last part). I walked down the hallway to teach my counseling class the following morning. Two students sat in the lobby. One ate some cookies and said, "This is my breakfast of champions." I laughed and said that I had just written a section in my book about the food of champions.

I then began class. A student who was preparing to present (who had not communicated with the previous two students from the lobby) took a last bite of her snack and similarly referred to it as her "breakfast of champions." The two initial students and I were shocked that she used that same expression that none of us had heard for years until this day where we heard it twice (which occurred the following morning after I wrote about the food of spiritual champions). I could only laugh at God's sense of humor.

CHAPTER 6

Perfect Dynamite

Yearning and Turning

I had seen the importance of me embracing the unintelligible voice of Christ wherever it came from, whether that was from myself, Kathy, others, or through what Christ seemed to be working particular circumstances for. But I had not yet crystalized or expressed the center of Kathy's and my counterpart identities that we were to embrace.

Then during my use of an earlier version of this book for teaching a spiritual class, I posed a question about these counterpart identities for my graduate students to consider. I did so because many of them could see the exact same dynamics with counterparts in their own lives. As we opened up to consider what the center of these relational dynamics were like, two students collectively arrived at the word "yearner" for Kathy's end, and instantly the word "turner" popped into my head for describing my end.

I knew as soon as those words emerged that they were the center of two primary counterparts, not only in Kathy and me, but in humanity. Since entering the counseling profession well over 30 years earlier, I had passionately watched and studied people and relational dynamics to learn all I could. Now, within my heart, because of the Spirit stirring within me, I instantly knew that these yearning and turning counterparts were the central stumbling blocks to, as well as the potentially powerful means for, fully functioning relationships. For God-designed relationships.

I have especially watched these powerful dynamics coming through couples, dynamics that were also clearly evident in Kathy and me. Somehow these forces had always seemed bigger than couples, just like they had seemed bigger than Kathy and me for a season. But, now, I felt like God was putting His finger on these counterparts as crucial identities or roles for establishing heaven's higher ways. I got the sense that, if people and couples in particular weren't awakened to participating with these two distinct roles, they would remain significantly incapacitated regarding God's works during trials.

You can see these dynamics very clearly when watching couples. One person (more often women) will be the yearner who feels the lack, weakness, and gaps where life is not working well, which then usually causes her to long or yearn for something more in that area. This was usually Kathy. The other person (more often men) will be inclined to hold a steady course during the waves, and to pay attention to what most makes sense to bring fulfillment in that area. That was usually me during our trials.

God works through the yearner to cause awareness of need where He wants to work further. Then God works in the turner to keep his eyes on how best to fulfill those needs, which ideally means remaining surrendered to His higher works for meeting needs. I now see the yearner's gift as centered on awareness, and the turner's gift as focused on fulfillment.

Time and time again during upheaval, Kathy and I were each inclined towards our underlying identities. Our gifts. Kathy could feel or sense a needle in a haystack. She felt lack or places of need very deeply in life, which also caused her to experience upheaval, emotions, and reactions more fully. Her gift allowed us to know where God wanted to work further, but being tossed in the waves was her disadvantage. I felt emotions too, though usually not as deeply, especially in the immediate moment of the waves. I often detached a little more emotionally during the storms (without trying to do so), which allowed me to stand firm and keep paying attention to what God might be after.

The only problem was, there was always somewhat of a gap between us emotionally *during* the storms. As I pondered the many couples I had counseled previously, as well as my observations about life, I saw that this powerful dynamic repeatedly occurred. Saying it bluntly, the yearner tends to think about the turner, "He doesn't seem present or in touch with the full reality of what I'm experiencing!" The turner tends to view the yearner, "She doesn't seem to be in touch with reality when her emotions and reactions overpower and blind both of us!" Both persons' experiences have partial validity, but both persons are also partially blind.

Kathy and I needed one another for further awakening into God's fullness, which could only happen by sacrificially loving one another through the gaps and rough edges. The felt gaps were not supposed to stop "once and for all" in life, but neither was the sacrificial love that was meant to prevail through those periodic but temporary felt gaps. We each already carried the fullness of Christ within us but could only awaken to that fullness through the other's area of strength. Kathy's yearning gift was necessary to further awaken that gift within me, and my turning gift was important for gradually awakening that gift within her.

Kathy had an uncanny ability to sense when family or extended family was encountering difficult situations. Sometimes her intuitive sense showed up initially as fear (again, this is usually the yearner who is in touch with gaps). While I was not to fully follow or react to Kathy's fear, I needed to validate that her heart was aware of an area of importance that we were to attend to. Previously in those situations, I would tend to detach when I experienced Kathy powerfully focusing on me to do something. But I gradually learned to sacrificially love Kathy at those times by first being with her more fully emotionally, which then tended to lead into me contributing my part. I could only be with Kathy well emotionally when she also learned to sacrificially love me, which meant accepting that I could not always be what she wanted me to be, and also accepting my "turner" contribution. My part, *after comforting her and validating her part*, was usually prayer and trusting God's time and ways regarding what He was working. If there was an additional step to take beyond prayer, Christ would show it through our sincere turning to Him in unity (although new revelations do not always come in the immediate moment, which especially makes it difficult for the yearner during felt gaps).

The more Kathy and I embraced our own yearning and turning identities, and also each other's, the more we saw spiritual birth through us as counterparts uniting. Sometimes that birth was immediate and other times birth came about gradually.

At one point, we received hopeless news about an extended family member, who I will call Joe. I am being vague to protect his identity, but normally, resolution for someone in his predicament was not expected. Kathy and I, and then my men's group, prayed for Joe. Some prayers came from the yearner perspective, which was a longing from a deep place of acknowledging lack and human weakness; these prayers arose from a deep place of anguish and knowing that nothing earthly could truly meet the depth of need. Other prayers came from the turner perspective, from knowing that God was working in the situation and that He was trustworthy and desired to meet that deep place of need. As those counterpart prayers went forth, I already knew in my Spirit that God had answered. I sensed that something spiritual had been birthed, and that at some point we would see the fruit.

Within two weeks God brought powerful awakening and higher goodness in Joe's situation. All who were connected to Joe new that God had worked a miracle. Not everything works out the way we might want at an earthly level, but God is always in situations and desires to awaken people to Him in new ways, one way or the other.

Through Kathy and me uniting in prayer about situations like Joe's and also through the long-term storms we encountered, I knew I was coming into a clearer sense of how spiritual birth occurs. I knew that many kinds of counterparts existed on this earth. I began seeing that the various counterparts working in unison caused spiritual birth and that the yearning and turning counterparts were the foremost catalysts of birth. That caused me to search the scriptures about marital counterparts as originally designed.

Suitable Help and Conception

Believe it or not, God taught me the following scriptural foundation about conception coming through counterparts *after* I had already written most everything on this topic. Because this discovery occurred afterwards, it powerfully validated my experiential learning through the Spirit and what I had already written about counterparts.

God gave Adam a "suitable helper," Eve (Gen. 2:18). Helper means support or aid, as you might expect. Suitable, different than many people might think, means "a part opposite, specifically a counterpart." That Hebrew word *neged* refers to "a part that is opposite, far off, or against, which means sometimes is an affront … oppositional." It is a complementary part that is experienced as uniquely different or separate from oneself so as to fill in gaps, complete, or vigorously awaken what one has not yet lived or known. I had never heard anyone preach about marriage where spouses are not only supposed to be helpful aids but also oppositional at times! Doesn't life experience verify this?

Interestingly, the Hebrew word *neged* sounds similar to the English word naked and conveys that we will walk somewhat naked unless counterparts work together as God intended. I see, now, how both Kathy and I would have remained blind and naked in certain areas had we not received what we were to gain from each other's differences.

God constantly works life so that we encounter "suitable" helpers whether we want them or not. The Spirit works within couples (and all relationships) in many ways to do whatever is needed in each person (like the terms yin and yang) to help each one awaken from nakedness. We walk in nakedness and think we are alone when we believe the lie of separation between us and others. Especially those who appear different from us.

Sometimes Kathy is meant to be support like I might want, which will help me to stand in the truth. In my Christ nature. Other times she is meant to be in opposition to what is very important to me. Why? The Spirit uses those times to shake away more of my flesh nature to ensure that I am walking forward by faith. The Spirit wants to awaken me more into my Christ nature through my primary counterpart Kathy, and He will use me in various ways to help Kathy awaken further into hers.

I had learned through my panic attacks that I did not need to be different or more than I was to be acceptable, which sometimes frustrated Kathy when she felt like she needed certain things from me that she thought I should be able to provide. My earthly inability was a counterpart and an obstacle to her at times, but God used my inability to cause her to have to turn to Christ being her enough in place of a man's earthly abilities. There were also times that I would have liked her to be more encouraging of my writing or of some of my spiritually "out of the box ways," but I saw God using those times to ensure that I would go forward by faith rather than in human strength or ability.

For me, learning that God set up marital counterparts to be oppositional at times, validated what I had learned experientially. Knowing this caused both Kathy and me to surrender more fully to whatever God was working through our differences that sometimes felt like sandpaper. I began seeing an overall pattern of God bringing upheaval through Kathy's yearning, which caused me "to come to be" in Christ in that difficult area. Kathy's yearning caused me to turn more deeply to Christ in the areas of struggle because I knew that nothing else would work. In those places of upheaval, Kathy initially experienced lack and not having what she felt she needed. But as she united with me in this turning process, both she and I came "to have." I eventually saw the scriptures as highlighting the woman's purpose as *causing the man to be* and the man's purpose as *causing the woman to have.* Said another way so that you don't limit this learning to man and woman, the yearner causes the turner to be, and the turner causes the yearner to have. Really, in the end, God's goal is that both would "be" and both would "have."

The scriptures describe conception as coming about through man and woman uniting, which symbolizes spiritual conception. Just after God said that conception and childrearing would be difficult, He stated to the woman (Gen. 3:16) "… Your desire will be for your husband, and he will rule over you." Conception, the woman's desire, and the husband ruling are all connected, and they are more about the spiritual than the physical.[1]

Woman *desiring* man, and yet, man *ruling* symbolized two crucial counterparts. Humanity's flesh nature has seriously distorted these scriptures for selfishly meeting needs, but much spiritual depth is in them. The Hebrew meanings add clarity and fully describe the essence of Kathy's and my struggles. They also describe the two counterpart identities or roles that we saw as necessary to participate with to overcome the struggles.

Desiring means longing or yearning, as well as the awareness of being unfulfilled (yearning for and needing Christ). Ruling represents governing or "causing to have," which is most about directing or turning that need towards fulfillment (turning towards Christ). These meanings verified the two core counterparts that I and the graduate students had recognized about couples at a practical level.

Yearning for and needing Christ, and turning to Christ for fulfillment of need, to me, are the two most significant counterparts to honor for restoration of couples and all relationships. The first two statements in the previous paragraph succinctly describe the center of God-designed relationships, where both unique identities must be fully embraced rather than resisted for achieving healthy relationships. Once you understand these two core counterparts, you will see them throughout the scriptures and notice them regularly in your relationships.

To me, unresolved conflict on this earth most relates to not understanding and participating with Christ's yearning and turning counterparts, where two must become as one. The more Kathy and I came to see these two parts that needed to work together as one, the more restoration occurred. We also sensed a tremendous increase in the power of our prayers during the unity of these two counterparts. I believe that that sense of power and completion or fulfillment was us experiencing conception during those unified prayers. I knew that those prayers would be answered.

Yearning and turning within humanity can occur in healthy or unhealthy ways, meaning with or without Christ. Yearning for fulfillment can be focused on the earth or on heaven, and turning for fulfillment can be focused on the earth or on heaven.

Another scriptural passage is crucial for understanding yearning and turning at a practical level: in Christ, there is neither male nor female (Gal. 3:28). This means that we cannot stereotype or confine the Spirit's meaning of yearning to "woman" and turning to "man." Labels cannot capture the full meaning. The Old Testament was not the true, but only a shadow of the true (Col. 2:17; Heb. 8:5; 10:1). Yet, these scriptures about marriage say what they do to provide direction about these two counterparts *that are evident within all people.*

One person may be more inclined towards yearning overall, and another one towards turning. Or, a person may fluctuate between yearning and turning depending upon the situation, but both parts are within all of us. Part of me yearns because of need at times (symbolized by woman), and part of me directs or turns that need towards fulfillment (symbolized by man).

Just as testosterone is higher in males and estrogen higher in females overall, so too, the Old Testament scriptures about males tend to be more true of males and the ones about females more true of females. Yet, both male and female counterparts described in the scriptures are within all people just like testosterone and estrogen are within all people.

If you are beginning to become fearful about everything not being in clear-cut, black and white boxes, that is okay. Many people were confused and sometimes afraid of Jesus' messages because He was beyond clear-cut boxes. The flesh nature wants to keep simple boxes and formulas as false ways to maintain security. Let go of earthly security and pay attention to what you sense from deeper within yourself. Watch life for evidence of these counterparts.

They are especially clear during conflict or disagreements. Life and God will continually teach you as you watch.

Two essential counterparts exist within all people, one that yearns and is aware of gaps, need, or weakness (to call forth Christ in places of need), and another counterpart that is designed to turn or direct that need towards fulfillment by holding fast during trials or felt lack (for Christ to fulfill those needs).

Just as the scriptures say that man and woman are not independent from one another (1 Cor. 11:11), similarly, these counterparts within us and between us as people must work well together for fulfillment. Yearning is necessary to call forth Christ, and turning is needed to direct the thirst towards Christ alone. Turning, without deep yearning, will not thirst well enough to call forth Christ from deep to Deep. This was more of my struggle during marital conflict. And yearning, without true turning, will focus on other places for fulfillment than on Christ alone. This was more often Kathy's struggle, where she would tend to focus on me to attain certain outcomes (just like the scriptures said would happen in Genesis 3:16).

Within couples who are in conflict, you will usually see yearning standing out in one person and turning standing out in the other. Two poles with uniquely different spiritual tasks, but, sadly, often remaining in opposition to one another. This has likely been the single-most significant dynamic that has kept couples (and all difficult relationships) from working together as one.

Conflict throughout this world and throughout time, at the most basic level, stems from the fact that two have not become one. Yearning and turning have not worked together as originally designed by God.

The yearner is supposed to exist to draw true fulfillment, but it must be directed towards true fulfillment. The turner exists to direct the yearning towards true fulfillment, but it must know and be one-with the yearner in that deep place of lack. Jesus demonstrated both for us, which I will address shortly.

During our marital conflict, God worked in Kathy to yearn for higher unity than we had, although she focused on me in many ways to try to achieve that unity. I believed that God wanted higher unity too, but I sensed that this was beyond either of our current abilities to achieve. I kept trying to turn us towards God to fulfill that desire, but I hadn't previously done so through first deeply yearning from a place of lack with Kathy. In the end, Kathy learned to surrender the timing and way of fulfillment to God more fully, and I learned to be weak and yearn from deep places with Kathy before turning to God. For now, that is about as simply as I can say the essence of our deepest learning about the kind of unity God desired, and this way of uniting required a lengthy season for God to birth or establish more fully within us.

Romans 8:18-27 and verses 28-39 beautifully illustrate these yearning and turning counterparts, with the first half focusing on groaning and the second half focusing on conquering or overcoming.[2] That is yearning and then turning. Both parts are necessary.

Originally, I had seen in the scriptures that the man would rule connected to the woman, which meant that he would "cause to have." That is also consistent with the New Testament's man being "the head" of the woman by laying down his life for her (1 Cor 11:3).

More recently, I was shocked to find when researching the New Testament that the word for "woman" comes from the base Greek word *ginomai*, meaning "to cause to be; to cause to come into being." Doesn't this understanding give new meaning to the expression "the woman behind the man"? In other words, the "woman" who initially feels the weakness and gaps is meant to cause the "man" to come into being, into his full identity. She feels the felt gaps and then focuses on the "man" for fulfillment (as it states in Genesis 3:16). The man, then, feels that strain, which causes him to know lack more deeply. Then he must lead the way of turning to Christ by laying down his earthly nature while still being united in awareness of need with the woman. The man comes into the fullness of his identity when he initiates turning to Christ in that place. He comes into being, which then causes both of them to have. This beautifully portrayed Kathy and me.

Being causes having. The woman causes the man to be, and the man then causes the woman to have. Remember that these counterparts coming together is often in accordance with the stereotypes of men and women, but you will see them oppositely at times because we all have both parts like testosterone and estrogen. That is why you will encounter both yearning and turning counterparts within yourself and others at times.

Sometimes I feel weakness and gaps (symbolized by woman or yearning), which causes me to turn to Christ more deeply (symbolized by man or turning). Yearning, whether from Kathy or within myself, causes me to turn to Christ. To be "in Christ." Being in Christ then causes us to have.

Overall, Kathy is more inclined towards yearning and me towards turning (although in wounded areas I demonstrate more yearning and in secure areas Kathy demonstrates more turning). Also, we have both awakened more in the opposite areas through all our upheaval. That is how counterparts are supposed to work. Counterparts are meant to further awaken one another into Christ's fullness that we already carry within us.

Dynamite Through Counterparts

Earlier in our fireworks Kathy and I could not see that God was making us into perfect dynamite for furthering His works in and through us. God's goal was not so much to expose gaps between us but within each of us, ones that could only be awakened through each other. God wanted to make these gaps evident so that He could occupy our soul in those places and become our heavenly strength in place of earthly ways. Part of how Christ further occupied those places within us came through our acceptance of, and functioning in, our counterpart identities. Those true Christ identities began to fill gaps that seemed impossible to fill.

People's poor treatment of one another demonstrates the need for love to fill many gaps. Humanity has not walked in unity. Christians have not walked in unity. Humanity's one body with its many parts has not lived as one.

We can also see that people as a whole have not walked in Christ's power. Power comes through unity. The book of Acts displays a glimpse of the power that is available when we walk in higher unity.

The Greek word *dunamis* in the scriptures means the power of God. The word "dynamite" originates from this word. Dynamite consists of packing together somewhat unstable explosive substances with stabilizing materials (like forgiveness) that absorb the explosive ones. The bonding of those counterpart materials must maintain enough stability until lighting the fuse at the proper time. The explosion then tears down unwanted obstacles. Dynamite detonates shock waves that move faster than the speed of sound for breaking through powerful barriers.

God's dynamite also produces shock waves to cut through fleshly dullness. God has not lit the fuse of His fuller power in His people but the acceptable time is approaching. The acceptable time will come forth as we unify with God's counterparts specifically designed for us. Many counterparts must work together for Christ's fullness to come forth, and the foundational ones are yearning and turning.

Like the two counterparts in dynamite, the yearner is the more unpredictable powerful part whose underlying faith draws attention to gaps that God desires to fill (even when the yearner demonstrates fear rather than faith outwardly). The turner is the stabilizing part whose faith holds fast until the acceptable time or way for the fuse to be lit. These yearning and turning counterparts are God's perfect dynamite for upcoming kingdom explosions.

Prior to our fireworks Kathy sometimes became very fearful about our boys' riskier ventures, which initially created more upheaval between us when I didn't equally demonstrate emotions and concern. Only after learning to fully embrace one another as counterparts did we work well together in those places. I became the trusting stabilizing factor combined with Kathy's powerful attention drawn to a particular area where God desired to work further (usually though unified prayer first). Thinking that we should be the same wasn't going to work. God desired to unify deep recognition of need and earthly inability with trust in His goodness, ways, and timing for meeting needs. One without the other would not work, and Kathy and I without each other would not work. Yearning and turning needed unified.

Counterparts exist not only between people but also between situations and people. God regularly uses unstable and even undesirable earthly situations that He wishes to unite with a person's stability of faith until the proper time to light the fuse. We see these dynamics portrayed when Israel conquered the Promised Land starting with Jericho.

The instability of an impossible city to be conquered was combined with the stability of Israel's faith for seven days. We often want difficulties resolved immediately, but we see unending scriptural examples of people's faith needing to stand firm for a season before God's proper time for lighting the fuse!

Israel's faith for "seven" days represents fullness, and faith was carried out to fullness. On the seventh day after circling Jericho seven times they blew their trumpets and shouted, and earthly walls tumbled. Earthly instability was combined with the stability of faith until God's time, and the spiritual fuse was lit. God's supernatural power through a unified people went forth and demolished earthly strongholds.

But what was the stability of faith focused on until the fuse was lit? Of course we would say "God." But let's consider it more practically. Leading into this supernatural event, the leader of the people of Israel, Joshua, saw a man standing with a sword in his hand. Joshua asked (Josh. 5:13), "Are you for us or for our enemies?" The man answered (vs. 14), "Neither, but as commander of the army of the Lord I have now come."

God is neither for nor against one group versus another, or one person versus another. He doesn't play favorites (Rom. 2:11). Humanity and the various religions have regularly asked that God would fight on their behalf during conflicts and wars. They have prayed at an earthly level for God's favoritism, but He does not show partiality for anyone of the earth (even though it appears as if He does at times).

We see that God was for nothing earthly by how the commander of His heavenly army responded to Joshua. God continuously awakens people to the heavenly realm one way or the other. Earthly outcomes may appear as if God is for one side or another but He is always for awakening people, which is beyond earthly purposes.

Joshua let go of earthly agendas and joined with faith that governed the earthly realm. Had Joshua's higher priority been to defeat Jericho he would not have surrendered to the "foolish" way of faith that relied on walking in circles, blowing trumpets, and shouting. He let go of the earthly ways of either-or and surrendered to the higher way of neither. Our loyalty is not to be oriented towards anything of the earth but to Christ and His higher ways alone.

God works sovereignly and powerfully through earthly counterparts. We must recognize God's counterparts and surrender to the higher way of neither. God was for neither Kathy nor me at the earthly level during our season of conflict. He wanted to awaken both of us to higher ways. We would never have gotten through our conflict had I viewed us as separate and as if God was for one *or* the other.

God continually and intentionally raised up Pharaoh to be at odds with Moses. Why? Pharaoh was Moses' counterpart to awaken higher faith. God was working to cause both of them to know that He was God beyond what either of them had known previously, which is why God said even about Pharaoh and the Egyptians, "Then they will know that I am God."

Earthly instability and upheaval always have purpose. God uses the earthly instability and conflict of two to awaken faith that produces the heavenly unity of One. Then God lights the fuse at the acceptable time and His fireworks become seen on this earth. His kingdom comes and earthly strongholds fall.

Kathy and I encountered many situations that seemed utterly impossible and beyond us to deal with effectively during our upheaval. But, somehow, God kept awakening us gradually through all those counterpart sandpaper situations (like certain people on her end not giving me a chance or certain people on my end not giving her a chance). Instability comes through difficult earthly circumstances, conflict, and even people's internal struggles. And we see that God releases extraordinary power through a greater unified faith (like all of Israel's unity for seven days to conquer Jericho).

God has many counterpart members within His body of people on this earth, but we have not yet learned to walk in the unity of neither (in the flesh). The instability of two very different counterparts can only be combined through a stable absorbing faith, which establishes unified relationship until the acceptable time to light the fuse. That faith often calls counterparts to love one another sacrificially.

God used Kathy's and my fireworks to establish greater vulnerability about weakness in me and greater trusting patience in Kathy. I see these two areas as central in humanity. *God desires greater vulnerability about weakness in His turners and greater trusting patience in His yearners.* Yearners and turners will not fully unify for kingdom fullness without awakening further in these ways.

Jesus said that God's answers come if two of you agree (Matt. 18:19) ... if two counterparts find the higher unity that exists between them. Like-minded people are already in agreement. Jesus' statement was more about powerful restoration through two (meaning those who are different) becoming united by a faithful love that fills gaps. Two counterparts agreeing in areas where differences or gaps had previously existed *is* answered prayer. That is God's fullness coming to earth through counterparts that love enough to lay down their lives to differences and embrace one another as oneself. That is the stabilizing material that allows explosive parts to be combined for higher purposes.

Love loves neither in the flesh and both in Christ. Love always pursues the heavenly rather than the earthly. Then the earthly becomes added or fulfilled as well, usually after patience and time.

Counterparts become God's perfect dynamite as love faithfully lays down its life for its friends. Christ's fullness is in the counterparts. Pursue them. Christ is called the Alpha and the Omega, the beginning and the end. Counterparts! Christ through His counterparts holds all things together like bookends that cause the books to stand upright. Let us stand upright.

Embrace the counterparts. Within a group of people you will find some who are like-minded and some who think or act counter to your ways. Each counterpart offers balance and higher spiritual sight than any one part alone. Be curious and learn about Christ in one another. Seek the kingdom within one another and all else becomes added. Counterparts often seem contradictory, but when combined they produce dynamite's higher unity and power.

I might be more scriptural and you might be more prophetic or experiential. I might be more cognitive and you more emotional. I might be more relational and you more task-oriented, and me more truth based and you more love based.

I realize that true boxes of one versus the other never actually exist but have varying degrees of emphasis in one direction or another. My main point is that God uses counterparts as a gateway for coming into greater love, unity, and power. Sacrificial love that embraces counterparts is the primary way to receive His greater works and power. Let go of earthly agendas and embrace Christ's counterparts that bring greater fullness. Heaven's gate becomes opened on earth through the fullness of Christ's body of people working together, which we have yet to see.[3]

Humanity could greatly benefit by learning to lay down agendas to the higher way of neither, and by no longer cutting off love from one another because of different beliefs, ways, or lifestyles. I have already addressed the way of neither and have also emphasized the importance of being safe for one another during differences to be able to awaken, but I want to say more about how people sometimes cut off love from one another.

Divisions quickly became evident between Kathy and me anytime different beliefs or positions were immovable anchors that we clung to more powerfully than love. Fear regarding one another's differences demonstrated when we felt threatened and needed earthly security through sameness. The fear exposed places where we could not yet sacrificially love one another well.

Love must be higher than positions or beliefs. I have encountered people immediately expressing a huge *but* right after I emphasized not cutting off love because of differences of beliefs or ways. I feel people's deep fear coming through them at those times. They act as if they will become contaminated when they don't hold at a distance whoever they think is believing wrongly or going astray in a particular area. They either avoid a person or say up front what is wrong about them. That is the same thing that the Pharisees did. There was no love.

People's first reaction of "I disagree with such and such" focuses more on what might not be Christ rather than on what is Christ. That response often shuts down life; it is not Christ's love. Quick responses of disagreement are an anti-stance, and they come from flesh's fear, judgment, and pride. Really, death.

Jesus focused most on who He and the Father were, not on who They were not. Let Christ pull up the weeds at harvest time. Do not hold others at a distance when you see one area that you deem deceived or misled. I understand that we are not to agree with an area that may not be God's direction, but that does not necessitate holding people at a distance. Jesus neither distanced Himself from prostitutes and tax gatherers nor from His disciples who showed differences of ways and beliefs at points. Jesus respectfully engaged with them, which continued everyone's growth.

Focusing on agreement or disagreement or on this *versus* that is the flesh nature's way that separates for self-glory. Separation cuts off love just like the religious rulers did with Jesus, which caused them to allow no relationship with Him.

We must attend to any stirring of the Spirit about what might be Christ rather than to what we distrust. That is faith-governed rather than fear-governed. Be patient through what appears to be weeds rather than immediately yanking them out (which would uproot any chance of discovering the precious wheat in one another).

Unfortunately, cutting off love runs deep, which frightens people's souls into hiding again. And what we do to others, we do to ourselves. Without knowing or intending it, we have cut off our foot and become lame, our hand so we could not help, our eyes and ears so we could not see or hear, and our heart so we could not feel. My message is to gather rather than to separate. God desires to awaken us to His greater love that embraces the precious among what sometimes has been called the profane. Seeking life in one another builds the kingdom.

Two Witnesses

Kathy and I came to see more fully with Christ's eyes the more we embraced that each other was a purposeful, godly-designed counterpart for our awakening. Any point of opposition or difference from Kathy was purposefully meant to further awaken me. To further establish me in the true. The reverse was also the case. All of my differences or unique aspects were meant to further establish Kathy in the true. While Kathy and I each demonstrated both of the yearner and turner aspects within ourselves at times, throughout our upheaval Kathy consistently demonstrated more of the yearner characteristics and me more of the turner characteristics. The more we embraced these purposefully designed counterparts, the more Christ's greater love and testimony were established in and through us.

God planted the crucial message of embracing counterparts in the mystery of marriage, which is the foundation of true testimony. Jesus said that true testimony could only be established by a minimum of two witnesses (Matt. 18:16). In a dualistic world, the truth of a matter becomes established through two unified witnesses, and truth about matters which require higher discernment are established through two or more unified counterparts. Opposite poles coming into unity regarding a matter yield a fuller truth. A greater testimony of Christ.

Jesus' words in the New Testament, "If two of you agree ..." not only addressed true testimony but also re-emphasized the way of two becoming one (marriage). The physical symbolizes the spiritual. The seen symbolizes the unseen. So I will temporarily parallel and keep connected the seen and unseen to help you carry that foundational understanding of "two becoming one" into the spiritual realm.

The way to give birth physically is through male and female uniting. That is also true for spiritual birth on this earth. The scriptures emphasize that at the spiritual level (Gal. 3:28), "There is neither Jew nor Greek, slave nor free, male nor female, for you are all one in Christ Jesus." While this is true, the spiritual essence of man and woman uniting still applies, which is about yearning and turning uniting to give spiritual birth.

These two core counterparts needed to come together during my journey, whether within myself as a person, or with Kathy and others who offered more of the counterpart I had yet to fully embrace. Upon further embracing these counterparts through others, I began awakening to more of those counterpart aspects that I already carried within myself. That is how spiritual birth came about, and it was often difficult as the scriptures had said that it would be.

At the physical level the woman gives birth by man planting the seed. At the spiritual level the yearner gives birth but only through the turner planting the seed. Why does the turner alone plant the seed (again, this is not just about males)? Because of Eve's or "woman's" distrustful way of taking during her time of desire or yearning (see Gen. 3:6; which is not just about females but about the yearner needing balanced or completed by the turner). I saw that Kathy's deeper times of yearning during our upheaval could not be fulfilled until she at some point turned to Christ more fully about those gaps, which often happened through us uniting and turning. We only made headway and sensed completion about various difficulties when God granted grace for Kathy and me to both come to a place of yearning together and then letting go of outcomes so as to join with (or turn to) what we sensed God desired.

The yearner cannot give spiritual birth without the turner just like woman cannot give birth without man. The yearner cannot give birth when her felt gaps cause her to rise up in the flesh nature's fear to demand or take what she feels is needed. That demand, at least initially, most often gets focused on the turner rather than on Christ.

The turner, likewise, is not to do what Adam did (see Gen. 3:6). The turner must not passively follow the yearner's distrustful way that takes or demands what is needed. The turner is also not to "rule over" the yearner by rising up and forcing her to do what he now decides. That would be the fleshly way of this versus that.

The turner is also not to try to go forward without true support, which the yearner feels the need for more than him. The turner's gift is to rule or govern the *way* forward by conquering worldly forces in the same way Jesus conquered – by laying down

His earthly rights and trusting the Father's love to fill earthly gaps. Jesus did nothing from His own (fleshly) initiative. Jesus conquered all forces through laying down flesh's rights so as to join with the Father's higher will during all things.

Jesus Christ walked the way before His bride. That is how He became the Head that is above all rule and authority. The turner is to walk the way before the yearner (not apart from). The turner makes a way for the yearner. That is how a husband is to be head of his wife. Turning is how he gains the true support that begins to fill the places of need that the yearner feels so deeply.

Even during Kathy's focus on me to bring certain tangible outcomes, my role was to lay down my earthly rights. I paid attention to Kathy's alertness to particular areas of need, and tried to validate that those places *were* areas that God wanted to work something further. At the same time I paid attention to not just following Kathy's or my earthly desires but what Christ seemed to be working in those places. Through that process that definitely paralleled intense labor at times, Kathy and I kept coming to surrendered places of unified prayer about what God seemed to be working.

These yearning and turning counterparts that Kathy and I continually experienced exist within the many counterparts across this earth. The yearning part experiences and sees gaps but must rely on her turning counterpart that plants the seed by laying down earthly rights. The turner is to lead in the way of laying down, but the yearner must lay down with him (although he is not to force her to lay down). Love always allows freedom.

True love lays down to give birth. Love lays down its life for its friends (counterparts).

Blessings Demanded and Impotence

Kathy and I came to see very clearly through our struggles that God did not bring deliverance through demanding blessings. Deliverance kept coming about through our gradual acknowledgment of human weakness and limits as well as surrendering to what we sensed Christ was working.

In the Old Testament Jacob demanded a blessing from the angel of the Lord and received it (Gen. 32:24-29). The angel could not prevail to speak to Jacob's spirit because his flesh nature was raised up in fear. Jacob was afraid because he thought his brother Esau was coming to kill him, and fear caused Jacob to demand a blessing from God. So the angel touched Jacob's hip and gave him a limp, and then he blessed Jacob. The angel struck Jacob with more human weakness and then changed his name from Jacob (one who supplants or takes) to Israel (a prince who trusts and prevails with God).

Jacob came to truly prevail with God's spiritual blessings *after* the angel struck him with human weakness. Kathy and I received spiritual blessings after being struck with human weakness.

Taking or demanding blessings from God in our time and ways is not Christ's higher way. That is the yearner's fleshly way when she feels gaps (whether in men or women). The turner's fleshly way of going forward tends to be in human strength without God's true support.

The angel made a way forward for Jacob by touching him with human weakness so that he would rely on God's strength and support. That is how Jacob's name or character changed to Israel, which brought yearning and turning together within him.

While it is good to question and wrestle with what is true of God, wrestling for the purpose of taking or demanding is not. We see that God had a problem with Jacob's supplanting and demanding ways when the scriptures say (Hos. 12:2-6), "The LORD also has a dispute with Judah, and will punish [judge] Jacob according to his ways; He will repay him according to his deeds. In the womb he *took* his brother by the heel, and in his maturity he *contended* with God. Yes, he wrestled with the angel ... *Therefore, return* to your God, observe kindness and justice, and *wait* for your God continually."

God meeting our needs during our struggles often requires us to come to a place of trust in Him, which usually means waiting through our fear until we again experience His grace and help. Early in our growth God gives blessings even when we try to take them. That was Jacob the supplanter. But young children will never truly know or trust their parents' love when they receive gifts in the midst their distrustful demands. They can only know love when they have let go of any demands, and love still gives. Then they come to rest, to trust. They come to know love when they ask, allow freedom, and wait on love's true answer.

The beginning and end of the prodigal son story demonstrates these two kinds of desire (Lk. 15:11-32): earthly desire that demands, and godly desire that allows love's free response. Love had always been available to the prodigal son but he could not receive it when he demanded to be loved in his lesser way. Yielding to and trusting love's free response finally allowed the true to be known and received.

As our spiritual walk matures God will not bless us in the midst of our forcing or demanding certain outcomes. If anything, God seems silent at those times.

I believe that we as a people have a long way to go in asking for blessings from a humble place that accepts and waits on God's answers. We have been an impatient people. I believe that God is currently stretching us in the direction of Him not blessing us until we learn not to force or demand blessings. The scriptures say

(Jn. 6:15), "Jesus therefore perceiving that they were intending to come and take Him by force, to make Him king, *withdrew* again to the mountain by Himself alone."

Christ will not allow us to use the world's ways of power to get what we want. Even pursuing heavenly outcomes will not result through power or force. Christ seems to withdraw at those times.

I was in the midst of talking about these revelations with a friend, and he shared about a situation where he felt lots of pressure from a yearning counterpart regarding a decision he needed to make. He told me how one person even described him as passive, and he said to me with a bit of reaction, "But I'm not getting anything from God!" Even as I listened to him I realized that I also had nothing further from God to offer him (and I often get some hint of direction).

As I paused I could feel the same experience coming through him that I experienced throughout Kathy's and my conflict. Kathy also saw me as passive and wanted more than I could give at times. Then I remembered the series of experiences with others who tried to help Kathy and me during our upheaval. Like me, they all seemed confused and blank. They seemed passive during the pressure, just like me.

I believe that God often withdraws temporarily when we demand answers or blessings. King Herod questioned Jesus at length and wanted Him to show him a sign but Jesus remained silent (Lk. 23:8-9). He appeared passive. Demands allow no freedom and choke out the life of the Spirit. The Spirit will not take orders from a lesser realm.

The hour of darkness appeared to prevail the whole time leading into Jesus' cross, and Goodness seemed silent. Jesus and His disciples appeared very passive while the world forced all that it wanted. Violent men took heaven by force and did what they wanted with it (Matt. 11:12). Zeal with wisdom is good, and we will feel a violence against our souls at times when we stand for Christ during the world's chaos. I think that that is the meaning of verse 12 but that verse has sometimes been misused as justification for demanding heavenly outcomes.

Force is the world's way, not heaven's. Jesus was not that way. He laid down His life. That humility and turning to the Father's strength is what planted the seed and made the way. Laying down our fleshly rights during difficulties makes a way by allowing freedom for higher authority to give its true response that firmly plants seeds. During trials we must first see what Christ is doing. Only then can we step in unity with His authority (which might result in being very bold when we've come to see with Christ's clear eyes).

The word "impotent" came to my mind when my friend described how he received no direction from God during the pressure. Impotence exists when we do not lay down. A couple's impotence remains when one or both individuals do not lay down (because they are really one). Spiritual impotence in God's people remains to the extent that we do not follow Christ's way that lays down fleshly agendas to allow absolute freedom for higher authority's response.

The yearner is less inclined than the turner to lay down earthly rights (not necessarily meaning woman versus man). Does this mean that everyone should be turner oriented? No. The turner needs the yearner because she more easily discerns felt gaps and need where God desires to awaken more of His kingdom.

God purposefully works through felt gaps and needs to bring souls into agreement with Christ. Our Christ nature already has and reigns over all things, but our souls must continually come into agreement with Christ and His will. We are already in agreement in some places but there are many areas we are not, and Christ starts with the yearner to expose places He wants to go higher.

When the yearner discerns gaps, however, she sometimes believes that she "does not have." Jesus said (Matt. 25:29), "For everyone who has will be given more, and he will have an abundance. Whoever does not have, even what he has will be taken from him."

We are not to fearfully strive from a place that does not have. That is the yearner's fleshly way. That is why the yearner must unite with the turner who is more inclined towards trusting that they already have what is needed in the Christ nature when they look to Him to awaken their souls in those places. Looking to Christ might mean waiting or stepping, depending upon what He is presently doing in a given situation.

During my experiences with Kathy I learned that the yearner must first know that the turner knows the reality of her experiences before she will lay down her earthly rights, or before she will move forward with the turner's part regarding how Christ may want to fulfill needs. Kathy needed to know that I knew the bigness of the gaps or lack she felt. The fear, abandonment, hopelessness, or emptiness, whatever it happened to be. Kathy needed to know that I was in touch with those places of felt lack. Those places of "death" that had no earthly answer.

Kathy usually experienced additional security when she knew that I knew, especially when she sensed that I still trusted Christ in that place. That security from me as the turner helped her join with me to trust that Christ was available and wanted to meet those needs. We were not on our own. My turner part was to "rule" by trusting that we already had Christ's higher goodness available in those places and that we mainly needed to lay down our earthly rights to join with how He wanted to bring fulfillment.

At one point the disciples told Jesus to send the thousands of hungry people away. Jesus told them (Mk. 6:37), "You give them something to eat." They said it was impossible. Can you hear how

Jesus wanted them to be fully in touch with earthly limits? After Jesus got them in touch with earthly impossibility He responded (Mk. 6:38), "How many loaves *do* you have?" Jesus didn't ask for more than they had even though it probably felt like that.

Jesus first got His disciples in touch with earthly lack and impossibility, and then He began heaven's work with the few loaves and small fish they already had. He broke the bread, gave thanks, and shared the fish and broken bread, which supernaturally multiplied for feeding the many.

Recognize earthly impossibility when it exists in your life. Then start with what you do have rather than with what you don't have, even if that is with small beginnings and brokenness. Allow yourself to be where you are and then trust Higher Help that is always available. That is what Jesus did. Don't believe the lie that you have to be more than who or where you are.

Kathy and I learned that the turner is to start with the yearner's expression of broken or barren places as God's purposeful source of thirst to awaken the Christ nature in those places. Don't try to fix your situations. Acknowledge earthly impossibility first, and then turn to Christ within who always has. Turner and yearner must unite and give thanks for what they do have, even if that is initially about the felt earthly places of lack. Life will become evident there and even multiply.

Gaps are never truly gaps. We always have what we need through Christ who reigns over all. All things have been created through Him and for Him (Col. 1:16).

Perceived gaps are merely places to participate with God's ongoing works to awaken more of what we already have within. That is how Christ's kingdom "comes" more fully on this earth. In actuality, the kingdom is already here but becomes awakened and visible on earth to the extent that we participate with Christ.

In any given situation, some people are more aware of gaps (yearners) and others are aware that we already have (turners). One should not judge or negate the other. Gap discerners are God's work through one aspect of the body, and gap fillers are God's work through another part of His body. We cannot walk independently.

In the flesh nature, the yearner and turner will remain separate and disagree with one another rather than uniting. The yearner's flesh fearfully expresses (though not through words), "We need to pray that Thy kingdom come because it feels like the kingdom is *not* at hand!" The turner knows that fearful prayers are not from faith. But the turner's flesh nature is often ignited by the yearner's flesh nature and may convey, "The kingdom is here; we are already full, so we do not need more of the kingdom" (though those words usually would not be consciously thought or said).

During difficult situations where Christ desires to expose gaps and advance the kingdom, I pray that we would not react with disagreement in the flesh nature. The verse "Be still and know that I am God" applies to these foundational counterparts. Turner: be still and become aware of unredeemed areas needing agreement with Christ, which your yearner counterpart is more aware of than you. Yearner: be still and become aware that you can trust during those places because you already have, which your turner counterpart is more awakened to than you.

Counterparts: Do not turn against each other. Do not turn against your help. Be still and unite about what each of you is aware of, and know that God is God. Lay down your lives for one another, and cleave!

The time has come where we cannot plant seeds unless we lay down our lives for our friends (counterparts). Only love that lays down its life for its friends plants seeds. Throughout all the counterparts across this world, a yearner part experiences gaps but will sometimes show fleshly edges because of believing she does not have. A turner part then sometimes tries to go forward in fleshly strength rather than Christ's. But yearner and turner must unite by acknowledging earthly impossibility and then trusting that they already have, which lays down the flesh nature to plant seeds. They must both lay down to God's rights and timing for what He desires to plant in those places.

The truth is that Kathy and I are dynamite when we lay down our lives during felt gaps and trust that God desires to awaken more of His kingdom there! But we are impotent when we are unaware of the areas God wants to redeem or when we try to take because of distrust in those places.

Advancing the kingdom requires Christ's discernment of gaps (yearner) and then trusting Christ's way that fills gaps (turner). Pay attention to Christ's exposure of gaps as well as His ways and timing for filling gaps. Both are necessary.

CHAPTER 7

Perfect Food and Clothes

<u>Allow Weakness</u>

Kathy and I gradually came to eat higher food during the struggles. The center of this "food" was joining with Christ's will and purposes for the struggles. The more we participated with how Christ wanted to awaken each of us during the struggles, the more we became lifted spiritually. We could not eat this new spiritual food without allowing human weakness along the way.

Within Christianity and humanity as a whole, people have generally admired steadfastness during difficult situations. But people have usually despised being in need. We as a people have despised weakness (really, it is flesh despising its own weakness).

People generally hide weakness. Yet, weakness is crucial. Weakness is my source for being drawn more fully to God. Weakness causes me to thirst more deeply for fulfillment in Christ. I desire more of Christ's higher invisible realm in place of the lesser realm when I encounter my human inability. Weakness brings out the yearner in me.

The rural Pennsylvania culture where I grew up has historically not allowed weakness as part of the growth process. Especially expression of weakness. My way throughout life was to be strong, believe I was strong, and to appear strong even when I wasn't! That also meant being unemotional.

My superficial shell of strength caused me not to be attuned to weakness within me or within others, except in various counseling roles that gave me permission to embrace earthly weakness. Then, because of my panic attacks, I had had no choice but to acknowledge human weakness personally. This caused significant growth in my personal life becoming more like I was in the counseling profession (in terms of embracing human weakness as God's path for restoration into Christ). Kathy's and my marital struggles then increased this growth tremendously. I finally embraced weakness as a pathway to true strength.

I started noticing how my prayers for our children, family, and friends would not have been nearly as powerful had I not been in touch with weakness, which Kathy did for me. Kathy not only caused me to acknowledge my weakness, but she also consistently honed in on places of lack or concern in our children and others. Although I trusted God with His love and faithfulness regarding the people in our lives, without Kathy I would not have been alerted to some of the issues needing prayer and would not have addressed the root of those issues as fully. Kathy's yearning regularly alerted me to the deep. I needed her razor sharp discernment that came from her yearning tendencies.

Likewise, Kathy would have been far less effective without me. Her deep felt sense of need on behalf of people and situations sometimes caused greater upheaval in her. Kathy needed my gift of knowing in the midst of trials that God was working higher good. Her yearning needed united with my turning to and trusting God's works and timeframe for those works. While we were each inclined in the ways we were designed, God constantly worked to develop me more in the area of allowing weakness so that I could initially be joined with Kathy more fully in crying out to God from a deep place of knowing need.

Do not despise the yearning of Eve in the Garden of Eden. God created us that way; yearning is how He draws our souls to become further completed in Him. Without earthly weakness and yearning, we would settle for less than Christ's fullness. The reason that Eve yearned for something more was because she didn't know fulfillment within her. Adam and Eve hadn't inwardly known the love and fulfillment of God from the very beginning. Had they known fulfillment they would never have been tempted by the serpent to try to be fulfilled through false means (Gen. 3:1-8).

Fulfillment had been available and "given" to Adam and Eve, but it had not become part of them. They still hadn't "possessed" or received that love within their souls *through their own choices* even though they carried that fulfillment within them.

God wasn't surprised by Eve's yearning for the forbidden apple because He already knew that Adam and Eve's souls had not yet participated in "possessing" His love and fulfillment through free will. So Adam and Eve's "nakedness" or emptiness within caused them to yearn to attain fulfillment. That's why Adam joined Eve in eating the apple.

After Adam and Eve chose a lesser way to try to fill that emptiness, they saw their nakedness (which had already existed!). They recognized the emptiness within them, and they hid from God in the Garden. They now demonstrated outwardly that they hadn't truly known God and His love.

Coming face-to-face with human weakness convicts us that something higher is needed. Weakness helps our souls let go of the lesser life to embrace Christ and His higher life within. Earthly weakness causes yearning. As yearning is "coupled" with turning in steadfast trust towards Christ, kingdom fulfillment comes. Spiritual conception occurs.

Please hear my caution as you continue reading. You could have a tendency, in spite of my cautions, to hear what I say as only about *man versus woman* because of destructive socialization or how the scriptures have been previously used in marriages or other relationships to justify selfishness or level difference. I do not view one counterpart as better or worse than the other, or man or woman as better or worse than the other.

Men and women are equally valued in the sight of God. Weakness and steadfast trust are both necessary, and these counterparts within us as people are equally valued by God. They are both necessary to draw us to and establish us further in the kingdom.

God works times of weakness on our behalf just like He did for the Apostle Paul (2 Cor. 12:7-10). Do not despise it. I emphasize this because I have despised weakness in myself most of my life. I also regularly encounter people looking down on others or themselves when they struggle with some ongoing weakness or "sin."

Embrace times of weakness so that you might yearn for and turn to Christ as your strength beyond your earthly abilities in that place. As your food. That's what Paul did. That was both counterparts working together in him to bring forth greater kingdom fulfillment. Once Kathy's and my eyes had been opened to this way that conceives more of heaven on earth, we regularly experienced fulfillment rather than disaster connected to our difficulties.

Equal and Opposite

Kathy and I kept learning more about the necessary balance of yearning and turning through every difficulty we experienced. It seemed as if God perfectly orchestrated my personal life to regularly teach and build upon the centrality of these yearning and turning counterparts for kingdom fulfillment.

In my writing I had initially described these two core counterparts as masculinity and femininity but through feedback had recognized how much destructive socialization was attached to these terms. I saw that I could clarify all I wanted but that people would continually disregard key points about these counterparts because of previous socialization. That's why I believe that God opened up the terminology of yearning and turning, which all people can identify with at a practical level.

I will emphasize the center of the learning again: both counterparts are in all people in varying degrees, even though yearning and awareness of need tends to be more evident in women, and turning need towards fulfillment by steadfast trust during trials tends to be seen more in men. One is not better than the other. Both counterparts are necessary and in all of us, and they are the primary way to fulfillment in Christ. We cannot have truly loving relationships that establish fulfillment in Christ without the yearning-turning counterparts uniting. This is the law that makes these yearning-turning counterparts visible: for every action there is an equal and opposite reaction.

High reactivity shows yearning. Reactivity in any given situation demonstrates how deeply the yearner (not necessarily women) feels experiences. The yearner is a fire alarm. She is less emotionally insulated than the turner. That is what is meant by the scriptures about "women" being the weaker vessel (which does not mean a lesser one; see 1 Ptr. 3:7).

You will see that I often refer to the yearner as "she" and the turner as "he." I do so for ease of communication and because that tends to be the more prevalent pattern of how these counterparts are expressed through people. But remember, both counterparts are in all of us.

Deeply felt experiences drive the yearner's expression. She feels intense experiences at times when the turner may not feel anything. That is her gift that inclines towards compassion, nurturance, relationship, and desire for unity. She is also the source of alerting the turner to existing gaps in unity and to unmet needs where Christ desires to further His work. Kathy regularly did that for me.

The yearner's gift within humanity comes with the disadvantage of insecurity. She is more easily tossed by life's waves. That upheaval causes her earthly nature to tend towards controlling outcomes or taking what seems needed for regaining security. That is the spirit of Jezebel referred to in the Book of Revelation (2:20). The more the yearner grows into the Christ nature rather than the earthly nature, the more she gains the security that tends to be associated with the turner.

The turner is less reactive and emotional than the yearner. He (not just men) is typically more emotionally insulated, which increases security for holding steady through storms. That is the advantage. Stand fast, hold firm, be courageous as the scriptures say. The turner's additional emotional insulation also tends to allow more freedom for others' learning and growth (although the yearner may see him as simply not being in touch with what happens in life at times!).

The turner is Christ's way to fill gaps by trusting during storms. Jesus trusted the Father during trials (Mk. 1:13; Heb. 4:15). The turner is to wait on or step with God's rights even when the way is difficult. Through security and trust he is to lay down his life like Jesus did. This was more of my role during Kathy's and my fireworks (although I was very afraid at points).

The turner is disadvantaged by being less aware of need than his counterpart. His earthly nature's tendency is to handle life without true support when gaps exist. The turner's earthly nature tends to perceive or communicate from an unemotional perspective, which sometimes invalidates the yearner's expression. Even when trying to hear and embrace the yearner's emotions, the turner's communication often leaves her still feeling a lack of unity.

The more the turner grows into the Christ nature, the more he grows into the yearner's godly inclinations: he becomes more relational and more sensitive to emotions, gaps, and need. He also becomes more aware and accepting of weakness (which also helps the yearner further accept her weakness).

The yearning counterpart is activated during awareness of gaps, weakness, loss, or need, which occurs when God works earthly lack so as to "leave" what one has previously known as security or fulfillment. We all need these ongoing works that cause us to leave the lesser to cleave to more of the greater. For furthering Kathy and me, God worked in Kathy to return to the Catholic Church, which caused less earthly security in us because of no longer attending the same place spiritually.

The only way for us to become fulfilled after God worked earthly lack was for us to turn to Christ to be that Unseen Security in those areas. That was the turning counterpart becoming activated, usually initiated through me for governing, focusing on, and bringing about need fulfillment by holding fast during upheaval and loss of lesser things. The turning counterpart paid attention to cleave and endure through situations while holding onto Christ and what He was working. This turner part was usually easier for me than for Kathy because I was designed this way.

Jesus fully demonstrated yearning and turning during weakness. Jesus left heaven's security and came to be weakness on our behalf (2 Cor. 13:4). Then, *from that place of weakness*, He fulfilled all righteousness by turning to the Father (Jn. 6:38; Lk. 22:42). That yearning and turning gave Christ the right to reign over all things. To fulfill all things. Christ's leaving-and-cleaving sacrificial love gave Him that right.

Christ is in us to continually work yearning and turning to expand His kingdom's reign through us. Christ first works weakness and yearning within us, and then He fulfills righteousness in and through us as we turn our eyes to Him as our food and comfort during trials. I know that receiving Christ as our food and comfort during trials is the difficult part to make tangible, but I believe that this will become more understandable as you continue to glean whatever crumbs of Christ you can from Kathy's and my journey.

The scriptural principles of leaving and cleaving and yearning and turning constantly worked together for Kathy and me. Christ worked further in our lives through sometimes causing some difficulties with lesser things to make us weak, which caused us to leave the lesser and to yearn for the greater. As we allowed human weakness and yearning (rather than despising it), and then turned to Christ during that weakness, He increasingly became our reward and fulfillment. We further awakened to Christ's peace, rest, and love in place of the material world.

The Garden Experience

At some point, everyone who is serious about living the life of Christ will go through what I call "the Garden Experience." I've had numerous Garden Experiences but my two main ones were panic attacks and my marital fireworks. Anxiety that increased into full-fledged panic attacks and then certain unseen gaps with Kathy that instantly escalated into an unlivable situation were each an "hour of darkness" to me, which reminded me of Jesus' statement in the Garden of Gethsemane about the hour of darkness that was coming upon Him (Lk. 22:53).

Each of my Garden Experiences was an hour of darkness where I initially felt blind, afraid, and out of control. For much of the panic attacks, I had neither learned that Christ was with me nor how to participate with His higher will during that season of darkness. By the time of my marital struggles I had learned that Christ was with me as well as how to keep readjusting to what I sensed His will was during any perceived darkness. The fuller learning for me centered on participating with Christ's yearning and turning counterparts. There were times I was to participate with Him in yearning, groaning, and crying out for whatever He was working in His kingdom and in Kathy's and my relationship (while often feeling totally blind), and other times I was to turn to and stand in trust of Christ carrying out particular works when I saw what those works were.

We can learn most about the yearning-turning counterparts within humanity from Jesus' Garden experience. Jesus overcame during the Garden of Gethsemane, as contrasted with Adam and Eve not overcoming in the Garden of Eden. Jesus yearned and turned.

Jesus prayed during intense agony and weakness in the Garden. He yearned and groaned for fulfillment during that place of agony (just like the Spirit within us continues to groan and intercede for us when we are in agony).

After yearning intensely in the Garden, Jesus gradually turned to and fixed His eyes on what the Father wanted rather than on what the earthly nature wanted (Lk. 22:42). Jesus *made peace through the blood of the cross*" (Col. 1:20). Jesus was the ultimate Peacemaker where there was no peace. He kept God's will that kept peace between Him and the Father above all, which established His Garden on this earth. Participating with Higher will in place of earthly will always establishes more of heaven's Garden of peace on this earth.

Adam, in the initial Garden, had been charged with "working and keeping" the Garden (Gen. 2:15). He had worked the Garden but had not kept the Garden. Adam had not turned to and kept God's will. Keeping God's will was the way to keep the Garden as well as inner peace. Paul's words in the letter to the Philippians about God working within us "to will and to act [work]" were a direct reference to God's charge for Adam to work and keep God's will in the Garden of Eden (Phil. 2:13).

We will initially experience a lack of peace every time God sovereignly causes us to leave lesser things through experiencing weakness and yearning. That is where Christ wants us to be peace-*makers*. Christ wants us to turn to Him alone as our reward and fulfillment in those places. Yearn and turn. As we turn to Christ as our strength and peace, we have kept God's will and have further established His Peaceful Garden on this earth.

Jesus initially kept the Garden and desires to continue that work through us. Jesus had brought the two counterparts together. He had yearned and turned, and two were made as One. Let man not separate what God has joined together. Let us keep His Garden of peace during all things.

Unity in the Passover

Jesus made and became the Way to unite the two core counterparts within humanity. You can initially see this Way that unites these two counterparts within the people of Israel during their bondage in Egypt. This Way is seen through the Passover, which was Israel's deliverance.

The people of Israel had yearned and groaned as slaves in Egypt, and with God working through Moses, they turned and fixed their eyes on the Passover Lamb, which pointed to Christ. Israel yearned and then turned to eat of their Passover Lamb (Christ) while death and its terror passed by.

I really relate to standing fast and holding firm while terror passes by. That was the essence of my experience with panic attacks. While I had awakened tremendously to Christ being with me and for me in all things because of the season of panic attacks, I still encountered initial spikes of terror during intense incidents early in the marital struggles. Because of certain people's treatment of me at points, I again fell for lies that I needed to be further or different than who I was to be acceptable. The difference was, at this point, I was no longer moved by those lies or fear to try in futility to fill those felt gaps. Instead, as soon as I received space to be with Christ alone or to gain support from Him through key people after those intense experiences, I quickly became grounded to either wait on or step with peace. I paid attention to not reacting in earthly ways and, instead, waiting on Christ's peace within me to lead.

Still, I fully relate to the people of Israel holding fast while terror passed by. Imagine the terror that they experienced when they remained in their houses and did nothing as death passed by. That is what it feels like to my earthly nature every time I am in an intense Passover experience. I am brought to intense weakness and agony during earthly stuck places. Both my earthly nature and my soul yearn intensely because of being deeply unfulfilled at the earthly level. I feel need, gaps, and weakness during these Passover experiences.

In spite of what things looked or felt like, I was to keep the Passover by eating of Christ rather than the world's food. What did eating of Christ mean? It meant participating with Christ (His will and works) as my way rather than fearfully following lesser earthly ways. Keeping the Passover in places that lacked peace kept Christ's will, which was peacemaking. Keeping Christ's will in places that lacked peace, then became my food just as Jesus said that His food was to do the Father's will (Jn. 4:34). (I realize that Catholics also view eating of Christ as directly eating of Him through the sacrament of communion.)

The scriptures emphasize that the Spirit within me is patient and longsuffering and longs to take what is of Christ and give it to my soul (which is really an awakening). I must patiently wait on the Spirit during difficulties because the word within me is tested. My soul must be found trustworthy to keep God's will and Garden so as to receive more of Christ's fulfillment in those places. I will most be found trustworthy when I have kept God's will and peace during difficulties where the flesh nature is most likely to be selfish.

The flesh nature impatiently yearns to find fulfillment in whatever ways it can. Will I react in my flesh to save myself while death passes by? Will I impatiently react to fill my needs in false ways? Or will I trust that death cannot touch the true but only the false, just like death could not touch the people of Israel as they trusted in the Passover Lamb (Ex. 12:12-13, 21-23)?

I have known these places of agony as death passes by. Have you experienced them at times? If you have, what do you do there?

These Passover experiences require patience and courage to be still while death passes by. You are to "remain in your house" as you trust alone in the Passover sacrifice, which is Christ. You are to remain in your true house, the Christ nature, rather than enter your house of flesh nature that does not trust. Israel, even though they were frightened, remained in their houses. They did not participate with distrust. You too, must not act from a place of fear and distrust. Your anguish, while death passes by, then becomes united with trust in Christ to be your true food. When you stand firm to wait on or follow peace alone, Peace has become your food. That is yearning united with true turning, which is the Passover.

Passovers, just like for Jesus in the Garden, are terrifying at times. Yet, Jesus was faithful, and He will be faithful to you to become your peaceful words of life as you wait through death stripping away more of the flesh nature. I learned to hold fast through the times that death passed by, and to wait on my sense of Christ's peace before acting or communicating. If I did not sense enough of Christ's peace, presence, and love to establish any goodness in difficulties with Kathy, I said so and conveyed that I could not go forward until I became aware of Christ and His peace in that place.

Each time I regained a sense of peace, I knew I had eaten of Christ in those places rather than selfishly needing the world to be what I would have wanted it to be. During each initial spike of terror, I learned to return to and trust Christ within as my Passover in those places of death to the flesh. I ate of Christ's sacrificial way rather than demanding that earthly life (or Kathy) become what I wanted. I ate of Christ's sacrificial way that became my true food and drink during life's trials. I participated with Christ's sacrificial love by loving Him above the world, and He became my unseen food at those times that kept building up my soul in my Christ nature. That awareness of Christ in those places became new food within me that also helped Kathy receive more of Christ at those times of death.

Jesus said (Jn. 6:53) "I tell you the truth, unless you eat of the flesh of the Son of Man and drink His blood, you have no life in you." Partaking of Christ as my Passover meal during trials brings yearning and turning together, just like what happened for the people of Israel.

People sometimes forget that Christ is with them and desires to be their food during those excruciating Passover experiences. Aren't your worst moments of fear, hopelessness, or abandonment where you forget Christ? Where death and its terror passes by? That is where we tend to forget Jesus and is why He said to eat the Passover "in remembrance" of Him. When you eat of Christ as your food in those places rather than of the world's ways, you become spiritually girded up in more of Christ and His strength. Doing Christ's will becomes your food just as Jesus said that doing the Father's will was His food. Then you have true life coming forth in you in those places of death to the lesser realm. That is resurrection life.

The Passover is your point of breakthrough. It is your deliverance and healing.

The people of Israel were transformed from fear to awe of God through the Passover, which initiated many of His miracles and wonders. One way or the other a new journey begins when yearning and turning join in the impossible places.

This new journey means experiencing Christ in new ways, not necessarily encountering immediate change in your circumstances. Christ wants most to build you up in Him inwardly, which may or may not mean changed circumstances at the time.

Will you break through into new places by waiting and trusting in Christ to be your perfect food, your food that further nourishes, awakens, and completes your soul? Or will you be impatient and "eat false food." You eat false food when you impatiently participate with the spirit of Jezebel's unfaithful ways to try to regain earthly control (Rev. 2:20). That is when the trials increase. Suffering increases when you demand your ways rather than being still and eating of the Passover Lamb as death's works pass by.

For me, earthly life did not change immediately when I participated with (or ate of) Christ during my Passover experiences. But I did quickly begin a new spiritual journey. I began to know Christ in far deeper ways every time I allowed death to pass by while I remained in my "house." Greater revelations continually emerged when I partook of Christ Himself rather than allowing my flesh to try to fill holes in false ways.

Yearning and turning came together in me and also between Kathy and me later as a couple. But the yearning and turning counterparts needed to leave earthly origins and cleave to each other and to Christ during the Passover experiences. These were our Garden experiences to keep God's will and establish peace where there was no peace.

Death is Our Healing

Why is the unity of yearning and turning so difficult? Why did Kathy's and my struggles feel like deep loss or even death at times?

We regularly needed to let go of earthly ways to receive heaven's higher ways. That is death. To eat more of our perfect food, which was Christ, we continually needed to lose more earthly ways that had been our sustenance. During these Passover experiences we did not even know what we were losing or grieving, but we knew that much of the process to come out on the other side certainly felt like enduring death or hell.

The Passover is death to the lesser nature and the awakening of the Christ nature. During Passover experiences our souls are further delivered from death into life. Death is our healing.

Many followers of Christ are aware that the Hebrew word *rapha* (OT 7495) means to heal, mend, or cure. Most people do not know, however, that *rapha* (OT 7496) also means "dead, deceased, in the sense of to slacken, fail, faint, or cease," which also comes from the first word *rapha* (OT 7495; to heal).

Are you starting to grasp the profound significance of this? The same Hebrew word and pronunciation are used for both death and healing. They are two sides of a coin; losing life to gain life. Counterparts. The only way that the Jews would have known whether someone meant death or healing when saying *rapha* was by the context of its use. This dual meaning of *rapha* is evident in many of the scriptures' paradoxical statements about being humbled to be exalted, becoming poor to become rich, losing life to gain life, becoming empty to become full, and journeying from nakedness to being clothed. All of these statements indicate that our healing is intertwined with death. Healing results from death.

That's why many people "jump ship" during Passover experiences, whether individually or in difficult relationships. People encounter death to earthly things during those experiences, and they forget that Christ is with them and for them working to bring higher restoration in those places. Death's lie is that we are separate from Christ and from each other, and that we are alone and abandoned during these experiences. But it's all a lie.

Even the words in the definition of *rapha* (as death), such as to faint or cease, automatically bring other scriptures to mind: cease striving and know that I am God (Psm. 46:10), and trading a spirit of fainting for a garment of praise (Isa. 61:3). We trade death of the flesh for abundant life especially during our trials. That's what Kathy and I kept learning to do during our hellish experiences. We continually traded hell for heaven.

I say "hell for heaven" because death to our flesh nature is not easy. It is sometimes hell on earth. Just like heaven is not about a geographical place, hell is not simply a geographical place. The way of heaven and its abundant life can be here or afterwards depending upon what we participate with; so too, the way of hell and its fruits can be here or afterwards. I could have caused more hell for Kathy had I participated with more of hell's ways during our difficulties (and vice versa). We reap what we participate with; we reap what we sow. This principle is an unending (ever-existing or eternal) spiritual law.

God taught me much about hell through my experiences, which I believe was very purposeful on His part. I believe that

God planted a deeply burning message in me about hell being different than what has traditionally been taught. I believe that much of the world's view of God's love has been seriously distorted through the still-prevailing view of hell (because people's view of hell automatically makes a statement about their view of God's love).

Earlier in my journey, Kathy and I had received a prophetic word from a spiritually gifted person that accurately predicted our trials and conveyed God as saying to me, "I've put some things inside of you that I intend to get out of you" (this prophetic word had been recorded and printed at the time but had not alarmed Kathy or me by the way things were worded). I believe that this book is part of what God intended, and that He especially wanted to uproot the prevailing view of hell that has historically tainted how people have viewed His love. How can people believe in a truly loving God that throws some of His children away into torment forever? I know that as I raise this issue many people ask, "But how can we reach any other conclusion when hell is addressed very clearly in the scriptures?"

I don't discount those scriptures. I just see them in entirely new ways because of how God's fire awakened me. I now see that the historical views of hell are through fleshly eyes that still buy the lie of separation. My own trials have powerfully uprooted old views that are based on death's lie of separation versus Christ being the truth of no separation. For all, whether that is during this earthly journey or afterwards. Christ's cross made a way for all.

Ways establish realities, and hell is a way just like heaven is a way. Hell is about believing, participating with, and experiencing separation, and heaven is about knowing and experiencing no separation (which is Christ). I experienced hell every time I was in my earthly nature during trials and thought that I was alone, abandoned, or unacceptable as I was. Separated. But that "separation" was because of my view, which sometimes increased after others treated me those ways. But I awakened to and experienced heaven every time the lies of separation were uprooted. Heaven was real when I knew that Christ was with me and in me, usually through inner peace.

The scriptures give a great definition for hell. The definition is tied into the dual meaning of "rapha," which I mentioned; and it portrays the way of death to life, empty to full, and naked to being clothed. I learned about this pathway deeply and experientially during my fireworks and was shocked to learn afterwards that this meaning for hell had been right before my eyes in the scriptures. But I had not been able to see this definition until I had experienced my personal journey through hell.

I was not researching the topic of hell at the time. I was researching "circle," which showed up in Job 26:10. Also, my heart had stirred when seeing the number 266 several times the previous day. So I had wanted to pause with the Lord about what scriptures He might want to direct me to, but I had forgotten about it.

Then "coincidentally" the next morning I was researching the word circle in Job 26:10, and the number 266 popped into my mind again. I immediately looked above to verse 6 and was shocked.

Job 26:6 states, "Death is naked before God; destruction lies uncovered." I then read verse 5, "The dead [*rapha*] are in deep anguish, those beneath the waters and *all that live in them*." As I paused about this passage, I intuitively knew that it was focused on hell.

The King James translation of Job 26:6 is "Hell is *naked before Him*." Hell means being naked before God. It comes from the root word "to be bare; to deal craftily." Haven't you experienced times of feeling utterly empty and alone? When your earthly nature scrambled in futility to fix or fill that emptiness? I have.

During my trials I encountered times where I knew that neither human nature nor any amount of crafty maneuvering could fill my holes. At those times I experienced no security. I felt alone, empty, and naked before God, at least until He awakened me again. Fortunately I usually awoke with greater revelations and fullness of Christ.

The shocking part is that "hell being naked *before* God" means that hell's nakedness is *suitable* for God … the exact same Hebrew word for Adam's suitable helper, meaning a counterpart. Do you hear the Spirit or essence of this? Hell is God's suitable worker, a counterpart that accomplishes His purposes. God uses hell to expose our naked areas. This parallels what God spoke through Isaiah (54:16), "See, it is I who created the blacksmith who fans the coals into flame and forges a weapon fit for its work. And it is I who have created the destroyer to work havoc."

God created the destroyer! That sounds harsh but it is only to strip away the false to awaken the true. God's counterpart destroyer ruins the flesh nature so that our souls awaken to the Christ nature within. The true cannot be hurt. That's why the following verse states, "No weapon forged against you will prevail … This is the heritage of the servants of the LORD, and this is their vindication from Me."

The servants of the Lord is not about person versus person or group versus group. The servants of the Lord pertains to the Christ nature within people, and the destroyer is only made to prevail against, and bring to ruin, the flesh nature within people. But nothing will prevail against or harm the Christ nature within us, which is ultimately who we are.

Hell could harm nothing that was true in Kathy or me, or in our relationship. Only the false. After we experienced hell's nakedness in areas that were not fully Christ's ways, Kathy and I could not return to relationship as it was previously. We could not return to certain beliefs and ways like thinking we should be the same as one another, or thinking that we were unacceptable or unlovable as we were, or, that we shouldn't have struggles if we were closely following Christ. Lesser rules and ways became broken through God causing the nakedness of some of our lesser ways to be exposed.

Hell is Spiritual Nakedness

Just like heaven is the experience of God's fullness, hell is the utter absence of that fullness. Hell is spiritual nakedness and emptiness, whereas heaven is True Clothes and spiritual fullness. Counterparts.

During my panic attacks and marital fireworks the Lord took me through many experiences of being naked before Him. That nakedness exposed and uprooted lesser ways in me such as striving in human effort, hiding weakness, not seeking support through Christ in others, not honoring inner experiences and nudges, and always wanting others to think highly of me.

Fortunately God's purpose for nakedness was to awaken my soul to more of Him, not just to leave me empty. Empty to full; naked to being clothed. One counterpart to bring forth the Other.

God works through both counterparts during our earthly journey. When we participate with Christ's ways, does more of heaven manifest on earth or not? When we participate with the ways of death and hell, does more of hell take place on earth or not? Had I condemned Kathy for any weaknesses during our struggles, wouldn't that have caused her to experience more of hell on earth? More nakedness and abandonment?

The astounding thing about many of my discoveries on the topic of hell is that they seemed to come upon me. They seemed to want to happen. I was not researching hell, but somehow God highlighted that topic to me through the number 266. When I saw the meaning of hell in Job 26:6, so much of my journey seemed to make sense practically and spiritually. I experienced more wholeness in Christ. I saw God's ongoing way of the cross, which brings death to lesser ways to awaken more of His heavenly life that is wider, longer, higher, and deeper than my earthly limitations. God used hell and death to further restore me.

The Hebrew word for "hell" in that passage is *sheol*, meaning Hades, hell, death, the pit, the grave, or *the world of the dead*. All of these meanings come together in the last meaning, which is "the world of the dead." That's why all are in deep anguish who "live in the waters" (meaning in the waters that will waste away rather than in the Living Water; hell is when you live in what wastes away – see the Hebrew word for "waters" in that passage). The flesh nature is hell's waters that waste away and all who live in those waters experience life apart from God. Empty.

The wasting away of hell's waters also parallels the Apostle Paul's words (2 Cor 5:1-5): "Now we know that if the earthly tent we live in is destroyed, we have a building from God, an eternal house in heaven, not built by human hands. Meanwhile we groan, longing to be clothed with our heavenly dwelling, because when we are clothed, we will not be found naked. For while we are in this tent, we groan and are burdened, because we do not wish to be unclothed but to be clothed with our heavenly dwelling, so that what is mortal may be swallowed up by life. Now it is God *who has made us for this very purpose* and has given us the Spirit as a deposit, guaranteeing what is to come."

God's very purpose during my trials was to continually expose and uproot any nakedness to help Kathy and me put on more of our True Clothes. The scriptures about put on love, put on the new self, and put on Christ directed Kathy and me to put on our incorruptible Christ nature. We kept enduring God's stripping works to become further clothed in our Christ nature. God's "wrath" in the Old Testament was only ever for one purpose: to strip away people's false clothes that hindered them from being clothed in the true.

Remove the grave clothes! We must come up out of the grave just as Christ came up out of the grave. That is humanity's journey.

God rightly spoke through Isaiah (Isa. 43:19), "See, I am doing a new thing! Now it springs up; do you not perceive it? I am making a way in the desert and streams in the wasteland." This is about Jesus, but also about the New Jerusalem coming down out of heaven (Rev. 3:12). The kingdom of heaven manifests on this earth as people take off grave clothes and put on their True Clothes. That's what Lazarus symbolized when Jesus raised him from the dead and exclaimed (Jn. 11:44), "Take off the grave clothes and let him go."

Kathy and I, as well as the others connected to us, all played a part in removing some of our grave clothes. That eventually caused streams to come forth in our wasteland.

The "dead being in anguish" and "hell's nakedness before God" in our original passage are deeply intertwined with the second half of that passage: destruction lies uncovered, or "has no covering."

I know that some of this is deep and not easily grasped but it is a crucial foundation for understanding God and His works more fully. I believe with all my heart that the prevailing view of hell has been through fleshly eyes and that God intends to uproot that view so that we can receive Him more fully as He is ... to know Love that never retreats one step during His stripping works of the false. So bear with me to consider the implications of this scriptural passage more fully. One way or the other, your view of hell shows what you believe about God's love. Does God throw people away? Or does God's love truly never fail? Is God's love faithful even when we are faithless, or not?

The Hebrew word for destruction is *abaddown*, which also means Hades, or a perishing. The root meaning is to wander away, lose oneself, be undone, or have no way to flee and is also the root for "something lost." Don't the scriptures emphasize how much joy God experiences when He finds what is lost (Lk. 15:6, 9)? How He will leave the 99 out of 100 sheep to ensure that all 100 are in the fold? Aren't His scriptures eternal? Never-ending?

That passage emphasizes that destruction "has no covering." Destruction causes people to experience no earthly protection or security, which causes them to feel separate and alone.[1] Destruction's purpose is to bring people to earthly nothingness. Emptiness. Naked. Isn't that what you feel like every time intense trials first come upon you? That's what I initially experience at those times. But that destruction of the false allows space in our souls for God to awaken and establish the true.

Space for new moves (and new clothes) came about regularly for me during my journey through hell. Hell in my life was the place of having no covering whatsoever. During my most intense trials my previous clothes – my put-together exterior, people being my enough in certain ways, a good reputation, or effective communication with people – no longer worked. I could no longer trust in those things or "loves" to be my security. They could be shaken away. I experienced nakedness and could no longer find comfort or protection in those clothes. I felt alone and afraid.

I knew in my head that God was with me and for me at those times, and that He was my clothes. But at a practical level I experienced "Why hast Thou forsaken me?" Fortunately God's purpose for the fireworks was for me to receive more of my true clothes in place of nakedness. Nakedness that I had not realized previously when the false clothes had been covering me.

Before I continue, I want to emphasize that losing lesser clothes to embrace true clothes is not a one-time event but an ongoing journey. God sees us as we "will be," which is who we truly are. That means He sees us with our true clothes. But our earthly journey is to continually awaken us into more of Christ through experiencing periodic lack or nakedness for us to let go of the old.

Adam and Eve were initially naked and not ashamed. Being naked meant that they were barren or unfulfilled spiritually. But they were not ashamed because they were not initially aware that they were naked. Then they participated with lesser ways, recognized their spiritual nakedness, and were ashamed. Hell's craftiness began, and they hid from God. Their actions simply exposed their spiritual nakedness within.

Kathy and I needed to be willing to see and acknowledge our naked areas but not be ashamed. We needed to turn to Christ and His comforting clothes in those places, but we could not do that when we turned against ourselves or each other in condemnation. Condemnation left us with nowhere to turn, and we hid. That was still part of hell's ways. But True Love's way was secure. True Love already knew our naked areas that were meant to be further clothed, and He simply wanted us to acknowledge any nakedness so that we would turn to the True Value we carried within us.

During the marital struggles God wanted to awaken me to the fact that I was afraid at times. That fear showed spiritual nakedness within me, and I could not be clothed further in that area without first acknowledging my fear and nakedness. Simply acknowledging the fear and nakedness allowed room for Christ (directly and through others) to comfort and clothe me further in those places.

Interestingly, God did not seem ashamed of Adam and Even when they ate the forbidden fruit that exposed their nakedness. I don't believe that God is ashamed of us either. I see God as wanting simple childlike acknowledgment of our naked areas so that we don't hold onto what is false. The scriptures teach much about Israel's journey from nakedness to being clothed and ends with Jesus saying (Rev. 16:15): "Behold, I come like a thief! Blessed is he who stays awake and keeps his clothes with him, so that he may not go naked and be shamefully exposed."

We already have our true clothes within, and we keep or put on more of those true clothes through our trials that test the word within us. You will keep (put on) your true clothes when you keep God's will ... when you remain as a child during times of difficulty and simply turn to be with Daddy at those times. Allow the trials to expose any naked areas for you to awaken and embrace more of your perfect clothes. That is our ongoing journey. Acting from fear, in contrast, temporarily keeps or puts on more of our false clothes.

The garden event that led to Jesus on the cross is one of the most significant events in history, and there in the midst of history, the gospel writer Mark seems to randomly and unnecessarily mention about a naked man. Although it seems irrelevant, it is crucial.

The scriptures say (Mk. 14:51-52), "A young man, wearing nothing but a linen garment, was following Jesus. When they seized him, he fled naked, leaving his garment behind." That's what the cross is supposed to do to us. The cross is supposed to expose the inadequacy of our earthly coverings so we leave them behind. During the cross we recognize our nakedness and need, and we turn to more of our True Clothing. Our nakedness is sometimes hell on earth, and, yet, it is the way to more of Christ's fullness.

I believe that Jesus stated the essence of this difficult way very openly when He said (Matt. 16:18-19), "... on this rock I will build my church, and the gates of Hades will not overcome it. I will give

191

you the keys of the kingdom of heaven; whatever you bind on earth will be bound in heaven, and whatever you loose on earth will be loosed in heaven."

The gates of Hades periodically come against us during our journey. They are meant to at times. That is the destroyer God created for His holy purpose. God's purpose is to periodically expose our naked areas so as to clothe us in those places. Christ continually becomes our Rock and refuge through an unfolding day of nakedness to being clothed. We receive the keys to the kingdom when we embrace this ongoing way.

Yearn and turn while leaving and cleaving. Our soul's journey is to loosen and leave the fleshly, which is the wasting away of hell's waters; and then we bind the heavenly to our souls, which is Christ as our Living Water. That is the ongoing journey for embracing our new name, which is ongoing marriage of our soul to the Christ nature within. Becoming married to a person on earth is a one-day event but our soul becoming married to Christ is an ongoing unfolding day.

By the way, I believe that the young man who had worn only a sheet and escaped naked from the Garden was the rich young ruler who had literally sold all he owned to follow Jesus. I believe that both characters were Mark, the gospel writer. I think Mark described this "young man" without sharing that it was himself, just like Apostle John had talked about "the other disciple" out-running Peter to the tomb without identifying himself. You can also see that only Mark's gospel about the rich young ruler mentioned that Jesus "felt love for him" when He told him to sell all that he had (Mk. 10:21). Mark emphasized Jesus' love for him because it was directed towards him personally, and he felt that love. That's why Mark walked away grieving about Jesus' directive for him to sell everything. But Mark loved Jesus enough to eventually sell it all and to follow Him … and, yet, the cross still came upon him so that he would leave even the sheet covering him so as to further embrace his true clothes. The symbolism of that mysterious event in the Garden powerfully portrayed the way of losing superficial earthly clothes to gain our true ones.

I have much more to say on the topic of heaven and hell, as well as about God's utter faithfulness to us. For now, you might want to give all of this back to God and let Him sift through everything in His time.

Chapter 8

Fire Furthers the Kingdom

Overcoming Perceived Separation

God wanted Kathy and me to overcome perceived separation in the midst of us feeling very different and separate about significant issues. Would we remain attending church at different places? Could we do much together spiritually now that our views seemed to diverge? Could we be safe and accepting of one another while being honest about our differing views? We had talked about working with couples in the future, possibly after retirement. How did we feel about retirement now that we might not connect as well in the most important area of our life? Did we both want retirement sooner than later, or did we feel differently now?

In the book of Revelation Jesus emphasized "Hear what the Spirit says to the overcomers." I heard these words this morning as I was preparing to write (the italicized words below stood out the most to me).

"Hear what the Spirit says to the overcomers. Hear what the Spirit of I Am Who is beyond borders says to those who are compelled to overcome earthly limits. *Earth cannot be as it is in heaven without going beyond earthly words, structures, systems, labels, and mindsets.* 'Kingdom at hand OR kingdom come' must fall away and be replaced with 'Kingdom at hand AND kingdom come.' 'This OR that' must be replaced by 'This AND that' which gathers. Through sacrificial love I gathered even those who did not want Me. Know Me who transcends the earthly. I AM greater. Leave and cleave. The Spirit of Christ calls to those who are willing, 'Follow Me. Cleave to Me who is beyond labels. Cleave to Me within you and your many counterparts on earth.' 'Come out' cries the Spirit. 'Come out from your structures and lesser securities and allow Me to gather you like a hen gathers her chicks under her wings. Allow love's fire to gather you. Be servants of the Flame. Allow wisdom's sacrificial love to burn in you to make two sides into one so that you would awaken into the fullness of My kingdom. See with eyes of no separation and then you will experience My greater love and works that bring true rest.'"

We are called to overcome perceived separation. I believe that Kathy and I were meant to symbolize the overcoming journey. We journeyed (and are still journeying) from perceived separation into knowing our oneness. I believe that this is meant to be everyone's journey. God constantly works to uproot our worldview to receive the mind of Christ, which is to see all things as one.

I do not own anything about Kathy's and my retirement, about where God leads us to attend church individually or as a couple, or about how He may want us to connect spiritually and relationally as we go forward. All is God's for the purpose of awakening us further to the fact that true separation does not exist. Treating whatever and whoever I am connected to as separate from me is a lie. Why? Because Christ is in and through all things to work all things together for my awakening. Life works together as one, for me, for Kathy, and for all of us until we fully recognize Christ's oneness in all things.

Heaven is One and cannot be separated. The earth's duality appears as separate but must become one as it is in heaven. In the beginning God "separated" light from dark, day from night, and then created an expanse to separate the water below from the water above (Gen. 1:1-10). God lastly separated one man (Adam) into two (Adam and Eve).

Separating all those things, including man, meant that they had previously been one. Pause about the implications of that. The water above the expanse (heaven) continued to be recognized as one, but the water below the expanse (earth) was not seen as one by humanity. Everything was prepared in advance for humanity's blindness to the unity of all things, because God's design was that only faith (not earthly ability or control) would see and participate with all things on earth as one just as it is in heaven. Then God's heavenly kingdom would awaken on earth through souls participating with Christ within who sees with eyes of no separation. That has been Kathy's and my journey.

The water of the earth (us), which was below the expanse that "separated" us from the water above it, was designed to experience through faith that there was no true separation. Humanity can only overcome blindness by sacrificially loving what seems separate. Our sacrificial love of Christ and one another becomes Christ's justice that sweeps away our false refuge, which is the lie of death or separation (Isa. 28:17-18). The lie of two, of separation, will come to ruin. [1]

Two on earth must become one as it is in heaven. The "separation" of either-or and "this or that" must become "this and that." Day and night, light and dark, and water below the expanse (humanity) must become one as it is above the expanse. "Be fruitful and multiply, and reign on the earth" means walking with Christ's sacrificial love that continuously makes two into one, which conceives heaven's oneness on earth.

While Christ works to gather "this and that" into one, people's earthly nature seeks separation and constantly pits "this against that" for self-glory. Haven't you seen people arguing with one another because of trying to elevate their own point above another's? Level difference for self-glory.

False scales try to cheat wisdom by adding weight to one side, but wisdom has two sides (Job 11:6).

The scriptures tell us that, in Christ, we have nothing and yet possess everything (2 Cor. 6:10). We must lose life to gain life, become poor to become rich, be aware of our fleshly tendencies and yet recognize our beauty, become empty to become full, and become weak to become strong.

Wisdom has balance just like the physical body maintains balance to be healthy. Physical sickness automatically means that something is out of balance within our body. So, too, spiritual sickness is because of "this *or* that" thinking. Spiritual sickness comes from lack of balance in the spiritual realm. We hold rigidly to one thing and despise the Other, whose name is above all names. Bigger and beyond all individual names. Beware of promoting one thing over another.

God kept stripping Kathy and me from this or that thinking through all that we endured. He kept stripping us from holding onto one thing versus another so that we would eventually embrace wisdom that had two sides. God kept awakening us to see Him who was not limited to the Catholic *or* the protestant church, or to people with Christian labels versus those with other labels. While we still maintained our unique spiritual biases, we definitely came to see that God was bigger and working beyond religious structures or labels.

I believe that one of the biggest obstacles to Christ's fullness is to have "camps" of this or that. Camps of one or the other hinder Christ's fullness. Fortunately, fire furthers the kingdom.

Embracing the fire burns away the rigidity and separation of camps and continually causes two to become one.

When you watch a couple in conflict, you will see that *all communication comes to a halt when one or both individuals hold on tightly to a view that will not also consider or allow the other's view.* Christ is more encompassing and uses conflict and perceived differences to expand us into more of His fullness.

During Kathy's and my struggles Christ wanted both of us to embrace whatever could be gained from the other person being exactly where they were. "Yin and yang" were to be embraced as one. Neither of us would be changed (or completed) regarding God's purposes for this conflict until we gained "this *and* that." Christ asked us to love sacrificially, to seek and hold onto the true while love's fire burned away the false.

This or that is only a shadow; Christ is greater. Christ's sacrificial love is wider, longer, higher, and deeper because it goes beyond individual understanding or abilities. Christ's love gathers.

Leave and Cleave, Go and Know

I feel compelled to express through my writing not only Kathy's and my journey into wholeness but also how I see God working to gather humanity into the unity of heaven. God further transformed me into the mind of Christ through encountering struggles designed to strip away my lesser worldviews. Limiting worldviews. God persistently worked to gather Kathy and me into a way that was bigger than this versus that. Even if you feel that your spouse is blatantly wrong about something that leaves you in conflict with one another, God wants to strip you from lesser ways and awaken you into higher ones.

Christ's kingdom on earth increases as you leave and cleave, and go and know. Leave the shadows. Leave the finite earthly identities and labels, and cleave to and know the Spirit of Christ who has no borders. Know Him who is beyond your previous knowledge. You must even leave some of the good things to go on to the better.

Family is good. Culture is good. Camps, or groups of like-minded people, can be good too. But we are called to leave and cleave to more. We must leave the finite and cleave to the Infinite so that Christ's kingdom can expand in us and through us. Christ gathers us through ongoing leaving and cleaving. What if the various peoples on this earth forever remained in their own groups without associating with anyone beyond their groups (Muslims, African Americans, Caucasians, Native Americans, Hispanics, Asians, etc.)? Research in the counseling field validates that people who interact little with others outside of their identified group remain less mature and less able to love people well. In fact, remaining only with their identified group usually leaves them in fear of others.

God said to be fruitful and multiply and to fill the whole earth (Gen. 1:22, 28). That is more about the spiritual than the natural. God didn't want us to simply fill the earth with endless numbers of unloving people. God wanted us to fill the earth with His image, which is Christ who is able to love beyond labels. Then the earth becomes as it is in heaven.

Although we must walk through the valley of the shadow of death, which is our earthly journey, we must eventually leave the earthly shadows. We must leave the earthly and partake of the heavenly, which is about honoring the unseen Christ in all people.

God told Abraham to leave his family and all that he knew to go to the land that He would show him (Gen. 12:1). A land not yet known. Go and know. Jesus also called His disciples to leave and cleave when He told them to follow Him. Jesus called them to leave all they knew and to cleave to and follow Him who moved.

Rules, systems, and even the scriptures do not move because they are not living and breathing. Only the Living Word that the scriptures point towards lives and breathes and moves. I love the wisdom embedded in the scriptures, and Christ's Spirit regularly quickens me to more of that wisdom. But those revelations come not from the written words on a page but from the Spirit of the living Christ within me. Jesus did not tell me to follow the scriptures but, rather, to follow Him.

Jesus told His disciples that if they left homes, brothers, sisters, mother, father, or children and fields that they would receive much more in this age and in the age to come (Mk. 10:29). That was not about the physical but the spiritual. Leave and cleave; go and know.

The "land" that God would show Abraham symbolized the land of Christ within us. Jesus told us that the kingdom was within us (Lk. 17:21). God used my marital trials for Kathy and me to leave more of the old that was limited and to cleave to more of the land of Christ within us.

Honor the Greater

Part of my worldview that became increasingly transformed through Kathy's and my struggles was that God and Christ are always greater than the individual. God birthed a deeper humility in me during struggles that were beyond me as an individual. I saw that Christ was in all and working through all things, and that I was one small but necessary part that was to be brought together into wholeness with other necessary parts.

The land of Christ is within all of us. The mystery of Christ is "Christ within you, the hope of glory" that was initially planted within us but had not been revealed throughout the ages until Jesus walked this earth (Col. 1:27). The scriptures similarly refer to Christ as the life of the light within all men (Jn. 1:4). Also, as mentioned earlier, the scriptures give evidence of Christ within all people through their consciences testifying of God, even if they have not yet been awakened to know that it is Him.

Jesus said that we are one with Him and that He is one with the Father. Our unity with Christ and the Father boggles my mind. But that unity must be balanced with the humility of knowing that Christ and the Father are greater than us as individuals.

The greater is always beyond the individual. The greater is beyond the earth, as well as in the collective Christ nature within humanity.

The scriptures say that there is "… one God and Father of all, who is over all and through all and in all" (Eph. 4:6). That is a profound statement and is likely tied into Jesus' instructions for people to pray "*Our* Father … Your kingdom come, Your will be done on earth as it is in heaven" (Matt. 6:9-10).

Jesus said numerous times that He and the Father were one but that the Father was greater. He also conveyed that equality with the Father was not able to be grasped and that the Father alone determined the times and seasons (Phil. 2:6; Acts 1:7).

The Father symbolizes the greater, and trusting the Greater's absolute sovereignty is the way to establish the Greater's rights on earth for it to become as it is in heaven. I don't believe that my marriage had any chance at all without Kathy and me eventually participating with God's ordained difficult works that were purposed to establish more of heaven on earth.

The Greater determines the times and seasons of particular works much like the sun and rain determine the time of the flower blossoming into its glory and fullness. Without the sun and rain that are greater than the flower that is connected to the earth, the flower cannot live or awaken into its design. That is why Jesus said that He could do nothing without the Father (Jn. 5:19). This mystery always causes the flower to depend on and humbly exalt the greater. The flower can do nothing by itself.

The greater is beyond our present grasp as an individual. Power is beyond the individual. In naivety the simple-minded think that power can be controlled by an individual. Even Jesus knew that He could do nothing apart from the Father. Shouldn't that say something to us?

Genuine humility is a crucial part of walking further into the fullness of our true identity in Christ. I believe with all my heart that I and God's people as a whole must walk with deeper humility before we are entrusted with God's greater goodness and mysteries. I sensed a deep connection between me becoming humbled through circumstances *beyond my control* and then being granted to know mysteries that were *beyond my current understanding.* Those two things go together.

Love that surpasses your understanding and abilities grants you wisdom. That is greater love, which humbles the individual. It humbles individual fleshly thinking that separates for self-glory.

Earthly "wisdom" foolishly believes that power resides in a geographical (separated) place, as if power is here *or* there, in me *or* you, or comes forth from one religious label *or* another. But Christ is in and through all things, and is above and beyond all individual names. Earthly wisdom and labels cannot describe or contain Him.

Jesus said (Matt. 11:25-27), "I praise You, Father, Lord of heaven and earth, because You have hidden these things from the wise and learned, and revealed them to little children. Yes, Father, for this was Your good pleasure. All things have been committed to Me by My Father. *No one knows the Son except the Father, and no one knows the Father except the Son* and those to whom the Son chooses to reveal Him."

The Father hid the mysteries from the earthly nature's craftiness and supposed wisdom. The way of awakening to these mysteries is hidden in the precious Father-Son relationship – humility connected to One who is greater. Jesus, the Son, was always alert beyond Himself as an individual and saw Himself as a child who needed to honor and depend on the Father who was greater.

How can we grow or awaken beyond ourselves without paying attention to and learning from One who is beyond our self? Jesus' whole earthly journey demonstrated this to us. The kingdom is revealed to little children. Really, to *sons* (meaning daughters as well) who walk in the humility of little children with the Wise Parent.

The True Son, Christ, chooses to reveal the Father and His mysteries to those who are true sons just as He was a Son in how He walked this earth. Honoring the Father honors His times and seasons.

Our flesh nature experiences extreme difficulty accepting times and seasons, especially long ones. Kathy and I could not force change in one another or ourselves ahead of God's time and works (which of course, we didn't handle perfectly!).

There were times of desperation when I tried new steps connected to Kathy, thinking that it was Christ when no action was yet going to work to bring change. Kathy also pressured me at points to take certain actions when Christ was not yet working in those ways. Doors were closed for a season. Had I tried to force my way forward before the Lord's time, I believe I would have created more pain and false mountains that prevented our awakening to Him who was beyond us.

The scriptures say (Song 8:4), "Do not arouse or awaken my love until she pleases." Love awakens in God's time, not our earthly times.

Human hearts are dull and insensitive to times and seasons when we want something too badly. Life always seemed to get worse when Kathy or I concluded that we should already have something beyond what we had, like when we expected that counseling should be able to work for us when it was not yet going to work. That is the flower demanding the rain or sunshine.

When you let go and no longer demand what you think ought to be, from deeper within you are able to sense whether God is presently working what you want or not. As humans, we cannot pick and pull at the flower's blossoms to open before their time or we will ruin the flower. The cool spring air must leave so the flower can cleave to and gain strength from the summer sun's warmer breezes and glory, which then awakens it to its own unique glory.

Only through humbly honoring the Greater does the flower become lifted up on this earth.

I am that flower. Kathy is that flower. You are that flower. Our true Christ nature within us is that flower, and we must regularly defer to the Greater just like Jesus did. We must also be aware that we are connected to the greater body of Christ beyond us as an individual.

We sometimes suffer and groan not just for individual awakening but also for the awakening of many others. That's why the power to heal is not fully under individual choice, but is interdependent with that which is beyond the individual.

I used to try harder to believe, as if turning purple from straining would cause healing for me and others. That is the earthly nature's naivety that wants power and control as a self-contained individual. Wouldn't that be great?

Fortunately God spares me from what my ego might do if healing power were under my own individual control. God can and will work powerfully through individuals, but not because the power was under their individual fleshly control. Those works will come forth the more we learn to walk in true humility that depends upon that which is greater than us as individuals.

Jesus only did what He saw the Father doing. He discerned and then acted. Jesus trusted the Father's times and seasons, even the hour of darkness that came upon Him (Lk. 22:53). That is true humility. Jesus neither changed nor tried to change the hour of darkness. He saw what the Father was doing and followed His lead even though they were One.

This does not mean that Jesus constantly asked questions to the Father about what He should do. Jesus did many things spontaneously when He knew He was at peace with the Father. Peace was the key. That peace already indicated His unity with the Father's nature and works. But Jesus could not have started His ministry or performed miracles before His Father initiated that season for Him (which began from outside of Himself, from His mother Mary). Jesus would not have sensed peace from the Father for that season until the Father's time.

Just like the flower needing to defer to the sun and rain that are greater for it to fulfill its purpose on the earth, Jesus emptied Himself when He came to the earth and deferred to the Father who was beyond the earth. The greater determined the times and seasons.

Is life at a stalemate for you? Notice that I said "for you." If life is at a stalemate, the Greater is reigning over it for His higher purposes. During difficult circumstances I ask Christ, "What are You working? What am I to join with in these works?"

Asking those questions starts you off with a good foundation. That foundation acknowledges up front that God is involved in your circumstances. That is prerequisite to anything else. In that way you don't fearfully approach your circumstances as if you are alone and that He abandoned you. If you believe that you are alone, you are already in the earthly nature rather than the true.

Likewise, beware if you have one particular outcome in your sights. Sometimes people only focus on physical healing or circumstances changing to "good" worldly ones. Instead, desire to be with Christ and allow Him to be with you. Then you begin receiving higher sight and knowing more fully that He is with you. Receiving your answers begins through desiring to be with Him rather than focusing on some outcome.

For me, my panic attacks were so severe earlier in my spiritual journey that I simply wanted them to disappear. I don't know whether or not you've ever experienced panic attacks. They were horrific. I just wanted them to be gone. That's what I fixed my eyes on without knowing it at the time.

Looking back, I am grateful that God gave me grace to let go of my demand that He simply heal me from the panic attacks. Without knowing it, deeper inside I was still driven to have everything in place so as to be acceptable. Loved.

Please understand that I believed all the right things in my head and knew that I didn't need to be different to be acceptable. But a deeper place inside my heart didn't know that. God was going further and He wanted to reach that deeper root before healing me from panic attacks. That might sound callous or harsh by God but it wasn't. It was greater peace and freedom for me in the end … after I learned to participate with Him (still through free will) that uprooted me from lifeless ways. Ways that I couldn't see about myself.

God knew that if He simply healed me from panic attacks that I would have continued forward still trying to become acceptable based on performance. I would have continued on a false foundation. I would still have been driven by a lie that would have never allowed me to rest in life. I am thankful that He persevered to get to the false root in me.

God's bigger purpose was to uproot my lie of needing to perform to gain acceptance and for me to be able to rest in His love that is not dependent on anything. He wanted inner healing and wholeness through me deeply knowing love first. That's how God uprooted the panic attacks. But it was God's order and timing, not mine.

Hear what the Spirit is speaking to some of you. Do you have your sights fixed on physical healing or changed circumstances? Without knowing it you are essentially demanding that God serve you in your timing or ways. Lesser ways. That is not relationship but expecting God to accomplish your earthly purposes rather than you paying attention to join with His higher works. And you will find that His difficult works are good after you let go of your time and expectations for restoration.

Please don't hear me wrongly. There is nothing wrong with asking God to heal you. But do so from a surrendered respectful place that acknowledges that He might know more than you! God always wants to heal but He may first want to heal you in a deeper way than what is visible. Like God did with me, He may want you to know love, care, and rest in a deeper way before He heals what you see at the surface level. Or, like me as well, He may want you to learn to be vulnerable with others and to receive emotional and inner support from them, which then helps you to know His goodness and comfort at an experiential level.

Ask, but let go of agendas, results, and expectations. New wine cannot be poured into rigid wineskins.

The Greater is the Creator

The Greater further establishes heaven on earth. The rain and sun in the sky must further establish the flower. The Greater is the Creator.

I used to think much about what I was going to accomplish. I now see that my view was earthly and that more of heaven on earth comes through the higher realm's initiative. I try to stay alert for that initiative from Christ within myself or others. In the scriptures you cannot find Jesus saying that He (apart from the Father) during His earthly journey created anything. Instead, Jesus said that the works He did were not His own but His Father's (Jn. 5:19-20). Jesus took no ownership of the works, partly because He took no initiative from the flesh nature. Then when the works came forth, He knew Whose they were.

Only to the degree that I saw my absolute need for the Greater did I truly depend upon the Greater Who further established heaven in me. I personally needed to hit impossible earthly walls to awaken me further to pray and act from this place of greater dependence on God.

During life I act spontaneously for the most part when I sense Christ's peace. Then I know that the works are His. But anytime I am not fully at peace, I become quickly alert to what Christ and His Father might be doing. Why? I believe that my lack of peace is God's signal for me to watch and reposition myself to be one with His works. That is when I am a peacemaker on this earth.

Peacemakers constantly lay down their lives to defer to, and make room for, the Greater so that He has space or emptiness from which to create. That establishes His works in place of earthly ones.

Our souls continually awaken by letting go of the false and taking up the true. Hear how the law of the conservation of energy is revealed in the scriptures: lose your life to find your life (Matt. 10:39); humble yourself that you may be exalted (1 Ptr. 5:6); seek first the kingdom and all else becomes added (Matt. 6:33); become empty that you would become filled (Matt. 5:6); and become poor to become rich (Jam. 2:5).

The Spirit's higher energy cannot regularly take place within my soul while lesser energy reigns within me. In every aspect of my life I trade one thing for another. My soul is an enclosed energy system. Which energy runs my soul? Earthly or heavenly? I was meant to function with Christ's limitless energy rather than the bondage of the earthly energy, and my choices make way for which energy governs through me.

Many other scriptures convey that you cannot awaken further into the true when you hang onto the false. Make way for Christ. Make space for the Greater to be the creator in and through your life. You become Christ's vessel that creates when your choices are in union with Him, just like when Jesus was in union with the Father.

The human soul is like a vacuum cleaner hose that sucks in life to sustain it. When our hose is turned towards earthly life and its limitations, we are filled with the earthly, which leaves no room for the Greater.

That is why we often need to encounter earthly limits where our earthly energy cannot sustain or give true life to us. That is Love's fire. Unending examples in the scriptures come to mind: Abraham and Sarah not being able to have a child; Joseph unfairly imprisoned for a long season; Israel enslaved in Egypt; Moses and Israel trapped by the sea with Pharaoh's army approaching to annihilate them; Jesus and His disciples with no food to feed the multitude; and Jesus in the tomb. These examples are predicaments of fire or "death." Predicaments of earthly impossibility.

We must encounter predicaments of earthly impossibility in the various aspects of our lives to continually shift our vacuum cleaner hoses to draw in and awaken to more of true life rather than the earthly. That is how we gradually walk in more of our incorruptible inheritance, our beyond-human Christ nature.

When my hose is turned towards and truly dependent upon the Greater, I come to know the Greater more fully in that area of my heart. I come to know He is trustworthy, and I become an enlarged vessel of His works and rights (righteousness). The Greater wants to be the creator through me to establish more of heaven's ways on this earth, but He needs His heavenly will to work through me rather than my earthly one.

One of humanity's greatest struggles is to honor God's times and seasons. I see humanity resisting seasons of weakness. Only as we continue to encounter earthly impossibility will collective belief on this earth truly shift to acknowledging God who is greater. Greater love will awaken as collective belief shifts and people's trust grows during the fire. As greater love awakens, we will see humanity become more ready to lay down their lives for one another.

Personally, my initial reaction to trials has been to resist acknowledging my human weakness and limitations. My tendency has been to hide my weakness from others and even from myself. I know that through all Kathy and I endured, Christ wanted each of us to allow seasons of weakness. She and I are now united about honoring seasons of weakness that remind us to honor the Greater more fully. I experience ongoing revelations especially during those seasons of weakness, as well as Christ's comfort in place of earthly security because I turn to Him more fully with watchfulness at those times.

I experienced a deep shift within me (sometimes during but other times a day or so afterwards) every time I hit a wall of earthly impossibility and then, out of that empty place, I fully opened up to the heavenly. To the greater beyond my present grasp. I began to see during earthly impossibility that Christ wanted to establish His kingdom beyond my present level of participation with Him. My vacuum cleaner hose shifted more fully to Him at those times. That was the overcoming journey that established more of heaven on earth.

It took a lot of earthly impossibility for Kathy and me to leave the lies of earthly control and to cleave to the Greater and His time. I encourage you to leave the lie of life being under your control and to cleave to and follow Him who moves. Seasons of ongoing weakness are not bad, though they feel bad to the earthly nature.

Honoring the greater is how Kathy and I awakened further into the fullness of God's flowers of Christ on this earth who give glory to the sun (Son). We now more consistently honor the Greater's timing that awakens a greater love than we currently know, and His greater love within us increases for bringing forth His greater works.

Faith is simply the gift of God (Eph. 2:8). A gift cannot be bought or earned but is simply given by the Giver. While the kingdom of heaven is already here on this earth, further establishing that kingdom is always a gift. Furthering heaven's ways in place of and beyond earth's existing ways is always a gift from the Greater.[2]

During difficulties, have you set aside earthly energy to join with God's energy that is beyond your earthly nature? Beyond your current ability or awareness. True humility is established when you have endured experiences where you knew that you could receive nothing unless it was given to you from above (Jn. 3:27). Granted as a gift.

The Golden Eagle and the Fox

Honor the greater who tumbles the earthly to make room for establishing the heavenly.

A friend had just told me about his dream that centered on a golden eagle. He was clear that it was a golden eagle, not a bald eagle, and he asked if anything had struck me spiritually about it. Nothing had come to my mind, but I made a mental note of it because it stirred my heart.

Coincidentally, three days later my dad sent me an email with pictures of a golden eagle grabbing a fox with its talons and lifting it off the earth causing it to tumble. Immediately the Spirit stirred within me, especially because it was a golden eagle. I knew that it was no coincidence and that God desired to teach me through it. I somehow knew that it would also relate to all that Kathy and I had endured. Had my friend not said anything about his dream, I would not have been alert to what God desired to teach me through my dad's email.

Certain scriptures about foxes came to mind as I pondered the pictures. Foxes are crafty and ruin the vineyard, and the Lord condemns a crafty man (Song 2:15; Prov. 12:2). The craftiness of fleshly man temporarily ruins the vineyard, but in the end the crafty man of flesh comes to ruin.

Jesus said to those who made excuses rather than following Him (Matt. 8:20), "The foxes have their holes in the ground and the birds of the air their nests, but the Son of Man has nowhere to lay His head." The earthly has its own securities, structures, and places of rest, but true followers of Christ will rely on no earthly structures or securities but on Him alone as their rest.

Jesus also said to those who told Him that Herod wanted to kill Him (Lk. 13:32), "Go tell that fox, 'I will drive out demons and heal people today and tomorrow, and on the third day I will reach My goal.'"

Herod represented earthly authorities and systems that restrict or kill what brings true life; he symbolized earthly things demanding honor instead of allowing people to honor and follow the Spirit of Christ directly. That's the crafty fox that ruins the vineyard. Focusing on or adhering to earthly authorities, systems, and rules does not honor or embrace the unseen Christ and His higher life, but following Him directly does. We enter Christ's higher realm by following His unseen Spirit in the midst of earthly systems and rules.

After contemplating these scriptures and the pictures of the golden eagle tumbling the fox, I was clear that we are in a season where the heavenly is tumbling the earthly. I saw that that is what had happened to Kathy and me and that God will continue these works in humanity. Kathy and I had become awakened from flesh's craftiness, and others are being awakened from their misplaced trust in the flesh nature and its false securities. The fox that ruins the vineyard is being brought to ruin. The comfort of earthly authority, structures, and labels is being tumbled and will continue to tumble in this unfolding season to increasingly awaken us to True Comfort beyond the earth.

The one who has "no one" or "nowhere" to go and trusts in the Greater who is beyond our present grasp will find True Refuge. True comfort in place of earthly security.

Research the scriptures about the above quoted words and you will awaken to the necessity of becoming an orphan, widow, stranger, or outcast (ones with no one at their side) to more fully enter and establish God's kingdom on earth. You will see those quoted words (no one and nowhere) regularly connected to Christ's unfolding day of trouble or "judgment" that strips away lesser securities so as to root us in more of His kingdom of love. That's why Jesus called Herod a "fox" that would be used to bring Him to His goal, which was the cross that would ultimately establish Him as heaven's fullness and way on this earth. That is our journey as well.

"The day" is an invitation to enter the kingdom further through the gate of difficulties. We will find grace and comfort to enter through those gates when we see and participate with whatever Christ is doing rather than resisting that day. Jesus told us that He would come at unexpected times. Often, "unexpected times" means situations when we don't think God is involved, when we find ourselves saying, "Where are You God?" Christ works these unexpected situations so that our human nature can no longer satisfy us and that only faith can get us through. The earthly is tumbled so that faith within us will rise.

God tumbling the earthly has nothing to do with Him being angry at us. He simply desires to awaken us from leaning on undependable earthly securities so that we will rest in His true comfort and grace. That higher inner comfort remains and is no longer dependent upon life circumstances. I continually come into more of that comfort as Christ meets me during trials.

Just as I was learning about this season of difficulties for entering more fully into Christ's comfort and grace, a series of gates showed themselves within three days' time to confirm to me that this season is coming upon us.

The first was a graduate student whose car slid gracefully in the snow between two bigger vehicles that slid off the road to the right and to the left just in front of her. I saw the parting vehicles in front of her as a spiritual gate where the gentleness of God's grace spiritually ushered her safely through it. I saw that God's gates of difficulties were open to all who were willing to enter and that His grace would usher people through into higher places.

The next day I was driving down a mountain road and numerous deer were in a long line crossing the road. I hit my breaks as the group of deer instantly parted, some to the right and others to the left, with me going safely through the middle of them. The day after that I was driving and noticed a flock of birds just to the side of the road. They all turned to fly across the road right in front of me and I thought my windshield would hit them. Suddenly, with tremendous beauty and grace they parted just before my windshield struck them, some to the right and some to the left. Their grace was breath-taking.

No matter what your difficulties feel like, desire Christ's grace and comfort through them. Do not resist Him who speaks and works in your life, and you will find the grace that ushers you into heavenly riches beyond what the earthly could have offered. You will likely feel alone if you resist His works. Embracing the works is the beginning of No-Longer-Alone in those places.

Pray that you would desire Christ's grace and comfort so that you would not believe the lie that you have been forsaken during Love's fire (though it sometimes feels that way for a spell until you are further awakened). Become aware that Christ is with you and for you during the fire.

Wherever and Whatever

The Lord wants us to walk in the Spirit's fullness, which powerfully establishes heaven on earth. God periodically works "no one and nowhere to go" in our lives to cause Christ within us to be everywhere. To fill, really, to awaken the whole earth to His goodness and glory.

God kept taking my fingers off of everything throughout Kathy's and my struggles. My ideals of having a great marriage, being a model for counseling students about effective communication and relationship, and persisting through all things for good earthly outcomes were all up for grabs. I could no longer hold onto these shoulds as "givens" and saw that I needed to surrender into whatever Christ was doing as the higher priority. I saw that sometimes His works meant letting go of conclusions like, "Surely God wouldn't be operating behind the scenes in fully uprooting my marriage."

People even said to me, "God would want your marriage to be good, so He can't be in what is happening right now." That statement would have meant that God abandoned us; it conveys that He is in the good earthly things and not the bad. Instead, I knew that God was fully working to uproot my marriage to the extent that He did. Kathy and I received so many enlarging, freeing life lessons, and I saw that receiving them depended upon fully participating with Christ in whatever He was presently working. Each of us increasingly learned to let go of all things, although we only let go through experiencing further safety. I have much more to say about how safety became established. But our learning to let go more fully allowed the Spirit room to establish whatever Christ was working. In time, the Spirit gained room to truly breathe new life into our lives.

Because of letting go and more fluently joining with the Spirit in the moment during difficulties, the words "wherever, whatever, whoever, and whenever" in the scriptures now hold great spiritual meaning for me. Just so you know, I don't randomly research words in the scriptures because of an endless joy of research. Rather, I sometimes hear the Spirit say a particular word when I am still, and I open up to whatever Christ wants to teach me about that word. Sometimes opening up meant sitting still in my living room, and other times that meant researching any related scriptures.

One morning after seeing the pictures of the golden eagle tumbling the fox, I sensed more fullness of the Spirit about Jesus having *nowhere* to lay His head. No structures, securities, or labels was the first part. After further stillness, the word "wherever" popped into my mind with the Lord's presence all over it.

I looked again at those scriptures and saw that Jesus having nowhere to lay His head was in response to a person saying to Him (Lk. 9:57), "I will follow You *wherever* you go." I immediately knew that the words "whatever, whoever, wherever, and whenever" were highly related and held great significance in the scriptures. I knew that the spiritual essence of these words was related to walking more fully in the Spirit, which I saw as central to lifting me above earthly structures, securities, and labels. I intuitively knew that I would find both freedom and higher authority in what these particular scriptures emphasized. Then I researched. I have included the more significant scriptures.

Following Christ beyond earthly systems, structures, and labels, especially during trials, is evident in Jesus' words to Nicodemus (Jn. 3:5-8): "I tell you the truth, no one can enter the kingdom of God unless he is born of water and the Spirit. Flesh gives birth to flesh, but the Spirit gives birth to spirit. You should not be surprised at My saying, 'You must be born again.' The wind blows *wherever* it pleases. You hear its sound, but you cannot tell where it comes from or where it is going. *So it is with everyone born of the Spirit.*" Can you hear the total lack of earthly control evident in those words about following the Spirit?

God wanted Kathy and me to be born more fully of the Spirit. He desired that we learn to walk more fully with the Spirit of Christ in the moment rather than following the shoulds, rules, and systems of the world around us. Christ wanted us to be *wherever* He was and to follow Him *wherever* He went with nowhere to lay our head. That is the meaning of the overcomers laying down their lives to follow the Lamb wherever He goes (Rev. 14:4). No earthly control governing their walk.

Being born of the Spirit is not a one-time event. Every time we follow the unseen Christ directly rather than worldly systems or rules, more of the unseen Spirit of Christ is birthed or awakened within our souls. Our souls join more with the Spirit of Christ who lives and moves, and we become further freed from the limited natural realm. But we must follow the Spirit like the wind.

Do you try to tell the wind what direction is right? So it is with trying to tell the Spirit what direction or outcome is right. Shoulds will not work.

Following the Lamb is about us being living sacrifices that surrender our earthly will just like Jesus did with the Father. This is not passivity but about discerning and joining with Christ's unseen works. "Wherever" is the essence of Jesus' meaning about Peter following Him with outstretched arms (that brings death to fleshly will and honors greater will; Jn. 21:18). That is Christ's ongoing sacrificial love that feeds His sheep and establishes the Greater on earth.

Jesus said to the Father (Heb. 10:7-9) "I have come to do Your will." That is to be our way as well. "Thy kingdom come" is accomplished through "Thy will be done."

Surrendering into "wherever Christ is" establishes in us whatever He is presently working. Wherever and whatever both refer to being joined with the Spirit of Christ. This was Jesus' meaning when He said (Jn. 14:12-14), "I tell you the truth, anyone who has faith in Me will do *what I have been doing*. He will do even greater things than these, because I am going to the Father. And I will do *whatever* you ask in My name, so that the Son may bring glory to the Father. You may ask Me for anything in My name, and I will do it."

Faith and belief in Jesus pertain to whatever He is doing and us doing likewise, not asking for and getting whatever we want just because we verbalized His name along with our requests! Faith or belief means asking *in* His name. In His character or way.

Hear Jesus' way that honored the greater and established the Father's works on earth (Jn. 5:19-21): "I tell you the truth, the Son can do nothing by himself; He can do only what He sees His Father doing, because *whatever* the Father does the Son also does. For the Father loves the Son and shows Him all He does. Yes, to your amazement He will show Him even greater things than these. For just as the Father raises the dead and gives them life, *even so* the Son gives life to whom He is pleased to give it."

The Father shows the Son all He does. For *just as the Father raises the dead and gives them life*, "even so," or in the same way, the Son gives life to us. "In the same way" has to do with dying to the fleshly life and honoring the Greater. Those who have died to their earthly will and participate with Jesus' higher will, in the same way, will receive higher life.

Kathy and I followed the Spirit within us to step in new ways at times, like communicating vulnerably beyond how we had previously. That is an example of joining with the life of the Spirit within us that brought new life to our relationship. Other times following the Spirit within meant letting go of something that was important to us, or, establishing a healthy boundary by taking space during difficulties rather than storming "forward" in unhealthy ways. These examples portray "dying" to various aspects of earthly life.

Following Christ's will regarding wherever and whatever He works in the moment is not simple. Flesh tries to make this walk simple by boxes or formulas, which then requires no faith. I feel compelled to address an all-or-nothing pendulum I have seen sometimes among those labeling themselves as Christians.

For centuries some people have unknowingly treated themselves and others as totally depraved and worthless, thinking that total annihilation of people's personalities was necessary for humbly walking with God, as if following Him meant only "death" in one form or another. That was definitely not the "good news" that Christ wanted His followers to express.

Recently more followers of Christ have emphasized that our true identity is beautiful and that all people are made in God's image. This thinking emphasizes being who we are for expressing Christ, and walking in His power and authority that have already been provided. I fully support honoring the true identity within one another, and yet sometimes this position has been communicated to the extreme of believing that we hardly need to pay attention to shedding the false things that keep us stuck. This over-emphasizes one aspect and negates the other, which is still "this versus that" fleshly thinking.

I learned much about the above two contrasting points through my difficulties. Kathy and I could not have overcome the impossible walls we encountered without engaging with the true *and* disengaging from the false. Both were necessary. Regularly!

Overlooking the flesh nature's constant desire to protect itself or to gain self-glory is foolish. That is why Jesus said that He did nothing on His "own" individual (meaning separate) initiative. Jesus' work was sourced from and unified with whatever and wherever the Father was working. Sometimes that was joining with heaven's higher life, and other times that was participating with the loss or death of the earthly life.

Two kingdoms are always within me. An ongoing battle exists. I must constantly disengage from the selfish flesh nature, which is not who I truly am. It is the false, but must regularly be laid down. I must also be alert to following the Spirit's lead to honor the true.

Overemphasizing one or the other is the flesh nature's blindness that hinders my ability to follow Christ.

Jesus said that He had received authority to lay down His life and to take it up again (Jn. 10:18). That is both. I pray this almost daily. Jesus laid down His flesh nature's rights and took up the true life by following the Father's lead. Both required the Greater's authority.

The flesh nature is unable to love with wholeness. It idolizes one thing or another. Even when flesh seems at times to embrace love or truth, it is really only a semblance of love *or* truth because love and truth come together in Christ.

Christ is whole and is both love and truth. Neither of these foundations, in Christ, ever disappears at the expense of the other. Also, both the false and the true nature are in us, and Christ continually works within us to lay down more of the false to take up the true. Only as more flesh nature is stripped away by love's fire do we come into more of Christ's completion that is beyond either-or. Ruined flesh nature always allows more of Christ's love within us that gathers greater love and truth, which surpasses present knowledge. Ruined flesh nature makes a way to receive Christ's love and truth that are always wider, longer, higher, and deeper than we presently know.

The one who abides in Christ's love maintains the humble secure balance of having nothing yet possessing all things (2 Cor. 6:10). Flesh nature cannot grasp that kind of wholeness.

CHAPTER 9

Love's Fierce Way

The Lie of No Struggles

Why is fire necessary? Kathy and I definitely asked this at points. Sometimes there are no easy answers. I know it's possible that God could have created us with His nature without us needing to take it on through participation with Him during life experiences. But it is evident on this earth that we only truly possess or take on Christ's nature by participating with His divine nature through choices we make. That is clear in the scriptures (2 Ptr. 1:4).

My best guess is that we would likely not be trustworthy with God's love if it was simply handed to us. I don't think we could ever know the true value or nature of God's love if it was easily, and always, within our human control.

I come to know the value of God's love when I am clear that it is a gift and beyond my human limitations. That is why the scriptures say (Song 8:6-7), "… love is as strong as death … Many waters cannot quench love; rivers cannot wash it away. If one were to give all the wealth of his house for love, it would be utterly scorned." Despised.

Money can't buy us love. It's always a gift. Love's value is far beyond any tangible thing we know. We only come to know love's value through experiencing times *without* being aware of love. Instantly handing love to us where we never experienced lack would be like children given money constantly by parents without them experiencing life apart from money. Those children usually waste the money selfishly like the prodigal son did because of not learning its value (Lk. 15:11).

Fortunately, we are the bride in the Song of Songs, loved dearly by the Bridegroom even when the Bridegroom seems to disappear for periods of time (to gather other lilies or brides). She occasionally feels His absence although He never truly abandons her or stops loving her. That is a picture of Christ with us.

The occasional periods of feeling agony about love's "absence" cause us to know love's value. We learn deeply the contrast of experiencing love's security or not.

During Kathy's and my struggles we both experienced times of knowing God's love deeply and also times of feeling empty and abandoned. But love never abandoned either one of us even though it felt that way at points. Had we believed that Love abandoned us, we would have quickly given up on trying to participate with Christ and, instead, tried to take control of establishing earthly goodness through unhealthy means. Fortunately Christ gave grace for us to know that He was still with us and for us, and desired greater goodness through the trials.

Accept the rhythm of life. Accept the good and the bad, like Job said during his horrendous experiences (Job 2:10).

Unless you accept the rhythm of life your earthly nature will convince you that you are doing something wrong or that you need to strive to fix something when you experience a "down-period" during life. Flesh tries to convince you that at some point, if you strive hard enough or walk perfectly enough, you will finally live in an ongoing ideal "high" in life … as if you can come to a place of no more fear, no more upheaval, or no more struggles with the sin of the lesser nature.

Suffering will be part of our ongoing journey as long as gaps exist between heaven and earth's ways. As long as areas exist where peace needs established on earth, we must be peacemakers. That means suffering and holding fast while Christ fills those gaps through us. That is the meaning behind Paul's bewildering words (Col. 1:24): "Now I rejoice in what was suffered for you, and I fill up in my flesh what is still lacking in regard to Christ's afflictions, for the sake of His body, which is the church."

Christ isn't lacking. What is lacking is afflictions because Christ's kingdom becomes further established during conflict with earthly kingdoms. More afflictions are necessary to establish peace where there is no peace. We must stand as peacemakers in Christ's sacrificial ways that establish peace where there is no peace. That means afflictions, whether they are tangible outer circumstances or inner unseen ones until earth becomes as it is in heaven. This is the perspective that Christ regularly gave me during the trials. He grounded me in the fact that I was not only enduring trials to birth greater love and works in me, but I was also being used as a peacemaker and vessel of God's higher will and rights to flow through me into others (because we are all one).

Like Paul, will we do our share of suffering to establish Christ's kingdom? Will we join Christ in the fellowship of His sufferings that establish His resurrection life in places of death to the lesser (Phil. 3:10)?

Flesh nature's lie about finally rising above struggles while on this earth will keep you condemning yourself or striving in the flesh nature to stamp out "once and for all" any difficulties. Why does flesh nature desperately want to arrive at some ideal place? Then, you could go on your merry way in the flesh nature without needing Christ. That means no further awakening into Him and His higher realm. It's all a lie. Suffering is an inevitable part of our journey into awakening. The rhythm of life will continue as long as gaps exist between earth's and heaven's ways.

As humans we usually don't understand that love is a fire and is stronger than death. Love burns away all else that is limited so as to awaken us to love that is unlimited. Wider, longer, higher, and deeper.

Transformation Through Fire

I encountered the lesser's limits to know the limitless value of the Greater. That's how the earth is transformed through fire (Job 28:5). That's why the present heavens and earth are being burned by fire (2 Ptr. 3:7). Love's invisible fire burns away the lesser "heavens" and earth to establish God's highest heaven in us ... Christ. As people walk more in their Christ nature, His kingdom continually comes and is established on earth as it is in heaven (though His kingdom is already at hand).

I took my dog Molly for a walk and saw papers blowing across our yard the very morning that God put the above scriptures about fire on my heart. I knew that I was supposed to see what was on those papers, so I quickly walked over to pick them up. Amazingly, the stiff wind did not blow them away before I reached them.

The papers, a school student's assignment, focused on the necessity of heat to transfer solids into liquids, and liquids into gases. Immediately, I saw the parallel of humanity's flesh nature being like the solid created matter that, when heated, shifts people's souls into letting go of rigid solid matter to participate with the flowing water of Christ within. I sensed how more heat would cause additional transformation where our souls would further participate with the supernatural unseen realm of Christ, symbolized by unseen gases.

I then googled the topic. Hear the incredible parallels to the spiritual realm.

The particles of ice, water, and steam are identical but just arranged differently when heated. That statement made me think about people who have expressed feeling heat when they were physically healed through prayer. Hmm … just particles rearranged through heat.

Solids are particles tightly packed together and separate from other solids. Each solid's tightly packed particles are rigid and cause each one to remain an entity to itself. That is just like our flesh nature, separate from others' flesh nature and from God who is Spirit.

Heating solid particles gives them more energy causing them to shake and vibrate faster, which breaks down their rigidity and ordered structure. Wow, doesn't quickening of the heart have new meaning? The heat and shaking are transformative, and that's what love's fire does to our flesh nature! The increased heat loosens the particles from one another so that they have enough space to be more flexible and can flow freely back and forth past each another. That sounds like free-flowing relationship with one another.

Each solid has a set melting point, which causes it to become liquid. God knows "the proper time" for each one of us. He knows the proper temperature regarding each aspect of our lives for our flesh nature to melt and come to ruin. That is when our souls let go of the lesser nature's securities and turn to Christ and His nature within, which is true security.

As I read these kinds of statements on Wikipedia, I couldn't help but think of how Kathy and I had become transformed significantly through the intense heat of what we experienced. Rigid particles had become heated through life circumstances causing them to shake and vibrate loose from their rigid positions. Solids became liquids and flowed more freely. The heat and shaking caused space that allowed the Spirit more room from which to create freer higher life within our souls. Kathy's and my fiery circumstances eventually made room for more of the Spirit's higher life and ways within us. More of heaven.

As I further read about transformation of matter, I saw that heating liquids then gives particles even more energy. They move faster with even more space and flexibility. Ordered structure further decreases and, at the right temperature, the particles become fully freed from one another. No longer bound. That full freedom for particles is gas. Fully unseen.

God had repeatedly shown me during earlier trials that He worked to create space in my soul so that I would open up and embrace more of my Christ nature. Here it was again, space.

Heat, or spiritual fire in our lives, causes space (which is in contrast to the religious rulers who had no space or room in their heart for Jesus' word; see Jn. 8:37). Fire transforms this earth into heaven. People's rigid rules that keep them in bondage become replaced with the unseen spiritual realm that is like the wind. Love's fire does that. It is necessary.

Then about a year after this learning about fire, I saw another paper blowing across the neighboring lot. It stopped blowing once it came to my lawn. My heart stirred. I thought, "I'm researching "fire" and "melting" just like a year ago? Could that paper be God's doing again?" I walked over to it and picked it up. It was another school student's assignment; this time, on thermal energy. Think about it. Out of all the students in the school and all the possible assignments that could have randomly blown across my lawn, and the only two that did so dealt with fire and heat. Right at the times I happened to be researching this topic.

Wikipedia's definition of thermal energy is the internal energy present in a system by virtue of its temperature. The description continued and stated that "particles' degrees of freedom within any system depend upon the temperature, and the more heat, the more freedom."

Wow, that is astounding. The scriptures frequently emphasize heat, melting, and fire as necessary for transforming the earth. That is absolutely true for humanity. The fire's heat frees us from our rigidity and is the central force for transforming the earth to be as it is in heaven.

Love's fire heats us up through trials, which then cause us to let go of rigidity that restricts us. Rigidity that restricts Christ's love and works through us. We can't love people well when we cling to our rules. We can't even know love when we cling to rules above the wind of Spirit. Rules cannot love us. And, yet, we cannot be freed from our rigidity so as to know the peace, love, and freedom of Christ unless Love's fireworks cause us to let go of our rigidity. Think about all the fiery trials you and others have endured. Doesn't that increased heat eventually cause us to let go of our facades or false loves, and of trying to control life? We become more flexible and more able to love after going through fire. Rigid particles loosen.

The day after learning this, I saw a clear picture in my mind during worship where I gather corporately. I saw all of us as candles with faces, which were really masks (kind of like the candle on "Beauty and the Beast"). The candles kept burning brighter as the flames increased in height and width, and the masks began to melt away. The flames became so wide that they touched one another causing a dramatic increase in the flames, as well as in the collective light. The joining of the flames brought tremendous brilliance and beauty that lit up all the darkness around them. I instantly understood the necessity of fire. Fire melts away our earthly masks that keep us apart, and greater fire increases our connections and collective light. That has definitely happened for Kathy and me. Various masks melted away and more light went forth.

Several days after seeing the paper on thermal energy, I saw a movie that portrayed a real story of how people gradually changed over the course of their lives. I saw how trials worked to soften people through life. They became less fixed in their ways and learned to love a little better after they endured fire. That's why the scriptures say that God will strengthen and establish us *after* we have suffered a little while (1 Ptr. 5:10). After the flesh nature can't control life to be what it wants and then becomes humbled, we become more flexible and are granted more of heaven's riches because we are more trustworthy to love.

Of course there were the few people in the movie who had not yet surrendered their fixed ways. They had not reached "the right temperature" and continued to go through similar trials because the fire had not yet been hot enough to bring humility and flexibility.

I now see all of life working this way. Love's fire transforms us to become part of the fire. We increasingly learn to move with God's wind and fire.

I see the fire's necessity for melting away masks and rigid ways so as to free people into love that is wider, longer, higher, and deeper than what they've known. Kathy and I are utterly thankful for love's fire. I fully believe that we cannot see much of the depth, truth, and love in the scriptures without love's fire burning away our rigid fleshly views. Unstripped flesh nature will cause us to perceive many of the scriptures as being for one person or group over another rather than about the flesh nature versus the Christ nature in all people. That fleshly view falsely authorizes level-difference and separation between people. But after our lesser nature has been further stripped by fire, we learn that no one has reason to boast. We're all in the same boat.

Embrace periodic fire as part of the rhythm of life.

Here's where you may conclude that I'm a little crazy. In the midst of God teaching me about embracing the rhythm of life, I saw a car's license plate "GPC – 3737." Without trying to think of anything the following words popped into my mind. "God Pours Christ through cross-completion, cross-completion." Scripturally, 3 represents the cross and 7 represents completion. I saw this as the afflictions of Christ that fill up what is lacking in humanity (God's church). I understood God as saying to me that He pours forth more of Christ in our lives through the pattern of flesh nature being emptied through the cross and then our soul being filled or completed with Christ in that place. (And, no, not every license plate stirs my heart or causes me to hear voices!)

God's fire is meant to be our companion during our journey. That is depicted by Moses speaking with the fire (God) from within the burning bush (Ex. 2:2-4). That bush's thorny exterior represents our flesh nature, and the fire on the inside symbolizes Christ in us.

God's fire kept speaking to Moses on his journey, and it wasn't because the thorn bush accompanied him. God's fire went with Moses because it was within him, which is also why God said that he was standing on holy ground. It wasn't the ground but where Moses would walk in union with God that became holy. Their intimate relationship was demonstrated immediately when God said "Moses, Moses" (an expression of intimacy) and when Moses responded to the call of I AM, "Here I am."

Israel's journey in the wilderness also demonstrated our journey with fire. The pillar of cloud during the day and the pillar of fire by night never left Israel and "searched out places for them to camp and to show them which way to go" (Ex. 13:21-22; Dt. 1:33). Campfires and wildfires again.

Thorns and Briers

The scriptures say (Isa. 10:17), "The Light of Israel will become a fire, their Holy One a flame; in a single day it will burn and consume *His thorns and His briers.*"[1] Remember my dream about the sewage plant and its lies that were hidden in the thorns and brush? These scriptures point towards the false thorny flesh nature gradually coming to ruin through "the day," a gradually unfolding one; and the fire within increasingly becomes our Light. Christ's light shall shine forth from darkness.

Jacob and Esau, as touched upon earlier, represent the spirit person and the flesh person within us, one who looks to God and one who doesn't. Obadiah (vs. 18) states, "The house of Jacob will be a fire and the house of Joseph [who also looked to God while imprisoned] a flame; the house of Esau will be stubble, and they will set it on fire and consume it. There will be no survivors from the house of Esau." That means eternal ruin for the false flesh nature so as to awaken the soul to embrace its inheritance, which is eternal life. That is soul joined with Christ.

That is humanity's journey. The spiritual person within us (symbolized by Jacob) will set fire to the fleshly person within (Esau). In the end, in "the last day" of flesh nature, there will be no survivors from the house of Esau. Only that which is of Christ will remain. God's eternal fire that continues beyond the earthly journey will have its way.[2]

Jesus said to tell John the Baptist who was in prison and would be executed (Lk. 7:23), "Blessed is he who does not take offense at Me." Jesus conveyed to us through this that we would be blessed or fulfilled when we trust Him even in the midst of Him doing or allowing difficult works in our lives. We experience more of heaven's fullness when we recognize and receive Christ even when He comes in an hour or way we do not expect.

I wish I could simply give you what I know deeply from within my heart about trusting and embracing Love's fireworks in your life. But all I can do is share what Christ's fireworks have done at a practical level in my own life. Fire loosened Kathy and I from some of our rigidity that then allowed us to know Christ in higher ways than previously. Heat further transformed us.

Jesus told us (Lk. 10:19), "I have given you authority ... to overcome all the power of the enemy; nothing will harm you." People sometimes see this verse as meaning that they will walk with invincibility on this earth. Yet, all of Jesus' followers suffered and died at various points! Can you hear that Jesus' meaning was about the unseen Christ nature planted within us? Nothing can harm our true self, though the outer fleshly person will experience hurt quite frequently!

I believe that we will know without doubt when we pass from this earthly life into greater heavenly life that nothing could have harmed our true self during the earthly journey. Fire merely awakens us into our true nature, though it is quite painful to the lesser nature.

Trust that God is always for our true self, even during difficult works. God is sovereign and loves us fully. He loves all, which is why the scriptures say (Psm. 145:9), "The LORD is good to all; He has compassion on *all* He has made."

God is good to all. Can you receive that? To divide ourselves into camps and say that He loves one group over another violates many scriptures, including this one. The "wicked" is always about the flesh nature and the righteous is about the Christ nature in all people. God loves all people and eventually burns away the false in all so that what is of Christ remains (whether that happens here or after the earthly journey). Because love remains.

All of love's fireworks bring intimacy with God and are symbolized in Elijah's experience with the Lord in the cave on Mount Horeb. Elijah found himself at Mount Horeb after heroically standing alone for God on Mount Carmel. Elijah had fled from there because Jezebel sent him a message that she would kill him. So he ran in fear.

Then God spoke to Elijah in the cave and told him to come out when He passed by. The scriptures say that God was not present in the wind, the earthquake, or the fire on the mountain. Those kinds of works were only His outer fringe (Job 26:14). God worked those works but Elijah didn't experience God's intimate presence till those works were completed. *After* those works, God's presence established the true Elijah in ways that he had not yet been established. This is consistent with my experience.

Those intense works (the wind, earthquake, and fire) were shaking and stripping works. They all caused faster vibration of particles like was addressed earlier (vibration that loosens the rigidity in created matter and causes space for God to fill with more of Himself). That's why the scriptures say that God came to Elijah afterwards in a "still small voice" (1 Kgs. 19:12, NKJV). The Hebrew meaning of "small" is "dust; in pieces or bits; crushed." God shook, heated, and loosened the rigid particles of Elijah's flesh nature. Until then, the particles were more rigid as in a solid, which is as an entity to itself. That's why Elijah thought he was alone and could not truly receive God's presence (vs. 10, 14). But after the vibration and heat loosened Elijah's rigidity, he was able to hear God's answer that he was not alone and that 7000 people still looked to Him (vs. 18).

Like with Elijah, those fiery works cause particles within us to become quickened, and the solid flesh nature within us is not able to stand and becomes humbled. Ruined. Our souls within are more able to let go of that flesh nature because of seeing its futility, and we awaken to the freer Spirit nature within us. In that freedom we recognize God and His presence. We recognize that we are not alone and that we were never alone. Too bad that it is usually afterwards, at least until we more fully learn to embrace the fire!

Are you currently going through fire? If you are, what might be perceived necessary outcomes that your flesh nature demands? What possible rigidity might God's heat be working to free you from? Sometimes that rigidity might even be ways and expectations that many of the people around you also think ought to be. Often God is not only working to free you personally but also to free humanity into His ways that are higher than our ways. God may use you as a vessel to awaken those around you. God uses fire to burn away or shake loose commonly accepted ways or expectations that are not His higher ways.

What causes "the beast" of our flesh nature to be rigid? Flesh nature does not know the security of love, so it always braces itself in fear and agendas to try to fill that hole. Agendas motivated by fear cause flesh to fix its sight on something, sometimes even on the *things* of God rather than on the presence of God Himself. That is the rigidity.[3]

We cannot recognize God or His works in our midst when our rigid agendas blind us. Our agendas cause God to come in an hour or way we do not expect, and then we are blind to His presence.

My dog Molly was bent on having her walk earlier than usual one morning. At first I could not focus well during my still time because of her obsession with what she wanted. Her obsession unusually irritated me. I saw obsession as an ugly turn-off in that moment. Then, as I paused further with God, I recognized that He desired to teach me about this very point when *my agenda* was disrupted by her agenda. I was humbled. I could neither love her well nor could I recognize God's presence when He came in a time and way I did not expect. My fixed agenda caused fleshly rigidity until His fire through Molly awakened me. After I recognized God's presence, I saw how He used Molly to again teach me to hold desired outcomes loosely. I saw the importance of giving thanks in all things. Fire awakened me. Fire caught my attention and caused me to experience and know Christ beyond where I had been.

Jesus said, "Zeal for Your house will consume Me" (Jn. 2:17). The precise Greek meaning for zeal is "Heat or zeal" from "to be hot (boil, of liquids; or glow, of solids)." I did not add my own words! You can look it up if you wish. Also, the meaning for house is "dwelling, house, family;" and the meaning for consume is "eat down or devour" (similar to the Old Testament's Hebrew meaning, "consume or burn away."

Do you hear the Spirit of these meanings? I chuckled at Christ's surprises again, as well as at His consistent reinforcement of what He kept teaching me. Transformation of us requires God's heat. Jesus walked this way before us and is now walking this way within us. Christ's heat and zeal greatly desire His dwelling place within our souls, and He shakes, vibrates, and burns away or consumes the rigidity of flesh nature so that He can abide fully within us. That's why Jesus also said about Himself and His body of people on this earth (Jn. 2:19), "Destroy this temple, and I will raise it again in three days." Destroying the one always raises the Other, so participate with seasons where Christ comes to burn away more of the false flesh nature.

Planting Seed through Need

I have lived most of my life not acknowledging when I was in need. I believe that that is the case for much of humanity. Even when some people are inclined to acknowledge need, they often do so expecting no help to be forthcoming or to focus on what needs changed about their outer circumstances. I have frequently done both, and so did Kathy and I early in our struggles. Neither is God's desire.

God planted more seed in Kathy's and my souls through need. Our souls became the open fertile ground for more of the Christ nature when God brought us to places of need. God desired to use our earthly upheaval for Kathy and me to squarely acknowledge *inner* need. That is where space was needed for Christ to become further established within us. God powerfully used our acknowledgment of inner need to shift us from our limited human capacity to our limitless Christ nature.

Squarely acknowledging fleshly limits disconnected me from the flesh and into more of my spirit nature (flesh gives birth to flesh, and the spirit to Spirit). My flesh could only perform human works but my Christ nature was able to perform greater, but often unseen, spiritual works. The key was this: I needed to continually let go of the lesser realm and come into union with the Christ nature during difficulties. That way of surrender most came through me periodically encountering times that were well beyond my earthly nature's control.

The scriptures' references to hardness of heart pertain to people not acknowledging weakness and, therefore, the need of God during their difficulties. That is spiritual blindness.

During my marital upheaval, God wanted me to acknowledge my *inner lack* when it existed and to turn to Him for what was beyond me in those places. I eventually learned to acknowledge my inner lack more fully. More regularly. This lack was sometimes fear, hopelessness, discouragement, and ultimately, a lack of trust in Christ. Kathy became better at acknowledging her inner need after I became better at acknowledging mine. She seemed more secure about becoming aware of her need when she saw me acknowledging my need (turners must grow in this to help the yearners!). I now see this as crucial for people experiencing intimacy in relationships. Really, godly love in relationships. This means simple honesty about felt need. Childlike honesty.

The world trains us not to acknowledge need and that need shouldn't exist. Rigidity is the result. The world also trains us to accomplish what is needed with little to no support. Especially inner support. That is what people most need in this life. Inner support. And Christ *wants* to provide that, directly and through one another.

God sometimes delays restoring outer circumstances and even physical healing for us to learn to acknowledge our need for inner support and comfort. From my years of counseling experience and recent fireworks, I believe that most (if not all) of humanity could benefit by seriously considering this previous statement. I know that it was the single biggest barrier to me being healed from panic attacks. I wanted God to fix the panic attacks without letting Him or anyone comfort me inwardly (of course I now see the absurdity of that). Even when I did share that terrified place with others, they either seemed too afraid of my fear or had no direction for how I could receive healing there. Inner support was not the acceptable way in the rural farmland region where I lived, so that was not anywhere on people's radar! But now, I see this way of receiving God's and others' inner support as central to all healing. Can you see that receiving inner support is Christ's avenue for awakening the rest of His heavenly riches, which are *inner* peace, rest, freedom, and heavenly security? Without receiving that inner comfort, peace, rest, and freedom, we are left with the braced flesh nature raising up in rigid (and usually outwardly focused) ways to try to fill those holes.

Please hear the deep learning that I suffered so tremendously to gain! Receiving inner support during fiery trials ignites the inner heavenly riches. Christ's riches. God wants us to pay attention to desiring inner support rather than staying behind strong shells that give the pretense that we're tough. As if we have it altogether. That was my normal individualistic way of life until my fireworks freed me from it.

During trials people tend to resort to what they've experienced and known in those places. Usually they've gotten no inner support along with expectations to become and provide what is "supposed to be" with no questions asked. So what happens later during similar trials for people as they go forward in life?

People brace and try to become more than they are able. That's the ongoing lie that runs people's lives, and it is fleshly rigidity. That's all I knew to do. Without looking for any help. Or, even if I did look for help, I usually didn't expect true help. Especially inner help and support. Even though I was spiritual, sometimes I initially *forgot* that Christ was available when fiery sparks shot forth. But then I would remember to "eat of Him" as my food and comfort at those times, whether that was directly or through Him in others as my support.

God uses places of need as opportunities to transfer power within our souls. From earthly to heavenly power. The beginning of that power is to know the security of Christ's love that greatly desires to support us at those times.

In certain areas of our souls, all people are still filled with the world's lie about achieving or performing what is needed to become acceptable. That root is way deeper than most people think. That lie usually includes the standard that we should perform without needing any support. That is earthly power; it is the world's way. God wants to uproot these lies that have filled our souls and to establish His comfort, security, and power in those places. God most establishes us in Him through periodically causing us to experience need at the earthly level.

My earlier season of panic attacks kept being the necessary pressure to cause me to acknowledge inner need for awakening to love in the places within me that had not known true comfort or love. Then, during my marital upheaval, God worked on Kathy that way and also furthered that work within me.

God knew that if He simply restored the difficult areas of our lives that we would still not know Him or His love in those aspects of our hearts. God was more interested in us knowing Him and His love in our empty places than for our circumstances to be changed immediately. The foundation was far more important than the exterior. Only then did His restful loving way take greater root within our souls.

God wanted full honesty and humility when I was afraid or in need. He desired that I acknowledge when I didn't know Him or His security in a given area and that He alone could gird me up in that place (whether directly or through others). Part of my journey included asking trusted individuals to stand with me and to help me focus on the Lord being my "enough" in those places.

During the marital struggles I learned to squarely acknowledge my own need first to myself, then with God, and then with Kathy. God further stripped away hypocrisy at a deeper level, *especially about my present state of security.* I regularly asked God for that grace during the fire. I believe that this was one of the most pivotal lessons that eventually restored our marriage.

Power is in the Gaps

People sometimes want Christ's kingdom on earth to be as it is in heaven without going through the process that establishes that kingdom. Jesus said that the kingdom is at hand. It is here and available but He establishes it visibly on earth through people participating with Him. Jesus highlighted His way to establish His kingdom when He taught us how to pray to the Father (Matt. 6:10): "Your kingdom come, Your will be done."

That whole prayer teaches us the essence of how to establish Christ's kingdom on this earth. "Your will be done" is the center of "Your kingdom come." That way of losing our will and life to establish Christ's is seen repeatedly in the scriptures. There is much more to say about Jesus' prayer and about following His will, but the most crucial times that His followers have tended not to follow His will is during trials.

I saw with great clarity one day that God desires to use places of impossibility as opportunities to transfer power within us from kingdom to kingdom. During a difficult moment between Kathy and me, I knew that I could not be what she felt was needed emotionally. She was not ready for a hug and I felt afraid as her focus intensely turned towards me to somehow meet her needs. So I was honest about being afraid and said that I needed space so that Christ could be our wisdom rather than continuing down a rocky path. I saw that it was an impossible place for Kathy and me to overcome through talk or anything we had known up to that point. I saw that it was impossible without something or Someone greater granting more to me, Kathy, or the circumstances to bring support or perspective.

During that stillness I knew in my mind that I wanted whatever Christ desired above anything earthly. Suddenly I became overwhelmed with grief. I saw Kathy's and my fearful reactive flesh nature. I saw it clearly as "hardness of heart" that had no clue of inner goodness, support, or security in that impossible place. I saw how our flesh tried to bolster itself to become more than it could be or to strive fearfully for something it could not get rather than us simply acknowledging our need. Our human limitations. I saw that that was the way of escape from this fiery circumstance. Acknowledgment of weakness and need was the way of escape from the flesh nature. Then I experienced what felt like an endless pit of grief in that moment, a grief that felt like mine and also way bigger than mine.

I saw how humanity misunderstands God and His purposes during places of impossibility. I saw how God desires to help us there and how we tend not to let Him help. God desires for us to let go of lesser powers and loves and to turn towards Him to know Him and His comfort more fully in those places. Those places of impossibility are places of power transfer – to establish Christ's endless comfort and goodness in place of our flesh's bottomless pit of suffering. I sat weeping deeply for several minutes and felt badly about my, Kathy's, and people's misunderstanding of God.

During that stillness I saw how I tried to be strong and brave when I wasn't! Hypocrisy. I saw how Kathy's and my fullness of the lesser "power" disallowed the greater power from being established within us ... because of free will. Our wills had held onto and remained in the lesser nature at that place of impossibility. Then I heard the Spirit say that those places of impossibility were the greatest opportunities of power transfer in our lives. The truth of that was sobering.

Those places of impossibility are places for exchange, from hardness of heart to humility that squarely acknowledges earthly limitations. *Square acknowledgment of human limitations causes clearer turning to Christ within who reigns above those limitations. That is the place of power transfer. That place melts away the candles' masks for the flames to come together to burn more brightly.*

Part of humility during lack is surrendering to Christ's time and way of answering rather than us having our sights on what we think ought to be. Focus on what Christ *is* doing rather than on what He should be doing. Do not fight the River's current.

After the stillness and being filled with the Spirt, I approached Kathy again and prayed with her from a humbled broken place. She immediately heard the Spirit's compassionate message through me about God knowing the gaps but wanting neither of us trying to be "the enough" in those empty places. He wanted rest and inner comfort for us during that place of need, and that we would trust like children who knew that Daddy wanted to provide in those places. True comfort came as we united there. A power shift took place. Earthly power to heavenly power. Kathy and I both opened up fully to receive Christ's comfort in that place rather than human nature trying in futility to fill gaps. That experience of shifting from rigidity to humility during the fire became a landmark for us.

That evening Kathy and I also prayed for wisdom just like Solomon asked for wisdom's discernment above all else (1 Kgs. 3:9-11). Solomon asked for this heavenly gift even above health or happiness. Kathy and I knew that we desired wisdom in our lives beyond any particular earthly outcomes. So we united and agreed with God. Uniting in this deeper way had only been possible because of our long season of gradually awakening through fire.

The next morning I felt like wisdom met me. Wisdom revealed deeper meaning when I read the scriptures about God's power residing in the skies (Psm. 68:34). I heard the words, "Greater power resides in the expanse." Remember that the expanse in Genesis chapter one pertained to humanity's perceived separation (between one another and us with God)? A few moments later I heard it as, "Greater power for you resides in the gaps." Christ's power to go beyond where we have been previously resides in the gaps, the places of perceived separation. Christ's presence and power are most available in the gaps for transforming earth into heaven (for peacemaking).

Felt gaps reveal where earth is not yet united with heaven. Gaps reveal people's participation with "the separation of two" rather than the unity of One. Gaps expose earthly fortresses where people cling to positions and lesser loves. Their kingdoms. That is where you see power tied up in people's lives, often untouchable power. Earthly power is always more intense where separating positions and kingdoms are sought above love and unity.

Gaps are the places where kingdom against kingdom collide. Felt gaps and perceived differences require faith. Christ "holds all things together" and especially makes His power available during perceived gaps and conflict for restoring earth to become as it is in heaven. But it is by faith.

We are called to trust that, in spite of any felt gaps, all things work together as one when we stand in faith about Christ's desire to restore gaps. Participate with Christ and His kingdom rather than earthly powers that fight for positions and lesser loves that separate for self-glory.

We experientially feel and see great power in the various places of "separation" on this earth: between us and God when He doesn't do what we think He should; when we don't feel God's presence; during relational gaps and conflict; when encountering differences in spiritual views with others; and between us and the difficult circumstances that do not cooperate with us.

Conflict says it best. Conflict between where life is and where we think it ought to be. Doesn't conflict give evidence of where significant emotion and power are tied up in our lives? Where bigger forces within us are loyal to things rather than to Christ. Those are the felt gaps where Christ's greater power is accessible by joining Him at those times. Christ wants gaps restored. Joining with Christ during conflict is the primary path for power transfer. What is He after at those times? We must let go of one power to embrace the Other.

Being a living sacrifice accomplishes this. The scriptural meaning about us being living sacrifices is about "not being conformed or fashioned by accompanying the world but being transformed or fashioned anew by accompanying God" (Rom. 12:1-2). That is about following one Will over the other during conflict and places of power. Let go of earthly power and you become a peacemaker in those places. I regularly saw God working to cause Kathy and me to let go of earthly power during conflict to embrace what He was presently working so that we would participate with His power that further establishes His kingdom on earth.

Strong emotions or reactions also give evidence of the power tied up in these places of perceived gaps or differences. But often we will not join with Christ to transfer power during conflict unless we pause or take brief space, at least inwardly, so as to unhook from the earthly power that wants to govern those times.

When someone judges you and you feel deeply hurt, much power is tied up there. Responding with defensiveness or hurtful words demonstrates that you do not know *God's* love at that moment. If you knew God's love, you would be at peace and be able to respond with love. Those fleshly responses only continue that destructive power rather than redeeming those felt gaps with Christ's power.

During my struggles with Kathy I began watching the places where earthly power dominated. I prayed that during conflict and experiencing pain between us that I would pause enough to *remember* love's security there rather than to continue with earthly power. And when I wasn't aware or able to respond from Christ's security, I vulnerably admitted my lack and need of Christ. I saw that God was training me through encountering times where Kathy was unable to remember or display love. I prayed that I would increasingly see with Christ's eyes and participate with Him in either responding with His security and love or admitting my lack. One of these two responses seemed crucial for unhooking from lesser ways, and earlier in the struggles, I mostly needed to respond with humbly acknowledging my lack.

Gradually, during conflict each of us became more able to respond with Christ's security and love, or with humble acknowledgment of lack. These new responses began causing a transfer of power in those places. Even though those shifts were not always or immediately visible, false power in those places gradually became uprooted and Christ's power and kingdom became further established. Participating with Christ's will over earthly will in those places further established His kingdom.

Watch for places of greater power during life and become a vessel that establishes Christ's will and power in those places. His kingdom comes through His will being done.

Let go of your earthly desires. Lose your earthly life to gain heavenly life in the places of impossibility. Humble yourselves in the places of perceived gaps and in God's time you will be exalted in those places. Allow felt earthly separation, and trust that Christ truly "holds all things together" in those places (Col. 1:17). That trust in Christ, as you let go of earthly power, further establishes His power in places of perceived gaps.

Although Kathy or I often could not see the power transfer in the midst of those difficult places, enduring them while initially doing nothing further in the natural realm often caused us to see through the lies. Stopping the old energy allowed higher energy to manifest. We no longer participated with or fed the lesser powers when we unhooked from them. We no longer fed the power of perceived separation when we did not participate with those lies. Fast from the lesser. That's what Jesus did when encountering His hour of darkness. He demonstrated to all that darkness was really a lie, and that He was still secure because He knew that He was not separated from His Father.

Be still and know that God is God during the fire. Only then can you participate with Him. The earthly loses its power while heaven's ways of peace and security increase within you. That happened for me through the panic attacks and then through the marital struggles. Kathy and I have increasingly trusted Christ's way of losing the earthly life during perceived gaps.

Earlier in my journey during the panic attacks I believed I would literally die if I did nothing about them. Only when I stopped trying to fix myself there and waited on Christ to be with me as inner support in those places did I see that I had been under lies. The lies fell away when I no longer participated with lesser energy to fix the felt gaps. Earthly energy to fill gaps decreased, which made room for God's energy to work all things within me. Power was transferred, although it was gradual for me. Those gaps became filled with awareness of Christ and His security. If you need help to trust Christ in those places, ask one or two trusted others to stand with you to believe in Christ's goodness.

Unending scriptures emphasize Christ's sacrificial love that makes two into one during the places of perceived gaps. Bear with, forgive, endure, stand firm, hold fast. Choose God's will above earthly will during gaps. Choose wisdom above all. Above marriage, finances, or even health. Then wisdom will gather all else. Seek first the kingdom and the rest comes along with it. I just hadn't known during my panic attacks how much I still believed lies, which had caused me to focus on outcomes more than learning to rest in love alone during those places. Resting in love during circumstances that humbled my earthly nature gradually brought security and wisdom into those places, which was more of Christ.

Heavenly power is established when we become living sacrifices unto God's will, which renews our minds and transforms us inwardly during perceived gaps. Greater numbers of people are beginning to choose that narrow gate during their walk, which restores the kingdom within their souls as well as in the world around them. My marital fireworks were an ongoing journey to come face-to-face with my limited human nature so that my soul would open up and receive more of my Christ nature. I saw the necessity of continually surrendering the power of the lesser realm and turning to Christ as my power, love, and fullness.

During trials the human nature wants to rise up like the Tower of Babel to be more than it is. *We cannot escape fleshly torment while still believing the lie that we "should" be better, different, or beyond where we are.* Believing that lie demonstrates the need for more stripping works to humble that fleshly tower.

In places of torment and helplessness, people usually don't know that Christ is with and for them because they *feel* abandoned. God purposefully emphasized that He would never leave or forsake us (Heb. 13:5). Why? He knew that we would feel weak and abandoned during the stripping of the lesser nature.

The Gap Filler

Experiences of perceived abandonment are inevitable. They are part of the journey.

During significant upheaval between Kathy and me, I happened to be reading Jesus' words about trials in the following passages: "But these things I have spoken to you, so that when their hour comes, you may *remember* that I told you of them. These things I did not say to you at the beginning, because I was with you" (Jn. 16:4); "But I tell you the truth, *it is to your advantage that I go away*; for if I do not go away, the Helper will not come to you; but *if I go*, I will send Him to you" (Jn. 16:7); "A little while, and you will no longer see Me; and again a little while, and you will see Me" (Jn. 16:16).

I know that Jesus was referring to the cross that would physically take Him away from His disciples, and that the Holy Spirit would be sent because of Him going away. I believe that too. I just know clearly between me and Christ that He *also* meant for that to be about His ongoing kingdom way of increase within us.

I saw this with clarity one morning. Without trying to work at anything in my mind, the bride's experience in the Song of Songs popped into my mind connected to the above passages. I saw the bride's intermittent experiences of perceived separation from the Bridegroom as a full parallel to Jesus' words about "going away and returning." In the Song of Songs (5:6-8; 6:2-3) the Bridegroom treasures His bride and yet periodically goes away "to gather more lilies" (meaning brides). I understand and fully relate to the bride's experiences of agony at points when she cries out "Where is my Beloved?" The Bridegroom, though "going away" periodically to gather other lilies, never betrays or abandons His bride. He is fully committed to her and treasures her the whole time. Different than the human body, the Spirit is many places at the same time.

Jesus told us that He never leaves or abandons us. He is in and through all things and is able to be with us as He gathers other brides. In fact, we carry Him within us! But our intermittent human experiences of knowing Love's security and at other times having no clue that we are loved demonstrate that the Lord may occasionally withdraw His *felt* presence. We definitely experience times of not encountering His felt presence even when seeking Him. This is purposeful. Why?

I am most convicted of flesh's futility when I periodically do not sense Christ's felt presence, because I then sometimes feel helpless or abandoned. The times that feel like Christ is not with me is how He exposes and uproots more of my flesh nature. Conviction of fleshly futility must come, not through a one-time event for me, but through intermittent periodic experiences. Then I continually shift from kingdom to kingdom.[4]

I don't believe that conviction and true spiritual awakening can happen without the false being exposed, which only happens through the periodic times of Christ withdrawing His felt presence. In those places of conviction, there is finally space for me to receive more of Christ into my soul. I'm sure that you're aware of the saying that alcoholics don't change until they first deeply acknowledge they have a problem. That is the flesh nature. During conviction my flesh nature finally becomes humbled enough for my soul to further let go of it and embrace more of Christ.

The times of felt helplessness remind me to accept the rhythm of life. Accept the ups and downs, the felt mountain tops and the helpless experiences. God subjected the whole world to periodic futility to transform people into true sons and daughters that walk in their Christ nature (Rom. 8:26-27).

The Spirit intercedes and helps us during our weakness.[5] The Spirit's groanings that are "too deep for words" relate to Christ's finished works that surpass our present knowledge or abilities. During times of weakness, the Spirit takes hold of us together with Him to shift us from kingdom to kingdom. From earthliness to heavenliness. Do not despise times of weakness.

Only through becoming like a child in places of lack can I further enter the kingdom. Only through squarely admitting human limitation and my need for Christ to give-for where I have nothing to give will I begin finding true comfort. The taskmaster's torment, shoulds, and accusations then stop. I stop. I cease striving in the flesh and become aware that God is God in that place. I have fasted from the old and then the New, the Alpha (initially like an infant within me), begins to take root in that place.

After holding fast through each trial I face, I come to see what Christ is working, which then girds me up with His grace. I come to say in that new place just like Jesus said (Jn. 14:30), "The prince of this world is coming, he has no hold on Me." I see that I do not need to save myself because I have awakened enough to know through experience that Christ and His love are greater than death. I also begin to see that the world's greatest power, which is death, has lost its sting. I see that death is only an illusion, a lie.

Patiently holding fast and trusting that Christ is with me and for me during the trials provides the space and time for the Spirit to work within me. Jesus told us that during the times that He "goes away," the Spirit takes of Him and gives to us (Jn. 16:14-15). He is the gap filler. Most of the time we will not *feel* Him giving to us in the midst of our weakness. It is by faith, but I fully know it to be true now through my experiences.

Even though many people are awakened overall and *carry* the fullness of Christ, Jesus told us to ask for more of the Holy Spirit. Why? Embracing more of Christ's infiniteness is an ongoing journey. We embrace more of Christ as we overcome more of the flesh during periods of weakness. The lies of the lesser nature fall away when we no longer participate with or feed that lesser nature. It further comes to ruin.

Dispossessing the false flesh nature from within me established more humility. I didn't simply dispossess more of the flesh nature during my journey. That was and is beyond me. Dispossessed flesh nature came through God-ordained trials. My part was to participate with God during the trials.[6]

Circumstances beyond my control caused humility. Flesh nature became further ruined, and automatically within, I more humbly looked to God as the Greater. He alone became my way of kingdom enlargement. Ever since being awakened further in this way, I can't help but to see the tremendous pressure people put on flesh nature within self and those around them.

Jesus emphasized the necessary process of us becoming broken to receive true authority. He said that we would receive authority in the same way He received authority and stated (Rev. 2:26), "And he who overcomes, and keeps My works [will] until the end [of flesh nature], to him will I give power [also translated authority] …" Do you want true authority? Overcoming and enduring the breaking of flesh nature is the way, just as it was for Jesus, and it is an ongoing work.

"The end" means "an impost or levy as paid." The price of true power or authority is the loss of flesh nature. The authority, works, and will of the lesser nature must be emptied for our souls to be filled with (or given) the Other. That periodic emptying of our flesh nature continually establishes humility, which then entrusts us with greater authority. Receiving more of the Greater goes hand in hand with losing the lesser.[7]

Jesus said (Matt. 12:8), "For the Son of Man is Lord of the Sabbath." The Sabbath is about rest. The Greater enlarges our souls only when we rest or fast from our earthly will, effort, and works. Resting during trials is the proof that God has established trust and humility within us, which allows space for the Greater to govern within us. Wisdom and humility, after being tested by fire, become our companions.

CHAPTER 10

Greater Help and Mysteries

Resurrection Doors

Greater help is from above as well as from the fuller body of Christ, which is beyond the individual. Greater help also feels good at times, and other times it does not.

God kept directing me during my journey to maintain a balance of gaining support along with embracing various difficulties and counterparts for fuller awakening. I learned the necessity of not only embracing Kathy's unique differences but also the contributions of the various people that God placed around me in my life. Some were support, some were sandpaper. (I chuckled as I was refining this section because I saw a train going by hauling many box cars labeled "Triple Crown," ... which again reminded me of spiritual champions receiving greater help through eating crumbs of Christ wherever they can find them!)

What is important to know about receiving this greater help? The writer of Hebrews (13:5-9) refers to a psalmist's words about the Lord being our helper and states this right after saying that Christ will never leave or forsake us (Heb. 13:5-9; Psm. 118:7-24).[1]

Why does the Hebrews writer directly connect God as helper and the fact that He won't leave or forsake us?

God most helps and delivers us through His stripping works, which is most when we *feel* abandoned. Sometimes as if we will die (just like the psalmist felt).

God especially helps us when we feel alone and forsaken. That's why the Hebrews writer then stated in verse 9 that God gives grace *to our hearts* (rather than providing the earthly things we sometimes think we need). Knowing this helped orient me towards opening up to Christ inwardly during the trials rather than looking outwardly.

Christ calls the Spirit our Helper. He wants to strengthen us by His grace in our inner being during life's difficulties. This directly parallels God's fiery works that take us from hell's nakedness inwardly to being clothed in Christ. From death to life.

The psalmist's and the writer of Hebrews' meaning of the Spirit as our Helper directly tie into God's first use of the word "helper." Eve was Adam's suitable helper and the Holy Spirit is our Suitable Helper, which means a Counterpart that is sometimes our support and sometimes being oppositional to cause us to become. All is for standing in more of who we truly are, which is true life.

Counterparts are resurrection doors or gates. Those doors are not only about a spouse but about the fuller body of Christ.[2] They are opposite sides that are part of God's discipline to us *where we must love sacrificially to receive our help.* We must first love and honor the spiritual over the natural, which is our door to resurrection life.

Several people around me recognized my need for them to simply stand with me in trust of Christ's birthing works that were happening through Kathy's and my struggles. That support caused me to stay more grounded in Christ and to hold fast even when the way was very difficult. Other people challenged the path I felt called to by Christ. That was the sandpaper that caused birth in areas I couldn't see at the time. The sandpaper caused me "to become." I came to stand in Christ in new areas because of again having to turn to Christ to be my enough. But awakening mainly occurred as I first gave Christ a drink (whether in myself or others), and then my thirsty soul found drink. This is symbolized in the scriptures when Elijah asked a starving woman and her son to first give him food and drink, as well as portrayed in Jesus' parable about the servant first serving the master before eating and drinking (Lk. 17:7-8; 1 Kgs. 17:7-13). Occasionally giving Christ a drink in others during their confrontations of me was through me validating them that they were risking to follow Christ's leading as well as they could.

Suitable help originally came from a rib, which was not just about Eve an individual woman. Adam called her "Woman" because she was bone of his bones, and really side of his side. "Woman" (*ishshah*) is the feminine counterpart for "man in general." In other words, Eve or Woman symbolizes the Church, which is about the true spirit person within all people. That is why Adam then referred to her as the mother of all the living (Gen. 3:20). We have many sides of our side, which are our counterparts throughout the body of Christ on this earth. Jesus said that He was the door, which means we as His body of people are also doors of Christ's fullness for one another.

I saw great irony in Christ initially working earthly separation between Kathy and me to gradually increase our unity, as well as with those connected to us. In spite of how much separation occurred relationally among various people during our upheaval, Christ brought higher unity and wholeness in the end. To me, that still leaves me shaking my head in wonderment.[3]

Christ desires that the bones in His body, the various counterparts, would rise as one. We must be knit together in love and gather "this and that" rather than remaining in positions of "this versus that." The body of Christ, like Jacob, will remain one-sided and walk with a limp until we learn to sacrificially love our counterparts. Others' truth should not negate ours, and ours should not negate theirs. An eye saying it has no need of an ear is foolish. Christ's kingdom will not fully come or be visible without us going through Him as the gate, which is also through the many sides, really doors, of Him as His body on this earth.

I was most frustrated during my seasons of difficulty when I encountered people that maintained strong opinions that disallowed others' voices. Especially when I was not allowed voice and treated as if only one of the two views was "right" (and it was not mine!). Consideration that both parties needed heard about valid points could not get received at times.

"This versus that" must eventually fall away because Christ's kingdom will not be in some inner room alone or only out in the desert. Stop chasing after one thing *or* another. When you get there He will be gone. Rather, Christ's kingdom will be like lightning that lights up the sky from one end clear to the other (Lk. 17:23-24). No gaps. Christ will manifest light from here all the way to there, and from this all the way to that. Christ is the beginning and the end, and He brings fullness to everything in between.

Some people will say to wait. Others will say to act. Some will work to heal people. Others will help people allow God's ordained suffering that births more of the kingdom. All have their place depending upon God's season or purpose. Ask for discernment so we can gather.

Christ wants to gather us, and yet, our differences, struggles, and wounds will still be part of the way forward as a body of people. Others treating me like only their point mattered was part of the struggle to birth Christ's higher ways, where life always comes after death. After the other disciples told Thomas that they had seen the resurrected Lord, Thomas said (Jn. 20:25), "Unless I see the nail marks in His hands and put my finger where the nails were, and put my hand into His side, I will not believe it."

Thomas' statement is prophetic and portrays the body of Christ as a whole. We simply won't believe in the fullness of Christ unless we've touched death and seen His resurrection life over the power of death.

Couples in conflict listen very closely when I share about Kathy's and my struggles. They understand and believe in life after death when they get to touch my real wounds and experiences that parallel theirs, and yet, they get to see me standing on the other side. That is what happened when Jesus told Thomas (Jn. 20:27), "Put your finger here; see My hands. Reach out your hand and *put it into My side*. Stop doubting and believe."

How do we stop doubting and believe? Jesus already told us. We must touch one another's wounds. We are to reach out our hand and put it into Christ's side. Just like Eve came from Adam's side, the bride (body of Christ) has come from Jesus' pierced side. Christ's wounded side is the bride, where there is profound healing. We are healed by His wounds, not just when He was physically on the cross, but also from us on our own crosses as we sacrificially love and touch one another in our wounded places.

Jesus wanted Thomas to *touch* His wounds, and He wants us touch one another's wounds. That is Jesus' deeper meaning about us touching His wounded side. We are His many sides (counterparts), and Jesus wants us to intimately know one another's wounds and resurrection life in those places, which then brings fullness and healing to each other. That's when we are overwhelmed with Christ who reigns over all death, and we will say just like Thomas said upon seeing the evidence of the resurrected Christ (Jn. 20:28), "My Lord, and My God."

Do you want to see the resurrected Christ? Regularly?

We will see the resurrected Christ to the extent that we begin knowing each other's death marks that become marks of resurrection glory. We only get to see the resurrection glory in and through one another when we reach our hand into the various sides or counterparts and touch their wounds. And we must be vulnerable and let them touch ours. That is true intimacy. Let us learn to love sacrificially like Christ loved the Church. Let us be doors of resurrection life.

Lust versus Trust

Sacrificial love is the foundation of the body of Christ rising as one. Christ' sacrificial love helps us to trust God's love that wants to be with us in spite of our inadequacies, blindness, and hurtful ways. Christ also works to express His sacrificial love through us with those who do not know His love in any given moment. Sometimes that was Kathy and sometimes that was me who did not know His love, which was when we needed others to sacrificially love us so that we would remember His love during the worst of the trials. Through others' love of us, Kathy and I gradually became better at serving one another in our wounded places that had not known love.

At times, when I knew Christ's unwavering love in the midst of upheaval, I was able to be a vessel that imparted that love even while receiving hurtful communication. I saw that the key for me being able to love Kathy (and others) sacrificially was whether or not I was grounded in Christ's secure love at the moment. Greater help was available when I was aware of greater love.

Knowing Christ's secure love personally allows you to become an avenue of His sacrificial love for others in their wounded places that have not known love. You are able to act and speak on behalf of the very people persecuting you when you know without doubt that God fully loves you regardless of your difficulties or inadequacies.

Clarity about being loved by the Father was how Jesus sacrificially loved others while being persecuted, and our clarity about being fully loved allows us to express Christ's sacrificial love. Through security we become able to discern and caringly respond to the deeper truth of a matter in a person rather than to their reactive hurtful flesh nature.

I would not have loved sacrificially very well during my struggles had I believed in an angry wrathful god (later I address a prevailing misunderstanding of God's wrath). Believing in an angry god actually *causes* fear and perceived separation, which is a root of all unloving behaviors. It is a root of all sin. I am more likely to hide, run, fight, control, deceive, or maneuver when I don't know that a truly loving God is for me. From fear I lust; I hold onto or covet (like the fearful servant in the parable of the talents; see Matt. 25:25).

Believing in an angry demanding god is also the source of conflict and wars on this earth. Why? That kind of god causes us to lust for what we don't have or think we won't get. I don't just mean sexual lust. I mean lust for whatever a demanding god might withhold from us.

Lust covets; it always wants more and says "I must have!" Lust knows no love. It cares not for the welfare of another but only that it gets what it wants. Most people view lust as only about sexual matters. But lust is the core of flesh nature. Lust is the reason for the lack of love on this earth. Lust even causes people to selfishly demand godly things.

I can walk in trust, however, when I begin with a truly loving God in my mind. I am freed from the desperation, lust, and sin of the flesh nature when I am secure. Just watch secure children who know they are loved versus insecure ones and you will see this spiritual truth.

We as a people will unfortunately encounter many stripping works to free us from our ways and views until we embrace a more loving God. I believe that God is moving more noticeably than prior seasons to awaken us to His greater love. As we are awakened corporately to a loving God through His stripping works, those difficult works decrease for those who are awakened (just like when the prodigal son awakened to love; see Lk. 15:17-20).

During my difficulties I experienced others being frantic for me, treating me as if God would harshly oppose me for my "belligerence." Some people pressured me to walk certain directions that I didn't sense as God's path (such as don't wait, act now, and work at pursuing and loving Kathy all the more). Some people said that the enemy got hold of us and caused havoc. Other people said that it was simply choice, that it was because of free will and stubbornness on both our parts. A select few who had been through extensive fireworks said that it was God going further and that He was trustworthy to bring greater spiritual good as we kept surrendered to Him.

I just know experientially that I would have stared outwardly at "problematic Kathy" had I thought it was simply because of her stubbornness, sin, or free will. Or, I would have judged myself harshly had I thought that my own sin and stubbornness was the ultimate obstacle. Both of those views would have treated us as if we were the center of the universe and that God was not greater (especially when we were crying out to Him). I also know that I would not have maintained peace through much of this fire had I believed the enemy was causing havoc beyond God's sovereignty. I don't believe that our marriage would have been restored had I viewed life in these lesser ways.

All I knew at a practical level was that communication could not work. Being together could not work. Nor was it going to work for a season. I knew that trying to force outcomes would only restrict or prolong our awakening. I sensed that a season of freedom from one another was needed to unhook from old familiar ways to awaken into higher unknown ones.

I also knew that our situation was beyond human control for both Kathy and me. I believed that this season was for higher purposes (for marriages, relationships, and this book). I didn't believe that Kathy should be beyond where she was. At the same time I surely wasn't perfect. I got frustrated and angry with painfully repetitive dynamics during times of contact.

My initial goal was not to engage with one another when fleshly reactivity was too heightened to allow any awareness of Christ. During heightened fleshly activity, lust for certain outcomes increased and sacrificial love decreased. I knew I was to stay surrendered and alert to what God was after in me (and regarding Kathy for my prayers for her). Space was also needed so that I wasn't as available to become Kathy's focal point. The space helped both of us to pay more attention to God and what He wanted to work in our hearts. But I greatly added to Kathy's and others' perceptions that I wasn't supportive of her when I encouraged continued space during the heightened upheaval. In spite of that perception I knew that being together and trying to communicate (even with help) was far more destructive. I was mainly convicted to pray regularly about God stripping away the false in both of us to awaken us more to the true.

Eye of the Beholder

My marital fireworks looked dark to many, as if there was no higher purpose in them. But I was in awe of the glorious life those trials regularly produced. I literally experienced a constant birthing of revelations. Those revelations occurred because I embraced the trials as purposeful for birthing greater heavenly life (which was also God's grace to me). Greater help was available as I trusted God's greater sovereignty, which, to me, meant that no lapses of God's involvement existed.

The cross was the center of God's eternal purpose carried out in Jesus. This eternal purpose is the way of laying down our lesser life during tribulations. Our tribulations awaken God's higher glory in us and in all who witness faith during suffering.

No darkness or trial occurs apart from God's sovereignty for stripping away the lesser to free us into the greater. God gave much grace to me for maintaining this perspective during my trials. God is after faith in His unwavering goodness through all things. That's the way Jesus walked.

Jesus warned us about what our eye focuses on and which master we will serve (Matt. 6:21-24). Will I serve the earthly life and its goodness (not just money) or will I let go of it and serve Christ's higher realm? My eye is bad and I become filled with darkness when I serve the earthly life. Then when it does not give me what I want, fear, hopelessness, and anger begin knocking at the door. Earthly events appear dark or evil when they do not cooperate with me; and it seems as if God has abandoned or betrayed me. My eye is bad and the darkness proceeds from within, as Jesus said.

But my body is filled with light when my eye is good. The word "good" means clear, single, or pure. No obstructions. No idols. Even in the midst of trials the pure in heart shall see God just like Jesus saw the Father during His trials (Matt. 5:8; Jn. 5:19). The way is clear for Christ's higher realm in me when I do not serve the earthly life.

I have looked through both good and bad eyes during my fireworks. I remained at peace when I maintained a position of letting go of earthly outcomes for receiving whatever God appeared to be working. That was difficult, but crucial. I instantly became filled with grief or anxiety when I wanted or could not hold onto an earthly outcome. My pain skyrocketed as soon as I focused on wanting my marriage restored, wanting people's understanding, wanting clear direction from God in Kathy's or my timeframe (this was a big one), or wanting people's judgment to stop. But my life and walk with God became peaceful as soon as I let go of all expectations of what "should be." I could see and know Christ during trials when I surrendered the earthly life.

Those who let go of the earthly can see and hear Christ because they hold onto no obstructions. The single in heart shall see God. Great unity is possible when we no longer see anything of this earth as ours. No individual ownership frees us to love one another more fully.

The scriptures say (Acts 4:32-33), "All the believers were one in heart and mind. *No one claimed that any of his possessions was his own*, but they shared everything they had. With great power the apostles continued to testify to the resurrection of the Lord Jesus, and much grace was upon them all."

Look at Christ's glory and grace that poured forth through His people! Their minds maintained no earthly possessions or identity, which caused them to have one mind. No obstructions existed; their eyes were clear. No separation existed between them and God or one another. Jesus' words had become true about them (Lk. 18:29-30): "… no one who has left home or wife or brothers or parents or children for the sake of the kingdom of God will fail to receive many times as much in this age and, in the age to come, eternal life."

Heaven had come to earth through losing the earthly life and serving the heavenly life.

In pondering these higher ways of heaven during my difficulties, I realized that much of my pain was caused by what my eyes focused on and not by what occurred in the world around me. I saw that there really wasn't any darkness outside me; outer darkness had no power over me when I stayed awake. Jesus' words came to mind (Mk. 7:23), "... evil things proceed from within and defile the man."

That is the flesh nature, not the true. That is what defiles people from within. All outer darkness is caused by people's inner darkness; it is *created* by our inner darkness. Fear of outer darkness (which leads to lust) causes all the fighting in this world. But the fear is from within.

Participating with fear causes separation and hinders communication and love. The only way for humanity's fear to be uprooted is Jesus' way of the cross that lays down one's life. Fearfully fighting for earthly outcomes stops through the way of the cross, and the cross awakens resurrection life. Love makes a way and defeats our fears through the cross' way of surrendering earthly rights. We are fallible and will experience fear at times. Accept our human weakness. That is not the problem. The problem is when we participate with fear ... when we allow fear to make our decisions.

I become a place of peace for the world when I no longer let fear lead me. I am a vessel of peace when I no longer fight against outer darkness. Some people fight an outward devil all the time, and it will never end except through the cross that no longer fights against outer darkness. Jesus didn't fight. He trusted and surrendered to whatever He sensed the Father was working.

I regain security during difficulties when I see all outer darkness as God's faithful trials to strip me from my lesser nature to awaken me further into who I truly am. *And whatever trials they may be, I miraculously no longer experience them as intolerable suffering when I lay down my earthly life.* Instead, relationship with Christ and His inner support gradually increase during the trials when I surrender into Him. I am no longer alone.

My inner experience of suffering was only unbearable when I wanted certain earthly outcomes. My one son said simply to me, "Suffering is horrible mostly when we want something different or more than being with Christ." Suffering occurred most when my eye was bad because of wanting the earthly life to serve me (which caused me to perceive outer darkness).

We experience on this earth Jesus' words about being cast into outer darkness when our fleshly eyes perceive outer darkness that will not serve us. Why? The darkness is really from within as soon as we lose all peace because of staring at "outer darkness" that won't cooperate with us.

The outer darkness that Jesus referred to is our fleshly outer man that decays and doesn't know love. Inability to know love or God *is* the scary outer darkness, which comes from being in a fleshly mindset.

Do you have difficult trials? Do you feel fearful, alone, or abandoned during those trials? As if God is no longer available? I did, and still do when I temporarily lose awareness. If you feel abandoned by God, it usually indicates that you are looking with fleshly eyes at an outer darkness that you think is beyond God's sovereignty. You are already in the outer darkness of your own flesh nature when you perceive something or someone outside you as outer darkness.

God powerfully changed me during this lengthy season of fire. I came to know during the midst of powerful out-of-control moments that God still governed. God wasn't dependent upon me, Kathy, free will, or sin. He was in and above it all. He worked *all* things together for Kathy and me in spite of *anything*. (I believe that I would convey this same message even if God had not ultimately brought Kathy's and my marriage back together.)

Perfect Prisons

When Kathy had moved out, I hadn't initially trusted God's sovereignty. I had felt betrayed like Joseph.

Joseph was sold as a slave by his brothers and eventually ended up in prison. Higher than his brothers' sins and free will, God governed Joseph's earthly prison to make him a refuge of wisdom and food for the world. God also caused Pharaoh to give Joseph authority over his princes. The scriptures say (Psm. 105:17-22):

"He [God] sent a man before them, Joseph, who was sold as a slave. They afflicted his feet with fetters, he himself was laid in irons; *until the time that his word came to pass,* the word of the Lord tested him. The king sent and released him, the ruler of peoples, and set him free. He made him lord of his house, and ruler over all his possessions, *to imprison his princes at will, that he might teach his elders wisdom.*"

Joseph remained in an earthly prison until the time that God's word for Joseph came to pass. It was a God-ordained time for awakening Joseph to wisdom beyond the world. Then Pharaoh released Joseph and gave him authority to imprison his elders to teach them wisdom. Wow, imprisoning people to teach them wisdom. Don't you have some people you'd like to do that with?

All joking aside, I see a higher truth about what God sovereignly worked in Joseph's life. We powerfully thirst for God's higher realm when earthly ways are made unattainable ... usually for a lengthy time, which requires patience. God sometimes gives special tasks to people who have already experienced His goodness and will hold the course during suffering. That was Joseph.

As I briefly mentioned, Kathy and I received prophetic words numerous years earlier that predicted our enduring through a difficult season. The only parts that seemed clear were that I would be immovable (standing fast) and that Kathy would be faithful through the difficulties. Only in the beginning of these fireworks did I "coincidentally" see copies of these prophetic words. They finally made complete sense to me and also provided additional encouragement for persevering through the trials.

We endured an earthly prison that caused us to thirst for and wait on God alone. You can see numerous psalmists in the scriptures who cried out to and waited on God during trials. They sensed when no earthly answers were available and waited. I, too, regularly received God's higher answers and mysteries through waiting on Him while He stripped away the earthly fog over a period of time.

Joseph endured prison for over two years (like Kathy and me). He attained God's wisdom and higher ways through his earthly prison. Joseph learned that earthly prisons were God's ways to gain unseen wisdom, to the extent that he imprisoned Pharaoh's princes to teach them wisdom.

Isn't receiving God's wisdom only for those who look to the God of the Bible? Or is it possible that all hearts are created to thirst beyond the earth for God when they encounter earthly prisons? Why else would Joseph imprison Pharaoh's elders to learn wisdom? Doesn't everyone who is open to learning during trials become awakened to God's deeper ways and wisdom? Regardless of label? I have witnessed many of my previous clients gaining tremendous wisdom when they embraced life's prisons to glean whatever could be gained.

That was my experience as well. Prison taught me wisdom that broke my current rules. That wisdom took me beyond labels and some of my traditional views. I saw that God's wisdom is not limited to a select few who hold to a certain tradition, view, or label. God's wisdom cannot be bound by words or boxes.

God's wisdom is wisdom. Christ is that wisdom that isn't bound by rules or labels. That's why He is referred to as the name above all names. People who may not know Christ gain more of Him as they gain wisdom through their earthly prisons (though they may not know they are embracing aspects of Him).

The poor are chosen by God to be made rich in faith (Jam. 2:5). I could not turn to and know God's fuller love when Kathy's and others' love already filled my heart. There was no room for me to know Christ's greater love when I experienced people's love of me as fully good.

I could not see beyond the world's limits and fullness till the Rule-Breaker broke those ways that filled me. The scriptures say (Psm. 69:33), "For the Lord hears the needy, and does not despise His who are prisoners." God heard the needy. He heard Kathy and me. We gradually awakened to His mysteries through earthly prisons where our prior ways no longer worked.

Wisdom teaches me constantly now because I no longer see trials as bad. When I see Christ in the midst of the trials, I begin to see Him everywhere. When I know Christ especially through "the fellowship of His sufferings," I begin to know His resurrection life that's greater than suffering or death. Earthly trials and loss then awaken me to the kingdom's greater love, and I am able to see Christ gathering all things into Him. Nothing is unreachable to Christ who is in and reigns over all things.

Joseph learned this wisdom when he no longer viewed his situation as if his brothers, Egypt, or Pharaoh were acting on their own against him. Even when acting from sin and free will none of them were beyond God's sovereign domain. No true conspiracy existed even though Joseph's brothers secretly conspired against him. It was not personal from God's perspective; it was God working higher goodness through all things. But you cannot see this when you value earthly life above heavenly life, or when you think that death or other tragedies can hurt the true.

God speaks about His utter sovereignty through Isaiah (45:6-7): "That men may know *from the rising to the setting of the sun* that there is no one besides Me. I am the LORD, and there is no other, the One forming light and creating darkness, causing well-being and creating calamity; I am the LORD who does all these." Isn't He saying that there is only one God Who is above all? I don't think that God could have made this any clearer.

Do you want to walk like Jesus did? Outer darkness could not touch Jesus, Who was Spirit within the body of flesh. He maintained power over darkness because He walked with security, love, and life. He trusted the Father's sovereignty and goodness even during catastrophic earthly darkness. Jesus' security was His trust in the Father's sovereignty and unwavering love.

God worked in the midst of every bit of darkness I encountered over the two and a half years of marital struggles. Whether or not it appeared like sin or the enemy governing Kathy's steps or mine, she was ultimately to be where she was. I was to be where I was. The earlier prophetic word about us enduring difficulties conveyed that. Only Christ frees and awakens us from the sinful lesser nature. We are to receive life's difficulties as God's works to awaken us, and we are where we are *until* He awakens us. We cannot rush the awakening of life or love (although we can ask and pray to be awakened to join with His works).

Nothing ever justifies or excuses sin and its harmful effects. But we are not freed from sin at a practical level until God gives grace to awaken us from those lesser ways. Whatever I am not awakened from is sovereignly purposed to affect Kathy and all who are around me. And vice versa. That is what is meant by Paul's statement that grace abounds all the more where there's sin (Rom. 5:20). That is why Paul also said not to receive in vain God's grace for working together with Him in all things (which often included seemingly senseless things; see 2 Cor. 6:1-5).

I will awaken from lesser ways in God's time, and meanwhile, He will use those lesser ways to work what He wants in Kathy's life (and those around us). God purposes our crosses and any accompanying darkness in our lives to bring greater light.

Mysteries

God taught me much about unity during my marital upheaval. God broke my old mindsets and restrictive rules about how the world worked, and He did that through me experiencing disunity with Kathy, the person I most cherished on this earth. I look now with hindsight and know that this disunity was to awaken me to an even greater unity than I had yet known. I saw how God kept using counterparts to teach me: lack of love to know love, emptiness to know fullness, and disunity to know unity.

Living in the realm of signs, wonders, and miracles like Jesus did comes through this greater unity that He lived. Jesus walked in a higher unity with the Father and with all people than we have yet walked.

The scriptures say (Isa. 8:18) "Behold, I and the children whom the Lord has given me are for signs and wonders ..." Kathy's and my marriage is a sign and wonder. I know without doubt that nothing earthly would have brought our marriage out of the pit, and I think that all who witnessed our fireworks would agree. I sensed that marital resolution would be God's sign that accompanied this book's message, kind of like the rainbow He placed in the sky after the storm Noah encountered.

Thankfully God gradually awakened me to what He was after from the beginning of our fireworks … a higher unity for Kathy and me, and for His people. We are all one, for good or for bad.

I had previously seen in the positive direction that there is only one Spirit and one body of Christ with the many differing members and gifts (Rom. 12:4-5). We may appear different but there is absolutely no separation even when we treat one another as different or separate.

I had also known intellectually that this spiritual truth of being one was true in the negative direction. But I had not known this truth at a practical level nor had I been awakened to the implications of this truth. I only awakened after extensive fireworks and believe that I would not have awakened without them.

The scriptures say (1 Cor. 15:39), "All flesh is not the same flesh, *but there is one flesh of men*, and another flesh of beasts, and another flesh of birds, and another of fish." This verse means that there is one body of flesh nature within humanity with its many differing members, worldly ways, and sins. It is the imposter, the counterpart of the true body of Christ. It is the man of lawlessness that is to be revealed to the world (2 Thes. 2:3-7).

Two natures exist within humanity: the Christ nature and the flesh nature (for choice). And the man of lawlessness is revealed to the degree that our Christ nature is revealed on this earth.

No separation exists within humanity's flesh nature even though we appear different from one another. Your sin (flesh's lesser ways) may look different from mine, but in actuality there is no mine and yours. I agree that I will awaken more when I take responsibility to face my individual sin at any given moment. But I am not to view myself as separate and unique from the rest of flesh nature on this earth.

Viewing myself as a unique defect only increases self-judgment. There is only one flesh nature that is behind all sin. One flesh nature connects and is in all of us even though that part is the imposter.

That is why the scriptures say that all suffer when one suffers (1 Cor. 12:26). We affect one another because we are all one. The closer the connection the greater the effect. I can say to my physical body that I hate my ineffective heart, hip, or knee, but those different parts are still part of me and affect me. *They only improve when I care for them.*

Forgive me God. Forgive humanity for judging and separating from one another because of our fleshly lenses. Forgive us for staring with bad eyes at perceived outer darkness, as if others' sins are different or worse than our own. We have looked with dark eyes at ineffective knees or hearts. Then while on this earth we were cast into outer darkness (our own flesh nature) because of staring at perceived outer darkness. We have made a mess of our whole body by judging and tearing it down.

We looked at the speck in our neighbor's eye while we had a log in our own. We judged and separated so we became judged and separate. That's why Jesus said to judge not lest you be judged (Matt. 7:1). We experience what we do to another because we do it to ourselves when doing it to another. We are one. That is also how we reap what we sow (Gal. 6:7).

Do you pray for another's cancer as if it were your own? Do you pray for another's emotional struggle as if it were your struggle? Do you pray for another's sins as if those sins were your very own?

I had not. But I do now. I am glad for love's fireworks. I am glad that God awakened me.

You may likely experience from me in these writings more acceptance and love towards people and their struggles than is normal. That is because I now see with eyes of oneness that do not separate from others because of perceived outward differences. I believe that no longer judging one another is part of Christ's greater love that is to come, but it comes through seeing with eyes of oneness. Seeing our oneness heightens unity. That is how we love our neighbor as ourselves.

I previously felt deep compassion for others who struggled. But if others outwardly blamed me for actions they were doing to me at the moment, I viewed it as only them doing it. I did not pray for them as if I were the one doing it. Now I pray that way. I forgive that way.

Jesus said that the Father does not forgive us when we have not forgiven one another (Matt. 6:14). Why? It is not because the Father is angry or conditionally loving us. Rather, the Father's self-correcting way is that we reap what we sow because we are one. We don't know forgiveness when we don't forgive.

I had neither known nor walked Jesus' way that bore others' sins. You may react to my statement and think that Jesus paid the price and already dealt with sin once and for all. And that we are to focus on true life rather than sin. True.

All sin has been forgiven through Christ. But we as a people have not fully embraced this truth. Heavenly life still needs awakened at a practical level in our places of sin and death. We bring life and love to each other when we sacrificially bear with one another's sins. That allows people to *experientially* know and embrace Christ's forgiveness. That is exactly what happened for Bob who went back to his wife after living with us for four months. Bob's wife knew the truth about his miss-steps in life and then forgave him, which allowed him to know God's forgiveness. I am clear that he would not have forgiven himself otherwise, and he would have remained stuck in life.

Although I have focused on sin in the last two paragraphs, I want you to know that I am life-oriented and love-focused rather than sin-focused. I also hesitate to use the word "sin" because of the mountain of abuse we have caused one another in the name of trying to be godly. Jesus said to a woman caught in adultery (Jn. 8:11), "Then neither do I condemn you ... Go now and leave your life of sin."

No condemnation. And Jesus' words about leaving her life of sin were not another standard for her to strive for. That is the flesh nature's view that always places standards on us. The law brings death but grace brings life. Jesus' words gave her grace. Spiritual power. Jesus' words girded up this woman with higher life *to empower her* to leave her life of sin. It's as if He said to her, "My words are life, and I give you the grace and power to leave your life of bondage."

I use the word sin simply to describe flesh's lesser ways (and it is what Christians most understand but have sometimes used in condemning ways). Condemnation restricts us. My desire is to uproot condemnation about sin so that we would find grace to embrace God's love during our struggles! That's what frees us. Jesus' love freed the woman caught in adultery.

We are to bear with one another's sins because the reality is that sin will be in my face and yours at times. Why is bearing with one another's sins necessary if Christ already bore our sins? *We have many false mindsets that have not yet been broken for us to be awakened to Christ's reality that already exists.* And Christ uses His higher nature within us to break the rules of fleshly mindsets in one another.

Jesus took up our infirmities and carried our sins as His very own, not just when He was on the cross but throughout His walk on this earth (Matt. 8:16-17). Jesus showed us the way to walk. The Christ nature within us continues walking His way. The scriptures say (Gal. 6:1-2), "Brethren, even if a man is caught in any trespass, you who are spiritual, restore such a one in a spirit of gentleness; each one looking to yourself, lest you too be tempted. Bear one another's burdens [sins], and thus fulfill the law of Christ."

We most fulfill the law of Christ by bearing one another's trespasses against us. Jesus told us to love others as He has loved us. That means sacrificially. We are to pray for and forgive those who persecute us. Can we pray as if their sin against us was our very own doing?

What has our flesh nature done when others have sinned in ways we can't imagine sinning? We have judged. I have judged. But the scriptures say (Hab. 2:10), "You have devised a shameful thing for your house by cutting off many peoples; so you are sinning against yourself."

God is presently working a higher unity in humanity to transform this earth. *Seeing people as one increases unity and love.* And increased love is greater love. Greater love lays down its life for its friends.

Greater love leaves earthly security and lays down its life to establish love in places of need. Are you willing to leave your earthly security and temporarily experience another's burdensome struggle as if it were literally your own? I know that this is what Kathy needed at a deeper level from me for her to break through certain areas in her walk. That is also what I need from Kathy and others for me to break through difficult areas in my walk. Are you willing to experientially touch the blind or hopeless places within others to call forth Christ's hope, sight, and presence there? Lovingly touch people's death marks and you will bring resurrection life.

I pulled back during accusations. I had not seen Kathy's sins as my very own. She had not seen my sins as her very own. As soon as I identified with her sins as my own, I saw flashes of those sins within myself. I came to see more clearly my unique ways of separating from her *after* I identified with her separating ways as my own.

After I identified with, and prayed for, her sin of staring outwardly at my flaws – as if it were my own sin – I came to see how I also stared outwardly in fear at an imperfect part in her. I began to see the flesh nature's oneness no matter who expressed it at any given moment. I now know experientially the truth of humanity's unity of flesh nature.

Forgive me God for separating eyes that have looked at outer darkness.[4] Jesus, You taught us to pray saying "… forgive us *our* debts, as we also have forgiven our debtors …" (Matt. 6:9-15). You who were sinless said to forgive us *our* trespasses … because You took on our sin as Your very own. You became one with us in those lowly places to redeem them. Now You desire for us to walk as You walked and to pray as You prayed.

Just so you know I don't view forgiveness as me pleading with God to hold back His wrath regarding bad behaviors! That would only be evidence of me not knowing His love. I view forgiveness of sins as God removing the obstacles that have interfered with me knowing Him and His love.

Jesus healed people in one of two directions: He proclaimed healing (such as to rise and walk), and He forgave their sins (Matt. 9:5).

People believed until encountering Jesus that being blind, lame, or deaf was God's curse because of their sins. They saw a harsh God and felt like victims. So Jesus uprooted those lesser beliefs by healing them or by telling them that their sins were forgiven.

Healing *meant* forgiveness of sins to the people. Forgiveness of sins also meant or implied that they could now be healed. The two were tied together in people's minds. They knew Jesus' love either way. They received no condemnation from Him.

Forgiveness of sins means the removal of obstacles. Forgiveness is the rule-breaking Christ who breaks through our lesser beliefs and ways to heal us.

All of us need forgiveness more than we know. Turners tend to be less sensitive to people's wounds and emotions. That hurts people. Yearners tend to feel emotions and wounds more deeply and will be more reactive. Their sin will merely be easier to see. But greater or lesser degrees of sin do not matter. Seen or unseen sin does not matter. Sin directed at self or another does not matter. All sin hurts people. All of it keeps the focus on the imposter rather than on who we truly are.

You may think that you would never be abusive like another person's abusive behaviors. I disagree. Maybe you're a rare person that's never been abusive towards others, but even if that were true, surely you've been abusive towards yourself at points. I know that I've abused myself. We've all been abusive, and all abusiveness affects people. What affects one affects all.

But I haven't murdered like murderers! The only difference between my flesh nature and a murderer's is the environment that shaped that nature. My lesser nature is just as capable of murder if all I knew as a child was crime, violence, pain, and murder, especially if those ways ensured survival.

God designed us to lay down our lives for our friends. All friends. All people. No exceptions.

Jesus laid down His life for all. Atheist, Muslim, Jew, Buddhist, Christian, New Age oriented, or other spiritually-minded people. Jesus laid down His life for Judas who He knew would betray Him. God in Christ loved the world so much that He laid down His life to carry people's sins as if those sins were His very own. Complete oneness.

Christ still loves people that much. He still wants to work through His Christ nature within us to carry people's burdensome sins. We are to identify with people's sins (like He did), and we are to bring Him as the Way, Truth, and Life to their places of need. That is tremendous intercession for others. No judgment. That's how Jesus walked.

Imagine humanity walking like that! Deeper unity in all respects ... initially deeper unity in the way of knowing that all sin is also my flesh nature's sin, and then deeper unity with Him who reigns above all sin and circumstances. That was and is Christ's way.

Love's Humility

Lesser nature falls away when I know the Truth of Him as the foundation of all people. Then I no longer view people according to the distinctions of the flesh nature (2 Cor. 5:16). That is their imposter. Instead, I am to touch people's places of need (while not being consumed by it) and then intercede for them through faith in God's goodness.

This Way is the essence of effective counseling. As a counselor I do not become so involved in the client's world that I forget who I am, but I momentarily take on their world to fully identify with it. Upon identifying with the client's world I am able to discern the valued true parts versus the destructive false parts. Through that temporary unity and identification I am able to bring higher support and sight to clients, which tears down the false and establishes the true in those places.

The principle is this: you cannot remain on a precipice higher than a heavy person and easily lift them. Beautiful people who have suffered know this. Like Christ they offer a healing love rather than separation or judgment. They do not heal people from a distance. These beautiful people come to the depths with others who suffer. They have deep compassion and "suffer with" them in those places. Then that greater love that's unified with them awakens and lifts them. That is Christ's way that lowers Himself to be with others to lift them.[5]

Different Functions

During my marital upheaval I often experienced Kathy as wanting me to meet her needs, and I could neither meet those needs nor did I know how to become one with her during the intensity of the gaps. I was to initiate Christ's way of laying down so that He could fill those needs in His way and time. But I could not see how Christ wanted to meet Kathy's needs even when I surrendered to whatever He might be working. Nothing seemed to meet needs or bring resolution.

The trials continued in spite of my attempts to lay down earthly ways. I sensed that God had ordained this season for many purposes beyond marital fulfillment or individual growth. I also believed that God wanted to use our trials and their outcomes as signs and wonders. I saw that Kathy and I represented God's recently increasing stripping works. They are works that I believe will continue to increase on this earth to bring a great awakening, and I believe that this book is to help people be awakened to participate with rather than resist the stripping works.

Over time I gradually began to see how Christ desired both Kathy and me to participate with His unique works through one another. Would I recognize and honor Kathy's fire alarm about gaps no matter what her flesh nature's inability to love looked like? Would she honor my initiative to lay down our rights for God to meet our needs in His ways and time regardless of how inadequate my flesh nature appeared? These two key questions seemed helpful to us.

The scriptures say (Rom. 12:4-5), "For just as we have many members in one body and all the members *do not have the same function*, so we, who are many, are one body in Christ, and individually members one of another." We are supposed to have different functions.

We are part of one another and only become awakened through the body of Christ's fullness. But we sometimes buy the flesh nature's lie that our souls are already complete in themselves. Our souls are "journeyers" not yet completed in Christ (please hear me further).

Our souls are further completed during life's journey by embracing more of our Christ nature that we carry within us (which *is* already complete). And we most need the body of Christ's counterparts to awaken us to more of His fullness that we carry. Our awakening in various areas continuously "completes our souls" and will seem as if we've always known what was just awakened. Why? Because we carried it within but only came to know and possess it through embracing that higher nature during our journey.

I thought I already fully embraced Kathy's unique contributions. But God wanted to awaken me to higher ways of embracing Kathy's Christ nature even when I could not perceive it. He showed me higher ways to join with her in the midst of heightened fleshly reactivity. I knew that as I learned these ways that God would also awaken Kathy in these ways. I was to lead in the way of laying down my life for my friend.

At the same time, I want to be clear that Kathy also did her best to lay down her life. She, too, focused on letting go of what was important to her so she could join with what Christ was working. Kathy regularly prayed for God to awaken each of us as much as I did.

This whole ordeal was not about right or wrong but about us trying to conform to what Christ worked these fireworks *for*. God is fully sovereign and works all of life to awaken us. Regardless of what Kathy and I looked like, we were counterparts being used by Christ to strip away the old so as to awaken more of the new.

Viewing one another through eyes of judgment and separation denies God's sovereign reign and unity over all. Christ is our unity even when things feel separate. *The Lord God is one,* regardless of our perceptions or labels of Him (Mk. 12:29). Embracing God's sovereignly-placed counterparts embraces Him, and it opens a crucial doorway to His higher unity, power, and love. And yearning and turning are the core of all counterparts.

Heaven's foundation is One. The world's foundation is two but is a false foundation. Two appears as two in this world, but they are really one.

As mentioned earlier this world was created with duality (God separated day and night, above and below; see Gen. 1). Then Eve was also taken out of Adam and they ate from the tree of the knowledge of good and evil. Our flesh nature has looked through separating eyes ever since. Our flesh nature has remained under the blindness of good *versus* evil, light *versus* dark, male *versus* female, and endless versions of this *versus* that.

The scriptures say (Prov. 11:3), "The unfaithful are destroyed through their duplicity." The unfaithful is the flesh nature in all of us. It is double-minded and always separates into two for selfishly elevating "mine versus yours." Unity is far easier when we see that there is no mine versus yours. We are all one.

The number "two" in the scriptures represents earthly division that God desires to awaken into the unity of One. Jesus said (Matt. 6:24), "No one can serve two masters." This statement means that we will experience earthly division until we serve only Christ, who is one. That means serving Christ directly, and Christ in one another. We are a house divided until then.

Marriage was God's foundational covenant about two becoming one that pointed towards Christ's cross ... towards Christ's sacrificial love that is necessary for any relationship to become one. All of God's other covenants with His people depended upon the sacrificial love of "marriage."

Duality is brought to unity in Christ. Two separated humans can only live as one by abiding in the Christ nature. This way of two made into One points towards Christ and His bride coming together and also earth becoming as it is in heaven. Two always become one in Christ. Only by abiding in Christ's way of laying down our lives for our friends (counterparts) do two become one. Only then are people awakened into completion and unity.

That is why Jesus said (Matt. 18:19-20), "Again I say to you, that if two of you agree on earth about anything that they may ask, it shall be done for them by My Father who is in heaven."

This agreement is not about like-minded people agreeing. They already agreed. Two who are "separated" coming into agreement is the power behind Jesus' words. That kind of unity is the power of restoration on this earth. It fills gaps. That unified place of counterparts working together demonstrates greater fullness and power of Christ. It is His greater love.

Then Jesus added (vs. 20), "For *where two or three have gathered together* in My name, there I am in their midst." This statement expanded the two-shall-become-one into the body of Christ walking as one. Jesus' statement exhorted us to embrace counterparts, and yearning and turning are humanity's foundational counterparts. That was the work God most did in Kathy and me to bring restoration. Often the yearner more fully discerns areas of need but then must embrace the turner's gift of pausing rather than reacting so they can join together with what Christ desires to establish in those places of need.

Resilience

People who are resilient come through trials and land on their feet. God gave grace to Kathy and me to weather our storms. A rapidly growing body of research on resilience points towards my emphasis on embracing counterparts, which I believe was foundational for us surviving. The center of resilience is "Be still and become aware." Doesn't that statement sound familiar? The scriptures say (Psm. 46:10), "Be still, and know that I am God."

During crises when you are usually not as aware of God I would say, "Be still and become aware that God is God … be still and become aware of Him and what He is working on your behalf during your out-of-control circumstances." That is your strength and resilience for learning higher skills that crises or trials call for. That is also why people on earth who look to God are referred to as "the called." They are called to learn and walk in His higher ways, and trials are used to awaken them.

On the one hand, resilience is about pausing or being still (putting on the breaks) during trials so as not to react blindly to one's situation or inner felt experiences. Military Special Forces individuals are more able to remain calm rather than to react in crises and, through training, become even more resilient. That most symbolizes the turner as well as my inclination during difficulties. That "way" of resilience is about learning to unhook from automatic reactions that are often less effective during crises.

On the other hand, resilience is about increasing one's awareness during trials by fully experiencing the reality of the situation, which then provides greater discernment about what the particular trials call for. That is the yearner's fuller awareness that must unite with the turner's pause during crises or difficulties to awaken people to higher ways. These two aspects of resilience are foundational for Christ's kingdom to expand within us.

God is after resilience in His people. Christ most embodies these two core aspects of resilience that are evident in yearning and turning. Christ emptied Himself to be in touch with need and then brought fullness through turning to His Father's higher rights. "Christ emptied" is awareness of need and gap (yearning), and then "Christ as sacrificial love for His bride" joins with places of need and holds fast to God's higher realm to fulfill those places (turning). That is the core of what Christ awakened in me during my trials.

CHAPTER 11

Wings in the Flames

Healing is in His Wings

During heightened periods of conflict Kathy and I often felt like we were on the fringes with nowhere solid to stand. But the fringes were are healing. The scriptures in this chapter have come alive for me because they very much validate my experiences of how deeper healing occurred for us.

Words are only symbols of the unseen, the real. The scriptures as a whole symbolize what is wider, longer, higher, and deeper than we can see or communicate. I now see powerful symbolism in the Malachi verse (4:2; KJV), "… the Sun of Righteousness shall arise with healing in His wings …" This is not about Christ equipped with a pair of healing-anointed wings. Deeper spiritual meaning is behind these words.

"Wings" means edge, extremity, wing, border, corner, end, feather, or uttermost part, and it comes from the root "to project laterally, to withdraw or be removed." Removed? Surprising isn't it? Malachi's statement about healing in God's wings means that we receive healing when we are put at the extremes. Removed to the fringes, where nothing earthly can heal us so that heaven can.

We are healed by being put in situations beyond our current ability or control. The fringes awaken us.

Although we carry Christ's limitless nature, our souls usually must experience the end of our lesser nature to awaken to that greater nature. In each aspect of our life God awakens or plants more of His Christ nature within our souls when we turn to Him in place of the earthly realm. That's why God's river that comes from under the threshold of the temple and pours into the desert increases in the latter days to a height that is beyond human ability to cross (Ezek. 47:5). That river symbolizes a spiritual unseen one.

What kinds of experiences do you most dread? I dislike situations that are beyond me, beyond my current abilities or comfort level. Why? Those extremes expose my weakness, and I feel naked and inadequate. Extremes cause me to have to depend on something or Someone beyond me.

I felt vulnerable and saw my inadequacy very plainly when Kathy and I brought Bob to live with us and were unable to heal him. Communication didn't work. Medication and counseling didn't work. Love and support and all the prayers we could muster up didn't seem to work. We knew that human effort could not touch the situation. We were removed to the fringes where we no longer experienced God's felt presence for extended periods. But those extremes produced healing for each of us beyond what any of us knew we needed.

Insurmountable circumstances forced us to acknowledge weakness, emptiness, and need, which made room for Christ to further awaken His wisdom, ways, and fullness in those places. I now see that God desired periodically to put us at the fringes, edges, and extremes – in situations beyond our current ability – so that He could establish more of His kingdom in place of earthly effort and ability. Current rules and ways got broken while God established more of His higher ways within us.

As is evident throughout the scriptures, stretching experiences are necessary to enlarge us. How can we awaken to Christ's *greater* love and works when situations remain within our current ability? God uses the extremes to call forth the greater within us. As our souls unite with the greater during the extremes, we are healed, restored, redeemed, spiritually lifted, and awakened into more of Christ. Each of those words points towards the exchange that happens as we unite with Christ during our extreme situations.

Here are a few key passages related to God healing us through the fringes or extremes: "touched the fringe of His cloak and was healed" (Matt. 9:20)[1]; "the train [hem or fringe] of His robe filling the temple" (Isa. 6:1); Boaz spread the corner (fringe) of his cover over Ruth (Ruth 3:9); and Jesus Christ is the cornerstone (the stone that heals us when we are placed in the corner, edge, or fringe; Isa. 28:16; Eph. 2:20). We are healed as other foundations no longer work during the difficulties and He becomes established as our true foundation. This is not a one-time event but an ongoing journey.

My initial reaction during difficulties was to think that I needed a situation to turn out a certain way for life to be good. I have found that Christ usually wanted me to surrender first and do nothing to make certain outcomes occur. As I did so and became still enough to simply be with Christ in those places, I became strengthened to see what He was working and to participate with Him there. Sometimes I saw that nothing needed done whatsoever. Other times I stepped with what I sensed Christ was working. Either way, I became lifted spiritually as I first surrendered to simply be with Christ.

Suffering in the extremes continually gave me knew eyes. The scriptures kept coming together into fuller unity the more Christ washed my feet.[2] I was to let Christ wash me through the extremes, which happened mostly through Kathy; and He most used me to wash her feet as well.

Christ used many extreme situations at my home and my job to wash away more aspects of my earthly nature during the marital struggles. My job included teaching, presenting at conferences and workshops, hearing others' deep struggles, and making many significant decisions, all of which occurred while my personal life had been shattered to pieces. That shattering had caused my regular job activities to be extreme situations where I could no longer go about life as usual. I could now only make it through those duties by constantly taking free moments to be centered in Christ again, as well as through finding support from others. I also became more real and vulnerable with people, to the extent that it was safe or right to do so.

Ironically during this time period, a particular site supervisor was appalling in how she treated two of my interns. I consider myself gentle and tactful in how I handle situations, but nothing could avoid the huge clash that occurred with this woman. She saw me as the enemy, threatened to bring a law suit against those who did not align with her, and continued to be an unnerving presence in my life at the same time that Kathy and I were separated and unable to communicate. Talk about being stretched?!

The extremes washed me. I began to connect with others more deeply in life than I had previously. I had become broken bread that fed others because of me demonstrating difficult life dynamics at fuller levels for their learning, which also caused deeper fellowship between me and them. The extremes washed away lesser ways to eventually cause wisdom to come forth in those places for all of us.[3]

We must be washed through the extremes. Extremes are out of control situations as well as counterpart people within Christ's body. That is how we are continually redeemed to walk in Christ.

Wisdom's Children

God changed my view of suffering through all the trials I endured. I believe that many people have stayed stuck in suffering because of equating suffering with immaturity, which then causes self-condemnation that hinders healing. Even if you don't equate suffering with immaturity, many people around you may treat you that way when you suffer. I am passionate about awakening people on this topic.

In a passage that most seems to capture the big picture for me about healing through the extremes and suffering, Jesus said to His people (Matt. 23:37) "… how often I have longed to gather your children together, as a hen gathers her chicks under her wings, but you were not willing."

Jesus' longing was clear. People's unwillingness was clear. How might we still be unwilling?

Wings again are evident in this passage. Jesus' message was about gathering His children through the extremes and that those are the times we are least willing to let Him gather us.

The word "children" also sheds light on what Jesus most emphasized in this passage. Jesus' word for children meant those going through trials. We tend to be less willing to be gathered during trials. That is when we are more inclined to have no part with Christ! I also want to clarify a longstanding inaccurate teaching about the word "children" that Jesus used for His message.

Two central Greek words for children have been taught as if they cannot go together. Correct teaching on Jesus' terms for children are foundational and provide balance for more accurately interpreting many of the scriptures (because He talks much about children). Please endure with me through the next few paragraphs to glean one of the more important treasures in this book.

The Greek word *huios* for children or sons has been taught as mature children, and the word *teknon*, also meaning children or sons, has been taught as immature children. These oversimplifications have hindered our willingness to allow Christ to wash us.

The root word for *teknon* is *tikto*, meaning "child or son as produced, as delivered through travail." I believe that people's flesh nature concluded (much like the religious rulers originally concluded) that suffering meant that people were not walking in accordance with God. That's why they concluded that Jesus was not of God. Jesus suffered. That's also why many people today still conclude that *teknon* means immature, which further causes judgment of self and others when encountering trials. The prevailing (often unspoken) view has been, "How can you be walking close with God if you are suffering? If you are suffering, it is because you are immature."

Prevailing understandings of *huios* and *teknon* have been fleshly either-or views that equate suffering with immaturity and non-suffering with maturity. No wonder many people have remained hidden. Nowhere in the Greek meanings of *teknon* or its root is immaturity stated or implied. People's flesh nature added that part.

One scriptural passage that quickly demonstrates that *teknon* should not be equated with immaturity is (Matt. 11:19, NKJV), "But wisdom is justified [proved right] by her children." The meaning here is that children (*teknon*) who glean wisdom through trials prove wisdom's ways as right. *Wisdom's* children are not immature but instead glean wisdom's fruit! Isn't wisdom gleaned most from trials?

I can be a mature child and yet encounter trials to make me more mature. Wasn't that Jesus? Wasn't He already mature? But He was granted more because of His sufferings (Heb. 5:7-10).

One profound change in humanity that I would love to come through this book is for people to embrace trials as the very times that Christ works most passionately to be one with us. I have learned that I am not delinquent or defective simply because I am experiencing trials but, rather, Christ is deeply for me and working to lift me further into His peace, rest, freedom, and glory at those times.

God grants us more through placing us in the extremes, especially when we trust Him there. We come to reign with Christ if we suffer with Christ. If we reject the suffering, we reject Christ, and then our suffering worsens anyway. That is the meaning of Christ desiring to gather us under His wings, though sometimes we are unwilling. Even the physical illustration of hens with their wings spread over their chicks points towards protection during times of fear and danger. That is when a hen, duck, or goose gathers her little ones under her wings.

During the extremes I no longer feel Christ's close presence and must keep paying attention to turning whatever way He moves while the scary extremes pass by. Paying attention to remaining under the shadow and power of His wings during the extremes is my protection. The shadow (or darkness, which is its meaning) of His wings is my protection and deliverance from lesser ways. Fearfully running in other directions because of staring at what I fear is my demise. Fearfully reacting causes me to leave the security and shadow of His wings.

Here is the spirit and deeper meaning of Jesus' message:

"O My people, how I've yearned to awaken you to be with Me, especially in the midst of the trials that are meant to free you. My desire has been to periodically put you into extreme situations beyond your present ability or control so that you would turn to Me as comfort that is beyond the world. But so often you have been unwilling to be gathered into more of Me during those times because you have not trusted Me to be for you, and so you have sometimes gone on your own and experienced greater suffering. My heart breaks for you when you do not let Me be with you during trials. Have I not said that those who suffer and are peacemakers are blessed? Be at peace with Me during trials. I am not against you. I have told you that I will never forsake you, even though I know that it feels like I do at times. I use trials in your life to continually bring you into My rest."

You may want to read the context of both gospels relating to Jesus' desire to gather us (Matt. 23:37; Lk. 19:41-44). You will see that the context emphasizes how God's people have traditionally stoned and killed the prophets who were sent to help them. That's why Jesus, after His statement of longing to gather us, emphasized (vs. 39), "For I tell you, you will not see Me again until you say, 'Blessed is he who comes in the name of the Lord.'"

I will not see Jesus in "the day of visitation" (my trials) when I stone and kill those meant to awaken me. I saw Jesus and His works regularly during my marital conflict because I saw Him in Kathy rather than stoning her. I saw Christ working through her even though her fleshly edges seemed more powerful at times.

The people and situations that we most feel inclined to stone are usually counterparts where the Lord wants us to say "Blessed is he who comes in the name of the Lord." Then we receive our help. God wanted me to say about Kathy, "Blessed is she who comes in the name of the Lord," whether she looked like that or not.

Your help often comes through the extremes. Do not stone and kill your counterparts meant to awaken you! Know that counterparts come in the name of the Lord whose name is over all individual names.

Set on Fire

You are set on fire by what you touch. The woman hemorrhaging for twelve years touched the fringe of Jesus' cloak and knew that it was the same as touching Jesus. Faith automatically proceeded forth from Jesus to heal her when she touched that fringe (Lk. 8:44-46).

"Touched" means touched or reached for, and the root of that word means "set on fire." That bleeding woman was set on fire by what she touched. Healing resulted and a fire within her was likely awakened to begin shining forth from darkness. Reaching or stretching to join with Christ during His extreme works increases the light of His fire on this earth. We are set on fire by what we reach for.

King David reached for Bathsheba and got burned, just like Adam and Eve reached for the forbidden apple that began hell's fire and death on earth. Again, I want to be clear that God is not against our true self but only burns away anything false that hinders us from awakening to His secure love.

Depending upon what I touch, I continue either hell's fire or Christ's baptism of fire on this earth. The fringes or extremes press me further than where I have gone in certain aspects of my life, and I encounter choices in those pressed places. What will I reach for? Will I reach for Christ in those places, or will I reach for false loves to fill the felt gaps? Whatever I reach for ignites more fire.

I ignited more hell within me and between Kathy and me when I reached towards earthly outcomes such as trying to have communication work when it simply wasn't yet time for it to work. Hell also continued when I tried to go on dates with Kathy at points and ignored the bad timing that my heart new by faith. Looking back, I could only learn some of what I learned through trial and error. But I am clear that more hell continued at times when I stepped in lesser ways. Those flames, though, still worked to clear away more of my earthly ways and eventually increase my discernment.

Christ's baptism of fire awakens His light and sacrificial love on earth so that He may be known, whereas hell's fire continues the world's darkness, torment, and deception that you are alone and must fend for yourself. The higher fire acknowledges Christ who is the truth of no separation, and the lesser fire does not. You will reap what you sow. Regardless, even if you choose flesh's lesser ways, those ways will draw the lesser fire to burn away that nature. Jesus expressed this in part when He conveyed that those who live by the sword will die by the sword. Why is that? You draw the sword to yourself when you live by it. You draw hell's fire to yourself when you live by hell's ways.[4]

Wings of the Dawn

Part of God's grace for me remaining steadfast through the trials was knowing that God was absolutely sovereign over all things, even the extremes. God wants us to know how sovereign He is during our extreme situations where our trust sometimes wavers. That's why He caused King David to proclaim (Psm. 139:7-10): "Where can I go from Your Spirit? Where can I flee from Your presence? If I go up to the heavens, You are there; if I make my bed in the depths [Sheol or hell], You are there. If I rise on the *wings* of the dawn, if I settle on the far side of the sea, even there Your hand will guide me, Your right hand will hold me fast."

God emphasized that He will hold us fast through all of the extremes mentioned in that passage. That's why wings is mentioned again. Can I escape His Spirit? Or His presence? No. Although I may not feel God's presence, He is with me regardless of my extreme situations. During those "wings," or extreme situations, I

293

may rise to seek and embrace the early light of heaven (the dawn); I may make my bed or have my stance in the depths (Sheol or hell); or, I may settle on the far side of the sea, meaning the latter or trailing part (rather than embracing the early light); but one thing is sure, God's right hand will hold me fast.

Unknowingly I have personally done, and then experienced, each of the above at times during my trials. Sometimes people ask regarding God holding us fast in spite of our circumstance, "But what about God's judgment and justice?" Just yesterday after writing the above paragraphs, God stirred my heart by putting the number 366 in front of me several times. I knew that I was to go to Psalms 36:6 and was giddy when I saw the extremes brought up again. Verses 6-9 give the full picture, "Your righteousness is like the mighty mountains, Your justice like the *great deep*. O LORD, you preserve both man and beast. How priceless is your unfailing love! Both high and low among men find refuge in the shadow of Your *wings*. They feast on the abundance of Your house; You give them drink from Your river of delights. For with You is the fountain of life; in Your light we see light."

We find refuge during the shadow or darkness of God's wings or extremes. The psalmist expressed that God's judgment and justice (both words apply here) are like the great deep, which means God's deep, or God's "abyss." As deep as the abyss is, as deep as any extreme is, God's justice and unfailing love are still a refuge for us. That's why the psalmist continued to say in connection to those extremes that God gives us a drink from His river of delights. That is what I experienced through the extremes I endured (although I usually didn't *feel* God's security and refuge while in the moment of experiencing the worst of the suffering).

We can see the "great deep" and the accompanying meanings emphasized again in another passage that conveys that the extremes and the depths are a pathway for us. Isaiah stated (51:10-11), "Was it not You who dried up the sea, the waters of the *great deep*; who made *the depths* of the sea a pathway for the redeemed to cross over? So the ransomed of the LORD will return and come with joyful shouting to Zion." These scriptures are comforting to me now. Anytime I experience the extremes, I am clearer that I am not alone and that Christ is especially with me to lift me into more of Him at those times.

God made the great deep, the abyss, as a pathway for the redeemed to cross over! For the people of Israel and for us. The redeemed or ransomed is not about person versus person or people versus people, but about the soul embracing the Christ nature versus the flesh nature during the depths. This is about the true self, not the false. The true, which is the foundation of who we are, is also what is meant by the remnant or "the stump," which is Christ within us (Isa. 6:13). The soul, after becoming trimmed from the superficial flesh nature, is the remnant joined with Christ. That is the redeemed. Married – soul and Christ nature. That is also our new self described in the New Testament.

The scriptures say that the ransomed will return, but how? The depths *are* the pathway. Any abyss we encounter is God's pathway where His justice is equal to the task of feeding the poor and afflicted (whether here or after this earthly journey).

We cross over from the flesh nature to the Christ nature through the depths. God symbolized this way of delivering His people from Egypt's (flesh's) bondage through the parting of the sea. The depths being our pathway and deliverance ensures that God rather than human effort builds His house, for the scriptures say (Psm. 127:1), "Unless the Lord builds the house, its builders labor in vain."

We must periodically encounter human limits to ensure that God alone builds the house. Because of the extremes Kathy and I encountered, we are both clearer than ever before that striving in human effort cannot build God's kingdom. Only participating with what Christ presently works accomplishes that.

I feel compelled to emphasize again what I had mentioned earlier about false messages of "no more fear or pain." I agree that there will no longer be pain, suffering, and therefore, no fear *after* the earth has become as it is in heaven. That is when the New Jerusalem comes down out of heaven to be here on this earth (Rev. 3:12). But until then, do not naively think that you will arrive at a place of no suffering or fear. You and I will occasionally experience suffering and fear as long as significant gaps exist between the ways of heaven and earth. Significant gaps will still cause fear or lack of faith at times when we are called to be peacemakers in places that have no peace.

For now, God wants to cause us to walk on the waves like Jesus did. He wants to give us wings to fly during the flames. Let us rise on the wings of the dawn rather than choosing lesser ways (Psm. 139:9). Let us rise as a kite during stiff winds.

The word "wings" in Psalm 139 is used on purpose. God wants us to learn to fly above our extreme circumstances. Grace during the extremes is how He lifts us spiritually. That is our healing.

The passage about healing being in God's "wings" is exactly the same word as Boaz redeeming Ruth with the "corner" of his cover. Boaz' redemption of Ruth symbolizes Christ's ongoing works to buy as back when we are placed in the extremes, fringes, or corners. Do you personally grasp the symbolism of Boaz redeeming Ruth by the corner of his cover? Christ wants to trade your flesh nature for His Christ nature in every place you feel cornered by your circumstances! Christ redeems you, especially at those times. The corners are the extremes and are always opportunities to be lifted. To fly.

That is why Christ is referred to as the Cornerstone. In the corners or extremes Christ works within our souls to replace the earthly limitations with His incorruptible, unlimited nature. Lesser kingdom must give way to the True Kingdom. Our inheritance.

Christ wants to use all of your extreme situations for Him to become your Cornerstone and foundation in those very places. His Rock foundation is given as you acknowledge and lose your weak earthly foundations. You must trade in your systems of security for True Security in every aspect of your life.

Don't the sayings "cutting corners," "being cornered," and being on the "cutting edge" have new meaning? Cutting corners comes from fear and earthly control. Being cornered or being on the cutting edge require risk and trust beyond earthly security. That is faith.

The book of Zephaniah (1:15-16) describes the day of the Lord as "… a day of trumpet and battle cry against the fortified cities and against the corner towers." The Lord places us in the extremes that are beyond our fortified earthly comfort and protection, and in those corners He tears down earthly towers so He can become our Cornerstone in those places.

Builders know that the cornerstone is the foundation and measure for constructing buildings. All is aligned according to the cornerstone. Christ wants every aspect of your life to be measured and established in His strength and love rather than created matter. He wants you to know that He is absolutely sovereign and with you during all of your extreme situations. There, upon acknowledging fleshly weakness, He begins to take root as the Cornerstone and continues with you on your journey until He becomes the Capstone.

Two Great Wings

Without knowing it, Kathy and I were nurtured during our marital upheaval. I was reasonably aware of that nurturance during the upheaval, but I can especially see the nurturance as I look back.

The scriptures say (Rev. 12:14), "The woman was given the two wings of a great eagle, so that she might fly to the place prepared for her in the desert, where she would be taken care of for a time, times and half a time, out of the serpent's reach."

The woman, symbolizing the Church, *was given* two wings of a great eagle to fly. The woman did not earn or go somewhere to obtain a set of wings. The wings were given to her. Beyond her ability, grace gave her wings and then grace nourished her in the wilderness. Grace gave her wings to choose the wilderness as well as nourished her during that time.

These graces (wings) parallel the two graces emphasized earlier (see Zechariah 4). One grace places us on Christ's foundation to receive His comfort, which allows us to *see* the kingdom, and another grace is for choosing the wilderness, to *enter* further into the kingdom through sacrificial love in the midst of tribulation, which builds or spiritually lifts God's greater house.

Two wings are required to fly. To be lifted. I also see these two wings as two extremes that must come together as one to lift us. I believe these extremes are humanity's two core aspects that have yet to become one: the yearning and turning of "marriage." As stated, yearning is frequently more evident in women and turning more evident in men, but these two counterparts are always in both and must work together in unison for humanity to be lifted into its true identity.

The felt gaps between the yearning and turning counterparts are part of the wilderness we experience in relationships. People feel isolated from one another because of these counterparts that have two distinctly different functions. But in those solitary places, God makes space where He nourishes us. Although the wilderness feels like a solitary place, God finds room and freedom to expand us there. Didn't God take Israel into the wilderness, where He fed them manna, which was Christ? Christ's desire during the wilderness is to feed our souls with more of Himself (which is also the Passover).

Kathy and I slowly received some nourishment during our wilderness. We began to see and embrace wider, longer, higher, and deeper than previously. Rather than seeing with either-or and right-or-wrong eyes, we began to allow God to make two into one. Somehow strawberries tasted great with shortcake, and peanut butter went well with chocolate. Peanut butter was not to conform and become like chocolate, nor chocolate to lose its flavor and become the same as peanut butter.

Unity in the body of Christ is not sameness. Unity is each person fully embracing their unique identity while embracing everyone else's unique identity. All counterparts are to be oiled (the trust of the Spirit), keeping them free and working well together as one. And the core of all counterparts, yearning and turning, are the two great counterparts coming together as two wings that allow us to be fully nourished by Christ in the wilderness. Have you viewed your counterparts and extreme situations as times to be nourished? I do.

Christ is able to become our food more easily and fully when no other food is available. That is why Christ sometimes puts us in extremes beyond our control, as well as utilizes the extremes of the yearning and turning counterparts.

Until I fast from my present abilities during the extremes, there is no space for the new. Until I stop striving to support myself, Christ will have no room to be my support. God's goal for the extremes in my life is to wean me from the lesser so He can nourish me with the Greater. He nourishes me directly as well as through His counterparts during those times whether it tangibly feels like that or not. That is what God did through Kathy, Bob, and the others during my fireworks whether they appeared as friendly or unfriendly pieces to the puzzle.

Overshadowed Back Pain

Just now while reading and refining this past section I have been experiencing chronic back pain, which resulted in this section. I have been experiencing severe back pain for two weeks after I helped someone move. I experienced no noticeable mishap while loading the truck but felt my lower back tightening a bit near the end. The following morning the pain became intense and it only increased since then. And, now, the pain is unbearable, even as I've been writing. Is Christ with me and for me during this or not?

Any previous intense back pain in my life had gone away after several days. This time I went to a doctor after enduring several days of pain that was too much to handle, especially with no sign of relief in sight. The doctor said I had muscle spasms, gave me muscle relaxants, and told me that walking would help bring oxygen into my back.

So after following his advice, as well as taking Aleve twice daily, I became afraid when the pain became even more intense. With no escape in sight I wondered if I had permanently injured my back. Without realizing it, I began feeling discouraged and was losing hope. Now I know how unending intense physical pain can cause people to feel utterly hopeless.

Then I realized how I was handling this trial alone inwardly, and that I was acting like Christ was nowhere to be found. Even though Kathy was supporting me, spiritually I had felt abandoned within me. As I realized my spiritual state, I "remembered" that

Christ wants to be my comfort in the places where I can find no true comfort in the earthly realm. I also told Kathy what I had been experiencing inwardly so that she could pray for me to receive Christ's comfort there, as well as for any other works He might want to accomplish through this misery!

As soon as I embraced Christ's desire to be my comfort during this trial, the pain seemed more bearable. I wanted to be one with Christ in that place and to know Him there even more than I wanted the back pain gone. I believe that knowing and being with Christ as one will accomplish all that's needed, for He will then be able to lead me if He wants some further steps on my part.

I then began experiencing Christ's higher presence. I passionately prayed for the many people who encounter trials that cause them to feel abandoned or hopeless, and for them to remember that Christ wants to be their true comfort in those places where the earthly won't work. The more I prayed the more I sensed Christ's higher goodness and comfort that caused my back pain to all-but disappear at that point.

I don't think that the pain actually disappeared, but it sure felt like it did. That's when I felt compelled to add this experience to these writings, and I knew right where it was to go. As I paused to let the Spirit bring words to what this experience was like, I heard "My goodness and comfort *overshadowed* your pain." The Spirit emphasized the word overshadowed, and I realized through numerous previous experiences that "the things of the earth will grow strangely dim in the light of His glory and grace" (the words from a song). Somehow, fuller heavenly Comfort caused earthly discomfort to fade into the background for me.

I've experienced Christ's support and comfort many times in previous areas where no earthly support would suffice. I have learned to turn to Christ there and have found that His higher support somehow overshadows the pain. In this situation, the word "overshadow" immediately caused me to think about the Holy Spirit overshadowing Mary to conceive Jesus (Lk. 1:35). The word overshadow is used only once in the scriptures. I genuinely believe that that word choice connected to my back, which happened very spontaneously as I wrote, was given to me (conceived!) by the Holy Spirit. Why?

Conception of, or establishing more of, Christ's higher realm on earth happens this way. Christ's kingdom is here but is conceived or established as the Holy Spirit overshadows us during the extremes. Life became more difficult for Mary at points, and life becomes more difficult for us when the Holy Spirit overshadows us to conceive more of Christ. Practically, overshadowing means experiencing some earthly difficulties while the Spirit conceives more of Christ within our souls.

The Holy Spirit had been overshadowing me regarding this back pain, but He made it utterly clear to me through this particular experience. I had already felt like God was birthing kingdom ways through me during this impossible pain (just like during Kathy's and my heightened struggles). I had felt like God was regularly using me to pray for many people to learn how to turn to Christ in the middle of unending humanly impossible trials. That's why I somehow intuitively knew that the back pain would not immediately be healed, and yet I knew that Christ would carry me through it.

I have been writing about conception all along – through marriage, fire, gaps, and the extremes – but, here in the moment, the Spirit added the part about Him overshadowing us. Just as it was initially with Mary, human nature cannot conceive or establish Christ and His higher nature and realm. God places us in the extremes where human effort and striving cannot work for filling gaps. During those gaps, Christ wants us to turn to Him as our true comfort and support in those places. As we do so, the

Spirit of Christ overshadows us and conceives more of His higher realm at those times. I had not planned on writing about this, but Christ graciously used my intense back pain to conceive something higher as I looked to Christ as my true comfort. Do not take this to mean that I should never go to doctors or make use of certain earthly helps as well. But the earthly helps should not be in place of looking to Christ as my ultimate comfort.

Part of the Spirit's conception during this back pain had been to cause me to pray much for these deep, fearful places in people's lives, and that we would all learn to rest and trust in Christ's comfort in the midst of impossible places. I have prayed that these deep yearnings during earthly gaps would be united with turning to Christ in trust for conceiving His higher realm in these places. Can you imagine the profound change that's possible as more people learn to participate with Christ and His Spirit in this way? Collective belief, in time, will cause Christ's kingdom to come on earth as it is in heaven.

Four Winds

The "four corners of the earth" and "the four winds" in the scriptures symbolize Christ's worldwide work using the extremes to gather all into Him.

Jesus Christ, the Root of Jesse, "… will assemble the scattered people of Judah from the four quarters of the earth" (Isa. 11:12). The four quarters (corners) of the earth? Again this is the same word for wings, corners, fringes, or extremes and symbolizes God using the extremes to wean us from the false and nourish us with the True so He can gather us. To lift us with His wings.

The number four in that passage has greater meaning as well. While the number four represents a worldwide work, what most people don't know is that the root word conveys being on all fours rather than on two legs and also means to prostrate oneself. This passage portrays God humbling humanity through the extremes so as to exalt Christ in all. The remnant or stump within will be left, which is Christ. All will be shaken away that is not Christ so that all that is of Christ remains.

God conveyed a consistent message to us through the cherubim in the tabernacle, through Ezekiel's vision of four living creatures, and through the book of Revelation's living creatures worshipping before God's throne. This overall message foretells of God's worldwide works that utilize extreme situations and counterpart people to gather us.[5] The extremes (wings) cause us to become connected and to touch one another more deeply, where gaps no longer exist. Touching the fringe of Jesus' garment sets us on fire. We become restored by touching or embracing Gods' sovereignly placed beyond-human-control situations as well as the extremes of His body of people on this earth.

The word "lightning" is also used in the Ezekiel passage and furthers the essence of God's message about how He will gather us. Jesus said that in the Son of Man's day, He would be like lightning. But He cautioned us not to go only into the inner room or only out in the desert as if to chase lightning once it has already flashed. Why? That is fleshly one-or-the-other thinking. Don't chase one truth at the expense of its counterpart. By the time you get to one place, He will flash in another part of the sky and you'll be running in senseless circles. Jesus continued saying that in His day, the whole sky would be lit up all the way from the east to all the way to the west (Matt. 24:27; Lk. 17:24). No gaps. Touching, just like the cherubim's wings in Ezekiel's vision.

God's extreme works in my life caused me to further shed the false and embrace the True. Upon embracing the True, I increasingly stopped worshipping individual names and "truths." I further lifted Christ's name above all and began to see the truth of Him within the various unique identities that come together to touch each other in fuller expression. Like a beautiful rainbow or a glorious symphony.

That's why those with insight mentioned in book of Daniel go back and forth to gather and increase knowledge (12:4). They do not judge or condemn differences. They do not exalt one individual name over another but go back and forth into the extremes *to gather* that knowledge, like marriage that makes two into one. Knowledge then grows and fills the gaps, and the whole sky is given light.

Those with insight glean and gather Christ's wisdom during the extremes. They will lead the many. Are you in conflict? Suffering? Ask fervently to awaken to what you do not yet embrace! Then you will become known as one with insight. Those with insight will rise above earthly labels, categories, and rough fleshly edges to glean Christ's wisdom, whether that is through the extremes of people or situations.

How does the Lord fill His temple? Through the extremes. The "train" of His robe *fills* His temple. The extremes fill Christ's temple on this earth. He who has ears to hear, let him hear what the Spirit yearns for in this day.

Prior to writing about Ezekiel's cherubim vision, while praying I had seen a great "bird" with its wings down near its sides. I instantly knew that God wanted the wings lifted and spread out to the sides, just like Jesus' arms on the cross. I did not know what to call this fierce bird. I knew that it was not an eagle. Then I saw a glimpse of the head and saw the face of a man. For some reason Ezekiel's visions had not yet come to mind, partly because the wings had caused me to think that what I saw was a bird even though I instinctively knew that it wasn't.

I did not initially tell anyone about this winged creature, even though I saw it during the prayer hour prior to the corporate

305

gathering where I attend. I didn't understand what I saw and wasn't sure what to share or if Christ even wanted it shared.

Only several days later when I was researching the word "fire" did I come upon Ezekiel's visions. As soon as I read about Ezekiel's vision of the living creatures that he later called cherubim, I read the verse (1:24), "When they stood still, they lowered their wings." Immediately I saw a flash of the "bird" with lowered wings I had seen previously, and my heart stirred. I realized that I had seen one of the living creatures or cherubim, with the face of a man and lowered wings ... wings that God wanted spread out or raised. At this point, I knew that God was conveying to me that He wanted us (man) to spread out or lift our wings.

Then when I read about Ezekiel's second vision where he named these living creatures "cherubim," I learned that wings spread out or lifted meant that they were moving or being lifted. I knew that God wanted to lift His people through wings. Through the extremes.

I also learned that the cherubim in Ezekiel's vision picked up burning coals to put upon God's people (10:2), similar to Isaiah's vision where the seraphim place a burning coal upon his lips for carrying out God's works. Then at my next corporate gathering for worship, I sat staring at the floor while being still with God. Right in front of my eyes a child's sandals landed on the floor. Before I looked up to see where they came from, God's words to Moses from the fire in the burning bush came to my mind (Ex. 3:5): "Take off your sandals, for the place you are standing is holy ground."

The sandals had fallen off a child who was being held by a parent just off to my side. The symbolism struck me. God wants to hold us as a father holding a child while removing our sandals. The Hebrew meaning of sandals is occupancy, and taking off sandals means marriage. As I paused, I heard the words, "It is time to take off your sandals. It is time to hear My voice in the fire. Hear My voice *from* the fire."

Do you hear God's voice from the fire? Or do you tend to decide "what's best" during the fire? Are you filled with what should or shouldn't be? Occupancy? Or do you remove your sandals in surrender to whatever Christ may be working so that you can become married to Him regarding what He is doing in the fire? In all that I went through, God continuously desired to take my fingers off of any preconceived "right" outcomes. Only with a totally surrendered and free heart could Christ work His greater love and works in me. Only in surrendering to His higher will could He overshadow me and conceive more of His higher realm through me.

God lifts us especially during the fire just like He did with Moses. God is presently transforming us from having the face of a man to becoming like an eagle with wings. That's why the third face of the living creatures in the book of Revelation is the face of a man, and the fourth looks like an eagle with wings. I did not realize any of this until after seeing the living creature with a man's face and lowered wings that were supposed to be raised. Lifted. I now see clearly that God is removing our corruptible human nature (the human face) and awakening us into His incorruptible Christ nature that flies with eagles' wings above the natural realm.

Awaken to your higher Christ nature during the fire. Let go of that which is merely human. Trust that the true cannot be hurt, and that only the corruptible flesh nature feels the pain of the fire. You are spirit beyond the natural realm. Embrace God's extremes. Embrace your trials as God's opportunities for you to be lifted. You begin flying when you embrace God's wings. When you hear His voice from the fire.

The fiery Rule-Breaker uses counterparts and extremes to break through the world's limits, rules, and ways. Our boxes of what ought to be lose their rigidity when we encounter the extremes that are outside of our current boxes. That is how our souls awaken to and embrace what is beyond human limits.

The four winds are from the north, south, east, and west. Worldwide extremes. The four winds of the Spirit are blowing through the extremes to strip away lesser nature and to awaken us into our Christ nature. That is how Christ gathers His elect, which is the unseen spirit person within our body of flesh. He breathes in and out, to and fro, and back and forth through our extreme situations to shake away created matter and to cause us to arise in our true inheritance, the Christ nature.

My back feels even better after writing this. I guess more of the load was lifted.

Chapter 12

Breakthroughs and a Dance

A Dance of Glory

I powerfully encountered the risen Lord within me about a year and a half after the initial explosion between Kathy and me. After all our attempts on our own as well as with outside help, we lost all hope in reconciliation through earthly means. All communication, and even any new steps, were completely futile. We were still separated with no signs of anything budging. I still remember my one son saying, "You two seem so different from one another; I don't see any hope of anything coming back together." I knew that this was true and that if resolution happened, it would simply be through a God-miracle. That's when God revealed Himself to me, or should I say "in me," through a profound higher-realm experience as I sat in my living room.

For several minutes my eyes were opened to see how Christ's authority had been working through me for many years. I saw that Christ worked exactly what He wanted to work within and through me during those years in spite of any blindness or felt inadequacies on my part.

After seeing Christ's authority through me, everything within me suddenly became awakened and spiritually heightened beyond anything I had known or encountered previously (even beyond the mountain of love that came through me on behalf of the flight attendant). I cried out immediately with great emotion, "I know who I am!"

I saw and experienced everything as if I were the fullness of Christ. I saw nothing through earthly eyes. I did not even think of myself as human but only knew myself as Christ in that moment. (Afterwards the experience definitely caused Paul's words to come to mind, "I no longer live, but Christ lives in me"; Gal. 2:20)

I experienced Christ's fullness and heavenly perspectives coming through me for at least five minutes. I felt like all earthliness within me was shut off and all heavenliness was released. That is the most accurate way I can describe it. I felt like Christ (rather than the earthly me) spoke with full authority as I prayed aloud about what I was seeing.

I saw God's kingdom on this earth with great clarity. I saw people's true Christ nature. I also saw how, at present, humanity's collective belief in a lesser god has maintained the spiritual forces and principalities that keep us in bondage to an earthly identity. I saw our many lies about a lesser love and a lesser Christ than He is. Humanity's love on this earth is primitive compared to Christ's never failing love that easily overshadows the greatest powers that exist.

Christ *is* fullness beyond us and in us. He is the Truth of who we are. All of life is a birthing process to awaken us out of the false flesh nature and into the Christ nature placed within us. That is our "hope" of glory planted within us and is God's *unchangeable* purpose (Heb. 6:17-20; Jn. 17:22; Col. 1:27).

During this heightened state I saw unending lies that govern humanity, especially about love. I saw the forces that maintain those lies within us as a people regardless of religious labels. I cried out with absolute certainty "I see you, and you *will* come down from your thrones. I command your false kingdoms to crumble." As I proclaimed this I recognized the parallel to the queen of Babylon in the Old Testament that symbolizes the forces within our hearts that govern our flesh nature, which cause us to see with eyes of separation. Death was the greatest deception. But I saw that death and its lie of separation would come to ruin on this earth.

You can read further about that queen, what she said, and how her words portray the forces in our own hearts that cling to the fleshly lies. That queen of our flesh nature has said (see Isa. 47:7-10): "I shall be a queen forever ... no one sees me ... I am, and there is no one besides me." These spiritual forces that work within the flesh nature want us to remain in bondage to our earthly identities, which means remaining in fear, doubt, and insecurity about who we are.

I continued commanding false kingdom ways to crumble and the true kingdom to be established by people awakening to who they are in Christ. I did not even consider the possibility of my words not accomplishing what was spoken. I believed with all my heart that those commands were being carried out in the spiritual realm as I spoke them. I believed this because I experienced Christ and not the earthly me commanding these changes to come forth during this season that is coming upon us. It is an unfolding day.

As I finished all that I was to proclaim about Christ's kingdom on this earth, I then commanded destruction to those false kingdom ways that had governed Kathy's and my marriage during this season. Again, I fully experienced me as Christ commanding this, not the earthly me doing so. I saw that it was God's time for a shift in all that had been humanly impossible for Kathy and me. I proclaimed restoration to our marriage and believed with absolute certainty that it had been granted in the spiritual realm (even though most everyone around me at the time would have believed this to be utterly impossible).

This higher-realm experience was more real to me than what I see daily with my natural eyes. I knew that I had literally experienced "I no longer live, but Christ lives in me." While still dark on a Sunday morning Christ within me had commanded strongholds to crumble. By Wednesday Kathy called me and said she wanted to talk. When we talked, she said that on Sunday while having time with God she had suddenly felt compelled by Him to move back in with me. Something had broken loose in the heavenly realm. A few days later following some intense conflict with Kathy, I had a vision of a principality on its throne. I saw this spiritual force's cracked throne wobbling and ready to fall. I knew that it was only a matter of time. But that principality had not yet fallen!

That vision of the principality matched my earthly experience. Kathy and I found that we still had a long way to go for restoration even though the principality's throne was cracked. But at least we were brought back together for God to touch us in new ways for restoring our marriage.

Near the two-year point in our marital fireworks I began to receive spiritual glimpses of a coming breakthrough for Kathy and me. Christ's commands were still being carried out, now at the earthly level!

The breakthrough seemed partly connected to me interacting and praying more for Kathy as if her sins were my own sins. It also seemed related to me feeding on whatever crumbs of Christ I could glean during the upheaval. I also knew that Kathy was regularly praying and trying to glean whatever she could glean from the trials. Many other people were praying for us as well.

Right at the two-year point of our marital upheaval I received a prophetic word from two different people (who did not know or talk with each other) about Kathy and me soon dancing a dance of glory. I also began seeing many UPS trucks just prior to the two-year point.

Then I saw another UPS truck while walking my dog Molly one morning. I had not realized that I had been staring at it. The Spirit stirred within me and I felt like my eyes finally saw the significance of these trucks. I sensed God teaching me that Kathy and I had endured many downs and that ups were now coming. The many earthly downs from these two years would produce many spiritual ups.

With capital letters, UPS! Spiritual lifting.

God seemed to emphasize that the spiritual ups were coming because of enduring earthly downs. Losing the earthly life would now produce higher life in Kathy and me. As I paused I was drawn to the words on the side of the UPS truck. They stated "Worldwide Services."

I sensed that God would use this increased spiritual life for touching the world whether that came through this book or not. I saw that Kathy and I could now be used as clearer vessels of God's rights that could come forth into the rest of His body even if that was unseen.

Daniel and his three friends in their captivity under the king of Babylon came to mind (see Dan. chapters 1-2). I saw how king Nebuchadnezzar's kingdom had been the greatest earthly kingdom that ever existed. I knew that the kingdom became great through Daniel and his three friends – unseen vessels of God's rights who prayed for and advised the ungodly king.

I believe that there are many other vessels beyond Kathy and me who have faithfully endured and overcome their trials. These overcomers will be used to advance God's kingdom on this earth. They will be unseen pillars of faith like Daniel and his three friends.

I believe many are at the point of breakthrough, and that breakthrough will come more powerfully for others as God's testimony begins to go forth through some initial overcomers. These breakthroughs cannot be rushed or forced. We can only hasten breakthroughs by laying down our fleshly rights and deferring to what we sense God is working during the fireworks, just like Daniel and his three friends did during their season of captivity.

Grace and trusting God's timing go hand in hand. I believe that God's single-most important work in this day is to help overcomers lay down fleshly rights during barren places. Laying down to Christ's times and ways is the way to higher authority. Do not awaken love until she pleases (see Song 2:7). I believe that turners, in particular, must pay attention to and honor God's times and seasons. That was my crucial part for Kathy and I being restored.

I experience greater fullness of resurrection life when I have truly lost my fleshly life. I see God move more powerfully in His resurrection glory that delivers many others when I face life's trials and say as Esther said, "If I perish, I perish" (Est. 4:16). Follow the Lamb wherever He goes.

Any impure motive or presumption about how my barren circumstances "need" to turn out will interfere with Christ's higher authority being established through me. I am a cup already full of the false if I maneuver, control, or demand that life turn out a certain way. I then make no room for God's rights and His Spirit. During trials I can feel within my heart when I still "need" certain outcomes. I can also feel whether or not I have truly let go unto a free and pure place for Christ's authority to reign through me. The pure in heart shall see God.

Do you include God's stripping works as part of His healing process for you? God is always present but you will not recognize

His presence if you do not accept His stripping works. You reign with Christ and He will reign through you especially when you recognize and join with His difficult works. That is resurrection life from death experiences. Resurrection life breaks through what is humanly impossible.

Foundations Sealed

God uses seasons of wilderness to seal me in more of Him. The barren places are for me. I become trusted with more when God finds me trustworthy during the wilderness. I will not panic at any point when I do not panic in the wilderness. I will refrain from selfish motives during good times when I don't react selfishly to save myself during bad times.

The Lord bestows heavenly riches during my barren places when I trust in Him (ask others to trust with you if you need help to trust). You can see in Isaiah chapters 61 and 62 in the NIV translation that God bestows comfort, beauty, gladness, and praise *into our barren areas.* That is a fuller planting of the Lord into our souls that makes us oaks of righteousness. Christ's fuller rights become established mostly in our barren places. He plants more of Himself there because He makes room within us there.

You know experientially those empty, alone places within your heart. That is Christ cutting off the earthly to establish fullness of Him there. Christ *wants* to be with you in those lost places. Only earthly emptiness makes more room for spiritual fullness. Your soul must have room to embrace more of Christ. Barren seasons do that.

In the midst of my barren places I receive a new name (my new self where more of my Christ nature is planted into my soul). I become married in those places and Christ speaks to me "My delight is in you." I am "no longer called Deserted or Desolate" (see Isa. 62). As you recall, the new name God gave Kathy and me was "Married," precisely on the date of 6/24, which was about Isaiah 62:4.

I encourage you to read Isaiah 61 and 62 to see God's great desire to bestow heavenly riches into your barren places. God seeks to be with you in your lost places but He wants to awaken you to Him as your comfort during those extended times of barrenness. That is *how* restoration into your Christ identity continues. God seals you more in Him through the barren places.

The Father affirmed Jesus when He was baptized in the Jordan (Matt. 3:17). That was the Father's initial seal of approval upon the Son. Then the Spirit led Jesus into the wilderness to be tempted by the devil (Matt. 4:1). Jesus was faithful to the Father in that wilderness and returned for ministry *in the power* of the Spirit (Lk. 4:14).

The Word was tested and found faithful in the wilderness. A noticeable shift occurred after Jesus was faithful through that wilderness.

The Father sealed Jesus with His glory and power in the wilderness. Then Jesus expressed the Father's glory to the world. Jesus changed water into wine for His first miracle. That miracle portrayed a change of substance, as seen by the world. Water changed to wine symbolized God's higher glory that would now become visible to the world. That miracle also represents the approaching season when followers of Christ fully embrace their Christ identity, where His glory within them will become visible to the world.

An initial seal of approval at the Jordan, and then a higher seal of glory and power after the wilderness! The Father did that for Jesus and does that for us.

But how was Jesus tempted in the wilderness? What can we learn about how we are tempted? I saw the importance of these questions because of Kathy's and my wilderness. I saw that our temptations paralleled Jesus' temptations.

The devil constantly tempted Jesus to *act* when, instead, the Spirit's purpose for the wilderness was for Jesus to *rest and trust* during temptation. The wilderness was to test Jesus about His identity and about whether or not He knew the Father's care, even during the hunger and thirst of an earthly wilderness. *If* You are the Son of God, then do such and such. That was the nature of the temptations. The devil tempted Jesus to act from a place that distrusted the Father's love just like he initially tempted Adam and Eve.

Would Jesus be moved selfishly by His hunger and thirst or would He trust in the Father as His enough in that place? Would Jesus hunger and thirst for righteousness (the Father's rights) in that place rather than for what the flesh nature wanted in the wilderness?

Following Jesus' wilderness experience He preached that all who hungered and thirsted for righteousness would be satisfied, and that the pure in heart would see God. Jesus had been sealed as the Living Word through the wilderness experience, which then prepared Him to teach what He had become in human form.

I am tempted most during barren places to believe that I am not God's child who He personally cares for. Kathy and I were tempted during barren places to believe the lie that we needed to be beyond who or where we were. We did not rest or know love at points because of that one lie. We were tempted to believe that we were not acceptable and that God was not truly with us in those places. As if we were totally immature, especially when the trials seemed unending!

That one lie is what causes panic, hopelessness, abandonment, anger, depression, and many other horrible emotions, which then leads to many fleshly reactions to try to fill that emptiness. All of these experiences come when I do not know Christ's secure love that allows me to rest in who I am and where I am (which establishes the security for true inner awakening).

Are those deeply emotional experiences real? Yes. But they only come from the lies I believe. Really, from the one lie that I have to be beyond where I am. That is my primary insecurity (which I believe is the root insecurity for humanity).

Believing that I need to be beyond where I am to be secure is what raises up the flesh nature. I *feel* separated from God, which then causes fleshly ways to try to fill those felt gaps.

Know that you can rest in the safety of Christ's cross that clearly shows that you are loved right where you are sin and all. Know that you can simply rest and watch for God to meet you in your wilderness places that seem impossible to change. That is what Jesus did in the wilderness (although it may take longer for us at times because of distrust or even because of God using the wilderness to work higher unseen works within us).

Jesus didn't react from distrust to get something additional to happen during temptation. Jesus trusted that the wilderness was there on purpose to test the Word – to see that He would not try to save Himself during the trials (where He didn't need saved from anything because He was already loved and secure). Most often we just need to know we are loved and acceptable during those places.

Would Jesus rest and trust that all was well between Him and His Father during that felt wilderness experience? Would Jesus trust that the wilderness experience was to seal Him in the fullness of the Father's glory? Yes. Would Kathy and I trust enough to be sealed? Barely!

God uses wilderness experiences for that purpose: to be sealed. To be married to Him in more and more aspects of our lives. Soul and Christ nature united like a bride and Bridegroom.

Your trust through the barren places seals you in more of your Christ identity. When you don't trust, find someone to stand with you to trust in that place. Just like with Jesus, you become sealed in love that is stronger than death when you do not rush the wilderness experience (Song 8:4-10). You become sealed and "return in the power of the Spirit."[1]

The scriptures say about God (Psm. 87:1-2), "He has set His foundation on the Holy mountain; the Lord loves the *gates* of Zion more than all the dwellings of Jacob." I must go through Zion's gates to rest on God's true foundation.

The gates of Zion *are* my barren places (see the root word for Zion). These barren places are where God establishes His foundation within me in place of my earthly ones. Then I am on the true foundation for Christ's glory to go forth through me.

Does this mean I am always to rest rather than to act? No. I am to act anytime I sense peace to act. That is stepping in my Christ nature. But anytime I am afraid or hopeless during barren places I am to rest and wait till I come to a place of trust. Deep yearning must unite with full turning.

Acting during barren places often comes from fear and distrust, and it strengthens the lie that I am alone. It strengthens fear. I have blindly stepped this way many times in the past. I will constantly experience leakage of spiritual power anytime I react during barren places. But I become sealed in more of my identity, love, power, and glory when I remain faithful in the wilderness. Part of that faith is to wait if I am not yet at a place of trust. Through trust or waiting when I don't trust, my holes become sealed at a foundational level in that area being tested. A storm can no longer wash away a house that is established on a rock solid foundation.

Security precedes authority. I heard these words very clearly one morning. Then the scriptures about "putting on love" came to mind (Col. 3:14). How do we put on love? The next verse (15) tells us how: "Let the peace of Christ *rule* in your hearts." Being in Christ's peace and security is where true authority originates. Stepping from peace continually puts on more of Christ's love in your life.

Christ's rule and authority are extended through me at a practical level anytime I step with peace. If I love God, and I sense peace in any action I am about to take, that means that His Spirit within me is at one with me in how I am about to step. Anytime I sense peace, I can step without questioning what is "right or wrong."

If I am not at peace, I am not yet in a position to act because I am not yet in unity with His Spirit within me. Lack of peace means that Christ is not ruling through my heart in that moment ... and that other things are ruling. If I am afraid at that point and then step because of fear, fear is governing me and wants to work through me to govern my situation.

Peace within me is the greatest signal as to whether Christ is ruling through me, as well as whether or not I am putting on love. Paying attention to whether or not we are acting from a foundation of peace or not is one of the most crucial ways for continually awakening into more of Christ. And I believe that much of humanity is deceived about how often fear operates from beneath our awareness, especially during difficulties.

Rest and trust in Christ during the wilderness without needing your circumstances or yourself to be different. Wait on Christ's peace before acting. Then Christ's grace will be more than sufficient for you because He will complete His power in you through that temporary weakness. Be still and know (or become aware) that He is God in those places where you haven't yet been aware. That is more important than all else during the wilderness.

If you can't trust during those barren places, acknowledge that with someone and ask them to trust with you at those times.

You are not defective because you are afraid or have barren places. Only the accuser tells you that. All who are serious about growing into Christ's fullness will experience fear and barren places. All experience this persecution. But that is where the planting of the Lord occurs to make us oaks of righteousness.

Master of Breakthrough

We accept rather than resist God's stripping works by His grace alone. Ask for it.

I was utterly blind and confused at points throughout my long-term upheaval. At times I was overwhelmed by the potential consequences regarding decisions I made (just like when Bob lived with Kathy and me). The stress at points was nearly unbearable until I again remembered that I needed no certain outcome. Then I would let go and trust that following my best sense of Christ's leading had to be enough. I regained peace and relationship with Him at those times.

I knew enough to know that I wanted to keep letting go of everything so that Christ's higher authority was free to govern during my trials. I knew that that was my only hope because everything was impossible in the natural realm.

God is the Master of breakthrough when I trust in Him alone to break through the impossible. King David saw that God didn't always want him to go to battle or to approach battle in the same way (like whether I am to act or wait during my trials). David saw that discerning God's desire during trials was crucial (2 Sam. 5:19-25). David experienced God as the Master of breakthrough when he discerned and followed God's wisdom.

That is what happened for Kathy and me. God was the Master of breakthrough as we kept trying to see what He wanted during the wilderness (although I often experienced Kathy as wanting certain earthly outcomes from me when things were heightened, which tends to be more true of yearners).

God doesn't work the immediate outcomes we often want in life. We find no resurrection power when we step in presumption or distrust to establish our desired outcomes. I have sensed that God has placed many people in earthly prisons to teach them higher wisdom during this season. Flesh won't work, and these prisons require patience, trust, and discernment for gleaning God's wisdom.

I will see God's works the more I let go; and the more I can see what He is working during ordained earthly prisons, the more I gain trust. Through trust I become the pure in heart who will see the Master of breakthrough and His glory.

I was mowing the grass one day and pondering what was causing the coming breakthroughs I sensed for Kathy and me. I knew that surrendering all control to God's higher authority was central. As I paused further I asked God "What is the capstone to this whole experience Kathy and I endured?"

Suddenly the word "Grace" came to mind. I realized that even my question was initiated by the Spirit within me (probably to uproot my flesh's tendency to cling to a concrete answer for its future security). The question highlighted the word capstone. That word is used in the very verse where God states that He will bring forth the capstone or top stone to His house "… with shouts of grace, grace to it!" (Zech. 4:7).

I believe that God wanted me and others to know above all else that His goodness comes through grace alone. I could do nothing to deliver Kathy or me, or to cause results ahead of God's works and ordained time. (I realize that people like to have more control over outcomes than what I convey here!) The most I could do during my blindness in these fireworks was to defer to whatever

I sensed Christ was working. I was to follow the Lamb wherever He went. Even that was a grace I asked for.

At a practical level, I frequently wrestled with whether or not other steps should be taken, especially given the length of the whole experience. Was there some new move that I was being dense about? One that I might not have wanted to take? I knew that I tended not to receive emotional or inner support, but how much reality should I share with those closest to me? Where was that line? What was right, healthy, and safe? What might be selfish? There were no easy answers.

Flesh wants a concrete plaque on the wall for direction rather than following the Unseen Christ by faith. All revelations I learned through these fireworks were God's gifts because of further entering His kingdom by faith. I received more of His kingdom the further I stretched by faith. No single way delivered me. The grace for following the Lamb by faith into unknown territory was His ongoing deliverance of Kathy and me.

A few days after asking for a capstone to this experience God emphasized another way for Kathy and me to come into His fullness. Here it is: don't try to communicate or go forward as a couple when you don't know true support. *Your heart will express distortions whether you want to or not when you don't know security and comfort.*

Be fully honest with yourself. Be aware of your inner experiences, especially when you have extra energy tied up in those places. Often, extra energy comes from pain or fear, and lies will pour forth from those places.

If you don't know God's support at the moment, stop! If the person you are in conflict with doesn't know support at the moment, stop! Don't continue communicating during serious conflict or pain when you experience significant lack of God's peace, rest, or security. That's what I learned very deeply through my marital fireworks.

You cannot lay down your earthly life during painful or volatile communication without first knowing Christ's security. Sometimes that means *not* communicating and, instead, paying attention to first receiving true support in those places. Security always precedes authority.

The yearner more deeply feels gaps and the need for support, and she sometimes reacts in fleshly ways to obtain outward security during difficulties without being aware of her inner state. Kathy frequently illustrated this dynamic. The turner does not feel the gaps and lack of support as deeply and in the flesh is often deceived to think he is more secure than he is and that life is not so bad … at least until he is touched by the yearner's deep places and then experiences the pressure from her to be more than he is. Then he feels the gaps as well. I illustrated this dynamic.

Christ wants both counterparts to experience His support and to unify in that place of need. As counterparts, we must acknowledge our need, and then be still and know that God is God in that place. We must first become secure in Him to know that He is. Only then will love's security make a way forward. Security brings authority.

CHAPTER 13

Hugs and Explosions

A Miracle Cure

A miracle cure exists for couples who endure conflict, pain, or trauma. The cure is a way that helps couples to become still and know that God is God where deep conflict or trauma exists. The cure helps couples to rest in the wilderness, so they can wait on peace that allows them to put on love in those places.

Here it is: hug! Hug rather than talk when those painful places are initially ignited. You may think that I'm joking. I am not.

Kathy and I literally experienced Christ's greater support awakening us when we united through hugs during the upheaval rather than talking. We first admitted that we both had need beyond what either could give, and then we held one another in silence. Humbly admitting inability and then hugging were both essential, and often we could not reach the point of hugging unless both admitted inability in the area of struggle. We learned to allow human weakness.

If either you or the other person feels unable to hug at times of upheaval, it is usually because one or both of you have not acknowledged human weakness, and, that you do not know

Christ's support within yourself. Acknowledge that you need support before you can do anything healthy or effective.

If you are not ready to hug, at least try to experience "withness" connected to the other person, whether that is through walking and holding hands, sitting closely beside each other while holding hands, or simply sitting still somewhat near each other while acknowledging your need of Christ's support. But if you are able, hug while being honest about your deep need of support. I can't emphasize these last four paragraphs enough! It is central to deeper life change in the stuck places.

As Kathy and I grew to trust hugs in those places, we were able to add this: the person encountering difficulty simply disclosed their inner experience like a child (which is usually about not knowing God's goodness or acceptance at the moment), and the other conveyed or prayed something like "I too have places within me that do not know goodness – you are not alone there; I will join with you to trust that God wants awareness of His goodness and support in these places where *we* have not known that."

Did you notice that the prayer emphasized the word "we"?

People typically feel alone, singled-out, defective, and abandoned in their places that have not known goodness. That is the accuser's lies from within. Unity in Christ overcomes all things, so the accuser especially works to divide and conquer. Love's enemy wants us to believe that we *can* be separated from Christ's love. That is why the accuser works his lies into us to believe that we are alone and separate.

Words *about* God or what is true cannot cut through in barren areas where we believe we are alone. Barren areas are the first three kinds of soil that Jesus described in the parable of the sower (Matt. 13:4). That soil is barren, hard, and rocky, where only thorns and thistles grow. Only after we faithfully endure difficulties that test the word within us does our soul's soil become broken, soft, and receptive. That was the fourth soil, the good soil that Jesus described.

Surrender, vulnerability, and humility demonstrate this fourth soil. That happens during the security of hugs while acknowledging your need of support. It opens up the soil where life has been barren.

In my heart's barren places my previous tendency was to not let others (or God) be with me there because I had believed that I was defective in those places. But through others *identifying and joining with me there*, I came to know experientially that I was not alone. I came to know God's goodness experientially through His hands and feet on this earth (which is His body, especially significant others). I came to trust God's goodness in the barren places through first encountering people's experiential goodness beyond words (withness), and this was true for Kathy as well.

Joining with another in the barren places is more important than trying to change anything! That is what is symbolized by Elisha the prophet laying on a boy body-to-body so as to identify with the boy in death to raise him to life (2 Kng. 4:32-35). That also symbolized how Jesus identified with us in death (sin) to raise us to life. Experiential joining rather than words.

Hugging, cleaving, or experientially joining with one another in the barren places awakens us to know we are not alone and that support is available; and after *experiencing* goodness through that unity we come to trust that Christ's higher goodness is available. We awaken to Christ and His support through waiting and resting at those times. Cease striving and know (or become aware) that God is God.

Become aware that God is still God during the bad places. That is always what is missing anytime you feel afraid, depressed, angry, hopeless, or abandoned. That, again, is "the fear of the Lord" (that knows He is absolutely sovereign and good, which then becomes the sanctuary of the Lord for you). That inner awareness causes your hopelessness and fear of the world to fade away.

The yearner is sometimes less ready to hug when she is afraid. The fear often causes her to want to talk and get somewhere different. An additional aspect that God opened up for Kathy and me during the stuck places was this: *if* the yearner cannot refrain from talk, the focus of any talk must first be "care-talk" rather than "fix-it talk." Fix-it talk led by fear leads to worse outcomes. Care-talk usually addresses the source of the fear at those times. Is care known or not? Not knowing care or love is the source of fear.

Often the yearner is initially less aware of care or comfort in the midst of the more significant gaps she experiences (because she was designed with less emotional insulation to experience greater awareness). The yearner's deeper experiences of gaps also adds to the potential distrust of God during the loss, pain, or lack, and therefore, she will not easily trust the turner either at critical points. Her distrust of the turner then sometimes becomes the dynamic that threatens him. Kathy and I displayed these dynamics.

This is the wilderness place for the yearner and turner counterparts, the barren place where God alone can comfort. Head knowledge won't do. Only experiential goodness helps counterparts to become more fully aware of God in that place. That's why hugs, and if needed, care-talk or other "withness experiences" open up awareness of God in that place.

Do not force one another to hug. Do not even force one another to go forward with care-talk. Your significant other may not be ready. Love is gentle and always allows freedom.

Kathy and I are both convinced that sacrificially cleaving through hugs is a miracle cure, which tangibly demonstrates the profound mystery of Christ where two become one. That is how Christ loved the Church – He experientially became one with us in the lost places. That is still how Christ desires to love us. Let us open up and receive Him and His care in those lost places. I have observed people's stuck places most of my life and have seen that they have received little care in those places. True care in those areas is what begins to free them.

Couples' painful lost places are where they must leave all else and *cleave* to one another in the Christ nature. Two counterparts who are at separate places in the natural realm must unite in a love that lays down differences so as to trust Christ's goodness that is always available. It is the place of neither in the flesh and both in Christ. Duality becomes unity.

Sacrificial love awakens us from death's lie of separation. That is how Jesus awakened us initially and is still how He awakens us, whether directly or through one another.

Profound restoration is always available in the barren places. Couples' gaps are filled by cleaving in the Christ nature, and that restoration is beyond what individuals alone can achieve. Dynamite is put in place when conflicted counterparts lay down their earthly rights and unite to trust Christ's goodness. Leave all and cleave.

Paul emphasized that cleaving was not merely about marriage but about Christ's love of the Church. Cleaving during conflict rather than trusting rational communication is the profound mystery that lays down earthly rights and exalts Christ. Like dynamite, higher power is stored up and compacted through this stabilizing sacrificial love. Christ's higher testimony then waits to be released through His "storehouses" at the proper time. Kathy and I definitely have a higher testimony of Christ's works in our marriage now.

What else happens when we cleave during differences? Christ's love replaces earthly love deep within our soul's barren places. We put on love through cleaving and waiting on peace to rule.

Kathy is very quick to support our boys during trials about not believing the lie that they have to be further, different, or beyond where they are. That was more of Christ planted within her soul during our prior barren places. Our boys have seen this greater wisdom coming through her because of all that we experienced.

Christ wants to keep replacing all of the world's lies and emptiness within our souls with more of Him as Truth. As adults we bring childhood wounds, lies, and abandonment into our marriages and other relationships. We all experienced abandonment during childhood at times because of earthly "love" in spite of well-meaning parents.

All adults have experienced incidents during childhood that were void of godly love. Goodness was unavailable at times. Sometimes parents communicated despisement, anger, or hatred; other times they unknowingly provided no support in difficult situations. We as children typically did not say "I need a hug" or "I need support" during deeper places of lack.

Then as adults we often re-enter those childhood states during our present difficulties. Many of us, like Kathy and me, haven't known that we could ask for hugs right in the midst of interactions going badly. When talking seemed urgent or necessary, we didn't know that we most needed care-talk!

Kathy and I now regularly say "I need a hug." Or we offer a hug to the other when we see that a hug is needed. We also acknowledge when we don't know support in the moment, and we join with one another by saying, "I too have places that don't know goodness; let me join with you there and pray that *we* would trust that Christ's goodness and support are available in our places that haven't known that."

Do you again hear my emphasis on "we" about places that haven't known goodness? I re-emphasize this because it is crucial. That kind of joining helps people not to feel defective and alone there, and they are more likely to feel safe enough to see truth and to let someone (and Christ) experientially be with them in that place. Then they are finally not alone. Their souls can open up and finally become the good fertile ground that Jesus mentioned. Then they "lift up the gates and let the King of Glory come into those places" (Psm. 24:9).

Unity in the lost places breaks open and makes fertile that barren hard ground. That is why Jesus encouraged us to pray "... forgive us *our* sins." We are one.

Cleaving allows us to receive the childhood hug we never got when we re-enter those childhood states as adults. Through hugs and withness we come to experientially know that goodness is available where we had not known that. We developmentally gain capacity to finally know Christ and trust love in the lost places. But that trust begins through cleaving. Experiential cleaving and hugging are the miracle cures humanity has needed in the barren places to become more fully awakened to Christ and His unwavering goodness. That is how Christ loved and still loves us in our lost places. That is how the good soil opens up to receive the loving rain during storms.

Cleaving during storms was the unity that initiated greater works to restore Kathy and me. This greater comfort and security during the storms was the beginning of Christ's greater love and works being built in us.

The Root Issue in All Things

Couples too often try to communicate further about "the problem" when one or both do not presently know Christ's inner support. The true problem needing addressed first is not knowing support. That was the root issue for Kathy and me. The yearner is often aware of lack in particular situations and then presses the turner (because of fear) to try to gain some kind of outward support. That pressure can cause the turner to become fearful where neither person then knows God's support. That is when communication has none of Christ's higher life in it; it becomes life-taking rather than life-giving.

Don't communicate when communication can't work. Don't talk about the problem when insecurity is too heightened. Your heart knows when this is the case. Christ's support is the way forward even if you have to be still in those places repeatedly rather than talking. Or, you may need to be still, talk just a bit, be still, and talk a bit more. But make sure you only go forward with Christ's security.

Kathy and I continually hugged without talking in the trauma places for at least several months before even bits of communication could work. If we did talk, it was mainly about acknowledging our inability in those places, along with our need to experience support. Through hugs and acknowledgment of weakness, Christ's unseen support literally kept causing lies to fall away. His support also established a base for talking further (but pay attention to whether or not both partners know support before talking; and a counselor or others are sometimes needed to hold you accountable to this).

Sometimes the deepest traumas in our lives occurred in childhood before we could think or communicate. Lies were planted experientially rather than through words. Support, then, can only be re-established through experience. Words or thoughts cannot undo the experientially-produced lies, even ones about God. Only experience can undo them. That is why support initially cannot be found through words about what is *supposed to be true* regarding the problem area.

I have observed many situations where people's words simply bounced off someone needing help in their stuck place, and that the suffering person only made headway once they experienced "withness" – knowing they were not alone, that they were not defective and the only one who experienced areas within that knew no goodness. The suffering person only moved on from their stuck place after someone identified with them about what it was like to feel helpless and unable to know goodness in a particular area. That unity strengthened the stuck person in the barren place and was a prerequisite before they could open up to anything further.

Hugs, or some kind of experiential withness, creates the necessary awareness that goodness is available and that God has not forsaken us in our desolate place. A counselor encouraged Kathy and me to begin pausing from all communication at the difficult places, and to just hug so as to know goodness there. We simply held one another while asking God alone to awaken us to His goodness. Hugs and experientially joining with one another communicated God's goodness to our traumatized areas. That security and goodness was a healthy foundation for being able to move forward.

Couples demonstrate the illusion of two when they painfully interact in either-or ways. Until each counterpart learns to cleave and receive support during painful areas, each person typically relies on some form of false security that increases both persons' experiences of separation.

The illusion of two is most transformed into the reality of One when couples cleave in Christ's comfort during difficulties. A larger, more secure perspective is then awakened in both.

Kingdom advancement cannot occur during difficulties without Christ's true foundation, which is His sacrificial love. That is His greater love that unites people. All will crumble that is not on the secure foundation of sacrificial love. Too many couples and people as a whole have tried to talk or act without knowing true support. Taking action when we are not truly secure is selfishness disguised.

Talking or acting apart from knowing God's support is lifeless and cannot help but be filled with fear, abandonment, rejection, and hopelessness. Lies are only confirmed and strengthened when couples communicate those lifeless experiences to one another.

Consider uplifting dating relationships you've experienced. Didn't you experience the power of being accepted as you were (which is often not the case for many long-term relationships)? Weren't you secure? You loved and accepted one another without needing any changes in the other person. That was higher security than you often experience in life. That loving security that demanded nothing further from you raised you to higher levels without extra effort on your part.

That is just a glimpse of God's love for us that we as a people do not yet fully know. Christ is powerful, loving security for us. That is how we are raised to higher life. His love that demands nothing further from us while fireworks strip away the false is *how* we are delivered from the lesser realm. Typically, we just have not rested in that kind of love that demands nothing further. We have not rested in that secure love that lifts us without any fleshly effort.

Surpassing Knowledge

I received more revelations as I awakened to the necessity of God's comfort and security before all else. About a week after asking for a capstone to my lengthy fireworks God revealed a little more about the yearner-turner aspect of my experience. This capstone was still God's works beyond my control. The words from Hosea (6:1-2) came to mind: "… He has torn us, but He will heal us …"

That is grace, grace. Grace supports us while we are wounded and stripped of the lesser nature and its lies, which places us on the true foundation; then grace supports us to sacrificially love and comfort others during their stripping works.

God wounded my flesh nature so my soul would let go of it to further embrace my inheritance – the Christ nature. I embraced the Christ nature as far as my trust allowed me to let go of the lesser nature. So God stretched me to the point of distrust. He stretched me to surpass my present level of trust and knowledge.

How far does your trust in Christ go? Through a bad day? A bad week, month, or year? Loss of job? Loss of marriage? Death of a significant other? How about when encountering a cross like Jesus did to bear the shame and sins of others?

God stretches us beyond the places where our soul still trusts in the flesh and the world's riches. Why? God wants to complete those gaps in our souls with Christ. So God wounds our flesh nature (which trusts in false leaves) to further awaken us into our Christ nature, which heals our soul.

I initially learned the way of the cross after experiencing panic attacks earlier in my life. I learned to surrender to whatever trials came along (at least at that point in my life!). I learned to be dead to the world and not in need of it in many ways. I was not as easily wounded in the flesh. But I still needed fleshly wounds to be further completed in Christ. So God went further.

God wounded Kathy's flesh as a way to further wound my flesh. He knew that He could reach me that way. God often wounds the yearner to wound the turner. The turner may unknowingly walk in fleshly security unless he is further wounded, and God sometimes wounds the yearner's flesh nature to further wound the turner's flesh. I sensed the gap Kathy initially felt and was unable to provide what she needed. She saw a steadiness that I walked in and wanted that.

Only after God wounded me further through Kathy could I truly join with her in a wounded area to ask God for support. Now I could cry out from "deep to Deep." Prior to my wound I only prayed from shallow to Deep about this gap (even though I felt much compassion for the gap Kathy experienced). But I had not fully identified or joined with her gap until I became further wounded.

God wounded Kathy and me to further complete us in Christ. He used each of us as counterparts to awaken our souls to more of Him. I came to know need and gaps more deeply like Kathy. Kathy came to know and receive more security as we united to cry out for awareness of Christ in the barren places.

Yearner and turner came to be one with both being deeply aware of gaps needing filled, yet with the security to be still and trust that Christ wanted to be with us and further awaken us in those places. Two became one. The trials we endured were necessary for God's higher ways to become established within us. We won't forget these lessons (unless God has temporary purpose in that at some point)!

Untested head knowledge wasn't enough for us to advance in the kingdom. Lesser ways needed stripped for us to open up from the deep to receive True Deep. Kathy and I have both expressed that every bit of the trials has been worth it. The initial breakthrough came one day out of the blue not long after I had asked for the capstone to the whole experience. My heart sensed it was coming but it was still like an awesome dream when it happened.

Just prior to this breakthrough we had experienced the trauma areas being touched again. We hugged and cried out to God together to know His support in that place. After we were still for several minutes I saw that Kathy seemed more secure. I also felt more secure and then shared the essence of the yearner-turner revelation.

Kathy responded "That is what my heart had known was missing in the beginning but could not express in words." She and I knew that we had come to the end of the locked-up season that was incomprehensible. We had come to the beginning of resurrection life in the barren places (though it was just the beginning of this new season that still had many hiccups).

Love and its fireworks caused us to surpass previous knowledge. We knew that each other knew. Our hearts were one in that moment for the first time in a long time.

Kathy then expressed what our hearts knew: this whole season was ordained by God for higher purposes and that no person but God would govern its conclusion. Nobody but God awakened us to His crucial revelation about embracing our counterpart identities. A counselor had especially contributed Christ's way of cleaving for inner support before talking further (which was God's grace through him), but no single person could be credited with deliverance.

We went to counseling previously and nothing had worked. Even with the present counselor, nothing seemed to take off until the revelation about hugs and security before talking. I also could have expressed my revelation to Kathy in part at earlier points (I had tried prior to the fullness of that revelation). But it was not God's time for us to enter through His doorway into higher unity until this point. His word for our lives needed tested. As we awakened experientially to God's desires for us, He released us into our higher destiny.

We were both clear that God was above all throughout our fireworks. The scriptures say (Job 12:14-16), "... He imprisons a man, and there can be no release ... the misled and the misleader belong to Him." Can you hear in that passage that God is always above all? We both fully believe that now.

We come to know Christ's higher works in every area where our flesh's lesser ones have ended. True awareness comes through being wounded to know flesh's utter weakness that causes the deep of the soul to turn to Deep, which then awakens or completes the soul in that place. That is both true awareness (most symbolized by the yearner) and true fulfillment (symbolized by the turner). That is deliverance. These two counterparts coming together is also true prayer and intercession for others.

In Christ is both awareness and fulfillment. Physically the woman represents the opening or gap, and the man represents the filling of the gap. Spiritually, too, the yearner represents awareness and expression of gaps, and the turner represents fulfillment of gaps. And the two shall become one in Christ. That is the power of Christ that births His kingdom on earth. That greater support in places of gaps is how Christ's greater love and works will go forth on this earth.

Fireworks awakened Kathy and me to a dance of glory. God lifted us. While Kathy and I do not hold the same spiritual views with everything, we experience greater unity than we've ever known. We are more unified counterparts, especially in places of differences or difficulties.

The Master of breakthrough definitely broke through and set off dynamite that had never been united in this higher way. Powerful explosions have already occurred. God's powerful explosions through us give testimony of Love's fireworks and the higher life they birth. Christ's glorious testimony that can never be silenced continues cutting through the murkiest of earthly fogs to keep awakening souls.

The time is approaching for Christ to govern through people with a higher authority than this earth has seen.

Historically, collective belief in a lesser god has maintained lesser forces or principalities that have governed "love" on this earth. Collective belief is powerful. We sometimes suffer not because of personal issues or sin but because of sacrificially withstanding humanity's lesser hurtful ways as well as the forces that maintain them. I sometimes suffer from the world's judgment that tells me I should have no weakness or fallibility, but standing in Christ's acceptance there continues to establish His kingdom and way through me. That was Paul's meaning when he said that he did his share of suffering on behalf of the Church (Col. 1:24).

We sacrificially love one another while suffering the forces of collective lesser beliefs. But collective belief is shifting. Sacrificial love continues birthing more of Christ's kingdom.

Principalities are falling because people are being awakened from lies. People are awakening to the fact that we can rest during trials or sin and trust that God's love is enough to reach us rather than the other way around. Fleshly efforts don't change sins in ourselves or others.

People are just now awakening experientially to a higher love that truly loves us where we are. We are beginning to believe that we don't have to be more than who we are (like when initially dating someone who is madly in love with us). We can rest where we are like children and agree with God to uproot the false while we dwell in His secure love that grows us. Love then works to align our hearts with Him and His fullness, which fills gaps while lesser things fall away.

Final Counterparts on the Last Day

In the last day God reveals the mystery of lawlessness and the mystery of Christ. The scriptures refer to these counterparts as mysteries because they are both kingdoms within us.

Didn't Jesus say that people are defiled by what comes from within? The true battle is within even if outward battles exist.

That is what God revealed to Kathy and me. This final revelation released us into Christ's fuller rest.

In each area of my life I must overcome the battle of kingdom against kingdom within me before I can overcome the battles outside me. I must be stripped and emptied of the lesser kingdom to receive the greater kingdom's fullness. Emptiness precedes fullness. Death precedes resurrection life.[1]

During trials, will I die to my lesser ways and allow Christ to be my strength there? Will I stop putting pressure on myself and, instead, walk in peace that demonstrates that His works are coming through me? His works, not my performance, is fulfillment in me, and I ask for that grace during times of need. My flesh's works then come to an end, which allows freedom for the Spirit to govern through me in those places.

God uses the man of lawlessness to put an end to flesh's futile ways. At some point during your journey God will raise up a power that opposes you beyond what your flesh nature can overcome, whether that is from within or outside you (like God raised up Pharaoh to oppose and oppress the people of Israel, and also like the thorn that was greater than Paul).

You must periodically experience powerlessness to receive more of Christ's power. God humbles you before exalting you. The word within you must be fully tested before you come to rest in sacrificial love. Then you are trustworthy to love as Christ loved.

Fuller tests also come after I initially embrace more of my Christ nature. These greater tests are the man of lawlessness, which is the counterpart to the Man of Christ. Didn't Abraham, Joseph, Moses, Job, and Esther go through trials that were beyond human ability? These tests are not meant to be scary but to stretch you beyond what you feel able to do through your human effort. "The last day" points towards these greater tests for receiving Christ's fullness. It is the last day of flesh nature and its lawlessness in certain areas of your life because the only way through them is to look for Christ being what you need in those places.

The lesser counterpart persecutes and awakens the greater counterpart within us. We as a people must go through the fullness of the man of lawlessness to receive Christ's fullness.[2]

In certain areas of my life I had to experience my flesh's full striving and futility before I let go of its works to receive Christ's fullness in those places. Some of those areas included trusting in my own strength such as my mind, communication ability, likability, achievements, and determination or will power.

Fleshly striving in those areas only came to an end to the extent that I believed that human strength was utterly useless to accomplish kingdom matters or true change. Flesh's end occurred through *experiencing* its uselessness. That is its last day or death. Those experiences cause my soul to awaken — to truly repent or turn from the flesh nature to the Christ nature.

Christ allows the gates of Hades to come against my flesh nature (Matt. 16:18). Death's power is allowed to strip away all that is not Christ to release His resurrection life within me. All that is not Christ is shaken away. That false part must eventually come to total (eternal) destruction. Forever ruined.

I recognized death's power through the man of lawlessness within me. The scriptures say (2 Thes. 2:3-4), "… the man of lawlessness … opposes and exalts himself above every so-called god or object of worship, so that he takes his seat in the temple of God, displaying himself as being God." This power was evident within me during the panic attacks when I recognized that nothing earthly could budge it. It bowed to nothing. Have you encountered this place within yourself? I have.

I have known Christ and His goodness in many ways but in my encounters with flesh's utter powerlessness I had experienced abandonment, aloneness, emptiness, fear, anger, and hopelessness.

That is death. Hell's weeping and gnashing of teeth. During those excruciating experiences nothing tangible reached or helped me (mainly because I had not yet let go of trying to achieve change through my own abilities; I had not yet let go of the world's lie or shoulds of supposedly being able to rise above everything through my willpower). Others' words or prayers did not free me from this power that bowed to nothing (partly because those prayers at that time were also mostly rooted in the fleshly lie that change would come if I simply tried harder). Nothing penetrated this desolate area within me.

The man of lawlessness within God's people will exalt himself against our will and bow to nothing. It is also the abomination of desolation that takes its stand in God's holy place, or temple, which is us (Matt. 24:15). Paul said (1 Cor. 3:16-17), "Do you not know that you are a temple of God, and that the Spirit of God dwells in you?"

This man of lawlessness was governing in place of Christ's Spirit within me. His power bowed to nothing during my panic attacks, and I was afraid and alone. I was desolate because of this "abomination of desolation" (Matt. 24:15).

I felt alone just like Christ's words about the Son of Man having nowhere to lay His head on this earth (Matt. 8:20). But Jesus knew He was not alone in spite of nowhere on earth to lay His head. Jesus went through earthly desolation but still knew the Father's comfort.

Initially I didn't know experientially that Christ was with me during the panic attacks. I felt alone even though I could say the "right" words about God. After gaining victory over this man of lawlessness through the way of rest, I again encountered this man of lawlessness, this abomination of desolation … within my wife Kathy and between us during the worst of our trials. We each felt utterly alone at times. No person could "be our enough" during this time of desolation. We found no answers.

But, really, we were not alone. Christ was with us during these difficult works even when we couldn't experience any goodness. Christ worked His counterpart, the man of lawlessness, to release more of our Christ nature's fullness.

Just like God raised up Pharaoh as Moses' counterpart, Christ raised up the mystery of lawlessness to release the mystery of Christ within Kathy and me. God revealed and glorified Himself through Moses, and Christ revealed and glorified Himself through Kathy and me (eventually).

Pharaoh appeared to win the earlier battles against Moses, and the man of lawlessness appeared to win Kathy's and my earlier battles. But God is always above all and grants authority to lesser forces at times just like He ultimately allowed authority for the beast to overcome the saints (Rev. 13:4-7; the beast is the power within humanity's flesh nature).

Who can withstand the beast? That is what the scriptures portray (Rev. 13:4). But Christ is above all authority. He grants authority to the beast for a time. For Christ's higher purposes (which is especially to raise up overcomers in this season).

Kathy and I were initially overcome and "made as a beast of the field" until the fullness of the times when the kingdom would be restored to us (like with King Nebuchadnezzar). The Spirit had said to me just like Daniel said to King Nebuchadnezzar, "… your kingdom will be restored to you *when* you acknowledge that Heaven rules" (Dan. 4:26-27).

Kathy and I are one, and we both needed to acknowledge that Heaven ruled. We strived in the flesh nature until we trusted and recognized that heaven alone ruled. Our willpower did not. The world's shoulds did not. Christ's higher realm and nature always governed the lesser. Christ had granted this "powerful" man of lawlessness authority over Kathy and me until His purposes were accomplished. Flesh's fullness needed reached, spent, and humbled for us to be released more fully into our Christ nature. The power of darkness had come from within, and so had the power of light come from within, which had the final say.

We were *supposed* to be overcome until we fully participated with Christ's way of the cross that rests and trusts during impossible trials rather than trying to save ourselves. The beast in the book of Revelation is granted authority to overcome the saints (only to the extent that God allows for His good purposes). Our flesh is supposed to be overcome until we truly rest in Christ's way of the cross, which is a sacrificial love for others even during persecution instead of selfishly hurting others to save ourselves.

Christ's purpose for the man of lawlessness within Kathy and me was to awaken us to the powerlessness of human striving. Flesh must experientially recognize that it cannot overcome the lesser kingdom's powers (because it is part of that kingdom). Flesh cannot reign over it. That lesser kingdom within us must decrease for the other to increase.

God wants us to recognize that no earthly power delivers. Prior to becoming king, David had already settled this truth within him when he went forth to battle Goliath and cried out (1 Sam. 17:47), "The battle is the Lord's." David was ready for the outer battle only because his inner one was settled.

You will know that no earthly power can help you when this man of lawlessness begins to exalt himself like Goliath did. In spite of this power that shakes all earthly foundations, the scriptures convey that the true cannot be hurt (Isa. 54:17). Ask others to stand in trust with you for receiving Christ and His higher comfort and works in those places. Even though God created the destroyer (vs. 16), he can only touch and ruin the flesh nature. That is God's purpose for him.

God wants earthly impossibility to come against us at times. The destroyer and his weapons *are* designed to prosper against our flesh, and it *feels* like he prospers during our flesh's desolation. Do not trust your feelings that tempt you to fight against these fireworks.

No More Fighting

The stripping works that came through this God-ordained destroyer freed me more easily when I agreed with Christ's purposes. I became freed when I walked the way Christ walked before me during trials. His way was, and is, to lose the fleshly life.

But beware. The man of lawlessness wants confrontation. Like Goliath, you will see at certain points that he arrogantly flaunts or exalts himself within you, within a significant other, or within an impossible situation you're encountering. He wants you to save yourself. He wants you to fearfully work at or strive for your perceived necessary outcome. He wants a fight. But engaging him through earthly means only increases his strength (our fetters grow stronger, as the scriptures say). Paul exhorted us to use spiritual rather than earthly weapons (2 Cor. 10:4).

Remember earlier when I asked God for a capstone to my marital fireworks? I believe this is the last part of the capstone: the man of lawlessness is not a fight we can win by anything earthly because "… not by might nor by power, but by my Spirit … he will bring out the capstone to shouts of 'God bless it! God bless it!'" (Or, "Grace, grace to it!"; Zech. 4:6-7).

Christ is the capstone. All Spirit. All grace. All love. No mixture. No flesh nature lifted up. All Christ. Jesus said about Himself (Matt. 21:42), "The stone the builders rejected has become the capstone." He Who is within is our capstone.

That full purity of Christ within us only governs when flesh knows its utter uselessness, which only comes through overcoming the man of lawlessness. The scriptures say about the man of lawlessness (2 Thes. 2:4), "...that he *sets himself up* in God's temple proclaiming himself to be God." Daniel foretold about this man of lawlessness who "sets himself up" as the abomination of desolation (Dan. 8:11; 8:25; 9:24; 11:31).

Paul exhorted us to pay attention to the inner battles with this man of lawlessness that "sets itself up" against Christ with arguments (meaning words of no profit or words with no power).[3] Paul also warned about its "pretension," which means falsehood. Paul cautioned us not to enter into fleshly fights with this man of lawlessness whose power is only through deception or illusion.

This man puffs up himself; he terrifies and accuses us through our thoughts and emotions that convey, "Where is God? Something is wrong; I feel no life, only emptiness and fear." The man of lawlessness deceptively draws our flesh nature into a fight to save itself, which strengthens him to become an even greater obstacle to us (sword drawing sword). That way is painful.

During those powerless places, God wants you to rest in your Christ nature that knows love. Trust. Then you see that no fight or striving is needed. This new way powerfully changed my panic attacks. It was a profound new move, one that I wouldn't have thought of in a million years. I had never tried the way of rest, of no longer working hard to change something! Until then I thought that willpower accomplished everything. When I rested I became able to know Christ within me more fully at that point, and that He was above this seemingly untouchable power. I had no way of truly or experientially knowing that Christ was greater than this scary unseen force within me until I fully halted my earthly striving. I overcame the man of lawlessness only through surrendering to Christ's ways that lost the fleshly life.

As part of Jesus' message about kingdoms being powerless when they are divided, He said that we must bind the strong man to plunder him (Matt. 12:29). The strong man is not about Satan but about the "strong" prideful man of flesh that must come to ruin (see Jer. 30:6 about this "strong" fleshly man, even though the flesh is spiritually weak). Bind the strong man. Rest, and fast from your old moves. You must empty the old wine before you are able to drink the new. You are a house divided until then.

Through trust you come to a greater knowing of the True Strong Man. Trust and rest in Christ's love that reaches you, which then breaks the strongest of chains as long as you give Him time. Trust Christ and you will learn of His trustworthiness.

Life comes upon me according to what I believe. Will I believe the lies that I am defective, unwanted, and abandoned during trials? During sin? The accuser works powerfully through the man of lawlessness during these times of desolation. I will feel singled out. Isolated.

The accuser wants to divide and conquer. He wants me to think that I am the only "defective" one, and that no one else experiences this power that feels untouchable. But we as a people are further delivered through the sacrificial ways of overcomers. Overcomers follow the way of the Lamb who endured the cross, they share that testimony with others, and they do not try to save or protect their earthly life (Rev. 12:11). Be vulnerable with others who are safe. Pray and ask others to stand with you in the fire, and stand with them in theirs.

The lack of love that we as a people have experienced in this world still causes us collectively to believe that comfort should sometimes not exist for us during trials or struggles with sin. We fail to believe that Christ truly wants to comfort us during the fleshly stripping, and we reject His comfort more than we know. Collective belief still overpowers us frequently in those places because we as a people have bought the lies that God is a lesser God than He is.

You cannot overcome the man of lawlessness in your time or power. The scriptures tell us that he will be stripped away "at the proper time" (that is, after Christ's purpose for him is completed; see 2 Thes. 2:6). The Spirit used the phrase "at the proper time" to alert us to another verse that pertains to the man of lawlessness.

The scriptures say (1 Ptr. 5:6-11), "Humble yourselves, therefore, under the mighty hand of God, that He may exalt you *at the proper time*, casting all your anxiety upon Him, because He cares for you. Be of sober spirit, be on the alert. Your adversary, the devil, prowls about like a roaring lion, seeking someone to devour. But resist him, firm in your faith, knowing that the same experiences of suffering are being *accomplished* by your brethren who are in the world. And *after* you have suffered for a little while, the God of all grace, who called you to His eternal glory in Christ, will Himself perfect, confirm, strengthen and establish you."

We become exalted after we've become humbled. Humble yourself and allow Christ to uproot this man of lawlessness in His time rather than yours. I wish I had known much earlier during my panic attacks this way of surrendering into Christ's higher goodness, comfort, and works. That would have saved me from seemingly endless periods of agony. But at least Christ used my futility to birth more of His ways for others to see. Pray that you would rest in Christ's peaceful arms until the proper time. Rest is the proof of your trust when you feel powerless. Die to the flesh nature's attempts to save yourself so that Christ can be the fulfillment within you in that desolate place. The perceived need to strive is a smoke screen that seduces you into trying to save your earthly life only to lose it in the end.

Christ is sovereign. He has the keys to death and Hades. Christ decides, not the man of lawlessness (even if it *feels* like he has the power). Christ alone decides when you are found trustworthy to sacrificially love others rather than to act selfishly to save yourself during trials, which actually comes to pass when you give place for Christ rather than worldly forces.

Daniel's words about the abomination of desolation in the last day indicate that Jerusalem will be rebuilt during times of trouble (Dan. 9:25). Jerusalem is symbolic of the spiritual true self within people. Christ rebuilds our souls during flesh's times of trouble and desolation.

Vultures

The Spirit stirred my heart one day about a huge swarm of vultures that led to my many revelations about the man of lawlessness and the abomination of desolation. I would not have seen what I saw scripturally otherwise.

Kathy and I had regularly seen swarms of vultures over our place for about two months as we were beginning to come out of the trenches. The surprising part is that we live in town with only a small group of trees behind our place! One day Kathy saw numerous vultures flying over us during a several mile walk on a country road. Jokingly, yet seriously, I said that they were probably flying to our house. I felt like I somehow knew this spiritually.

As our house came into view we saw vultures flying towards it from all directions, almost as if they had no other purpose than to get there as fast as they could. I could only laugh at this totally unexplainable scene. Then as we came closer I saw two huge swarms of vultures "side by side" over our house. I counted 35 in the smaller group and saw that the other group was significantly larger. I knew that 75 to 100 vultures swarmed directly above our place.

"Side by side" stood out to me as somehow paralleling Kathy and me as counterparts side by side. The Spirit stirred my heart to look up the word "vultures" in the scriptures. Coincidentally, I had just read about the man of lawlessness during my time with God the previous day.

Also during this time period I heard a man speak about how Peter realized that Jesus must have summoned the multitudes of fish into his nets. That's how I felt about the many vultures over our house, to the point that these vultures swooped low into our yard exciting our dog Molly about all the action above.

I saw in the scriptures that Jesus said (Matt. 24:28), "Wherever there is a carcass, there the vultures will gather." I immediately sensed the meaning but wanted to see all of Jesus' words leading into this statement (I realize that some people translate this passage as meaning eagles rather than vultures, but I see valuable points to be learned from each way of translating it). My heart quickened as I saw Jesus' words about the abomination that causes desolation (vs. 15). I knew that the vultures represented death of the flesh. The flesh nature raised up by the man of lawlessness within Kathy and me had been getting devoured.

Many revelations overwhelmed me in that moment, which had led to most of what I had written about the man of lawlessness to this point. The vultures played one additional part in the revelations I received. Kathy and I went for a walk one morning near our house and she said, "I walked here last evening and heard loud sounds coming from the tree tops, and I saw that it was the vultures."

My heart stirred about the scriptures when Kathy described the sounds coming from the tree tops. I remembered that sounds from the treetops represented God's supernatural power going forth to deliver from humanly impossible situations. The scriptures say about King David's upcoming battle with the Philistines (2 Sam.

350

5:23-25), "And when David inquired of the LORD, He said, 'You shall not go directly up; circle around behind them and come at them in front of the balsam trees. And it shall be, when you hear the sound of marching in the tops of the balsam trees, then you shall act promptly, for then the LORD will have gone out before you to strike the army of the Philistines.'"

God used the sounds in the tree tops to signal David that His delivering power was now going before him. My heart stirred about God signaling me that His power was now going before Kathy and me as we learned to rest and look to Him for comfort and goodness during encounters with the man of lawlessness.

Kathy and I joined later that morning to agree with God in prayer about what He had shown us. We prayed that we along with God's people would rest from the earthly and look to Him for comfort during encounters with the man of lawlessness. We trusted that Christ's power was going before us in those prayers. I was surprised when I looked out our kitchen window that very evening to see and hear many vultures shaking the several tree tops right behind our house! Instantly I knew that the Lord's delivering power was going forth answering our earlier prayers.

Kathy and I had become fully united in prayer about God's way of resting and looking to Him for comfort when encountering the man of lawlessness. Christ had gathered us. Astonishingly, that night was the last we saw the multitudes of vultures. Coincidence?

People in the community had commented about these vultures hanging out over our place for almost two months, and after Kathy and I had united in prayer with the revelations about overcoming the man of lawlessness, the vultures suddenly disappeared. Completely. I saw this as a clear sign that "the vultures" went elsewhere to devour flesh nature. Probably other overcomers!

I knew that Christ would continue these works in His people and I also knew that He had trained Kathy and me in His Way.

We would still encounter pruning as part of our continued walk with Christ, but He had humbled us to cause us to rest and trust during the fleshly stripping that comes through the man of lawlessness.

Humble yourselves under the mighty hand of God and He will exalt you at the proper time. Kathy and I have lived this. Christ's ways are true.

Do not wrestle with or fight this man of lawlessness within you or others. You will sense when this higher power seems untouchable. Allow the weeds among the wheat. Allow the thorns in the flesh. That is what awakens Christ and His resurrection power within us. We learn pure trust through these encounters.

I do not mean for us to be passive during our many life difficulties. But I do mean with all my heart for us to allow the man of lawlessness that exalts himself above all earthly powers. Christ allows that thorn to humble the flesh nature within us, and at the proper time Christ will strip away that unwanted powerful presence ... but only after Christ's grace has become our enough in that place. We receive resurrection power when our flesh nature has reached its end and we come to know that heaven alone rules. Christ alone reigns over all power, whether that is outside or within us.

The battle is never earthly; it is never about or because of people. Do not judge yourself or anyone else regarding this man of lawlessness. The battle is kingdom against kingdom, about Christ's higher, loving ways versus flesh's unloving ones that continue our suffering.

This heightened kingdom battle within us ends when fleshly efforts stop. The scriptures say (Job 37:8-9), "He seals [God stops or makes an end of] the hand of every man, that all men may know *His* work. *Then* the beast goes into its lair, and remains in its den." Do you remember that Jesus had said that we had made

His house a den of thieves? That was about us participating with the beast of flesh nature within us, rather than participating with Him within who becomes prayer through us. Then we become a house of prayer rather than a den of thieves.

May our fleshly beast remain in its den! That's my prayer. Silenced humbled flesh. I come to believe Christ's higher works when flesh's lesser ones have ended. Then the world's beast has nothing in me. It has no power to deceive or control me any longer in the areas I have encountered flesh's futility.

Only Christ awakens love in His time as He pleases. Christ alone has the keys of death and Hades. He alone governs the proper time. Pray that you rest and trust Christ's comfort when you encounter the man of lawlessness. You will reign and govern with Christ above the earthly realm after you have walked His sacrificial ways to receive this greater love that cannot be shaken.

Christ is the way, the truth, and the life. The scriptures state this order for a reason. You must first know Christ as the way. You must know His sacrificial way of the cross that lets go enough to see Truth during trials. Only after you see and know the Truth during those times can you find Life in those desolate places. Knowing and resting in Truth and resurrection Life come only through walking His sacrificial way.

We become Christ's beautiful people who reign with Him after we have suffered with Him. Greater love and works are released through beautiful people who have suffered the loss of their lesser ways.

CHAPTER 14

Love's Fire Works ... the Rule-Breaker

Shared Brokenness and Power

Higher heavenly ways break our earthly rules. Gaps and weakness are supposed to exist for us to call forth Christ's strength. That establishes His kingdom through us. God wants us to be vulnerable and express our need with Him and with one another during felt gaps. Jesus told us that we must become like children to enter the kingdom. Counterparts must unite and cry out for Christ's true support in those places.

Our crosses are meant to uproot our independence from one another so that we can unify. The cross is meant to uproot perceived separation. But we cannot unify when we hide our struggles or brokenness.

We must no longer hide like Adam and Eve in the garden. The cross is meant to humble our fleshly pride that pretends it has it altogether, which portrays no need and then continues perceived level differences between one another. It also continues the worldly lie that fleshly perfection is attainable.

We continue independence from Christ when we maintain independence from one another. One morning I heard the words,

"Shared brokenness is the way forward. That is My broken body, My bread that feeds the multitudes."

Sharing should not be a one-way street where others try to fix the struggling person. I have encountered that, and it hurts. We are most deceived when we think that we are the only one with significant struggles.

Shared brokenness is meant to be a shared journey of overcoming, one that we can all relate to. It is amazing how much strength we find when we see that we are not alone in our struggles. We see there is no separation, and we are far less able to be deceived. By shared brokenness I do not mean for us to stare outwardly and grumble about what is happening to us or about what is wrong with the world. Rather, shared brokenness is about sharing our struggle to trust and know what God is after in our heart during difficult struggles. That is the true struggle for all of us.

We as a people will discover greater unity and power through shared brokenness. That is what was symbolized by Jesus sharing the five loves of broken bread and two fish with the multitude (Mk. 6:41). The broken bread represents His body of people becoming broken and shared with the multitudes (just like Jesus had been broken for the many). Our brokenness is to be shared as food for the many, rather than hidden. The number "five" represents grace, and the number "two" represents earthly division. Earthly division and brokenness that become blessed by heaven transform into supernatural substance for the many. True food.

Heaven blesses the sacrificial love during shared brokenness and it reaches and satisfies the deep in people. The people sought Jesus not because of the miracles but because they ate and were truly satisfied (Jn. 6:26). That's my desire behind sharing my broken places and marital trials. We often think we have to give from a place that is altogether for others. But Jesus wanted His disciples to start sharing even if that was from little and brokenness, trusting that He would bring increase.

I have come to find that true life supernaturally multiplies through shared brokenness. One with another. Not a one way street. We all have broken parts that are meant to be spiritual food for all.

I facilitated a growth group where all people in it shared significant unanswerable life issues. Each of our barren broken places was met with deep acceptance and honesty. Me included. It was the safest yet most honest group I have ever experienced. People's barren places lost their rigidity and became soft enough to experience comfort for the first time. Love was received and lesser ways shed. The soft ground within had allowed Christ to plant new life within people's souls. But the good ground was ground that became soft through the safety of shared brokenness.

Supernatural growth occurred in that group. Life multiplied. Shared brokenness made it safe for people not to feel singled out and defective in their barren places. That lie could find no place when all were vulnerable and in the same boat. No longer fearing judgment, their souls opened up and received comfort and love in aspects of their heart that had never known true comfort. But they only opened up when they saw others' broken places, which brought them the security to know that others would not judge them.

Shared brokenness has not been the norm in the body of Christ. *Christ is after His broken body being shared with one another*, which He portrayed when He fed the multitude. Only earthly brokenness (death to the flesh nature) brings forth resurrection life, and it multiplies when we share vulnerably with one another.

Be vulnerable and cry out with others from deep to True Deep. Cry out in unity for Christ's higher nature, authority, and name to be further established in places of weakness. Kathy and I love uniting to trust during areas of weakness now. We experience wholeness and fulfillment of God's purpose for those weaknesses and struggles when we sacrificially unite in trust.

Jesus told us to ask for whatever we want in His name, and He will give it (see Jn. 14:13). That sounds like we can be selfish children who get whatever we want. That's not His meaning.

There is power in Jesus' name, but His name is only present in truth during our situations when the lesser is broken and stripped away. All other "names" that we trust or believe in within our heart must bow to the name of Jesus. The lesser nature must give way and honor higher nature within us.

Success, power, reputation, independence, and earthly loyalties must bow. Power in Jesus' name only comes when we have trusted Him through trials and have surrendered the lesser places of security and significance.

What do you stare at because of fear during trials? *What other names are you afraid of losing?* During my marital fireworks I feared losing my reputation of being a nice guy. During the writing of this book I was afraid of Christians judging me and questioning my soundness of mind when I stepped beyond the commonly accepted ways and rules of what should be. We exalt above Jesus' name whatever we stare at in fear.

Trials are for learning to see, stare at, and exalt Jesus' name above all names so that the power of those other names becomes humbled during trials. We overcome when we surrender other names and remain in steadfast trusting relationship with Him during trials.

That was my constant task during my fireworks. I saw that God wanted to further complete my soul in various areas. Christ established His name and higher nature within my soul when my sight remained fixed on Him.

Christ's kingdom comes when I surrender to what I sense He is working during my trials. That is praying in His name and higher nature. He answers. Maybe not immediately but His higher goodness comes. I gain true peace and security at those times – heavenly riches. He causes those other names to bow to His name in my life, and His reign increases.

But fear leads me and increases when I remain distrustful about what God is working during trials. Those "bigger powers" remain in my life when I stare at them as bigger than Christ. The battles continue.

Jesus disarmed all powers and authorities through His cross (Col. 2:15). Lesser powers became disarmed when Jesus surrendered to the Father's goodness and higher ways as above all else during trials. Those other powers lost their power. How? They could not control Jesus when He followed the Father's name and will alone.

Christ disarms those powers and authorities within us personally when we trust that He still reigns during trials. Trusting that He reigns during our trials gradually establishes His kingdom within us and around us (even when it doesn't feel that way at the time).

God is after trust. The spiritual place of trust in God alone through trials is Zion (see Psm. 125:1; Isa. 31:4-5). Zion represents a finished Jerusalem. That is why the scriptures refer to Zion as "… the place of the *name* of the LORD of hosts, even Mount Zion" (Isa. 18:7).

Zion is our place of trust in God where He desires more than all else to come and abide (Psm. 87:2). That is the power of His name, and He answers us in full when we pray from that place of trust that has been stripped of lesser ways through fire.

That is why the scriptures say (2 Cor. 1:2), "For no matter how many promises God has made, they are 'Yes' in Christ." We always receive God's promises when we are stripped of the lesser nature and rest in the place of *being in Christ*. Sometimes during fire we need to ask others who are safe to stand with us in trust. That is shared brokenness. That is also realness and intimacy.

Being in Christ means utter realness. In one of my counseling classes I give students an article about a man that saw a car hit his wife and son, killing them right in front of his eyes. I role play that man sharing in a detached unemotional way about the tragic incident, and I ask students to hear and support me in what I share. Then I role play the man sharing, instead, from a raw emotional place about that horrific event. The second scenario demonstrated utter realness whereas the first portrayed the man sharing from behind an invisible shell where he could not be touched.

After discussing the differences, the students realize that the man could receive no true support if he did not allow real relationship. Others hearing that man would not be able to truly support and connect with him if he kept the real and raw experience locked up and still alone within him. He would have still felt alone inwardly. Only disconnection would have occurred had he not been utterly real. The students knew that real relationship and connection would not have existed unless the man shared the raw emotions and experience that he kept hidden within him.

Our connection or disconnection with Christ happens the same way. Sharing our raw and real emotional experiences allows connection with Christ, and hiding that utter realness does not. Disconnecting from those real experiences will cause us to experience Christ saying to us, "I never knew you" in those places, just like He portrayed in His parable (Matt. 7:23). Christ wants to connect with us and to be with us, but we reap what we sow. We reap disconnection when we do not allow real connection. He honors free will and allows us to cut off relationship with Him.

If you look at the scriptures leading into and surrounding verse 23 in Matthew 7, you will see that Jesus is focused on whether or not we experience heaven's goodness and enter through an open door or not. Will we enter through the narrow gate of utterly real relationship with Him, or will we walk in false hypocritical ways (which is the common, wide gate that will draw more destruction to ourselves)? This whole section of scriptures focuses on these dynamics. We encounter disconnection from Christ (I never knew you) when we walk in falseness, and we encounter connection with Him when we walk in utter realness. That was Jesus' whole point in how we further enter the kingdom. Utter realness. No falseness. Study that whole passage and you will see that the focus is about intimate relationship ("Lord, Lord") versus falseness and hypocrisy (trying to pick figs from a thorn tree). One path is an open door and the other is not.

Jesus said to Nathanael that he was an Israelite with no falseness (Jn. 1:47-51). Then He said to him that he would see heaven opened. Why did Jesus emphasize that Nathanael would encounter an open heaven? Because Nathanael walked with no falseness. No hypocrisy. We experience open heavens when we walk in utter realness rather than falseness. There is no disconnect relationally when we are real. That was Nathanael. But we experience disconnection and aloneness in our "relationships" with one another and with Christ when we are not fully real and raw with who and where we are in our walk. (Sometimes this is as simple as us pretending to ourselves that we trust God's goodness at the moment when, in reality, we don't.) Then, unfortunately, Christ will need to break through our falseness to reach us. He will need to break through our false ways with its rigid rules so as to bring forth genuine real relationship, which then results in us experiencing with Him, "I know you." That is an open heaven with no barriers on our end.

God Keeps Breaking My Rules

In the first chapter I shared about God's greater love that touched a flight attendant and then a woman in group counseling. What would have happened if my flesh nature had responded in each of those situations?

Each woman would have encountered fleshly works and words that wouldn't have lifted their loads. Neither of my encounters with those women had to do with the words I spoke. My flesh nature was out of the way and Love's fire worked the Rule-Breaker. The Spirit's fiery wisdom spoke and burned away those women's earthly rules to awaken higher life.

God's fire breaks through the death in people's lives. Earthly ways become broken by Love's eternal fire that is unstoppable. The flight attendant's glowing face still showed evidence of God's burning fire as I left the plane. The woman in group counseling shone brightly with that fire the following week.

That is the difference between earthly testimony and love's fire that continues to give higher testimony. The higher works cause an encounter for people. Eternal works leave an ongoing impact rather than empty words. That's what Jesus portrayed when He asked the leper He healed to show himself to the priest rather than to use empty words *about* healing. Encounters with people who have been healed by Christ always show His higher works through them, and there's an impact because lesser rules and ways have been humbled.

God's fireworks take us beyond our current ways. Upon someone's recommendation I almost titled this book, *God Keeps Breaking My Rules*. At a practical level this title emphasized much of what this book is about. Our rules keep getting broken as the Lord continues to awaken us. Love's fiery works awaken more of Christ's finished works within us, works that came through the cross and defeated death and all other powers. Christ is alive, and He is in us for establishing His works in place of earthly ones.

Christ's finished works break death's rules. They have defeated death and *cannot* be stopped. They are the power of resurrection life that has no equal. There is no voice that is higher, purer, or more powerful than this unstoppable resurrection voice.

After Christ's resurrection many "powerful" people, voices, and other powers tried in futility to stamp out any trace of these finished works and voice of Truth. But the gates of Hades could not overpower Christ's finished works that had defeated all opposing powers. These powers had no control over Life that found a Way even after death.

Christ's finished works are built up within our souls every time we unite with His Way of death to the lesser nature. That is life after death while on this earth. This higher life within us that is in union with Him is His finished works that continue to burn away the earthly fog.

I Feel the Earth Move

During the writing of this book I encountered many signs and wonders. One of these coincidences was a song I found myself humming while writing one morning. The song was Carole King's *I Feel the Earth Move*, the first song on her album *Tapestry*. At the time I didn't know that the song was by Carole King.

Feeling the earth move under my feet was exactly how I had felt during my fireworks. I felt like the Lord had moved a tremendous amount of earthly ground (ways) under my feet spiritually. He gave grace for me to overcome lesser ways like striving and performing to attain God's riches. God had moved numerous earthly mountains.

That is the Rule-Breaker's work. Through the fire God also led me to pray for other people's earthly ground to be put under their feet. That means broken rules. I prayed that Christ would break through people's lesser ways to awaken the true. That is the new earth that comes while old views of heaven are burned away!

Humming the Carole King song was mysterious to me. I had heard her songs years earlier but had never focused on them. God brought her songs to my attention because they emphasized key messages burning in my heart. God is putting under our feet the earthly ground within us, and that battle is also seen in the following Carole King song. I have provided key lines from her song below, but I would encourage you to look at the rest of the words in that song.

Tapestry

My life has been a tapestry of rich and royal hue
An *everlasting* vision of the *everchanging* view
There came *a man of fortune, a drifter passing by*
Once he reached for something golden hanging from
a tree
And his hand came down empty
It seemed that *he had fallen into someone's wicked*
spell
A figure gray and ghostly beneath a flowing beard
Now *my tapestry's unraveling*; he's come to take me
back

Wow, I am amazed at the pointed spiritual truth in this song. Our lives are a tapestry of rich and royal hue, and they are also God's everlasting vision of the ever-changing view. We experience through Him an everlasting vision and we ever-grow into seeing Him as He is.

The words in this song are powerful. We regularly encounter within us this "man of fortune, a drifter passing by." That impermanent drifter is our flesh nature, which is not who we truly are.

We sometimes fall for this man of fortune's deceit about riches even though that fleshly imposter can gain no true wealth like the man portrayed in the song. That stranger was the one that reached for the gold with his hand coming down empty, just like our flesh reached for the forbidden fruit in the Garden of Eden and found emptiness. That fleshly lair within us still reaches for the apple.

This man of fortune was under the spell of a dark stranger, which caused him (our flesh nature) to suffer. We can hear in this song our same struggle of not wanting our tapestry to unravel. We don't want to be taken back to a place that we've known and disliked.

We can hear the constant pull towards that old familiar place where this drifter keeps trying to regain a foothold over our soul. But we only experience sorrow and suffering when we fall for his deceit and fail to let go of the lesser. We suffer and unravel when we do not journey onward with our impossible-to-hold tapestry of rich and royal hue, one that is an everlasting vision of an ever-changing view.

We are ever-growing tapestries of love. We are meant to ever-embrace and awaken to the wonders of who we truly are. I opened a fortune cookie recently and found the message "It takes courage to grow up and become who you truly are." That is profound.

"An everlasting vision of an ever-changing view" describes our process of growth connected to our two natures. We become aware of the everlasting vision every time we join with our Christ nature; and every time our soul further embraces God's everlasting works, our rule-oriented flesh nature experiences an ever-changing view of God (as if He changed the rules)!

Peals of Thunder

This section's title came about because I heard thunder rumble just as I was beginning to write about God's stripping works or "judgment." I felt sad as I thought about how greatly humanity has misunderstood God's judgment. That is when I heard the thunder rumbling outside. The phrase "peals of thunder" immediately came to mind, which caused me to glance at several of those phrases in the book of Revelation.

I was shocked as I read Revelation 4:1-8 about God's rainbow fully surrounding the throne. I knew that the throne and peals of thunder in that passage symbolized God's judgment, but I never remembered that a rainbow encompassed that judgment. Do you hear the meaning? Even from the Old Testament, God's rainbow symbolized His faithfulness, and here it is, encompassing His judgment. In other words, God's love endures through or beyond His judgment, beyond the stripping works. That is what He had been teaching me earlier in my journey when I found myself in the end of the rainbow. I knew at that time that His stripping works would continue until He found the gold, but now He provided scriptural understanding of what I had known initially through the Spirit directly: that His judgment is for us, not against us. God's love is bigger than and faithful through the stripping works. I was giddy when I saw that the rainbow surrounded the throne! I was also overwhelmed when I again saw His sovereignty regarding how He alerted me to the passage about "peals of thunder" that demonstrates His utter faithfulness during and through His judgment that strips away the false.

God had previously revealed some scriptures to me in Isaiah 28 (particularly vs. 2, 17) that portray God's judgment and justice as His hail *for sweeping away the refuge of lies in our lives.* That is the purpose of His judgment. This judgment is a spiritual hail of destruction to the fortresses of lies that have kept us blind to God's love as our true refuge.

God knows that we typically will not let go of our lies until they no longer work. That's what happened to me. That's how I let go of lies and lesser ways to go on with Christ's higher ones.

This last lengthy period of fireworks led me to pray tenaciously to uproot lies in me, as well as in those I'm connected to, and within humanity. This book is a direct result of those prayers.

The lies we believe are the source of our bondage. They are the true powers that hinder us from peace. We have freedom and know God's love to the extent that our lies have been uprooted. So hail, hail to God's hail that strips away lies! (Sorry, I got carried away here.)

Another coincidence happened on a golf course while learning about judgment that strips away our lies. It involved hail. Looking back I see it as a sign and wonder.

My son John and I were caught in the onslaught of a tremendous hailstorm. Hail larger than our golf balls poured down upon us. Fortunately a nearby woman waved for us to come for shelter in her garage. The hail fell so heavily that it blocked the garage door's sensor so that it could not close. After the hailstorm stopped we found many dimples in our van from the hail (not from our golf balls!). Huge hail might be common where you live but I am 55 and this was the first time I experienced such a powerful hailstorm.

Many coincidences occurred during the writing of this book, and they brought life and further understanding to the messages I share. These occurrences were mind-blowing. In hind sight I see a comprehensive work in my life that began well before these writings; and all of God's spiritual work "just happened" to line up completely with the title of this book. All these works illustrate how sovereign and good God is. In spite of often being blind to God's works and what He was doing in my life He brought unity to many seemingly unrelated events.

I have no doubt that my personal life's fireworks played a crucial part in birthing the depth and unity of what I share. Now I see the book's title as perfect for the messages within me that feel like a burning fire needing released.

Even when I decided on the book's name I questioned whether it was right … until the next coincidence occurred. It happened two days after deciding on the title, which was about two months into the writing.

I asked God again if the title was right. In the midst of wrestling with the Lord about it while driving my car, I "happened" to see a large bill board with the huge word "FIREWORKS." I stared at it in disbelief. Slanting up towards that bigger-than-life-word from underneath it was the smaller word "BRAVO!" I remember nothing else on the bill board; just that. It felt like God spoke directly to me as I read it … right when I was in the midst of asking Him!

The further I worked on this book the more I became overwhelmed with the thought, "There could have been *no* other title for this book!" I saw that the title was meant to be before the writing had ever begun.

My own personal fireworks and experiences of God's sovereign goodness worked together for me to see His faithfulness during and through His judgment. He desired to free me into His higher goodness, and now I can't help but to see the scriptures and His judgment with eyes that trust love's faithfulness.

Heavens Are Ways

Have you surrendered to God's works during impossible trials and experienced being awakened with new spiritual sight? I leave go of the lesser realm and thirst for Christ's higher realm during trials, and I regularly receive revelations about life and the scriptures at those times. Those new revelations birthed through fire are higher heavens.

"Heavens" consist of ways and views that establish realities. The highest heaven is God's purest Way. That is Christ and His surrendered way that constantly clear a pathway in us for abiding in God's unending higher nature and will. God is infinite and Christ is the sacrificial way for continuously awakening into Him who is greater. Christ's surrendered way within us during trials keeps birthing God's higher ways and views. That way establishes "Thy kingdom come on earth as it is in heaven."

God spoke through Isaiah (55:9), "For as the heavens are higher than the earth, so are My ways higher than your ways, and My thoughts than your thoughts." All parts of this passage are about the same thing. Our earthly views of heaven and goodness are our present heavens, and they are one with our earthly ways. That is why Jesus said that what we bind on earth will be bound in heaven, and what we loose on earth will be loosed in heaven (Matt. 16:19).

Jesus said to let things be done according to our belief. We experience shame about sins if we believe sins are inexcusable. We then also experience "God" as ashamed of us and justify any harsh ways or outcomes connected to us as right.

Our views and ways are our heavens. The scriptures say (Prov. 17:15), "He who justifies the wicked, and he who condemns the righteous, both of them alike are an abomination to the LORD."

Justifying the wicked is an abomination because it distorts righteousness and reveals our view of God and righteousness.

Consider our views about discipline. Excusing or justifying a parent who severely paddles a child for a wrong behavior supports that way as right. That is a view of righteousness. That belief regarding righteousness on earth will also be a person's view of God's righteousness with people. That is why God desires to burn away our current earthly ways and views of heaven.

Before all of my fireworks I had believed that kingdom advancement always required significant effort, my inward struggles shouldn't exist, and that I shouldn't need support. During my fireworks those ways no longer worked for me; God broke them so I could leave go of them.

My earthly ways corresponded to my views of heaven. They were connected, and they no longer worked. Love's fire broke my rules to awaken higher views of heaven.

God burns away lesser views of heaven to make room for higher views of heaven as we learn from Him during trials. He burns away those lesser views by ensuring that our corresponding earthly ways don't work. Burning away the lesser makes room for the greater.

God through Isaiah foretold this day that burns away our present views of heaven and earthly ways (65:17), "For behold, I create new heavens and a new earth; and the former things shall not be remembered or come to mind." That's why I believe that God wants us to view His ways in the Old Testament as only shadows, really, symbols, that merely pointed towards higher unseen spiritual ways. Those ways were not the real and are "not to come to our mind" as truly God. That is also why the scriptures emphasize that God saw something "wrong" with the old covenant when He established the new (Heb. 8:7).

There is more that stands out to me about the Isaiah passage. A new earth always made sense to me, but new heavens? New heavens and a new earth happen at the same time because they are connected, and the present heavens and earth become burned away by fire.

Views and ways establish reality. We encounter a taskmaster god who demands no mistakes when that has been our earthly experience, way, and view. But as our present views and ways are burned away we come into a new reality. New heavens and a new earth. The past is no longer to be a standard for us.

If I believe that I cannot have peace until my earthly circumstances become what I desire, that is my heavenly view of how things work. With that view I will not walk in peace until the outside world becomes perfectly what I want. That lesser view or way establishes a reality. Fortunately God is burning away our lesser views and ways of heaven to create a new earth.

Peter stated (2 Ptr. 3:7-13), "But the present heavens and earth by His word are being reserved for fire, kept for the day of judgment and destruction of ungodly men. But do not let this one fact escape your notice, beloved, that with the Lord one day is as a thousand years, and a thousand years as one day ... But the day of the Lord will come like a thief, in which the [present] heavens will pass away with a roar and the elements will be destroyed with intense heat, and the earth and its works will be burned up ... But according to His promise we are looking for *new heavens and a new earth, in which righteousness dwells.*"

"Judgment and destruction of ungodly men" is not about person versus person but about flesh nature versus true spirit nature. Know that the scriptures symbolize the unseen. The ungodly man is the lesser flesh nature that is burned away when we participate with that nature. Judgment of the old is to free us into the unity, goodness, and love of the new self. The Christ nature.

This gradually unfolding "day" of God's spiritual fire burns away our earthly ways and views of heaven so that righteousness dwells on this earth. That is the new earth where God's rights rather than fleshly rights dwell. One nature becomes humbled and the other exalted.

Why is there a need for new heavens? The need for new heavens tells us that lack currently exists. The scriptures say (Job 15:15), "Behold, He puts no trust in His holy ones, and the heavens are not pure in His sight." The need for new heavens and a new earth where righteousness dwells communicates that righteousness has not existed as things are presently. Part of the lack of righteousness is our lesser views of heaven that maintain our unrighteous ways on earth.

Our views of heaven and of the scriptures about heaven have not been God's higher views, and our present views along with the resulting ways are being burned away by fireworks!

We must no longer view heaven as some faraway place that requires certain simple confessions to arrive there where only a privileged few enjoy. All nations will see His righteousness. Heaven is to become known as a surrendered, trustworthy Way that people are to come to know and walk. Ways establish realities, and the Way of heaven is to become established wherever we are.

New heavens birth a new earth! New views of heaven bring higher life to this earth. That is the heavenly Jerusalem coming down to this earth. Christ's Way becomes established on this earth.

The scriptures say (Isa. 64:1-4), "Oh, that Thou wouldst rend the heavens and come down ... For from of old they have not heard nor perceived by ear, neither has the eye seen a God besides

Thee, Who acts in behalf of the one who waits for Him." That is a surrendered Way.

God worked love's fire in my life to burn away my earthly striving. Christ moved to restore me when I stopped striving in my earthly strength and joined His higher works. I no longer reacted by striving and effort to fill felt gaps. Christ then established new heavens or ways within me as I no longer participated with old moves. Then His fire awakened me to more of His higher ways during my marital trials.

Heaven had changed for me because my views and ways had changed. God didst rend my previous heavens and come down to me! God became to me a personally loving and powerful Person that reached me during the impossible. I discovered His greater love deeper within my soul. He more than took a camel through the eye of a needle for me just as the scriptures say (Matt. 19:24). Heaven to me was now a powerful pursuer that delivers through fire burning away the old to make all things new.

I no longer view trials as God's judgment for punishing a wrong. I now see His fire as always faithful to birth more of His ways, not just within me but within all people. I see His relentless pursuit of people's freedom, even though my earthly eyes temporarily cloud the truth at points. He faithfully burns away present heavens for us to see Him more as perfect love with the intent of fully casting out fear and judgment (1 Jn. 4:18). I never experienced that verse so deeply before.[1]

Wider, Longer, Higher, and Deeper

We as a people will desire to lose our life to gain true life the more we are stripped of the flesh nature's lies. I desire that now. I trust love more and have less need of a Thief to take the lesser from me.[2]

As we grow we will begin to know a love beyond definition and boxes, a love that is living, breathing, and growing. A love that is wider, longer, higher, and deeper than we imagined. An example comes to mind.

I used to live in Scranton, Pennsylvania. I remember driving through that city and encountering various streets such as Maple, Washington, Monroe, Ash, Jefferson, and others. Not until about my third year of living there did I have a revelation about those streets in the center of the city. All the streets running one direction were names of presidents and all the streets running the other direction were names of trees.

That bigger picture was always there. Nothing had changed. The only difference was me coming into a greater realization of what had always been. That greater realization helped me to find my way through the city far easier. That is how we awaken more into God's kingdom.

How can we believe that we have a great and final knowing of spiritual realities when it takes that long to see natural ones? That is especially true when we account for Christ's works to make those who "see" blind and those who are blind to see. That is why I tell people that I don't have a period at the end of my sentence spiritually (in spite of how much I temporarily embrace what God reveals to me). We keep gaining awareness of His higher ways over time.

Let's look at the topic of pleasure and what it might mean to see higher than we currently do. God created us to enjoy pleasure. Some of you may think that that statement goes against everything you have ever been taught.

Understanding this whole spiritual principle depends entirely upon our lesser or greater view of pleasure. Whether we look with fleshly eyes or Christ's eyes. Jesus called Peter "blessed" for receiving his revelation from the Father about Jesus being the Son of God. Being blessed means experiencing or receiving heavenly pleasure, fulfillment, or satisfaction.

God placed the desire for pleasure within us. Pleasure drives all people in various ways.

The problem is when we follow our flesh nature's lies about what satisfies us. No room is left for God to complete us with heavenly pleasure when we keep filling our cup with earthly pleasures.

We were created for true pleasure and joy, which come from the bliss of unity with God. That blissful unity is the highest form of love and pleasure.

We hinder our awakening by seeking and settling for lesser pleasures. Our hearts are like vacuum cleaner hoses towards pleasure. We will not draw to ourselves heavenly pleasure when earthly pleasures are available and desired above God. A rich person finds it impossible to further enter the kingdom – as impossible as a camel going through the eye of a needle.

Paul's discovery of being content in all circumstances came from learning to draw his pleasure from the Lord alone (Phil. 4:11). Then it did not matter whether Paul's earthly circumstances were great or little. His vacuum cleaner hose was not turned towards earthly pleasures whether they were available or not. But our flesh usually needs to experience significant stripping before our heart becomes like Paul's that freely inclines towards God's higher pleasure.

We cannot attain pleasure and satisfaction through God in the same way we attain earthly satisfaction. We gain earthly pleasure or fullness (success, status, or other rewards) by following all the worldly shoulds and rules.

People are often confused by their lack of fulfillment when they experience a season of being motivated by shoulds to serve God. I used to do that. Shoulds cause us not to be in relationship with God but with a taskmaster who cannot sustain us. Our relationship with rules leaves us empty and unfulfilled. God and love feel distant.

The more that shoulds and rules move you to "serve" God, the more powerfully you will be drawn to earthly pleasures to gain the missing satisfaction, which often results in earthly addictions or habits seemingly impossible to break. Watch and pay attention to your life and you will see that your struggles with earthly pleasures and addictions relate to being moved by shoulds and rules rather than by peace and freedom.

True satisfaction only comes through freedom and direct relationship with God as love. That is why the scriptures say not to do anything "under compulsion" (2 Cor. 9:7; Philem. 14).

Earthy pleasures keep us blind and "satisfied" until we are made poor of the world and then turn to higher love. We cannot see wider, longer, higher, or deeper when pursuing earthly pleasures. Lose the lesser life, which includes rules.

CHAPTER 15

Unsurpassed Love

Higher Ways of Love

God has done more than I thought possible in certain areas of my life. While I'm still waiting on some of my more outlandish dreams to come to pass, God worked the impossible through my lengthy trials.

The scriptures state that God is able (Eph. 3:20) "… to do immeasurably more than all we ask or imagine, according to His power that is at work within us …" Do you believe the fullness of His word about this? More than all you ask or imagine?

I don't know about you but I can imagine a great deal.

That is love that is infinitely beyond what our earthly minds can hold. It is a love beyond the bounds of many Christians' traditional interpretation of hell, which I believe has been through fleshly eyes rather than spiritual ones. I believe that God desires to awaken people from the traditional view of hell, and I am deeply passionate about that awakening. These last chapters expand beyond the traditional view of hell, as well as about God's love that is greater than all.

Have you ever meditated on Paul's words in the verses immediately prior to him telling us that God is able to do beyond what we think or imagine? These scriptures, which I believe are among the most significant in the Bible, seem to be God's foundation for His greater works that are beyond the world's ways.

Let's pause with these verses (Eph. 3:17-19): " ... I pray that you, being rooted and established in love, *may have power, together* with all the saints, to grasp how *wide* and *long* and *high* and *deep* is the love of Christ, and to know this love that surpasses knowledge – *that you may be filled* to the measure of all the fullness of God."

I hear several profound implications in these scriptures. Above all, we are not yet filled to that full measure, and God desires to fill us. How?

Being rooted and established in love is the foundation *so that we may have power*. I have said before that love is the security and way for embracing more of the kingdom. Being grounded in love is the beginning of greater power. But what is the power for? So that we may be filled.

The power is for receiving greater measures of God's infinite love. And by embracing that love, together with fellow journeyers, we attain fullness of Christ. It almost sounds like a play on words. We need rooted in love to grow in the power of love. And we need to grow in the power of love *to attain Christ's fullness*. We are at a stalemate without love.

Those who have ears to hear and eyes to see will approach everything with eyes of love. Being able to receive this book's messages, to me, depends upon whether or not you see with eyes of love as your foundation.

What does each word "wide, long, high, and deep" really mean? Don't they indicate that God's love is in some way *actually* wider, longer, higher, and deeper than our current knowledge or scriptural interpretations? Further in each of those directions!

Even beyond our wildest imagination. And mine can be pretty wild at times!

The scriptures say (Job 11:7-9), "Can you fathom the mysteries of God? Can you probe the limits of the Almighty? They are higher than the heavens – what can you do? They are deeper than the depths of the grave – what can you know? Their measure is longer than the earth and wider than the sea."

What is God trying to say to us in that passage? I hear God conveying that His love and mysteries are higher than the heavens we know, deeper than the grave or pit, longer than our earthly journey, and wider than our sea of troubles. His mysteries and reach go beyond our current understanding. Let's begin with higher for a start.

Ezekiel was shown in the spiritual realm the temple's measurements, and he stated that "… the width of the temple *increased as it went higher*" (Ezek. 41:7). Are the implications of this verse causing your head to spin?

The further we go into God's kingdom, the more expansive it is. That reminds me of my vision about being invited into a higher spiritual room that was still like kindergarten compared to the rest of the kingdom.

The temple's measurements were about the fullness of Christ and the expansiveness of God. They are infinite. The more we come to know the Lord, the more we encounter His ways that are beyond us. Our flesh nature has limited God in many ways, but we increasingly shed those earthly limits the more we know Him (just like God seemed to expand from the Old to the New Testament).

Doesn't this awareness about God's expansiveness begin to explain why we encounter more questions after answering certain ones? We find no concrete finished boxes that make everything neat and tidy (like the flesh nature wants for security). True love surpasses knowledge. Do we truly believe this? Will we accept this greater love?

Greater awareness of Christ brings greater love, freedom, and enlargement. Everything good increases the more we know Christ. That is why the Ephesian verses encourage us to receive power *for* embracing the width, length, height, and depth of God's love. We need greater power to embrace what has been beyond our present knowledge.

Don't prophets and others who embrace wisdom through trials come to see the kingdom in ways that are incomprehensible to others? Love's higher ways break people's current rules and knowledge.

You can see this kingdom increase throughout time, which much of this book has already indicated. God seems to expand, broaden, and break our rules the more we come to know Him. That is the kingdom increase that is supposed to happen. We awaken to His infinite fullness little by little.

The scriptures say (Isa. 9:7), "There will be no end *to the increase* of His government or of peace." Not just no end, but no end to the increase! Even the fullness and security of peace increase the more we enter the kingdom. Wow!

Many people are familiar with Isaiah's words about God's higher ways (which I brought up earlier; see 55:9): "For as the heavens are higher than the earth, so are My ways higher than your ways, and My thoughts than your thoughts."

What comes to mind when you hear that the heavens are higher than the earth? I hear that we shouldn't place earthly limits onto God's higher ways. Most people initially agree with what I just stated. But some people's messages are not in accordance with this truth. I don't say this in judgment because we are only able to see to the extent that God has opened up revelation of Him and His scriptures. How have some people's messages possibly placed limits on God?

I believe that fleshly scriptural interpretations have limited God's word to our earthly journey, but His word is eternal. Doesn't Jesus say that heaven and earth will pass away but that His words will *never* pass away (Matt. 24:35)? His words work beyond this earthly experience.

Wouldn't that mean that God's spiritual principles work on this earth and continue to work until *all* is brought to completion? Christ's words wouldn't simply stop working because our earthly journey comes to an end.

If God is infinite and His purposes don't change, wouldn't His purpose of growing us into His love and likeness be about here as well as after here? And if we are not oriented towards growing into His likeness, wouldn't we experience His refining fire to reorient us towards that purpose, whether that is here or after here? If the scriptures and the spiritual truths contained within them work towards certain ends here and now, wouldn't those same spiritual truths be upheld after here no matter where that is?

I thought God didn't change. That's at least what the scriptures say (1 Sam. 15:29; Psm. 55:19).

Higher Scriptures

I know that I am asking challenging questions. But the more I've grown the more I've been astounded that I had limited God's word and His works to people's earthly experiences … as if people could physically die and God's word (or works) would simply stop with certain people.

Who said that God's spiritual laws and ways stop for many people when they die? Why did I believe that? Why have many people believed that? People are eternal beings that go on living after this earthly experience. God's ways, as well, are living and eternal. The scriptures say (Psm. 119:160), "All your words are true; all your righteous laws are eternal."

Who made the rules that some of God's spiritual truths change after this earthly life? The scriptures surely don't say or imply that. All of God's spiritual laws apply to *everybody all the time* (although He is more active with those who are awake and honor His works in their lives). God meets people to the extent that they accept Him in their lives and He keeps trying to make Himself known. God's works are eternal or continuous, and He shows no partiality. Sooner or later, His fire strips away the impurities to reveal the gold.

Jesus' story about the rich man in hell surely looks like the spiritual laws of earth continue. Unloving people reap unloving experiences whether on this earth or afterwards. Longer than the earth, as the scriptures in Job said.

In Jesus' story the rich man in hell still wanted Lazarus (in heaven) to serve him by relieving his suffering. The rich man also wanted Lazarus to go warn his relatives about the path they were on. I believe that the rich man's desires were his prayers to God, to the God of Abraham.

Apparently the rich man had not yet been stripped of his unloving flesh nature. He still wanted others to serve him. Abraham answered the prayers of the rich man in hell (Lk. 16:25-26): "*Son,* remember that in your lifetime you received your good things, while Lazarus received bad things, but now he is comforted here and you are in agony."

Jesus used that story to symbolically communicate that Lazarus had gone through earthly fire that stripped flesh nature and was now receiving greater heavenly goodness. The rich man had participated with no stripping while on earth and was now encountering those stripping works. You can hear (as long as your eyes have been opened more fully to love) Jesus' compassion towards the rich man as portrayed through Abraham in that story. (Is that the Jesus you know? It's the Jesus I know!)

Abraham calls the rich man who is in hell "son." In a gentle teaching way Abraham helps the rich man learn from his earthly experience and also about the stripping he was now enduring (represented by God's eternal fire continuing its refining work beyond the earthly journey). Jesus portrayed Abraham as helping the rich man understand the spiritual principle that had always been in place ... *during and after* his earthly experience.

Even though the story portrays a "fixed chasm between heaven and hell" (which I address shortly), it illustrates that all people must experience God's refining fire that strips away the flesh nature, whether on earth or afterwards. Both Lazarus and the rich man encountered flesh's stripping works. No one avoids God's works designed to awaken us. God has subjected *all* creation to futility and frustration to awaken us (Rom. 8:20).

If Abraham's instruction is for the rich man's learning and awareness, why? To awaken him!

But if the rich man is in hell, aren't all bets off? Isn't it too late? Didn't the rich man make his bed, and shouldn't he have to lie in it even if that is in hell forever?

That has been the traditional view of hell. To me that sounds like earthly parents when they reach the end of their patience – when they reach the end of their "love" with their children.

Who made the rule that all bets are off after the earthly experience? Who made the rule and interpretation that eternal destruction was about a person's soul and spirit being stuck in torment forever versus the flesh nature being in torment because of being eternally ruined (flesh completely ruined, forever destroyed – every last cent to bring freedom and restoration to the soul)?

Why did I believe that lesser version of love?

Why would Jesus communicate a story that portrays a compassionate Abraham spending time helping the rich man gain understanding? Even if some people view Jesus' story as simply for people's awareness of hell when they read the scriptures, He wouldn't have conveyed compassionate instruction towards someone in hell. Why would Jesus portray Abraham calling that person "son"?

I believe that he was called "son" because he still was one! He was simply going through difficulties to strip him from the lesser nature and its ways. Some of my prior beliefs about hell could not account for Jesus' word choice of "son" in this passage. The only option under my prior beliefs was to conclude that Jesus' word choice was irrelevant. Exclude what I couldn't understand. This lack of explanation revealed that the story's meaning surpassed my current knowledge; it went beyond what I had been taught. It broke rules.

It also struck me that the "fixed chasm between heaven and hell" sounds a lot like the flaming sword guarding the entrance to the Garden of Eden (Gen. 3:24). In other words, flesh could not enter the garden – symbolic of flesh nature not being able to enter heaven's goodness. That *is* true; that is a fixed chasm. The flesh nature that sees with eyes of separation will continue to experience separation (hell) until it comes to ruin, which then frees and awakens the soul.

The fixed chasm between heaven and hell is a fixed chasm between the flesh nature and Christ nature. Set apart. Our soul cannot enter heaven's goodness or the true Garden when it is joined with the lesser sinful nature that is to come to eternal ruin (or eternal damnation, as other translations put it). Our soul's journey is about eternally growing to know God and our Christ nature while eternally losing the lesser nature. That's what Jesus conveyed to us: lose our lives to find life. Lose the flesh nature to find our Christ nature.

Jesus had preached to the spirits of those in "prison," to those who had died and did not enter Noah's ark (1 Ptr. 3:19-20). *The door had been closed on earth.* Wasn't it too late? Hadn't they made their bed and shouldn't they have to forever lie in it? The door was shut and their spirits were under guard. In prison. Why did Jesus preach to them?

The scriptures continue (1 Ptr. 4:5-6), "But they will have to give account to Him who is ready to judge the living and the dead. For *this is the reason* the gospel was preached *even to those who are now dead, so that* they might be judged according to men in regard to the body, but *live according to God in regard to the spirit.*"

Wow! That is clear to me about people's flesh nature being judged to free them to live with God in the spirit. I never heard a single person preach on that passage. I don't think people knew what to do with it. Even after people who had rejected God died, Christ continued to work to strip away the flesh nature so that they might live in union with God in the spirit. It's stated very clearly!

There is also more to the story about Abraham talking to the rich man, especially when we understand the Greek meaning of Jesus' word choice for "son." God blasted opened these scriptures in new ways when I saw this.

I wrote about the two Greek words for "sons" or "children" much earlier, but I re-emphasize it here because it is crucial. The Greek word for "son" used most frequently throughout the New Testament is *huios* and pertains to kinship or family. That is what we tend to think of when we hear the word "son."

The unique word for "son" that Jesus chose in this parable, however, is *teknon*. While *teknon* also means son, it is from the root word *tikto*, which essentially means "son as produced" or "son-in-the-making." Is this stirring your heart from within! All of the related words for describing the root meaning of son point directly towards a son-in-the-making or a *son birthed or delivered through travail.* I was amazed by this discovery. It expanded my view of God and His faithfulness tremendously.[1]

Why did Jesus choose that word *there*, in *that* story about Abraham talking to someone in hell? Could the rich man in hell have been a son-in-the-making? Needless to say I wasn't convinced by one example because of all the previous teachings I had encountered. I researched other instances where the scriptural meaning of "son" was son-in-the-making versus kinship or family.[2]

I discovered that *teknon* was the meaning for son or children anytime trials, difficulties, and suffering were evident. I saw that the intent in those passages was to portray God's fire that produces or makes children who become more like Him. *Teknon* was always connected to God's refining fire to birth the true gold, which is our Christ nature.

Don't you find this awareness overwhelming? Jesus' story about hell symbolically depicted fiery experiences to produce sons. Jesus portrayed hell as travail to deliver or birth true sons. His refining fire is eternally consistent and purposeful during and after this earthly journey. His word does not change. His fire does not change.

Doesn't Jesus' story point towards a love that *truly* endures all things, bears all things, believes all things, and hopes all things?[3] Doesn't it point towards a love that never fails and is faithful *even when we are faithless?*[4] The scriptures have told us this but we have often contradicted them in our minds. *Isn't it possible that this is what the gospel of good news was really intended to be, that God's love will find a way to do what the scriptures say He will do?* With God all things are possible.

Love's Eternal Fire Works

I pondered the discovery of sons-in-the-making for several days to let it sink in and give it back to God. Then I felt peace about continuing, so I researched a little further. Well, actually, a lot further. I will summarize for you.

I searched to see if there was any difference between the Greek word for "fire" when referring to hell's fire (Matt. 13:50 for example) versus Jesus referring to Him "casting fire upon the earth" (Lk. 12:49). I'm sure you already guessed it. In both cases the Greek word is the same; the word is *pur* and interestingly is pronounced like the English word "poor."

God's fire makes us poor ... for a purpose. His refining fire makes us poor of the lesser to become rich in the greater.

More eye-opening to me was when I discovered another place that used that word *pur*. John the Baptist said (Lk. 3:16-17), "As for me, I baptize you with water; but One is coming ... *He will baptize you with the Holy Spirit and fire ... He will burn up the chaff with unquenchable fire.*" Unquenchable fire? That sounds like hell again, but John speaks here not to two different people groups but he says "you." He speaks to those being saved, and that their flesh-natured chaff will burn away so that the true wheat of who they are will stand.

The purifying fire (*pur*) that the Lord baptizes and refines us with during our earthly walk is exactly the same refining fire that burns away the chaff, whether here or after this earthly experience. No difference in the nature of the fire. No difference in the purpose of the fire.

The fire is holy for the purpose of bringing holiness or completion in Christ. Only His nature survives hells fire here or after here. The fire ever-works to burn away the chaff to free the wheat. This kind of fire sounds exactly like the fiery passionate love I experienced coming through me with the flight attendant. Love's fire ever-pursues us, and I knew this in the Spirit without question during that experience. I just couldn't yet understand or explain it scripturally.

But wouldn't some of God's attributes like judgment, justice, righteousness, and holiness have to be cast aside to believe this greater love? (These are questions I asked myself along the way.)

I was surprised after researching many of God's attributes in the Greek and Hebrew languages. Shocked is probably more accurate. I found that God's meanings behind His various attributes all pointed in the same direction. I will say this as succinctly as I can, although you may want to read this next paragraph slowly for it to sink in.

God's judgment makes the flesh nature poor; it is stripped of its rights. Righteousness is God having His way and rights in His people through Christ within. Central to God's rights is justice, which is one of the first ways that judgment is often defined. Justice is most centered on *bringing relief to the oppressed and the poor.* Justice works to make the poor or incomplete soul to become rich in Christ. God passionately hears and desires to redeem the poor. God redeems the poor by buying back the poor, paying for them from His own wealth – Him giving-for where we are unable to give. And all of God's attributes work together towards His ultimate goal, which is holiness, another attribute of His. Holiness is wholeness and completion in Christ. It is unity with Him, which is also love.

All God's attributes are a circle of love that gathers all into the unity of Christ (Eph. 1:10).

Have you noticed that the word for God's fire is always singular in the scriptures just like the fruit of the Spirit is singular? That is because His fire has one nature and purpose just like the fruit of His Spirit has one nature and purpose. All is for gathering into the unity of Christ.

Love's fire burns away, separates, shakes, and makes us poor of all that is not Christ, of all that tries to keep us from Him. Why? Not to stop there and leave us poor! I now believe that that is the flesh nature's separating perspective of hell because it *does* become separate and poor! Flesh is supposed to be separated from the true (that is "the chasm"), just like a parent shapes children to lose their bad behaviors to establish them in the true. Good parents want the loss of their children's ineffective and hurtful behaviors, not that they be fully destroyed!

We are made poor of the false to establish our true self. Why would *any* true love leave a child poor? Love's fire ever-works to bring us into holiness, wholeness, and completion in the bliss of His love.

All I can say is that through the extensive fireworks that Kathy and I endured, God revealed Himself as a defender of the poor! I would not have come to know this without enduring. I know with all my heart that this is who God is: a lover of the poor. Some people might think that they were poor and that He has not loved them, but that is not true. Being truly poor means having nothing else to give. Many people continue their futile energies to save themselves in their fiery circumstances. That is not yet truly poor. That shows that they still have more to spend and have not yet become truly emptied of the false. Being poor is when you finally stop all of your false ways when encountering fire. You stop and patiently cry out to Christ alone because you recognize that there is no other hope at all. That is being poor. And He answers when given time.

Kathy and I were poor, and He defended us. He defended our true selves. He gave grace so that our hope would not turn away from Him in spite of all that had happened. Even if our marriage would have ended badly at the earthly level, He awakened us to see that He is good no matter what. That He is God and is in and through all things.

God defends the poor sooner or later, even if that means after this earthly journey. Love's fire does not fail. Love is faithful even when we are faithless. Love's fire *works!*

Certainty of Justice

What about justice? What about those who are sent into "eternal punishment, torment, and destruction"? The sheep separated from the goats? What about free will and people choosing never to turn to God? Wouldn't this higher view have to ignore some scriptures?

People have asked me these questions. They reference certain scriptures like I mentioned above. They have asked, "What do I do with those scriptures? Shouldn't justice be maintained?"

My first thought and sometimes first response is "Exactly! Those places *are* about justice and they still *are* true. Justice is certain. But I no longer interpret eternal destruction as about the true spirit person. The flesh nature *is* supposed to come to final ruin. Eternal destruction. Eternal damnation. Ruined for all time. Complete justice to bring complete freedom." This process is just about a long-term ongoing one.

It is like Jesus said about going into prison (hell) and not coming out *until* every last cent is paid (Matt. 5:26). You will find upon checking the scriptures that Jesus used the word "until." That is because the flesh nature will not escape its sentence, and a soul is not freed from the flesh nature's prison until the flesh comes to ruin. For everyone. No partiality. As mentioned in the scriptures the sword will devour *all* flesh nature in the end.[5]

Every last cent of the false must be paid; it must be lost to gain the true. That is how we are freed sooner or later.

This may be the first time you've thought this way. If so, you may continue to see certain scriptures about eternal destruction, and because of deeply embedded training you will likely interpret them according to what you've always known. Why? We have experienced unending teachings in those directions *as if they were from God Himself* (when many people and earthly authorities concluded similarly about hell being torment forever, which caused people to believe that it was the same as God saying it).

Those earlier teachings are a mountain that is difficult to move (just like it was for the Jews when Jesus seemed to teach contradictory views from what they had always believed). But I believe that Christ wants to use us to move this lesser mountain of belief that "certain people are tormented forever," and to cast that mountain into the sea. Only after a season of considering God's greater love do those often-troubling scriptures become seen as His faithful works to free us rather than being about Him forever tormenting people.

Some people might ask, "But I thought God's word was final?" God's word *is* final, but our interpretations and views of His word are not. The Jews' interpretations weren't final and neither are ours. That is why we are to go on with God, growing into a fuller revelation of who He is over the course of time.

The mystery of Christ is within *all* people and is who we are to participate with and become, sooner or later. Would God destroy the portion of Himself placed within us, which is ultimately who we are?

I realize that not all people join with Christ's mystery or His stripping works while on this earth. People who have avoided God's stripping fire on this earth, those not predestined to know Christ during this earthly journey, will experience the stripping later to be awakened. All are to be freed into God's love. God will never forsake a child He created. His scriptures are true.

But why are some people not destined to know Christ during this earthly journey? We must always have free choice, and we cannot even see choice during this earthly journey without the contrast of up and down, dark and light, lesser and greater, and flesh nature and Christ nature. We only know love through the contrast of not-love on this earth. We are only able to experience loving the unlovable because of encountering the unlovable. Choice only exists through encountering those counterparts on this earth. All is needed as it is for our awakening. Sooner or later God's fire will reveal the false and give testimony to the true in all people. God's fire always has purpose.

None of God's ways are without purpose. Treating even some of God's ways as purposeless is like trying to make wisdom as nothing. God always has purpose, and He will have His way.

Stronger than our free will, the fire eventually causes us to say "Uncle" (that is a common expression of surrender if you didn't know). The story of Jonah illustrates that God will have His way, one way or the other.

The One Sign of Jonah

God kept revealing scriptures in new ways to me during the writing of this book – all during my personal fireworks. My fireworks are *how* the Lord birthed, confirmed, and made more powerful much of what is written in this book. Remember the scriptures about us being established *after* suffering a little while (1 Ptr. 5:10)? That is true for me. God restored my marriage and established greater ministry to others through the testimony of His higher works that came through fire.

God revealed the story of Jonah to me in a whole new way during this season. Do you remember that God asked Jonah to preach to the rebellious city of Nineveh? Remember how Jonah rebelled and ran from the Lord because he didn't want Nineveh to be saved from destruction?

A rebellious Nineveh and a rebellious Jonah. Interesting. Did God get His way? If you know the story you realize that God did, in time, get His way. Think about that. In spite of everyone's free will and total rebellion throughout the story, God got His way with all of them.

God got His way even when Jonah fled on a ship. The storms raged and the sailors knew that Jonah was the reason. They asked Jonah what they should do. He said to throw him overboard to calm the seas.

The ship's crew could not bring themselves to throw Jonah overboard (even though God desired that). The scriptures then state (Jon. 1:13), "*Instead*, the men did their best to row back to land. But they could not, *for the sea grew even wilder than before.*" So the crew finally threw Jonah overboard and the sea became calm.

Jonah and the crew's wills opposed God's will. But Jonah and the crew finally surrendered. God increased the pressure on flesh nature and in a short bit of time got His way in spite of many united opposing wills. Didn't I say that God is more able than effective parents to shape circumstances to bring desirable choices in children? Even while allowing free will? That is what happened in the story of Jonah.

More than God having His way, He wanted to use Jonah as a sign for humanity in the latter days. God even achieved His preplanned purpose *through* Jonah's rebellion. Sovereign? After Jonah rebelled and was thrown overboard, the Lord "provided" a great fish to swallow Jonah. Jonah remained in the belly of the fish for three days and nights. That was the sign that symbolized Christ in the belly of the earth for three days and nights.

Rebellious Jonah went through fire to become God's ambassador to a rebellious people. Jonah had no compassion for the people and did not want them saved. So Jonah (God's unloving ambassador) endured his own cross to birth higher love in him that could reach others who were rebellious.

Jonah first going through his own cross symbolizes the scriptures about judgment beginning with "the house of God" (1 Ptr. 4:17). Why does judgment begin there? People who look to God must go through their own crosses to lose the unloving flesh nature. Only truly awakened people love with God's greater love (regardless of the label they may happen to use).

Jonah's rebellion is a picture of *all* flesh nature, which centers on rebellion against God's love. Flesh resists true love. God wanted to love and free people but Jonah, in his flesh nature, did not. Jonah's rebellion represented God's "loving" ambassadors, and rebellious Nineveh symbolized the fullness of flesh nature.

God had said to Jonah about Nineveh (Jon. 1:2), "Its wickedness has come up before Me." Nineveh was a picture of hell – only the flesh nature reigned there. All flesh, nothing good.

And what was Jonah's attitude after he finally preached to Nineveh and God saved them? Happy, right? Not at all. Jonah pouted and was extremely angry after God saved Nineveh. His attitude conveyed "Don't save them; leave them in their wickedness."

Jonah's attitude is similar to many people's views about what happens to people who "go to hell." It was their choice, as if God's way should be to let people suffer in agony forever because they rebelled.

God's compassion and love were beyond Jonah's. God wanted to reach people caught in hell's fleshly ways and lies. Jonah did not, so God took His ambassador Jonah through his own cross to awaken him to His greater love. Jesus said that the sign of Jonah was to be the one sign given to our generation (Matt. 12:39).

Perhaps God wants to awaken His ambassadors today into His greater love through their own crosses. That's what happened to me. I now believe in a greater love. My own cross caused me to believe that greater love wants to and is able to reach people beyond free will (like Jonah's cross showed him).

Haven't many people conveyed that free will is the clincher, that free will simply obstructs God's ability to reach us (as if it is more powerful than Him)? People have their chance on this earth but will forever be tormented in a geographical place called hell if they are still disobedient when they die. Wow.

That treats God as if He and His love are not powerful enough to cause people to surrender. God caused Jonah, a whole ship's crew, and all the people of Nineveh to surrender while free will had been going full blast in another direction. God also did that with Saul who became Paul, who then wrote the majority of the New Testament. I can no longer be convinced by the lie that God is held hostage to our free will. Our free will can delay God's works, but we can see through Jonah's story that God is greater than our free will. He is patient and longsuffering as the scriptures say, and He will have his way.

Don't the scriptures say (1 Jn. 3:20), "… for God is greater than our heart …" and (Prov. 21:1) "The king's heart is like channels of water in the hand of the LORD; *He turns it wherever He wishes*"? Just like God did with Pharaoh's heart? The scriptures also say that God is able to humble those who walk in the pride of the flesh nature (Dan. 4:37).

Is God able or not?

God Delivers from the Pit

If the scriptures are true about God being greater than our heart, doesn't that mean God *could* work life to have the outcome He wants all the time? Couldn't God work the necessary circumstances to cause *any* person to surrender to Him? Like He did with Jonah, the crew, and with Nineveh? In spite of their opposing wills He worked change in them and had His way.

If hell is a place of unending torment *and* God can always work to move hearts how He wants, wouldn't that mean He *wants* some people to go to a place of torment forever? And God who is love wants this?

Nineveh and the story of Jonah point otherwise. Not merely because of what was already mentioned but also because of some other noteworthy aspects of the story. The story does not mince words. The word choice during Jonah's prayer is striking. The scriptures say (Jon. 2:1), "Then Jonah prayed to the LORD his God from the stomach of the fish, and he said" (vs. 2-9):

"I called out of my distress to the LORD, and He answered me. *I cried for help from the depth of Sheol; Thou didst hear my voice.* For Thou hadst cast me into the deep, into the heart of the seas, and the current engulfed me. All Thy breakers and billows passed over me. So I said, '*I have been expelled from Thy sight. Nevertheless I will look again toward Thy holy temple.*' Water encompassed me to the point of death. The great deep engulfed me, weeds were wrapped around my head. I descended to the roots of the mountains. The earth with its bars was around me *forever,* but *Thou hast brought up my life from the pit,* O LORD my God. While I was fainting away, I remembered the LORD; and my prayer came to Thee, into Thy holy temple. Those who regard vain idols forsake their faithfulness, but I will sacrifice to

Thee with the voice of thanksgiving. That which I have vowed I will pay. Salvation is from the LORD."

Responding to Jonah's prayer the Lord commanded the fish to vomit Jonah onto dry land, and he finally preached to Nineveh.

Wow! To me, we can say all we want that Jonah was speaking figuratively, but he didn't have to choose the unified collection of words he did. That collection of words pointed very clearly to hell. Jonah could have said, "I'm in this dark place," but he said "I have been *expelled* [banished, in another translation] from Thy sight." Isn't that an exact reference to hell? Isn't that exactly what people have believed to be the essence of hell?

Expelled. Banished. But it was really Jonah's fiery cross to awaken him from the pit of lies!

Jonah could have said "Bring my life up from this cave, fish belly, or sea monster" but he didn't. The Spirit caused him to choose the words "from the depth of Sheol" and "from the pit." In fact, the King James Version is "Out of the belly of hell I cried"!

Why those words? The story of Jonah symbolizes the rebellious flesh nature that must come to ruin in the pit of hell, now or later. It happened to be now for Jonah. Jonah's prayer portrays his soul crying out to God from hell to be delivered, and God delivered.

The Womb of Hell

Please be patient with my teaching on this topic. The current view of hell has caused a greatly distorted view of God's love on this earth. Understanding the Hebrew root words strengthens and reinforces the deeper meaning of Jonah's prayer. The Hebrew word for "belly" of hell is *beten* and means "to be hollow, belly, *especially womb.*" Does the word "hollow" jar your memory about me saying earlier that the scriptures define hell as "being spiritually naked"? Hollow?

Through further research I had seen that numerous other Hebrew words in the scriptures depict God as "filling in the hollows." In fact, the alter in the Old Testament was hollow, which means to be foolish, to pierce, and is from "to sacrifice" (Ex. 27:8). Then the word "throne," as God's response to the alter, means covered and is from the root *kacah*, meaning to cover or fill up hollows (Psm. 9:7). Isn't it interesting that we are to lay down our fleshly lives as a sacrifice upon God's alter? And that the foolish and hollow flesh is to be pierced so that God can fill up the hollows? That's what Jesus did on His cross, to be and to show the way.

The word "womb" struck me even more powerfully than hollow. The womb of hell. Wow! The womb of hell causes space for God to fill. That is what happened to Kathy and me. The womb of hell caused us to lose lesser rules and ways, which made space for God to fill up those hollow places with His higher ways.

That's what happened to Jonah too. Jonah had said "By reason of my affliction" he cried to the Lord from the womb of hell. Jonah's affliction was a womb of hell. Jonah's hellish affliction *caused* him to surrender his shoulds or idols and turn to God again. Jonah said in the midst of him believing he was banished from God's sight (vs. 4), "I will look again toward Your holy temple."

Jonah was a sign and wonder, and Jesus emphasized that he was *the* sign and wonder. Jonah portrayed enduring the experience of hell, just like Jesus did. But Jonah experienced hell because he was angry at God's compassion and love for the people of Nineveh. Jonah believed that God's love should not be as far-reaching as it is. As if some people should be permanently separated from His love. So Jonah drew to himself God's works that stripped away that lesser view of love. Jesus, in contrast, endured His hellish cross because He believed that God's love should and does reach all people in their places of death to the flesh. He knew the Father's love was infinitely far more reaching than Jonah or humanity has believed.

Jonah experienced hell against his conclusion that God's love should have limits. As if love should not be a greater love. We too, upon questioning Christ's love and desire to reach people, will find ourselves in His stripping works *because of believing that His love has limits*. That is hell, just like it was for the rich man in hell. As if Love picks and chooses with partiality who will forever be loved and who will not. Believing that love cannot reach its desired goals because of limits is fleshly thinking. Hell is the place of believing separation. Aloneness. That is spiritual nakedness; it is not knowing the Truth, and then we experience what Jesus said, "Let it be done according to your belief."

I feel compelled to express another definition for hell, which I believe the Spirit taught me. Here it is. Hell is not knowing Christ who is the Truth of no separation (Rom. 8:38-39). Isn't that the source of all hellish suffering for everyone regardless of their label? Trials feel bad to me, but I only experience hell in those trials when I believe the lie that I am alone and forsaken. Unloved.

All suffering is unbearable when we believe the lie that we are separate or alone. Fear, depression, anger, and hopelessness are all rooted in believing we are separate from God and each other. That's when Kathy and I most experienced the anguish of those destructive emotions I just mentioned, which was hell. All those horrendous emotions are rooted in believing that we are somehow shamefully worthy of being thrown away and forgotten. That is why Adam and Eve hid from God when they recognized they weren't perfect. They were in the flesh nature and already believed death's lie of separation. That was the beginning of their blindness. Humanity's blindness.

Isn't your suffering severest when you think you are the only one, which then causes you to see yourself as defective and worthless? That's why the saying is true that "misery loves company." Then you know you're not alone. I have watched and worked with clients' struggles most of my life and have seen that people usually remain in their stuck places and cannot embrace help until they first know they are not the only one. That they are not alone. They first need to know that others have similar struggles too. Someone relating with them right where they are without trying to get them somewhere else allows them to finally experience not being alone, and that is usually the first glimpse of them being able to grow or awaken from their hell.

To know love is to know we are never alone. We were never designed to be alone. We are never separate from Goodness even when it feels that way.

We experience hell when we believe we are separate from goodness. That was the experience of the rich man in hell (Lk. 16:26). He was in the flesh nature, which will always experience the chasm of separation from goodness. That nature cannot help but believe the lie of separation and is why it must come to eternal ruin for our awakening.

The womb of hell awakened Jonah. During prayer Jonah said that God had cast him into "the deep," which is the same as the word *tsuwlah,* meaning abyss. The greater symbolism and meaning in Jonah's prayer simply cannot be denied.

Jonah continued to say that he had descended to the mountains and that the bars of the earth had been around him *forever* ... until the Lord brought him up from the pit. Jonah during his three days of trials had descended to the roots of the mountains of his flesh nature and had seen how that earthly prison of flesh had forever kept him in bondage (until the Lord resurrected him from that flesh nature). Flesh nature had surrounded and imprisoned the

Christ nature like a womb. That womb of hell birthed more of Christ in Jonah because Christ *is* always the resurrection.

Jonah undergoing his three days of "death" is the way of the cross that delivers us from flesh nature. God hears and answers us when we are made poor of the flesh, poor enough to cry out to Him. But sometimes we are not yet poor enough in the flesh nature to truly let go of lesser things and to turn to God. Then He will compassionately convey that the stripping works will continue for a season just like they did for Kathy and me. That is also true for the rich man in hell who cried out to Abraham during the trials, and the compassionate response was that it was his time to endure those stripping works like the poor man had already done (Lk. 16:25).

Jonah being resurrected from the pit points towards Christ's power within us that overcomes all that is. Christ overcame *all powers* when He was resurrected at the end of the three days in the belly of the earth. Jonah is the one sign given to us that clearly portrays Christ as our resurrection life that is greater than the power of death and hell. Christ is greater than those lies.

Did Christ and His resurrection power overcome death and Hades or not? Do death and Hades make decisions about people's souls or does Christ? And is Christ greater than our hearts and free will, like in the story of Jonah, or not? The scriptures say (Rev. 1:17-19), *"Do not be afraid; I am the first and the last,* and the living One; and I was dead, and behold, I am alive forevermore, and *I have the keys of death and of Hades."*

Christ boldly said that we are not to be afraid. That statement was related to the fact that He is the first and the last, and that He has the keys to death and Hades. Really. He means it!

Fear is what causes us to step in distrustful and unloving ways. Fear and not knowing secure love are what *cause* us to sin. There is no need for the false when we are filled with the true. I repeatedly saw this during my trials. That is why Christ wants us to know love and to not be afraid. Be filled with the true!

Immediately after telling us not to be afraid Jesus emphasized why. He is the beginning and the end, which means that He got the first word and He gets the last one. Doesn't it seem clear that Christ is saying that hell *isn't* the end, and that *He is*? Christ is saying that *He* is the beginning and the end regarding us – He who has no beginning or end. Eternal. That is our true nature.

What does Christ have the keys of death and Hades *for*? Just to jingle?

Keys symbolize authority, which is Christ's authority over all that is. He decides. Hell does not decide, and neither do our limited earthly views. The scriptures say (2 Sam. 14:14), "Like water spilled on the ground, which cannot be recovered, so we must die. But God does not take away life; instead, He devises ways so that a banished person may not remain estranged from Him." Another translation states that God devises ways so that banished persons would not be expelled from Him. That was Jonah and Nineveh, and that is us.

God doesn't want any of our lives ending when our earthly journey is done. He doesn't want us banished, expelled, or estranged from Him forever. God wants relationship. That's why He created us. His love was and is far more compassionate than Jonah's or ours.

Jonah was God's ambassador of love to the people. But Jonah had not grown enough to share God's greater love. The house of God (those who look to Him) is also God's ambassador of love to people. But how can we be ambassadors of God's love if we believe that His "love" casts people into hell for no other purpose than for banishment into unending, meaningless torment?

By the way, are you experiencing condemnation or concluding that I am judging you about any of your views? That kind of judgment tears people down; it is void of God's love. Turning against ourselves or each other with that lesser judgment is simply another tail of that same "love of God" that judges only to punish a wrong.

God's judgment, justice, redemption, holiness, and righteousness all work for a purpose. None of God's attributes are meaningless; they work for the purpose of restoring us into holiness, wholeness, and completion in Christ. That is His-story that never ends. An Eternal Story.

God's story of Jonah shows His greater love that reaches beyond earthly compassion and love. Christ delivers from the pit. And Jesus told us that Jonah is the one sign given to this generation.

Chapter 16

Inescapable Love

The Fear of Hell

God wanted Kathy and me to be awakened to His greater love, not to be afraid of hell. Knowing greater love filled us, which then further freed us from lesser ways that tried to fill holes. Being afraid of hell, whether about here or after here, would have kept us empty.

But isn't the fear of hell needed? If God's love is so inescapable and we communicate that love to others, won't people simply go wild thinking they can do whatever they want? Doesn't the fear of hell more or less keep people under control?

That is the flesh nature's way, not Love's way. If people take up the sword of fear, they'll have to die by it. Get stripped of it.

Love allows total freedom accompanied by the consequences of our choices. The flesh nature *only* performs to gain what it wants and to avoid what is unwanted. Using fear as a motivator only activates the flesh nature. There's no heart change.

You are more likely to believe that God needs the fear of hell if you personally have been raised under threats and punishment to keep you under control. Using fear to control others' behaviors is the world's way, which historically has been as much in religious people as in the rest of the world.

But God has no fear. He is secure and never moved by fear. We are to be like Him in that way. Perfect love casts out fear. Why would God use fear as a motivator? It is not in Him. God met His people in the lesser ways of punishment and wrath because that is the only way people initially recognized or honored Him … just like when they only wanted an earthly king (1 Sam. 8:19; 12:12). Then He gave them what they wanted so as to learn through experience to let go of lesser things. But you can hear in the scriptures that God's higher desire is for love to cast out fear and punishment (1 Jn. 4:18). That shows His higher way that humanity and religion have yet to agree with!

Some people argue that Jesus used fear when He spoke about potential consequences for not heeding His word. There is night and day difference between Jesus peacefully stating spiritual truths and their consequences versus Him using fear to control us.

The world and the flesh nature are filled with fear and often use fear as a motivator. That is why we sometimes think God relies on fear and that He even wants us to do so. Fear is not God's foundation. You will not find fear as part of His nature in the scriptures.[1]

Being afraid of God causes us to hide from Him. That strikes me funny – hiding from God. Hiding from God is what we try to do when we are afraid of Him. The reality is that we come out of relationship with God when we are afraid of Him.

I remember talking with a close friend about my perspectives on hell. This woman powerfully changed her dynamics with her children because the Spirit seemed to awaken her when I had expressed this more loving way than tradition had taught. Previously, she had nagged her children about making Christ important in their lives, but she had often done so from a place of fear. The children only resisted. Only after she saw hell in this new way did she approach her children from love rather than fear. This higher view had included God's love, which allowed that higher love to touch her children. This more loving way allowed communication about God rather than causing distance or resentment of some taskmaster. Love with security, rather than a bottomless pit of fear, now moved her.

Jesus was clear, "Do not be afraid." He wanted no part of us being afraid. Jesus didn't want fear to control our actions. Being moved by fear reinforces and strengthens fear. Jesus wanted us moved by the security of love rather than by the fear of hell. You will find no exhortation in the scriptures to "fear hell." We would focus more on hell had such an exhortation existed. God wants us to focus on Him to know Him. That is our security and freedom.

Some people are clear about not using the fear of hell to influence people and might even ask, "Why raise difficult questions about judgment or hell? Why even make hell a topic of discussion at all?" True, we could avoid difficult topics altogether. But *our views of hell and love are connected*. God's judgment or stripping works and love are connected. God is one and over all. He cannot be divided into parts. "This or that" negates a fuller accurate picture, and it brings imbalance.

We avoid seeing the reality of our beliefs about Love when we avoid facing our beliefs about hell. Viewing hell as God's meaningless unending torment for people powerfully reveals our view of Love! How would we view a parent who threw away children into literal flames and agony when they didn't listen – never to be with the parent again?

We would gasp with horror at the parent. We would immediately report them to protect the children from such abuse and horror! Yet that is what many believe about a "loving" God.

If you're honest with yourself, part of you knows that those views cannot go together.

How could I ever be secure with a "love" that does that? I might say the words "God loves me" but I would never be secure. What might "love" do to destroy *me* when I mess up?! Out of fear I would likely hide my mess-ups, even from myself. Kathy and I would have had no chance at restoration had we thought that God was angry at us throughout our upheaval. Coming to know a greater secure love is what allowed us to come to a place of peace, which began healthy communication again.

The traditional views of God's judgment and love were always confusing to me during my journey to know God. The disciples asked Jesus how many times they should forgive a person, and He conveyed that it should be limitless (Matt. 18:22).

Limitless forgiveness sounded great but I was totally confused by traditional views that forgiveness absolutely ended when a person died and "went to hell forever." It seemed like God was saying "Do what I say and not what I do." That was the very hypocrisy that Jesus confronted in the religious leaders who lived by harsh rules that tried to annihilate Love. The traditional view of hell had always been an incomplete revelation of God.

Whether you agree or disagree with the traditional view, the topic of hell is worth wrestling with to come to a place of peace. It may be the single-most important issue, which when resolved, allows a deeper security and trust in God's love. It may be the single-most important factor for collective belief to shift and allow God's greater love to awaken on this earth.

The Nature of Hell

Really, the nature of hell? Do we need to pay that much attention to hell?

Not normally. But if we don't squarely deal with this issue, I believe that a lesser view of God's love will remain. Understanding the nature of hell actually awakens us to God's inescapable love. It may be that hell is as much about awakening people here as after here and not so much about a geographical location. Isn't that similar to what people have been learning about heaven?

Maybe hell is an eternal truth that doesn't change (just like the rest of the scriptures!). Learning more about the nature of hell might enable us to participate more fully with the Lord's stripping works that free us.

As we mentioned in an earlier chapter, the scriptures define hell as being spiritually naked before God (Job 26:6). *We experience hell in any aspect of our life where earthly clothes have been stripped away and we have not yet embraced the Christ nature. We experience greater hell when we fight the cross and Christ's works that are designed to free us into Him.*

Haven't people believed that Jesus' agony as He encountered His cross was hell coming against Him on earth, which the Father allowed for completing Christ (Heb. 5:9)? Isn't it hell for us, too, when we experience our crosses during life?

Isn't flesh nature that utterly refuses to let go of its ways, rights, and clothes the essence of those who are "thrown into hell" after the earthly journey – those who haven't surrendered to Christ's higher ways? Hell is God's judgment of the flesh nature to free us, here or after here. It's the Sword that comes against our flesh's sword. Doesn't hell on earth increase to the extent that we fight God's stripping works? Didn't Jesus say that we must take up our crosses daily and follow Him, which is about losing the earthly life to express Him and His higher rights (Lk. 9:23)?

That is certainly when Jonah's hell increased. Jonah didn't want to be awakened to what God was working and that is when he experienced the three days of his cross. Hell increases when we fight God's present works. Here or after here. Pain increases to the extent that we fight His will that works to free us.

We most experience pain and separation from God when our will goes one way and His another. That is hell. That is the tearing experience we feel, the weeping and gnashing of teeth. We are never separated from God because the mystery of Christ is always within, but we most *experience* separation when our fleshly will opposes His will. When we hang onto the lesser as He tries to free us from it.

Doesn't separation and gnashing of teeth occur when two wills clash? Especially when it is a clash of flesh and Spirit? Whether here or after here?

This next story from the scriptures is incredible and gets to the heart of the battle between flesh and Spirit. That battle is what the experience of hell is most about. The story is about the demon that the disciples could not cast out. For later reference it is important to note that the disciples and the teachers of the law were arguing about this situation when Jesus approached them (Mk. 9:14).

A father told Jesus that his son had become possessed by a spirit that had robbed him of his speech. The man said to Jesus (Mk. 9:18), "… he foams at the mouth, *gnashes his teeth*, and *becomes rigid.*"

Various places in the scriptures use the exact phrase "gnashing of teeth" to represent hell's suffering. These same words are used here to describe that suffering in someone on this earth. But why the intense suffering?

Jesus said that "this kind" from childhood only comes out by fasting and prayer (Mk. 9:29). Jesus conveyed that these childhood strongholds held significant power.

People's flesh nature throughout humanity has place impossible expectations on children. That impact establishes a core lie within us: flesh nature should be greater than it is able to be, which is about being perfect. All children's flesh nature experiences pressure to be perfect and is trained to believe that it should be greater than it is rather than to humbly accept its fallibility. That is the rigidity in humanity.

Children come to believe this lie and then become angry at themselves when they experience the imperfection of that lesser nature. They experience a kind of gnashing of teeth and rigidness regarding those high expectations and rules within them. They experience "God" or life as a taskmaster.

The greater the lie that they should be more than they are, the more they experience drivenness, harshness, hopelessness, or judgment within themselves when high expectations are not met. That is why the demon-possessed boy became rigid when it overtook him. The battle with unmet rigid rules *was* the spiritual demon that overpowered him. Self-hatred and despisement overtook him.

I look back about my panic attacks and fully relate to these experiences. I froze. I became rigid because of underlying rules and demands that part of me knew I could not meet.

You will see that people demonstrate rigidity rather than a sense of knowing love in their stuck areas in life. The rigidity centers on some "necessary" performance to become accepted or loved. That is the very bondage that Christ works to free us from during the fire.

As children grow, they gain adult-like status when their flesh nature has become trained to appear more competent or perfect than it is. That is the flesh nature becoming established in people. That is why the disciples could not cast out this particular demon. This rigid spirit is at the core of all flesh nature. Only by prayer and fasting from the flesh nature could anyone cast out that spirit.

That is why Jesus' first statement about the situation centered on the unbelief of all who were present. We neither believe nor have spiritual power when we are joined with the lies of the flesh nature. That is especially the case when we view those deeply ingrained lies as true.

There is still more to learn about this spirit that caused weeping and gnashing of teeth. Remember when I said that the disciples and teachers of the law were initially arguing about this situation?

The disciples continued to argue following their unsuccessful attempts to cast out the demon. Aren't arguments usually about the flesh nature rising up to magnify itself? Isn't it peculiar that the disciples argued before and after this event? Everyone's flesh attempted to magnify itself when dealing with a spirit that demands perfection in the flesh.

Wait till you see what the disciples argued about after this event. Jesus asked them what they had been arguing about (Mk. 9:33). The scriptures state (vs. 34), "But they kept quiet because on the way they had argued about *who was the greatest.*"

That's amazing to me. Children are trained to strive for fleshly perfection. To the flesh nature, that usually means trying to be the greatest. Competition to magnify itself. The flesh nature in the demon-possessed boy hooked the flesh nature in the disciples as well as the teachers of the law.

The disciples knew that their flesh nature was raised up during their arguments; that's why they became quiet when Jesus questioned them. The competitive flesh nature rose up like it had been trained to do since childhood, and it wanted to be great. Look at the clash of wills!

Jesus then emphasized that if they wanted to be great, they needed to be last and a servant to all. Only through humbled flesh nature could they become great.

This story demonstrates that people's core flesh nature that rises up cannot cast out that same nature in others. Think about when you speak the truth in love to someone close to you and they cannot receive it. What sometimes happens at that point?

If you're like many people, you try to convince the person and often they still can't receive it. Then that person walks away frustrated with you and stares more at your flesh nature than at the initial truth you shared. Had you let go after sharing your initial truth with them, the Spirit of that truth would have had more freedom to work. With more freedom the person sometimes connects with you later and you find that the Spirit continued to enlighten them because your flesh nature hadn't interfered. Why does the work continue upon letting go?

The Spirit's eternal fireworks (finished works) continue their ever-advancing holy work to make us complete, especially when we do not become an obstacle to the Spirit's work. The Spirit and love always allow freedom, whereas flesh nature does not.

Love and freedom are not maintained when flesh tries to cast out flesh. Comparing, separation, expectations, and judgment are the fleshly spirits and works that are stronger than the words we use. I saw these fleshly ways at various points with Kathy and me. The only thing we could do once flesh was activated was to fast from that lesser nature ("this kind from childhood comes out only by fasting and prayer"). All of those fleshly spirits and works are limited to that which is of hell (whether on earth or after the earthly experience). Only Christ's finished works are eternal and continue to burn away that which is not Christ.

The demon-possessed boy's experience and his gnashing of teeth are a type of hell. That is why those words were used to describe his tormented condition. *And that torment was more about an experience than a place.*

Jesus' love was great for this son who was tormented by fleshly lies and demands. Doesn't Jesus' love demonstrate the Father's love for those *who are tormented by lies and unable to choose otherwise?*

Like Nineveh being unable to choose? And also like Jonah initially being unable to choose God's ways? Don't the scriptures say "With God all things are possible" (Matt. 19:26)?

Wouldn't people experiencing hell after this earth eventually become poor and needy, and then surrender? The scriptures say that God hears the poor, afflicted, and outcast. But what if those experiencing hell *still* didn't recognize they were poor and needy?

The demon-possessed boy was poor and needy and didn't know it … and yet another (his earthly father) interceded for him so that Jesus *still* delivered the son from his place of need. God says that defending the cause of the poor and needy is what it means to truly know Him (Jer. 22:16). Since my fireworks, this verse makes me emotional. I believe it with all my heart.

Have we truly known God? How could we have known Him and also believed that He would utterly abandon the poor and needy in hell forever? That is far from what my heart believes about God now. Many religious people may conclude that I'm crazy, misled, or a heretic. But I don't care. I went through many fireworks to become a voice that awakens people to God's greater love, and there's no way I can go back to what I see as a lesser, destructive view. Many people who have rejected religion have done so especially because a part of their heart has known that a God of love would not throw people away in torment to be forgotten forever!

Have we believed that God's stripping works are to make people poor to remain that way? He tells us plainly that that is not what it means to know Him.

Bringing relief and redemption to the poor and afflicted is to know God. Knowing God in that way is the beginning of understanding His greater love. It's the beginning of understanding that His love reaches wider, longer, higher, and deeper than our present knowledge. God *wants* to be our fulfillment in the places that are poor and unfulfilled. That is always who He is. Let Him be that to you!

God would not say to those experiencing hell, "My goal is to make you poor of the flesh nature for the purpose of ... well ... to make you poor and leave you there." That doesn't sound at all like God or love to me. That is neither the nature nor the love of the Christ I know.

God's attributes and patterns throughout the scriptures reveal Him as One who greatly desires to feed the hungry, clothe the naked, defend those who have no one else, break the yokes, set the oppressed free, and to make the poor rich (Isa. 58:1-8). This nature of His is repeatedly emphasized throughout the scriptures. And the scriptures are eternal. How could I have thought that God suddenly changed when it came to the topic of hell?

Many have somehow thought that the purpose of hell was to make people poor simply to leave them poor. *Why would God's ways about hell unexplainably and totally conflict with the essence of His nature that is repeatedly emphasized in the scriptures? God's nature doesn't change!*

Didn't we see earlier that God's spiritual pattern throughout the Bible is the two works of grace-grace? One work is to *cause lack* of the flesh nature to establish us on our "house's" true foundation (which is our Christ nature), and the other work is to *bring completion* to His larger house (the bride).

Made poor, then completed. Isn't that always God's spiritual pattern? Lack of the lesser nature to be awakened and completed in our Christ nature?

Why would God suddenly be inconsistent about hell? Wouldn't God's nature need to be completely different from what is revealed throughout the scriptures for hell to be what many people have traditionally believed? That would mean that God works towards wholeness and completion on this earth and then that He absolutely stops His eternal ways for some after this earthly journey.

I believe that traditional interpretations of the scriptures regarding hell have come from people's separating, flesh nature – a nature that uses earthly boxes and rules for its own elevation. This group is good; that group is bad. That is the simple way of flesh. The Jews had treated others as less, and many religious people have done the same in spite of having good intentions. We are all children of God. We are all objects of His love, just like Jesus treated people (and the flesh nature in all is the object of His "wrath" because those stripping works free us). Jesus treated no one as an outcast (although the religious leaders would have encountered serious stripping works because of their flesh's rigid rules and great distrust of Love).

We are all made of flesh and spirit, and hell's purpose is God's judgment of the flesh whether here or after here. That judgment is not against any true spirit person but against the flesh nature that has been our prison. God wants to free us – that is the nature of hell and its judgment whether here or after here.

Hell is flesh's agony of defeat (a phrase used in the winter Olympics)! That is the weeping and gnashing of teeth. Have you considered the meaning of that phrase?

I researched the word "gnashing." It means grating one's teeth *because of pain or rage.* The flesh rages when its desired outcomes don't occur. Its rights are denied. The flesh also experiences pain when its rights are stripped from it. That is hell's weeping and gnashing of teeth, whether on this earth or later. What do we sometimes act like when life does not turn out how we want? Don't we give a sigh, groan, or expression of disapproval? That is about flesh's rights. When we have put great effort into attaining a certain outcome that does not occur, don't we sometimes weep or become angry?

Traffic going slowly when we are late for an appointment. Spilling a drink. Accidentally breaking something valuable. Someone treating us poorly. How do we act? Or, really, react? Don't we sigh, groan, or react like our rights are not met as they "should be"?

Those reactions come from our flesh's rights being denied. The demons of the flesh groan and cry out. That is hell for all humans. That's why the demon shrieked when Jesus casted it out of the demon-possessed boy (Mk. 9:26). Then that boy's free will knew what to choose.

If God's spiritual principles are eternal, then wouldn't flesh's weeping and gnashing of teeth simply continue after this earthly experience if it had not yet surrendered its rights? Like for the rich man in hell? Doesn't hell after here point towards that? Bigger sighs, groans, and weeping where the soul that had clung to fleshly lies and rights finally begins awakening from that lesser nature's dominating blindness.

Wouldn't freedom from the flesh after here happen in same way that Christ's baptism of fire works on the earth? We said earlier that heavens are ways. Hell also is a *way* that works the loss of flesh's rights here and after here. It is an eternal way that burns or shakes away all that is not Christ so that we would continually awaken into more of Christ's infiniteness.

In the end, hell is God's passionate fireworks to free people from the flesh and its tyranny, a tyranny that we have often blindly called good when flesh achieved what it wanted. The scriptures say (see Isa. 65:1), "I permitted Myself to be found by those who did not seek Me." God makes Himself found and known one way or the other. Sooner or later.

Withering the Flesh Nature

Many scriptures begin to make fuller sense when you see this never-ending work to bring about Christ's finished works in all of creation. That is the new heaven and earth.

Jesus cursed the fig tree and scourged those who were buying and selling in the temple. That doesn't sound much like love, does it?

Jesus saw no fruit on the fig tree and cursed it so it withered. Then He said (Mk. 11:14), "May no one *ever* eat fruit from you again." Some people might conclude that Jesus got irritated when He didn't get what He wanted, or that maybe He got angry similar to the Father's wrath in the Old Testament!

But Jesus' actions (like all of His other actions) were purposeful. Cursing the fig tree symbolized cursing the flesh nature. This paralleled God in the garden of Eden cursing the ground that Adam's flesh nature was made from because he and Eve had participated with that lesser nature (but be clear that God did not curse the true spirit person Adam!).

A tree is known by its fruit, and a tree that doesn't produce fruit is good for nothing except to be burned. That is the flesh nature. Jesus said (Jn. 15:2), "Every branch in Me that does not bear fruit, He takes away; and every branch that bears fruit, He prunes it, that it may bear more fruit." Every soul abiding in the mystery of Christ within will be pruned and bear more fruit. But every soul abiding in the flesh nature cannot produce fruit and will be taken away (so the flesh can be withered or burned).

Cursing the fig tree cursed the flesh nature that keeps us in bondage. Jesus' words about no fruit ever being found on the fig tree were a prophetic prayer about our flesh tree producing no fruit. We finally become freed into the Christ nature when the flesh nature withers and we no longer believe that our fleshly fruit is good.

Christ's followers and humanity as a whole continually encounter the eternal fireworks of Jesus cursing the flesh tree. We continually come out from under the deception of that tree and become further freed into the life-filled Christ nature.

Jesus scourged those who were buying and selling in the temple. That is another prophetic action about the same issue. Not only those selling in the temple to make money were scourged, but those buying were also scourged. (I don't believe that Jesus actually hit people with His whip but, rather, overturned tables and scourged near them to disrupt the buying and selling.)

Jesus scourged humanity's flesh tree. After the scourging Jesus proclaimed (Mk. 11:17), "My house will be called a house of prayer for all nations." Jesus did not mean a building of stone. He meant you and me. All people.

Our "house" or "temple" was to become a house of prayer continually in communion with God. But we have made our house a "den of robbers," as Jesus said (vs. 17). We have participated with the flesh nature that buys and sells for self-gain.

The flesh nature does nothing without doing it for individual gain. So Jesus scourges those who buy and sell. That is what continues happening to our flesh nature so that we are further freed into the true nature that finally satisfies our soul.

The withering of the fig tree also parallels the Bible story of Jonah. Jonah finally obeyed God and preached to Nineveh, and the people were saved. Then Jonah became extremely angry and pouted about it. Jonah's continued freedom and maturity required his lesser nature to encounter more of the cross.

Jonah was like Job before all his trials. Jonah and Job both intellectually knew God's nature. But after Job went through all his trials he eventually said (Job 42:5), "I have heard of Thee by the hearing of the ear; but now my eye sees Thee." Job had only known God from a distance, but he came to truly know Him and become more like Him through trials that withered his flesh nature.

Jonah also needed to go through intense sun and heat connected to his pouting about God's ways, and God "provided" a worm to wither away the vine that shaded him. While we would likely call that difficult earthly experience "bad," God used it to further teach and awaken Jonah about God's sovereign goodness with all people. God emphasized how much more He cares about people who "cannot tell their right hand from their left" (Jon. 4:11).

"People who cannot tell their right hand from their left"? God had great compassion for people who didn't know any better, for people who could not yet make a wise choice (just like Jesus did for the demon-possessed boy).

God's nature hasn't changed in Father or Son. God has great compassion for those who don't know any better, and He works on their behalf. Hell is about those who don't know any better, whether here or after here. God cares and is still faithful to those who don't know any better. God at times provides fiery works and at other times relief from those works. The pattern and purpose of those works are consistent: to awaken us from our fleshly prison.

One other point just now struck me about Jonah's story. The word "worm" was used. God had provided a worm, which alerts us to further spiritual meaning. Where else do we hear about a worm in the scriptures? Several scriptures refer to "the worm that never dies" for those encountering hell.

Is your spirit starting to grasp the significance of this? God *provided* the worm. God's provisions are always for His good just like they were for Jonah, though they felt bad to him going through them. The never-dying worm continually devours the flesh tree so that it withers.

What is the worm's never-changing purpose in hell? To cause withering to the flesh nature like the worm caused *for* Jonah to further awaken him. Same withering, same purpose.

How far does the worm go? The worm never dies. Like the sword that devours all flesh, the worm that never dies represents God's stripping works till all flesh nature comes to ruin. Eternal destruction. Every last cent. All must be withered with no more false fruit.

The worm that God provided Jonah was no longer needed in that aspect of Jonah's life after it performed its purpose. The worm could eat no more after the vine withered and had been used to awaken Jonah from his flesh nature. That is hell's worm that devours flesh. To accomplish God's purpose. To make poor so as to make rich. That is God's never-ending history with us. How could we have concluded that God's unchanging nature and ways somehow changed regarding hell?

God's love and fireworks are inescapable. They never give up. Love's fire continually devours all that is not Christ so as to free us into all that is Him.

Inescapable Love

How inescapable is God's love? We have already considered His love that is higher. What about His love that surpasses knowledge in ways that are wider, longer, and deeper? What about God's mysteries that are "... deeper than the depths of the grave ... longer than the earth ... and wider than the sea" (Job 11:7-9)? Those specific words are used for reasons.

God's mystery of love that is wider than the sea (of troubles and trials) refers to His narrow gate. The gate is narrow for stripping all flesh, and no flesh nature will enter through that gate. But love that surpasses knowledge is far wider. Even in all of our blindness and fallibility during our trials, we find that nothing can separate us from Christ's love. Love that is wider is the sacrificial love of the cross that ever reaches us. It reaches across chasms. Flesh perceives chasms, but Christ's love that has no separation shakes away the false and reaches across chasms. We then surpass present knowledge and come to know Christ's greater love as we trust and surrender into Christ's outstretched arms during trials.

A surrendered way that lets go of earthly rights and limits begins embracing Christ's kingdom that is wider. We gain more of our inheritance every time our arms are stretched like Christ's in surrender wider than our trials. That is the cross. Upon surrendering and entering more through the narrow gate we awaken to a greater love that embraces with an infinitely wider embrace. We come to see a profoundly secure love.

The wide surrendered way during trials is the ongoing way to see higher, longer, and deeper. Ongoing surrender means that Christ has become our way, our strength, and our salvation into His ever-increasing kingdom.

Many of the scriptures seem to be a paradox. Turn the other cheek, yet restore a person. Lose your life, yet gain life. God's love is wider even though His gate is narrow.

Remember how the measurements of God's temple got wider as it went higher (Ezek. 41:7)? That sounds like the more we enter the kingdom and know Christ's love, we continually surpass present knowledge and will look back and recognize how blind we were to God's fullness. That has surely been the case so far in the journey of God's people historically and has also been my experience after my fireworks. I now see Christ's love as far greater than before those stripping works.

The scriptures say (Eph. 2:17), "And He came and preached peace to you who were far away, and peace to those who were near." Peace is meant to reach those far away. Further, wider.

Something new just struck me from the Old Testament while writing the last paragraph. I never saw this previously. God said at two different points in the scriptures (Ex. 14:4, 18), "Then the Egyptians will know that I am the Lord." The Egyptians? Why the Egyptians in the Old Testament? Who cares if people who were against God were going to hell, right?

God does! But many people have believed that the Egyptians at that time would all end up in hell forever. Truly, if those Egyptians were going to hell forever, *why would God care whatsoever that they come to know that He is Lord?* God wanted them to learn similar to how Jesus portrayed Abraham wanting the rich man in hell to learn (Lk. 16:25). The journey continues.

If the Egyptians were going to hell forever, the only reason for God wanting them to know He was God would be to rub it in their faces like some authority trying to show them who was boss. Only flesh nature does that. Not God who is love. Not God who is holy, whose actions are centered on holiness, which is wholeness and completion in Christ.

God wanted a testimony for the Egyptians. He wanted them to know Him though their trials, just like all of us. Why? Love is wider than we have thought. Isaiah prophesied of the kingdom, "Your gates will always stand open, they will never be shut, day or night ..." (60:11).[2]

The symbolism of gates never being closed represents no more separation in our minds. Perfect love will have cast out flesh nature along with fear and judgment. The narrow gate that separates flesh from spirit will no longer be needed because all will know God's love.

No more separation needed. No more narrow gate because flesh nature won't exist. Nothing is to separate us from the love of Christ (Rom. 8:39). All nations will see His righteousness. That is love that is wider. That love surpasses our current knowledge, limits, and labels.

Love is also longer. Longer than what?

Love is longer than Christianity's label or history. It is longer than the Jews' history. Love is longer than death and the earthly journey. It is longer than what we have known as time. God is eternal, and His love is eternal.

Love is longer than our earthly name and identity. God said to Jacob (Gen. 32:28), "Your name shall no longer be Jacob, but Israel ..." Earth's finite names come to an end, but God's love loves us longer. We are given "new names," really new identities that become one with Christ.

God's love is longer than our pain. We will weep for a night in the flesh nature but His everlasting joy comes in the morning of release from that nature (Psm. 30:5; Isa. 30:19-20). In that place there shall no longer be any weeping or tears (Rev. 21:4). Love is longer.

Love is deeper. Deeper than what?

Love is deeper than the pit of our troubles. We cannot hide from love at the bottom of the sea, in a forest, or in a multitude of peoples. Love reaches beyond any depth and finds a way. Love is deeper than Sheol, the pit, or hell (whatever terms we use).

There are numerous scriptures (beyond Jonah's prayer) that describe being lifted up from Sheol or the pit. Isn't that amazing? I researched the word "pit" in the Hebrew language and there was no way to tell whether that word was used to symbolically portray a pit of earthly trials and destruction or a pit of hell's destruction after this earthly journey. That is completely left to our interpretation. So pit could actually mean one or the other, or both.

Then why did we limit redemption? Why did I limit redemption as if it was not an eternal way? Why did I conclude that redemption was only an earthly choice to protect against a later hell or only to deliver me from my pits of earthly troubles? Why did I make God and His goodness so small and earthly?

The scriptures say (Job 33:28-30), "He has redeemed my soul from going to the pit and my life shall see the light. Behold, God does all these oftentimes with men, *to bring back* [or turn back, depending upon translations] his soul from the pit, that he may be enlightened with the light of life." Isn't this exactly what Jesus did when He preached to the souls of those who had died and were shut out of the ark in the days of Noah? Doors were closed "forever," and Jesus still preached to them that they would live according to God in the spirit (1 Ptr. 3:19-20; 4:6).

The word "pit" in the Job passage is *shachath* and means pit of destruction. That word also comes from the root word *shuwach* and means to sink, humble, or bow down.

Can you hear the purpose of the pit? That's incredible to me. The pit's purpose in the scriptures, including *the* pit of destruction, is to cause a sinking, humbling, or bowing down. Redemption through bowing down here or later. Every knee shall bend. Isn't that what the scriptures say? Why did we limit it?

The bent knee is not just to force people to bow but to humble the flesh nature to exalt all that is true. Souls bowed and humbled become exalted. That is God's unwavering good news.

The scriptures say (Phil 2:8-11), "And being found in appearance as a man, *He humbled Himself* by becoming obedient to the point of death, even death on a cross. *Therefore also God highly exalted Him*, and bestowed on Him the name which is above every name, that at the name of Jesus *every knee should bow, of those who are in heaven, and on earth, and under the earth*, and that every tongue should confess that Jesus Christ is Lord, to the glory of God the Father."

Under the earth? Meaning people who have gone to the grave, or those who are under the weight of flesh nature and earthliness?[3] The knee of all flesh bows so that all souls will exalt, and become one with, all that is Christ.

Every knee bowing! That is clear. I am amazed again. Humbling is *always* for the purpose of exalting. Poor to become rich.

The selfish flesh nature will be uprooted one way or the other. The point is this: the Lord constantly redeems us from the pit. Psalm 103:2-4 says, "Bless the LORD, O my soul ... Who *redeems* your life from the pit; who crowns you with lovingkindness and compassion."

The word "redeem" means to buy or purchase back. Doesn't God have the ability to do that here or after here? We don't have to remain in any kind of pit because Christ made a way for all. And Christ rules over all. His higher life *for* our lesser one. His finished works in place of our fleshly works. He is to become our way and righteousness in any place we have surrendered the flesh nature. Then we become a vessel of His rights and way.

Our selfish flesh nature cannot make a way, but Christ's finished works within us are able any place we surrender to His higher nature and way. Love reaches into the depths of any pit and eventually causes all to bow to Christ.

Every knee shall bow. Inescapable love is wider, longer, higher, and deeper.

CHAPTER 17

Divine Inescapable Government

Until Completion

When I have lost or misplaced something important to me, I experience a sense of incompletion until I have found it. A deeper place in me seems drawn towards finding what has been lost. That is Christ and His eternal way, and that is what this last chapter addresses.

This book would have been overwhelming had I kept all the previous parts within it (well, way more overwhelming than it might already be for you!). I had originally addressed much in depth about "some taken and others left" as well as God's fire continually working "until one thing is lost and another found." There are many scriptures about these topics. You will likely find that researching the word "until" is especially fruitful for seeing God's eternal way that never gives up on anyone.

God's eternal fireworks never stop working in either direction. Heaven always works until. Hell always works until. Love's fire works always and until.

How inescapable is God's love? Until that which is lost is found. Until completion! Is *until* clear enough for you? None of

Jesus' parables stop short of the happy ending! His message is consistent.

Here are just a few verses:
- *until* he finds it [the lost sheep] (Lk. 15:4)
- *until* she finds it [the woman's lost coin] (Lk. 15:8)
- he [the prodigal son] was lost, and has been found (you can see that the father intently waited and watched *until* the son awakened through trials and returned, see Lk. 15:24)

If you look at those passages more fully you can't help but to hear the immense joy and rejoicing that Jesus expressed about finding the lost. He will not stop short of it.

Prison Until

In my time of marital separation, God had initially met me and conveyed that the trials would birth further heavenly life and that He would bring resolution to the marriage in the end. I knew that He still wanted the marriage but that it would be like closed doors for a season, where everything would be locked up until He accomplished what He desired.

I related to the first part of Jesus' parable of the unmerciful servant, where the servant initially cried out to the master for mercy and received it (Matt. 18:21-35). I related to the impossibility of a task before me. That servant's impossible task was an unpayable debt; mine was impossible communication no matter what I tried. My abilities to accomplish the task at hand would not suffice, and the only thing left for me was to cry out for mercy and grace like that servant initially did with the master. The Master met me and conveyed that He would work what was needed but that it would require a lengthy time of being hedged in. Imprisoned.

Because of what I endured, I came to see much hidden meaning in Jesus' parable of the unmerciful servant (Matt. 18:21-35). I realize that people have typically taught this parable in a way that emphasizes this servant's inability to pay an unpayable debt, especially given the fact that he was thrown into prison (which represents hell).

People have traditionally treated the word "until" in this parable as meaningless because of believing that a person in hell could never pay their debt. (The truth is flesh never could for anyone.) I have researched the scriptures and found that the word "until" is used with the same theme throughout and is not used meaninglessly. The whole slant and spirit of this parable is about mercy and forgiveness, and then to conclude that the master will have no mercy – forever – disregards the context and nature of the whole parable.

Why do I say this? Do you realize that this whole parable immediately followed Peter's question about how many times he should forgive a brother who sins against him? Peter offered the number seven as a possibility to Jesus. What did Jesus say?

Jesus said (Matt. 18:22), "I do not say to you, up to seven times, but up to seventy times seven." Wow! Who forgives someone up to seventy times seven? Why did Jesus say that high of a number? Who even keeps track until that number is reached? Will you? I never have.

Jesus meant endless forgiveness. Endless mercy. That is the stage set by Jesus for telling the parable, and that is the nature and spirit of the parable. After Jesus' emphasis on endless forgiveness, He began His next statement about the parable of the unmerciful servant with "Therefore." This word meant that the parable's purpose was to teach further about endless forgiveness and mercy.

The confusing part for most people is that the master ended up throwing the unmerciful servant into prison (hell). That doesn't

427

seem like endless forgiveness and mercy, which was the whole point for Jesus' parable.

But what if someone's heart does not budge? What if their heart neither desires repentance nor forgiveness for wrongful actions? That was the case for this unmerciful servant. For immediately after that servant's debt was considered paid by the master, the servant choked a fellow servant and demanded that his debt be paid to him. When that debt was unable to be paid, the unmerciful servant threw his fellow servant into prison.

We can learn about Jesus' fuller perspective on this parable in the parallel scriptures on forgiveness in the Gospel of Luke (see 17:3-5). Here we see that Jesus emphasized forgiveness and mercy *if* their brother repented and desired forgiveness. Having mercy on another person was related to whether or not that person desired to walk the way of forgiveness and love.[1]

But the unmerciful servant's actions towards his fellow servant in Jesus' parable were intentional and hostile, even after the master's earlier mercy with him. This forgiven servant demonstrated no interest in learning the master's way of forgiveness and love.

By his standard of measure he was measured, so the master threw him into prison (like that servant had done with his fellow servant). For how long? The words say "*until* he paid back all he owed" (vs. 34). Did the master's nature and purpose for throwing this servant into prison suddenly change? Did he now legally want all his money back, every cent?

Not at all. The master's reason for throwing the servant into prison was not to punish a wrong (which is the traditional view of hell). If that were the case the master would have thrown him into prison the first time. The master had not required what he legally and rightfully deserved from the servant. Either time. That was not his focus.

The master, instead, wanted the servant to learn to love with the same mercy and forgiveness that he had shown him. That's why the master emphasized (vs. 33), *"Shouldn't you have had mercy on your fellow servant just as I had on you?"* That was the master's teaching and focus with the unmerciful servant. He was instructional just like Jesus' example of Abraham with the rich man in hell. The master's love and forgiving nature were unchangeable (like with God).

Seeing that the servant had not yet learned to love that way, the master threw him into a type of hell *until* he paid every last cent. Not materially! Every last cent meant every bit of the servant's unloving flesh nature that needed stripped *until* he was freed from it to love like the master loved.

We draw to ourselves and are measured by the standard we use. A sword draws a sword. We encounter hell's ways against us when we act in accordance with hell's ways. The unmerciful servant would experience the standard of (and consequences from) his own measure until that fleshly standard within him came to ruin.

You can be sure that the master's nature had not changed from mercy to legalism! The master's love and goal were unchangeable. You can be sure that what the master portrayed from the beginning with the servant was there at the end. The master's goal would be reached upon that servant becoming broken and learning to love with his love and mercy.

"Shouldn't you have had mercy on your fellow servant just as I had on you?" That was the master's goal.

Love would have been fulfilled. Completed. Love would have reigned. The master would have viewed every last cent as having been paid. He simply wanted all his servants to love with his love and mercy.

Prison is for hard hearts until they let go of lesser ways. Jesus' parable spoke about our need to learn to love with His love and forgiveness to receive that limitless forgiveness that He had just conveyed to His disciples. But, like with the prodigal son, His love and forgiveness will be watching and waiting for those with hard hearts to budge through the stripping works. He never gives up and will have His way one way or the other. Love's fire works until.

That Nothing May Be Lost

Christ used fireworks to further free Kathy and me from our restrictive rules so that we would live life more fully by the Spirit. Christ broke many of our rules, to the extent that we came to see that He always governed no matter how out of control the situation felt, and that nothing was wasted in the process. We both gained security about Christ reigning over all things, but He broke our rules to open our eyes.

Do you live by rules and standards rather than by the freedom of the Spirit, whether that is religion's or the world's rules? If you live by rules, you'll die by rules. That's what happened to us. We died to many rules that we had been "living" by.

Jesus had called the Pharisees and teachers of the law hypocrites when they questioned Him about His disciples eating with unclean hands. Jesus quoted Isaiah to them (Mk. 7:6-7), "These people honor Me with their lips, but their hearts are far from Me. They worship Me in vain; their teachings *are but rules* taught by men."

Then after feeding the four thousand Jesus warned His disciples (Mk. 8:15), "Be careful, watch out for the yeast of the Pharisees and that of Herod." That yeast was about the teachings and ways of men. Jesus meant for His disciples to guard their hearts from following earthly authorities' teachings that were but rules and limited earthly ways. Jesus was exhorting His disciples about following the free higher way of Him and His Spirit that had no limit.

The disciples further questioned Jesus about His warning. Jesus responded to them (Mk. 8:17-19), "Do you still not see or understand? *Are your hearts hardened?* Do you have eyes but fail to see, and ears but fail to hear? And don't you remember? When I broke the five loaves for the five thousand, *how many basketfuls of pieces* did you pick up? ... And when I broke the seven loaves for the four thousand, *how many basketfuls of pieces* did you pick up? ... Do you still not understand?"

The disciples had gathered twelve and seven basketfuls of pieces. Why was this answer so significant? Why did Jesus press them about this issue? You may conclude that Jesus said those words with a condemning tone but I believe He was simply conveying that they should have known something obvious about gathering twelve and seven basketfuls. The meaning of those numbers comes from an earlier point in the disciples' walk with Jesus.

The scriptures say (Mk. 3:20-21), "Then Jesus entered a house, and again a crowd gathered so that He and His disciples were not even able to eat. When his family heard about this, they went to take charge of Him, for they said, 'He is out of His mind.'"

Jesus' family thought He was crazy! Why? They had heard that He called to Himself *twelve* disciples (Matt. 3:16). Everyone in that culture looked for the coming Christ, so they knew immediately what picking twelve disciples meant. Jesus outright conveyed that He was the Christ, and some who knew Him thought He was crazy. A prophet is without honor in his hometown.

Twelve disciples meant divine government. So Jesus was surprised that the disciples hadn't recognized the significance of gathering twelve basketfuls of bread. That culture also recognized that the number seven represented completion. They all knew the story about God's people marching around Jericho seven times for the walls to come tumbling down.

Divine government and completion.

One other point is significant before being able to grasp the full picture. After Jesus fed the five thousand we find in the Gospel of John that He told His disciples (6:12), "Gather up the leftover fragments *that nothing may be lost.*"

"That nothing may be lost." All of this – Jesus' warning about religious leaders and His peculiar focus on the numbers twelve and seven – was about Him contrasting limited earthly ways with divine government that always brings completion. Earth's ways have limits. Heaven's ways do not.

Jesus broke bread that fed the multitudes. The pieces of broken bread represented His way of brokenness that brings greater life. The bread also symbolized us. Our brokenness brings greater life for us and for others. Divine government always expands and creates resurrection life through death and brokenness. All the shattered pieces become our food. Nothing is wasted.

Jesus asked the disciples to gather up the leftover fragments that *nothing* may be lost. Jesus didn't care about every bit of bread! That wasn't the point; Jesus did nothing without purpose. Jesus conveyed that nothing is wasted during our journey. But more important than that, the bread represented His broken body – us. Nothing being lost was about people! That is a greater heavenly government than we have known.

All must be brought to completion, and divine government works to ensure that nothing is lost. People sometimes overlook those who are broken like sheep without a shepherd, but greater love cannot. Greater love gathers *all* that is lost and broken. Love gathers all who are poor, afflicted, orphaned, outcast, and naked. That is divine justice that completes what is incomplete.

At one point or another the sword cuts into pieces the flesh nature that hinders our souls from embracing our Christ nature. Greater love then comes behind the sword to comfort our souls, and brokenness gives way to love's greater life. Love that misses nothing gathers and binds the brokenhearted, whether here or after here. Love gathers all the broken "bread" so that nothing may be lost. That is divine government that completes our souls. That is God's love that made sure that Nineveh wasn't missing. Let us learn from Jonah's hell to make sure that nothing is lost.

The Prodigal Son's Hell

Kathy's and my hell caused me to recognize some parallels with the prodigal son's hell. The story of the prodigal son has been told and expanded upon in many ways throughout the ages (Lk. 15:11-32). I mentioned it previously and expand upon it here. It is a moving story about a father's unfailing, unchangeable love for two sons that had taken two very different journeys ... where each son finds that their position with the father was the same.

Loved.

This story is *not* about one son who is worthy to be called a son and the other losing forever the privilege of being called son (as is the traditional view of hell). The story is *not* about one son who obeyed and received the father's goodness and another son disobeying and never receiving the father's blessings.

It's also not a story of one son truly knowing the father's love and the other one rebelling and being sent to hell forever. Rather, the story of the prodigal son is about a father's love for two very differently behaving sons (representing two kinds of sons of God).

The story is about one son who was awakened enough to know that it was best to be with the father and to do the father's will; and it is about another unawakened son who selfishly thought it was

433

better to chase after the material world and all the other potential loves of the world ... only to come to the end of himself. The end of his flesh nature. Isn't coming to the end of ourselves one of God's main goals with us during this earthly life? That we would come to the end of the fleshly nature to be freed into the true?

This story is also about a father's never-failing love for both sons, *neither* of whom truly knew the father's love *until* both sons experienced the father's unfailing love for the son who had gone astray. *That* is when both sons encountered the father's love that surpassed their knowledge.

The first son stayed with the father, and the second son asked for his inheritance, received it, and left home. This second son lived sensuously and cared for nothing but himself. In this prodigal son's mind, he had no father or brother. There was only self and what he wanted, and so he spent his whole inheritance. Every last cent of his worldly riches (the symbolism here is clear).

Famine had come, which caused him to experience the fruit of his ways. By his standard of measure he had experienced from others. No one cared about his needs or comforted him, which was hell. He was naked and alone.

This son came to see his selfish ways more clearly through experiencing a type of hell – a void of tangible love while in great need. That hell accomplished its work; he experienced his nakedness, which humbled his selfish flesh nature. Pride was stripped from him. Every last cent, which caused him "to come to his senses." He awakened.

This son told himself that he would say to his father when he returned (Lk. 15:19), "I am no longer worthy to be called your son; make me as one of your hired men." But great compassion and joy overwhelmed the father when *his son* returned home; the father didn't treat him as unworthy like the son had expected.

Unwavering compassion, joy, and love. The father waited, watched, and longed for this son *until* the son awakened through his trials and returned. The father was so earnestly looking towards this day that he saw the son coming from afar. No accusing questions shot forth "How could you spend … or how could you be so selfish …." The father's all-embracing love simply overwhelmed the son. Unwavering love, in spite of the son's selfishness and total lack of care for the father over the years.

The prodigal son symbolizes one kind of son of God. The older son symbolizes another.

The older son stayed with the father and seemed to think that he was better than the prodigal son. This older son saw the father's compassion and joy about the younger son returning home and became angry rather than celebrating *his own* brother's homecoming. Doesn't that sound kind of like Jonah pouting about the Father loving Nineveh who had gone astray?

This older son spoke with anger to his father (Lk. 15:29-30), "Look! All these years I've been slaving for you and never disobeyed your orders. Yet you never gave me even a young goat so I could celebrate with my friends. But when *this son of yours* who has squandered your property with prostitutes comes home, you kill the fattened calf for him!"

This older son desired preference over the younger son and conveyed separation when he said to the father "this son of yours." The older son evidently did not love the younger son like the father did.

The older son, looking through fleshly eyes, thought that all of his works "slaving" for the father should have given him preferential treatment and love. He simply could not believe that the father deeply loved both sons equally. This older son's separating view now caused him to feel separate and excluded. His sword drew an invisible sword to himself.

But the father made clear his love for both sons and tried to help his older son regain a sense of connection with his brother when he said with great compassion (Lk. 15:31-32), "My son ... you are always with me, and everything I have is yours. But we had to celebrate and be glad, because *this brother of yours* was dead and is alive again; he was lost and is found."

"This brother of yours," the father said. No separation. No judgment. No partiality ... even after the younger son's total selfishness and rejection of them. The father looked through spiritual eyes that did not separate one from another. Nothing could separate his sons from his love. Isn't every truly loving father that way with all their children?

The only judgment the younger son received was from his own standard of measure that became his hell. Likewise, the only judgment the older son received was from his standard of measure as well. No judgment or negative attitude came from the father. The father's love was faithful.

For an angry older son and for a younger son who had been through hell and back! A hell that brought the son to his senses. A hell that had made him poor so as to make him rich.

What a picture of the Father's love that Jesus portrayed. The prodigal son's father was patient and long-suffering, with a love enduring and bearing all things just like the scriptures say about God.

Have we possibly separated ourselves from our brethren like the older brother did – thinking that we deserve more love and are somehow better than those who have lived selfishly (as if we haven't)? Maybe, more than we know, the older brother was also a prodigal son who hadn't yet come home within his heart to the father's greater love.

Perhaps, we too have not yet come home to the Father's greater love. Have we possibly viewed the scriptures from our flesh nature that always wants preferential treatment like the older brother did regarding his initially selfish brother? It's as if the older brother believed his younger brother's hell should not have ended! Have we been the older brother concluding that hell should not end for *our* brother ... with us trying to tell our Father that our rebellious brother should not receive His love? Isn't that what Jonah did?

Do we see the Father's love as contingent upon anything at all? For the scriptures say that love endures and bears *all* things. Is that true or not? That's what the prodigal son story shows us. The story points to a greater love than we have embraced – a love that welcomes home the lost sheep, even (and especially) the lost sheep who have been humbled through the pits of hell.

Lesser nature, like with the prodigal son, is meant to be eternally ruined. But it's for the purpose of bringing home the lost sheep. Even 99 of 100 sheep are not enough. The Lord works to bring 100 percent of the sheep into the fold so that nothing may be lost!

Higher Truth, Higher Love

There is always more to come. There is always higher Truth and higher love. I know that there are further questions that have yet to be answered. Bring those questions before Christ and let them sit with Him. He continues answering them in His time when we bring them to Him with sincerity and surrendered hands.

I have received far more revelations than I have shared in these writings. But this is plenty to digest for now. One more thought strikes me before I bring things to an end. (Or should I say "to a new beginning"?)

Perhaps you still wrestle with the belief that hell is not just further fiery experiences but a single physical place with literal flames for "all the bad people." Maybe you believe that picture of hell because of various people's visions or spiritual experiences of hell. Or possibly your own experiences.

How real are people's experiences of "reality" in this world when they believe something strongly? How real was *your* experience of reality when you strongly believed what you discovered later was lies? Jesus said "Let it be done to you according to your belief."

Don't you encounter people on this earth who experience certain realities that you can tell don't exist (because you are on the outside of their beliefs)?

Strong beliefs in a taskmaster god like in the parable of the talents cause us to actually experience a taskmaster god. Strong beliefs in a hell with actual flames that will torment people forever cause people to encounter various experiences related to those beliefs (at least until Christ's stripping works uproot those beliefs). Self-fulfilling prophecy is very real and powerful. Extensive research verifies that. The sword comes against the sword … *until* we stop believing in and using the sword. That is why God continuously works to cast out our flesh's sword of fear and judgment. People's flesh nature *is* the sword that draws the sword until it comes to ruin.

Our experiences manifest in accordance with our deepest beliefs. They are established by what we place our faith in. People who are terrified of certain events often stare at and then experience the very situations they fear. Faith in rejection somehow brings the experience of rejection. Perhaps we are coming into a time where we will no longer place faith in a "loving God" who leaves people in an unending place of torment and agony.

People who are merciful receive mercy according to their beliefs and ways. The unmerciful do not experience mercy because of their unmerciful ways. We all have certain aspects within us that believe in mercy and other aspects within us that do not. All lack of mercy is to be burned away by love's fireworks. God is merciful. He judges all that is false and unmerciful, and that is what frees us!

All people have to stand like Daniel's three friends in the fiery furnace until their fleshly bondage is stripped away to reveal Christ. That's what the furnace did for Daniel's three friends! That's also what it does for us.

The mystery of Christ placed within all people is to stand. Who will stand in the day of the Lord? None in the flesh. Only the Christ nature, who we ultimately are, will stand. We are to put on Christ (Rom. 13:14); we are to put on the imperishable (1 Cor. 15:53-54). Only Christ is imperishable but that is who we truly are as our souls turn to and unite with Him who is within. It is no longer to be the earthly I, but Christ.

We cannot walk in God's greater love that establishes a new earth without receiving His higher heaven – Christ as the Way, Truth, and Life that *never* fails. Secure love precedes authority. Let us believe in a greater love that is truly secure.

How can we walk in unwavering security when we have not trusted love to be utterly faithful? How can we express a greater love to the world when we have not received a love that is actually higher than the world's?

We will love like Jonah or the prodigal son's older brother if we do not embrace the Father's love that is faithful even when we are faithless. Love has no separation. Alienation can *only* occur in our minds, as the scriptures say (Col. 1:20). We can only alienate the Father in our minds (like the prodigal son demonstrated), but He does not alienate us (Jer. 6:8).

You may want to dwell on the following scriptures (Rom. 8:35-39):

"Who shall separate us from the love of Christ? Shall tribulation, or distress, or persecution, or famine, or nakedness, or peril, or sword? Just as it is written, 'For Thy sake we are being put to death all day long; we were considered as sheep to be slaughtered.' But in all these things we overwhelmingly conquer through Him who loved us. For I am convinced that neither death, nor life, nor angels, nor principalities, nor things present, *nor things to come*, nor powers, *nor height, nor depth*, nor any other created thing, shall be able to separate us from the love of God, which is in Christ Jesus our Lord."

No powers can separate us. It's true!

We have believed in a lesser Christ than He is. We have seen Him as a lesser Truth than He is. That has been our lesser heavens. Fire will continue to burn them away. I say none of this in condemnation. How could we do any better without yet knowing Christ in this higher way?

But now is the acceptable time. We are in a new season. Let us receive Christ's fullness that releases His greater love on this earth.

We have not yet walked in Christ's greater works because His greater love is the foundation for those works. Higher testimony comes through this greater sacrificial love that is beyond earthly ways. Let us freely receive His greater love so we have a higher love than the world's to give.

Either way, love's faithful fireworks will continue to break our rules and burn away our lesser heavens to establish His highest heaven, which is Christ. Christ desires to make all things new within us in the midst the world's chaos.

He who has ears to hear: *Christ wants to make all things new through us! Let Him!* Christ will use us powerfully to establish His kingdom outwardly as we allow Him to clean the inside of our cup to be aligned with who He is.

True Authority, True Rule

Christ is in and through all things, not just those with a Christian label. I recognize aspects of Christ in other cultures, religions, or spiritual labels because His glory fills the whole earth. I focus on Christ because all Truth comes together in Him and His cross, which is His sacrificial love that never fails. Christ's sacrificial love is the centerpiece of Him who is the Way, Truth, and Life, and overcomers become one with Him as they embrace Him as their way, truth, and life.

In the beginning, God created us in His image for ruling the earth with His righteous rule that expresses Him and His love, which we initially failed to do (Gen. 1:26-28). In the end, Christ tells overcomers "I will give you authority *in the same way* that My Father gave Me authority," which was by the flesh nature being "dashed to pieces" (Rev. 2:26-27). He does not mince words. Overcomers will stand fast through the breaking of flesh nature to receive true authority.

True overcomers will bring true rule. They will have gone through the wilderness and learned to drink from the True Spring of Life. God makes this way of ruling clear (Isa. 32:1-3), "See, a king will reign in righteousness and rulers will rule with justice. Each man will be like a shelter from the wind and a refuge from the storm, like streams of water in the desert and the shadow of a great rock in a thirsty land. *Then* the eyes of those who see will no longer be closed, and the ears of those who hear will listen."

Do you hear the essence of true rule? Those who have endured and overcome wind, storm, desert, and thirst will receive authority to become shelter, refuge, streams of water, and "shadows" for others in parched places. That resurrection life is what causes others to hear the overcomers. The overcomers know that God's never-changing purpose is to make the poor rich, gather the outcast, feed the hungry, give drink to the thirsty, and establish life in those who lost it. Why? Because they have lived it.

Jesus walked this way of the cross during His life and many people then and since have heard His voice over earthly voices because He has been a wellspring in the desert. Jesus was not deserted by the Father even though it looked that way to natural eyes, and He does not desert us though it feels that way at times. Jesus demonstrated God's way of being made empty to receive fullness. Eyes and ears were initially opened by The Overcomer, and eyes and ears will be opened by overcomers in this season. True authority.

Who are the overcomers with ears to hear and eyes to see? Who will answer the call to be vessels of Christ's greater love, a love that is finally greater than the world's love?

Who will be Christ's bold vessels who stand in faith through His fire to establish His highest heaven that ushers in a new earth? Who will trust this greater love that establishes a divine justice that gathers all the sheep into the fold – the poor, blind, naked, widow, orphan, stranger, and outcast?

Who are the overcomers who become love's flames that burn away the old and establish the new? Who will be used to let love loose on this earth?

I say to all who hear, embrace Love's fire works. I say to all:

GRACE, GRACE!

Notes

1. Love's Passionate Pursuit

1. "You were taught, with regard to your former way of life, to put off your old self, which is being corrupted by its deceitful desires; to be made new in the attitude of your minds; and to put on the new self, created to be like God in true righteousness and holiness" (Eph. 4:22-24).

2. "But while his [the landowner's] men were sleeping, his enemy came and sowed tares among the wheat, and went away ... [to which the landowner then told his men not to pull out the tares and explained] 'while you are gathering up the tares, you may uproot the wheat with them. Allow both to grow together until the harvest; and in the time of the harvest I will say to the reapers, "First gather up the tares and bind them in bundles to burn them up; but gather the wheat into my barn"'" (Matt. 13:25, 29-30). Christ is the landowner and the land is our souls where both tares and wheat have been planted. Jesus conveyed to us that we must not pull out the weeds in ourselves or one another in our time but, instead, wait on Christ to pull out the weeds at the time of harvest. By the Spirit and Christ's peace within, we will sense His harvest time for establishing the true and uprooting the false in the various aspects of our lives.

2. Fire, Fire

1. My term for God's "judgment" is stripping works. Many people have misunderstood God's judgment in the scriptures. God's judgment has always been about stripping away the false from people to awaken the true. His judgment is not like the world's judgment that condemns and throws you away (although I realize that many people have interpreted the scriptures as God throwing people away when they don't agree with Him). God's

judgment and justice constantly work to strip away your refuge of lies that prevent you from knowing Him as He is (Isa. 28:17-18). As He strips away your lies so as to know Him, you see Him clearer and come into inner peace, rest, and the freedom to be. Do you equate God's judgment with freedom? With justice that restores us? That is His unwavering purpose, which does not stop until He leads justice to victory (Matt. 12:20).

2. The scriptures state (Rom. 8:28), "And we know that in all things God works for the good of those who love Him, who have been called according to His purpose." People usually interpret this passage to mean that God will work everything together for good for those who have embraced the Christian label. God is beyond labels. "Those who love God" versus those who don't (as well as the godly or ungodly person referred to in the scriptures) has nothing to do with labels. Interpreting the scriptures with higher eyes begins through knowing that no person is all good or all bad. All have the Christ nature within (the godly person) and the flesh or sin nature within (the ungodly person). Only the Christ nature love's God; all else will be shaken away.

3. God's two fiery works are most visible through the words "grace, grace" in the book of Zechariah (4:7). In 2007 I experienced a vivid dream where Christ showed me two distinct kingdom works. In the dream, He called each set of works a grace, one that places people on His true foundation (Christ within), and another one that uses that foundation to continue building or raising His spiritual house on this earth (Christ within others). Following that dream, God opened my eyes to His two works of grace in the Zechariah passage.

The first grace is God's stripping works to shift us onto Christ's true foundation within us. That is why that passage continues and directs us not to despise the day of small beginnings, which is often people's experience when foundational work occurs.

Foundations alone don't look like much. The second grace is the work of building or expanding God's spiritual house. These fiery experiences can occur in fully visible ways like with my panic attacks and marital trials, but more often they are ongoing cyclical experiences in smaller aspects of our lives that are beyond our human ability to resolve. This is illustrated by Paul's thorn in his side that left him periodically feeling weak so that Christ's strength in him would further awaken (2 Cor. 12:7-10).

These two works of grace (or fire) are also evident when God said that He works within us to will, and then to work according to His good pleasure (Phil. 2:13). These two distinctly different God-works are in accordance with grace, grace. His one work shifts me over from earthly to heavenly will (the difficult foundation work), and the other one works His kingdom ways through me (raising His spiritual house). Both ongoing works are necessary in our lives. God expressed these same two ways in the Garden of Eden to Adam about keeping or guarding the garden (of God's will), and then working that garden (of peace) that would continually produce God's fruit on the earth (Gen. 2:15).

Peacemaking and walking in peace also relate to the Philippians and Genesis passages, as well as to God's two fiery works. The scriptures tell us "Blessed are the peacemakers" and to "Let the peace of Christ rule our hearts" (Matt. 5:9; Col. 3:15). We become peacemakers when we participate with heavenly will rather than earthly will during the fire, which establishes higher will and peace on earth where there is no peace. Then we are able to walk in that established peace that touches others with that higher peace, which continues Christ's works of heaven on earth.

These two graces are also seen in the scriptures through the words "comfort, comfort," "gather, gather," and "trust, trust" (Isa. 40:1; Zeph. 2:1; Jn. 14:1). God's fire first works His works in us, and then His established works in us continue on behalf of others.

God works comfort in me to bring true comfort to others, which gathers me and then gathers others. He also works higher trust in me during the fire that then allows others to know that He is trustworthy during their encounters with fire.

4. We are all united in this ongoing awakening process. There is one Spirit, one body, and one baptism (Eph. 4:4-6). The Spirit baptizes us with fire during our earthly journey (Matt. 3:11; Mk. 9:49).

5. I decided to put all my hope into following Christ in His way of the cross even if died. Esther had said "… if I perish, I perish" when she risked her life to approach the king on behalf of the Jews (Est. 4:16). That was very real to me.

3. Behold Love's Fiery Testimony

1. Sharing with others what this book worked in you gives a testimony of the fruit; it is the kingdom way that continues its unstoppable works. But telling others (kind of like gossip) about the content's final destination without giving testimony to the fruit is not the kingdom way. In fact, that was the way that the demons testified about Jesus.

Jesus taught in a synagogue and a demon-possessed man cried out (Mk. 1:24), "What do you want with us, Jesus of Nazareth? Have you come to destroy us? I know who you are – the Holy One of God!" The demon-possessed man gave testimony didn't he? Isn't that good? Isn't any kind of testimony better than no witness? Apparently not. That's why Jesus then said (vs. 25), "Be quiet … come out of him!"

Jesus didn't want this demon giving witness to Him. Why? The witness came without the fruit of the Spirit. Works and spirits communicate more powerfully than words. A witness without life-filled fruit does not give testimony of the true works of the Lord. In fact, it often hinders God's works.

I can tell others about Jesus with harshness and they will hate Jesus. And me. The fruit coming through me is what powerfully impacts others, not the words or labels I use.

Intellectual discussions about beliefs are often fruitless when separated from testimony or deeper meaning because they come from a place of final outcomes. They have nothing to do with intimate knowing and give no testimony. Intellectual knowledge alone tends to puff up the human nature.

4. Servants of Conscience

1. The scriptures say (1 Jn. 4:1-3), "Dear friends, do not believe every spirit, but test the spirits to see whether they are from God, because many false prophets have gone out into the world. This is how you can recognize the Spirit of God: Every spirit that acknowledges that Jesus Christ has come in the flesh is from God, but every spirit that does not acknowledge Jesus is not from God. This is the spirit of the antichrist, which you have heard is coming and even now is already in the world." This passage continues and then describes these spirits as "the Spirit of truth and the spirit of falsehood" (vs. 6).

2. Jesus told us to worship in spirit and truth. He stated (Jn. 4:23), "God is spirit, and His worshippers must worship in spirit and truth." That was about a way of walking in life. Worshipping in spirit and truth is about beholding Christ's unseen reality as we journey, not just physical realities. We must worship the unseen Creator (by walking with Him as our sustenance) rather than worshipping creation.

Without knowing it, I worship creation when I focus on the physical realities as the true rather than on Christ and His unseen ways of the Spirit. The scriptures about Christ, Jerusalem, Israel, sheep, orphan, outcast, the poor, marriage, moving mountains, and the song of the Lamb all point towards spiritual realities. Their truth and meaning are beyond the physical.

3. True sacrificial love is following the Lamb (Christ and His way of sacrificial love) wherever He goes. The scriptures say (Rev. 14:4), "… they kept themselves pure. They follow the Lamb wherever He goes …" That is following conscience, which is peace between you and Christ within.

5.   Kingdom Counterparts and Crumbs

1. The more complete passage states (1 Cor. 1:26-31), "Brothers, think of what you were when you were called. Not many of you were wise by human standards; not many were influential; not many were of noble birth. But God chose the foolish things of the world to shame the wise; God chose the weak things of the world to shame the strong. He chose the lowly things of this world and the despised things — and the things that are not — to nullify the things that are, so that no one may boast before Him. It is because of Him that you are in Christ Jesus, who has become for us wisdom from God — that is, our righteousness, holiness and redemption. Therefore, as it is written: 'Let him who boasts boast in the Lord.'"

6.   Perfect Dynamite

1. "Woman" and "man" uniting, conception, and childrearing are clearly portrayed as painful and inevitable in the Genesis 3:16 passage. Some people say that these scriptures no longer apply because of Christ's works on the cross. I would say that the majority of Christ's messages about sacrificial love, endurance, and standing firm (as well as observing life!) say otherwise. Aren't marriages still difficult even when looking to Christ? Isn't sacrificial love still necessary in marriages? Isn't it applicable to relationships as a

whole? We all have flesh nature that interferes with relationships during our journey.

Some of you might also think that I am a bit off in my translation because those scriptures have predominantly been translated as "woman" and "husband." Here is one example of many where the scriptures have not been translated as accurately as they could have been.

The precise translation for "the woman" is already accurate, which is "the feminine of man, or woman." But the translation for her counterpart should have remained equivalent throughout this passage. The translation should have been "man," not "husband." The Hebrew words are *exact* counterparts within humanity just like Adam and Eve as individuals were exact counterparts (where Eve was *taken from* Adam to make each a counterpart; see Gen. 2:22).

God's words were to the "woman" and about the "man" and pertained to woman and man in general. Even the earlier Genesis passage about a "man" leaving father and mother and cleaving to his "wife" should have been translated as cleaving to his "woman." While the Hebrew meaning points to this broader translation, it does not lessen the importance of what God desires in marriage on this earth. But I do want to emphasize that these passages have traditionally been limited to earthly marriage when the scriptural meaning or application was about the difficulty, and yet necessity, of two core counterparts within humanity unifying.

When you look at life, aren't counterparts the way God designed life? Throughout life we encounter suitable helpers, sometimes support, sometimes sandpaper to awaken us. That is the groaning of all creation that continually awakens more of Christ within people on this earth.

2. Romans 8:18-39 portrays the yearning and turning counterparts better than anywhere else in the scriptures. I share

the essence of this passage, but if you are not familiar with these verses, you may want to turn there to fully grasp its fullness. Romans 8:22 states, "We know that the whole creation has been groaning as in the pains of childbirth right up to the present time." That statement is in the midst of verses 18 to 27, all of which emphasize yearning. God causes frustration at the earthly level that causes us to yearn for Him who is beyond the earthly.

Then, suddenly, the focus switches to turning (Rom. 8:28-39). Verse 28 states, "And we know that in all things God works for the good of those who love Him, who have been called according to His purpose." That verse ushers in turning to God by focusing on His utter sovereignty and continues until its conclusion (vs. 37-39) "… in all these things we are more than conquerors … For I am convinced that neither death nor life, neither angels nor demons, neither the present nor the future, nor any powers, neither height nor depth, nor anything else in all creation, will be able to separate us from the love of God that is in Christ Jesus our Lord."

Yearning and turning must work together as one, which conceives or awakens more of Christ's kingdom on earth as it is in heaven. Groaning and standing firm to overcome must unite.

Another way you can see the yearning and turning counterparts emphasized in the scriptures is through various psalmists. You will see psalmists crying out to God in anguish and expressing much feeling from deep places within them and then, suddenly, they come forth with a huge "But …," which begins their expression about how faithful, good, and trustworthy God is (Psm. 13:5; 31:14; 69:13). This Dr. Jekyll and Mr. Hyde contrast portrays these two counterparts from within the psalmists that are part of the necessary process of awakening into more of Christ. That is conception when those two counterparts come together to be one.

3. Jacob dreamed that "… a ladder was set on the earth with its top reaching to heaven; and behold, the angels of God were

ascending and descending on it" (Gen. 28:12). That was a dream about the kingdom coming on earth as it is in heaven.

Then Jacob said (Gen. 28:17), "How awesome is this place! This is none other than the house of God, and this is the gate of heaven." The house of God is the fullness of Christ within humanity. That is the gate of heaven. But we have much to learn for walking as a unified body of sacrificial love that becomes God's true gate.

7.   Perfect Food and Clothes

1. The Hebrew word for "no" is *ayin* (meaning, to be nothing, a non-entity, fatherless) and *kecuwth* means cover or garment, which comes from "to be filled up." These meanings point towards destruction as being times where we will experience nothing good or fulfilling; nothing earthly whatsoever will fill or satisfy us at those times. The result is feeling separate and alone.

8.   Fire Furthers the Kingdom

1. People's flesh nature can only see through eyes of separation, which causes competition, conflict, and power struggles for self-promotion. But self-promotion is a lie because separation is a lie. The lie of separation *is* humanity's blindness and bondage. Humanity's flesh nature with its lie of separation is the second "beast" referred to in the Book of Revelation. That's why the number of the beast is man's number, 666 (Rev. 13:18). Lesser spiritual powers only have their power because God ultimately grants it, even if it is only temporarily granted to achieve higher purposes. God allowed these beasts to overpower the saints (Rev. 13:7). Why? God desired that only faith would overcome that false power ... faith that sees with the eyes of Christ and His sacrificial love that loves all that is "separate." Separating eyes are

blind eyes, ones that act and speak arrogantly. But eyes that see with no separation are Christ's faith-filled sacrificially loving eyes.

2. Part of God's gift to us is providing the way of escape when you hit earthly impossible walls (1 Cor. 10:12-13; 2 Ptr. 1:4). The Way of escape for us is to partake of the divine nature by humbly acknowledging the limited earthly nature and opening up to more of Christ in that place. Humility is the sure way of ushering Christ into His rightful place within your heart.

The above Corinthians passage states that no temptation is "beyond" us. Certainly many temptations exist when life is beyond the earthly nature. That is supposed to be that way. But the Greek root of the word "beyond" is *huper*. That is the same Greek word in the verse (Jam. 1:17), "Every good and perfect gift is from above (*huper*)."

Can you hear the connection? When we hit humanly impossible walls, no temptation is *huper* because every good and perfect gift is from *huper*. From above or beyond. Our part is to squarely acknowledge our human limits. That is the humility that allows us to escape the earthly and to genuinely turn to the Greater who is beyond those places that *feel* beyond us, not for an outcome but just to be with (or in) Christ who is beyond! That is how power shift occurs. Cease from the lesser and turn to be with the Greater who is our reward in those places beyond our present abilities. Usually this gift comes when we let go of our perceived necessary outcomes so as to be with Christ who is peace, love, and true authority inwardly.

Paul later emphasized this message about participating with God's higher works using the same word *huper* that pertains to what is beyond or above us (Eph. 3:20). Paul explained that the kingdom becomes further established in and through us as we join with God's energy at work within the inner man rather than with human energy. Christ is within, not at some distant unreachable place. Turning to Christ during weakness is how heaven's abundance, especially love, is further established in place of earth's "goodness." Ask someone to stand with you to trust Christ's desire to be with you in that place when you don't currently have that trust.

9.   Love's Fierce Way

1. We can see in Acts (7:30, NASU) that the burning bush was a thorn bush. Isaiah (55:13) also stated, "Instead of the thorn bush will grow the pine tree, and instead of briers the myrtle will grow. This will be for the LORD's renown, for an everlasting sign, which will not be destroyed." In other words, God's fire destroys the thorny flesh nature to raise up resurrection life in its place (the Christ nature). Another way of saying this is that God uses an earthly wilderness where the fleshly thorns cannot grow, and miraculously He brings life into those deserted places where it seemed that nothing could grow. That's why the scriptures convey that this new life in barren places is an everlasting sign. It is resurrection life in places of death.

2. In the Old Testament, God's people couldn't decide who was truly God. Elijah told them (1 Kgs. 18:24), "The god who answers by fire, He is God." God answered by fire, and the people acknowledged Him. Then, much later, Elisha asked for a double portion of Elijah's anointing. Elisha received that double portion because he had seen (and accepted) Elijah being taken away to heaven. Elijah saw the horses and chariots of fire that took Elijah to heaven in a whirlwind. This symbolized that those who accept God's fire even when it takes the people or things closest to them will receive a double portion. That is what God desires in the overcomers of this day.

3. You can see this strong, obstinate rigidity in the demon possessed boy and in the legion of demons (Mk. 9:18; Mk. 5:4). Human effort cannot budge intense fleshly rigidity.

4. Right after Jesus emphasized that He would send the Spirit *if He goes away*, He continued (Jn. 16:8-11), "And He [the Holy Spirit], when He comes, will convict the world concerning sin and righteousness and judgment; concerning sin, because they do not believe in Me; and concerning righteousness, *because* I go to the Father and *you no longer see Me*; and concerning judgment, because the ruler of this world has been judged."

I am convicted of my unbelief in Christ *when* I feel utterly helpless and abandoned. Flesh is humbled and comes to ruin in the area of my trial. I am also convicted of the necessity of encountering periods of "no longer seeing Christ" for me to experientially know that His righteousness and works are necessary to accomplish what my human nature cannot. I see in that helpless place that human strength has nothing to give, and that Christ simply gives-for as a gift. That causes a humbling of earthly power and an exalting of heavenly power within me. In those difficult places I am convicted that judgment (stripping works) of my flesh nature is necessary to see its futility so as to unhook from it, which also further unhooks me from and judges the worldly ruler. Conviction about fleshly helplessness causes me to see through the dominating worldly lies.

5. Help is available from beyond, especially during weakness. In our places of weakness the Spirit helps us attain what is beyond human nature and will entreat or deal with us "in favor or against." But don't let that frighten you.

The Greek word for "helps" is stronger than the word "accompany" and means "to take hold of opposite together." One way or the other the Spirit intercedes on our behalf by taking hold of us even when we are at an opposite place … usually when we are in fear or unbelief. The Spirit will gird us up in Christ if we have come to a place of emptiness and humility. Or, the Spirit will work His fire to strip away more flesh nature so as to cause us to surrender and, still through free will, to embrace Christ in that area of struggle.

6. We can give nothing to attain (or awaken to) more of the Greater in our places of impossibility. The only cost for attaining more of the Greater is to lose the lesser. *Our soul attains more of the Beautiful Land within not simply through possessing it, but through dispossessing the false from residing in those places.* God portrayed this way of overcoming through Israel dispossessing other nations from the Promised Land so that they could possess it. That was a picture of God's works within human souls. We must dispossess the flesh nature from within our souls so as to have our true Christ nature abide there. Us in Him, and Him in us.

7. Jesus walked with incredible humility with His Father and said that He came not to do His own will but the Father's. Can you hear Jesus' utter dependence upon the Greater? Even the Father said in advance about Jesus walking on the earth (Matt. 12:18), *"I will put* My Spirit upon Him ..."* The Greek meaning of the words "put" and "upon" is "I will place or superimpose My Spirit regarding time, place, or order." That's why Jesus said (Matt. 12:6), "... something greater than the temple is here..." That's also why Jesus said that the Father was greater than Him and that the Father alone determined the times and seasons (Jn. 10:29; 14:28; Acts 1:7).

People's flesh nature participates with the lesser kingdom that wants "to change the times and seasons." It does not want to let go of its will and "power" that try to govern life. That's why trials are necessary. Lesser nature must be burned away which then becomes our spiritual food or wisdom where no proud lion prowls (Job 28:5-28). That is also the highway of holiness where no devouring lion is found (Isa. 35:8). Holiness is the wholeness in Christ that becomes established wherever the fleshly is ruined within us. Ongoing or eternal ruin of the one further awakens and establishes the eternal life of the Other within us.

10. Greater Help and Mysteries

1. God is our helper through "the day" described in the scriptures. We all go through an unfolding day. The Psalms state (118:24), "This is the day the Lord has made; let us rejoice and be glad in it!" But how does God help us in this glorious day? People have heard and sung the related song many times.

Verses 7 and 17-18 give fuller context for understanding this glorious day that many people sing about. Verse 7 states, "The Lord is with me; He is my helper. I will look in triumph on my enemies." But how did the Lord work triumph for the psalmist? We see in verses 17-18 how the Lord helped him: "I will not die but live, and will proclaim what the LORD has done. The LORD has chastened me severely, but He has not given me over to death." This was Kathy and me!

Then in verses 20-21 the psalmist refers to this discipline (stripping works) as the gate of the Lord where He finally answers and becomes his salvation, his way. This is similar to Jesus calling Himself the gate or door that causes the blind to see and that those who think they see to become blind (Jn. 10:6; 9:39). Jesus makes us blind in our fleshly places where we think we already see.

That is what happened to the psalmist. He called the Lord His helper and then described how he felt like he would die. But the psalmist knew that the Lord's discipline was upon him as his help.

2. As I paused about our help being oppositional at times, I felt compelled to research the fact that our suitable help was made from a rib. Rib means "a curve; figuratively *a door*; a side (of a person); a chamber; a beam or plank," and its root means "to curve or to limp as if one-sided; to halt."

Wow. Many implications are popping like popcorn for me right now. Ribs cannot function properly without counterparts. None of us can function properly without counterparts. Counterparts bring balance to us, and we limp otherwise. God's suitable help for us (beyond support) is that we would find beams, planks, or closed doors in our way at times, and that true wholeness becomes possible only when we take the plank out of our own eyes before trying to refine our "opposing planks" or counterparts (see Matt. 7:5).

Jacob's limp symbolized the need for us to depend upon something beyond ourselves as individuals, and the limp only disappears as we depend more fully on Christ directly and in one another.

3. God desires to gather His many counterparts, His helpers, into one with His breath of life. That is why God told Ezekiel (37:4) to prophesy and to breathe life into the dry bones so that the bones and joints would gather together and rise. Bones coming together restores us regarding Christ's bones that have been out of joint on the cross, which King David prophesied about Christ (Psm. 22:14). That is still us, the body of Christ with our bones out of joint. But God is currently breathing life into His dry bones to come together on this earth. Pray that His bones come together as one with His life in them.

4. Placed right in the middle of Isaiah 58 is God's exhortation not to hide or turn away from our own flesh and blood (vs. 7). Do not separate from others. Others' struggles are our own struggles. Others' burdens and sins are ours whether we see them that way or not. We are all connected, for good or for bad. Those scriptures tell us to feed the hungry, clothe the naked, and to remove the pointing of the finger and *then* our light will rise in darkness.

Our light rises when we love others because we are one. Israel could not go into the Promised Land unless they battled as one (Josh. 1:14-15).

5. Jesus had always been with the Father in heaven's higher realm. The Father could have simply told us how to walk the way into that realm. But He didn't. God descended from heaven at the appointed time and walked out the way with us through Jesus. He humbled Himself. Now He wants to do that through us with one another.

The scriptures say (Isa. 57:14-15), "And it will be said, 'Build up, build up, prepare the road! Remove the obstacles out of the way of my people.' For this is what the high and lofty One says – He who lives forever, whose name is holy: '*I live in* a high and holy place, *but also with* him who is contrite and lowly in spirit, to revive the spirit of the lowly and to revive the heart of the contrite.'" You can see that God's purpose is to revive us in Him. These scriptures also demonstrate high and low and "this and that" held together.

I am able to see others' sins with clarity and compassion when I'm in my Christ nature (rather than seeing with eyes of separation). From that place I see the futility of their sins and know the forgiveness and comfort needed there. Christ's higher presence desires to *be with* the contrite and lowly for reviving the lowly. Jesus said that He came to seek and be with us in the lost places.

Right in the middle of me telling a friend about this way of lowering myself to go higher, a neighbor tripped and fell while ascending some outer stairs to her second floor apartment. Within two minutes another neighbor fell while ascending a six-foot step ladder. He was probably 70-75 years old and fell onto the side walk. My heart stirred spiritually as we raced over to check on him. Miraculously he was not hurt beyond a cut and several bruises.

My friend and I then returned to our discussion. We both felt that the timing of those falls was to emphasize the significance of Jesus' love that lowers itself to bring unity. And we will likely fall at some point if we try to help from a high place.

11. **Wings in the Flames**

1. Healing through the extremes is powerfully symbolized by the woman who hemorrhaged for 12 years. No one could heal her, which makes clear that the situation is beyond human control (Lk. 8:43). By faith she believed she would be healed if she touched the fringe of Jesus' cloak (Matt. 9:21). *Kraspedon* is the Greek word for "fringe," which means border, tassel, hem, margin, or fringe. The meaning is the same as the word "wings" in the Old Testament: we are healed through the extremes. Through difficulties.

That woman represented those who look to Christ for healing during the extremes rather than looking to the world. She touched the fringe or extremes while having faith in Christ. "Touched" is an experiential word, which Jesus later emphasized with His disciples when He told them to touch the wounds in His hands, feet, and side (Lk. 24:30; Jn. 20:27). Jesus again emphasized the need for us to experientially encounter the extremes where our flesh becomes wounded. Where we come to know Him in those places as the resurrection who is beyond the flesh.

I was shocked at how many scriptures pointed towards healing coming through us being put in extreme situations beyond our control. That is what Christ did with Paul when He left the thorn in his side. Christ's goal was to expose more of Paul's weakness or nakedness so as to awaken more of His strength in Paul. Christ placed Paul at the edge, fringe, really, in an extreme where he could not meet certain needs in earthly ways. The above passages about the fringe or corner are only a few of the many related scriptures.

The fringe requires faith that God is good and fervently wants to be our *inner* help in that place. The fringe is where Christ helps us to lose more of the fleshly life and to raise us in more of Him. That is what is meant by Jesus saying to His disciples (Jn. 13:8), "Unless I wash you, you have no *part* with Me."

2. We have no part with Christ when we do not let Him wash our feet (Jn. 13:8), which symbolizes Him washing us through the extremes. Jesus' word for "wash" means only washing a part; an edge or portion, such as hands or feet, physically or symbolically. I chuckled to myself as soon as I saw this Greek definition that "coincidentally" lined up with all that Christ had been teaching me about Him healing Kathy and me through the extremes.

Jesus indicated that we have already bathed our whole body upon knowing Him as Lord, but that He must wash our feet. Christ periodically washes a part, portion, or aspect of our lives. He also works through us to wash certain parts or aspects of others' lives. Every time I suffered further in my marital fireworks, Christ washed my feet. I continually awakened every time I trusted during trials. Rather than resisting or having no part with Him during those extremes, my goal was to embrace Him even if it meant suffering to do so.

3. The Old Testament scriptures about the priests always washing their hands and feet before entering the Tent of Meeting symbolized people's necessary washing to gather together corporately (Ex. 30:19). This indicated washing as the only way to enter the "Tent of Meeting," which means a covering through assembling or gathering. Connecting together with one another and with God depended upon washing hands and feet. That Hebrew word comes from *yaad*, meaning to summon to trial; to engage for marriage; or to agree, or betroth.

Unity in a corporate gathering requires numerous washings of two coming together as one. Gathering is sometimes a trial, just like marriage. And enduring through more trials brings greater connection. The more I understand the scriptures, the more easily I see the necessity of the sacrificial love of marriage that continually gathers people into the unity of Christ.

4. Fortunately God will work His baptism of fire to forge jewels, which is about our new self in Christ coming forth. The whole chapter of Isaiah 54 emphasizes God's desire to enlarge us and how He will use fire to produce jewels (meaning us, who will reflect His beauty). God conveys that He will open our windows, battlements, gates, and *all our walls or borders* by fire and forge us into the Lord's jewels that give testimony to His higher works (vs. 12). The word for walls or borders is *gebuwl*, and like the word *kanaph* for wings, also means coast or quarter (extremes) but adds the aspect of God opening us up in areas we have been bound or limited. Then chapter 55 focuses on the comfort that the Lord brings during the fiery works, resulting in the *everlasting* sign – life birthed in the wilderness (vs. 13). That is resurrection life in places of death.

5. Ezekiel, by the Kebar River (1:4-18), saw an immense cloud with flashing *lightning* and (vs. 4) "... The center of the fire looked like glowing metal, and in the fire was what looked like four living creatures." Each of these four living creatures had four faces and four wings, "and their wings *touched* one another" (vs. 9). No gaps between the wings parallels the cherubim's wings that touched one another in the Old Testament temple (1 Kgs. 6:27). Each cherub had one wing touching a wall and the other wing touching the other cherub's wing. From wall to wall, two connected as one. No gaps.

Ezekiel had a similar vision of four cherubim with *human hands under the wings*, and he said that the cherubim were the living creatures he had seen earlier by the Kebar River (10:8, 15). The human hands under the cherubim's wings symbolizes our abilities coming under God's governance through the extremes He brings.

The cherubim or living creatures that Ezekiel saw are also the living creatures that worship before the throne of God and

461

the Lamb (Rev. 4:6-8; 5:6-14). These living creatures symbolize Christ's works to bring us into the sacrificial unity of the Lamb. That sacrificial unity that honors the Lamb's way above all else becomes our holiness. We become whole and holy in Christ through that sacrificial way. That's why the living creatures never stop crying out "Holy, holy, holy" to God while giving all praise and honor to the Lamb.

12. Breakthroughs and a Dance

1. The Apostle Paul also endured an ongoing barren place to further seal him in the power of Christ's love. Paul had entreated the Lord three times to take away a thorn in his flesh (a barren place) but the Lord said to him, "My grace is sufficient for you, for My power is perfected in weakness." Then Paul continued, "Therefore I will boast all the more gladly about my weaknesses, *so that Christ's power may rest* on me" (2 Cor. 12:9). Christ's power rested and remained on Paul because He allowed an ongoing place of fleshly weakness.

Fleshly weakness causes my soul to thirst for more of Christ and His strength. Then that yearning further establishes Christ in those places as I continually turn to Him in trust.

13. Hugs and Explosions

1. In each area of my life I must die for Christ to fulfill the law in me (Gal. 6:2). I don't mean physical death. Christ always was the fulfillment of the law on behalf of people. The victory was always won. But I won't allow Christ to fulfill the law for me in any area where my flesh nature hasn't died.

2. The scriptures indicate that "transgression must run its course (fullness of sin)," and "the fullness of the Gentiles must come in" before we receive Christ's "fullness of the times" (see Dan. 8:23; 9:24; Rom. 11:25; Eph. 1:10).

3. Paul gives instructions for dealing with this man of lawlessness without giving name to him (2 Cor. 10:4-5), "The weapons we fight with are not the weapons of the world. On the contrary, they have divine power to demolish strongholds. We demolish arguments and every pretension that *sets itself up against* the knowledge of God, and we take captive every thought to make it obedient to Christ."

14. Love's Fire Works ... the Rule-Breaker

1. God will cast out fear and judgment by shaking the heavens and the earth once more (Heb. 12:26). That shaking is to shake away our present views and ways that we've known as heaven. The open heavens referred to in the scriptures come from having the old burned away to embrace heaven's higher purer Way, which is Christ the Truth of no separation (Jn. 1:51).

The passing away of the old is seen in the book of Revelation where the New Jerusalem comes down from heaven and is established on this earth (21:1-5). That is God's ways coming upon the earth as it is in heaven, where no pain or suffering exists. The first things pass away. Current rules are blatantly broken. Earth shattering change comes. That is the marriage of the Bridegroom and His bride that gives testimony of His higher works. That is a new heaven on this earth, which creates a new earth.

2. "But if you do not wake up, I will come like a thief, and you will not know at what time I will come to you" (Rev. 3:3). "Behold, I come like a thief! Blessed is he who stays awake and keeps his clothes with him, so that he may not go naked and be shamefully exposed" (Rev. 16:15).

15. Unsurpassed Love

1. People can be both *huios* (kinship) and *teknon* (son being birthed), which is different than how these terms have been

traditionally taught. Usually, people have referred to *huios* as mature sons and *teknon* as immature sons. That is not fully accurate. Nowhere in the Greek meaning or even in the root words for *teknon* is immaturity stated or implied.

The Romans (8:19-21) passage about creation being subject to groaning for freeing us into the "glorious freedom of the children of God" first refers to these children or sons as *huios* (family) in verse 19. Then in verse 20 they are referred to as *teknon* (sons as produced). Glorious freedom sounds like maturity. It is. But the word *teknon* (sons being shaped) is also used because the context is about enduring trials to further shape sons into a fuller likeness of God. The Greater always has more infiniteness for us to awaken into. Sons (just like Jesus was when He walked this earth) are always being completed through suffering, and Jesus was anything but immature.

The implications of Jesus' word choice for son about the rich man in hell are astounding. Other words used to describe "son as produced" are "to bear, be born, bring forth, be delivered, and be in travail."

2. One other place where I found *teknon* for son was in Jesus' story about the father with two sons regarding which one had done the father's will. The whole slant of Jesus' parable was about which son was being made in the likeness of the father. Both sons were kinship, but Jesus used the story to portray that our choice to do the Father's will or not is for the purpose of being made into His likeness. Son-in-the-making.

I also researched the words "child" and "children" to see what those words revealed. I discovered many scriptures where *teknon* was used. In fact, I soon recognized the meaning from the context of its use before I looked up the Greek word, which always had to do with encountering trials.

3. "Love does not delight in evil but rejoices with the truth. It always protects, always trusts, always hopes, always perseveres. Love never fails." (1 Cor. 13:6-8).

4. "If we are faithless, He will remain faithful, for He cannot disown Himself" (2 Tim. 2:13). I realize that verse 12 in this passage states that if we disown Him, He will disown us. That is true in any given circumstance, just like when we do not forgive others, He does not forgive us. We reap what we sow, and He allows us to do that because of free will. We often do not experience His presence or support when we shut Him out. But even when we disown or deny Him like Peter did, He will pray that our faith may not fail (Lk. 22:31-32). Faith, which is and comes from Christ ultimately, carried Peter through the fire to reawaken him to the Lord at a later point. Christ was faithful even though Peter was faithless, and that is true for us as well. Even after we have denied Christ in any given moment, He will faithfully work to bring further circumstances to keep awakening His faith within us. He is more than able to work circumstances like an effective parent to bring the child around to effective choices again (whether during or after the earthly journey). Love faithfully pursues us and never gives up, even if it means using fire to cause awakening like had happened with Peter.

5. "... My sword will go forth from its sheath against all flesh from south to north. Thus all flesh will know that I, the LORD, have drawn My sword out of its sheath. It will not return to its sheath again" (Ezek. 21:4-5).

"All flesh is grass, and all its loveliness is like the flower of the field. The grass withers, the flower fades, when the breath of the LORD blows upon it; surely the people are grass. The grass withers, the flower fades, but the word of our God stands forever" (Isa. 40:6-8). Can you hear that flesh nature is like the grass that withers away, but Christ, the word within us, eternally stands after the flesh nature has become ruined?

16. Inescapable Love

1. The fear of God that was encouraged throughout the Old Testament was the Hebrew word *yare*. Several English words combined like "reverence, fear, and dread or awe" are necessary to gain a fuller picture of that Old Testament phrase. The fear of God was a sobering reality that all things come from His hand.

God wanted His people to know that He was absolutely sovereign and worked all things together for their good. That healthy reverential fear of God was to cause His people to turn their needs towards Him rather than to the world. God wanted their trust in Him, not that they would be afraid of Him.

2. The book of Revelation says (21: 10, 25), "… the holy city, Jerusalem, coming down out of heaven from God … And in the daytime (for there shall be no night there) its gates shall never be closed …" The gates will never be closed in the New Jerusalem that comes down to this earth. That is our new earth with its new heaven.

3. Every knee will bow and every tongue will confess that Jesus Christ is Lord. The Greek word for "confess" is *exomolgeo*. The translation means to profess, promise, acknowledge, or agree fully. That word comes from the root word *homologeo*, which means to assent or be in covenant with. Wow, nobody ever taught me that before!

17. Divine Inescapable Government

1. The issue of forgiveness was symbolized in the Old Testament by the cities of refuge, which gave refuge (forgiveness) to people who unintentionally wronged someone versus those whose wrongs were intentional or hostile in nature (Num. 35:16-25). That

contrast depicted the difference in people's motives and whether their heart needed purified or not. People that sinned intentionally or with hostility were required to encounter the consequences of their sins. Those sins were deeper, love was lacking, and their hearts needed purified.

People that sinned unintentionally were provided refuge, and the persons they wronged needed to live with that fact (representing forgiveness of people that unintentionally hurt them). Unintentional sins showed no heart motive needing purified. In fact, the wrongful person who had unintentionally sinned was brought to safety.

CPSIA information can be obtained at www.ICGtesting.com
Printed in the USA
BVOW08s0616180516

448544BV00001B/14/P